Government and Law

An Introduction to the Working of the Constitution in Britain

T. C. HARTLEY, B.A., LL.B., LL.M.

Lecturer in Law at the London School of Economics and Political Science

J. A. G. GRIFFITH, LL.M.

Professor of Public Law in the University of London
Of the Inner Temple, Barrister-at-Law

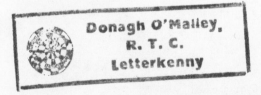
WEIDENFELD AND NICOLSON

London

Weidenfeld and Nicolson
11 St John's Hill, London SW11

$$\frac{A}{342.41}$$

ISBN 0 297 76791 7 cased
ISBN 0 297 76792 5 paperback

Printed in Great Britain by
Cox & Wyman Ltd,
London, Fakenham and Reading

CONTENTS

Foreword

There has been a tradition in England to see the politics and the law of the constitution as two distinct systems. Books on Constitutional Law have normally been written by lawyers for lawyers or law students; books on Government have usually been written by non-lawyers for students of politics or for a wider audience. The lawyers focussed on legislation, political decisions and rules based on custom or convention; writers on Government have tended to neglect the work of the courts and, to a considerable extent, the detailed content of constitutional rules. In this book two lawyers have tried to bridge the gap by writing a contextual introduction to Government and Law in England which treats students of law and of politics as a single audience.

The authors bring a rare combination of skills and experience to this undertaking. Professor Griffith's distinguished work in Administrative Law and more recently in administration and the workings of Parliament is well known. It is based not only on many years of research and teaching but also on extensive practical experience of local government. Mr Hartley brings to the study of Government and Law in England a specialized knowledge of Constitutional Law and a broad experience of other jurisdictions. Both have a special concern to present their subject in a manner attractive both to the student and the non-specialist.

RBS

WLT

Preface

Government and law are not separate matters but two aspects of one matter: the regulation of society and of individuals in society. This is a vast subject and anyone who tries to introduce it in a short and elementary book can select only those of its parts which seem most important from his particular standpoint. We have omitted much that other writers would have dealt with (including the special provisions of the law relating to Scotland and Northern Ireland) and as lawyers we have included some material which others would no doubt exclude. This book is designed to be of use to students of law and government.

T. C. Hartley wrote the first drafts of Chapters 3, 5, 7, 8, 9, 11, 12, 13, 15, 16 and 17; J. A. G. Griffith wrote the first drafts of Chapters 1, 2, 4, 6, 10 and 14.

We would like to thank our colleague, John Evans, for reading and commenting on, drafts of Chapters 15 and 16; we are also grateful to the civil servants in various departments who assisted us by their prompt and helpful answers to our inquiries. We owe a further debt to our research assistant, Carol Lilley, who compiled the table of cases and statutes and helped to put right numerous errors. The book is based on the situation in July 1973, with up-dating on certain topics only.

J.A.G.G.

London School of Economics
and Political Science
March 1974

I

Introduction

The distinction between groups of people and what groups of people do is elementary. But it is not always kept when government is spoken of. 'Government' itself is deeply ambiguous for the word is used to describe both a group of people (sometimes also called, with variations of meaning and of definition, the executive or the administration or even, simply, the Cabinet or Ministers of the Crown) and a function: that of governing. Prime Ministers are fond of saying, because it sounds a good and firm thing to say: the Government must govern. And this means both 'We shall govern' (and not someone else) and 'What we shall do is govern' (and not something else).

There are other ambiguities at the outset. We talk, for instance, about 'the separation of powers'. As with government, so powers may mean groups of people (as when we speak of Great Powers, meaning certain nations) and even an individual ('he is a power in the land'). But powers also are used to mean functions: the legislative power, the judicial power, the executive power.

At this point the confusion becomes worse confounded for we find that traditionally writers have often referred to, particularly, three groups of people: the legislature, the executive, and the judiciary. And they have also referred to three categories of activity or functions: legislating, executing or administering, and adjudicating. Thence it is easy to bring the two together and to assume that the legislature legislates, the executive executes, and the judiciary adjudicates. Simply as a general, very rough and ready, description of what each of these groups of people do most of the time, this bringing together of people and functions is not harmful, though it conceals many difficulties of analysis. But a yet further step is often taken – and this is the ultimate confusion – for it begins to be asserted that the legislature and only the legislature legislates, that the executive and only the executive executes, that the judiciary and only the judiciary adjudicates. And when it is observed that this is untrue, that on any reasonable definition of what each of the three functions means in the English language, the legislature has functions which involve execution and adjudicating, the executive has functions which involve legislating and adjudicating, and the judiciary has functions which involve executing and legislating, then a political controversy arises and it begins to be asserted that if any of these bodies exercises functions which are primarily associated with another of these bodies, this is improper or dangerous and ought not to happen.

The introduction of this idea of what groups 'ought' and 'ought not' to do suggests some rule or principle brought in from outside, some yardstick by which we can determine whether one group has gone beyond its function. This cannot be derived from the history of these groups. For the story of the development of the functions which these groups perform begins in a time when our present concepts of the distinction between the three functions was unknown.

The royal power which grew until it welded Britain into a nation was a power that partook of all these functions. The functions of the group of people we now call Members of the Commons House of Parliament were developed at the expense of the royal power. Similarly the independence of the judiciary – which means not being dependent on the executive – emerged out of its struggles with that power. In a famous case in 1607 the question was whether the King could himself be judge in a dispute: 'Then the King said that he thought the law was founded upon reason, and that he and others had reason, as well as the Judges.' To this Sir Edward Coke, Chief Justice of the Common Pleas, replied that:

His Majesty was not learned in the laws of his realm of England, and causes which concern the life, or inheritance, or goods, or fortunes of his subjects, are not to be decided by natural reason but by the artificial reason and judgment of law, which law is an act which requires long study and experience before that a man can attain to the cognizance of it.

We are told that the King was greatly offended and said that 'then he should be under the law, which was treason to affirm'. But Coke replied in the words of Bracton that the King should not be under any man, but under God and the law.[1]

The three groups of people whom we call the legislature, the executive and the judiciary, together exercise most, though not all, of the public political power in the United Kingdom today. If we wish to be more precise, as a matter of definition, we must list more closely which persons we mean to include in each group and which we mean to exclude. 'The Legislature' carries its own special difficulties of meaning. For it is more than the House of Commons and the House of Lords. Those two Houses are the Houses of Parliament. But the ideas both of 'the legislature' and of 'Parliament' carry with them and involve the Queen as head of the executive. The Queen is not a member of either House but the 'parley', the conversation, is between the members of those Houses and herself. And most certainly 'the legislature' involves the Queen. This is not a lawyer's quibble. Acts of Parliament begin with these words:

Be it enacted by the Queen's most Excellent Majesty, by and with the advice and consent of the Lords Spiritual and Temporal, and Commons, in this present Parliament assembled and by the authority of the same.

To examine the meaning of each word in that phrase is not appropriate here but it is important to realize that the enactment is 'by the Queen's most Excellent Majesty', buttressed and supported by the members of the two Houses.

Within the group called 'the executive' must be included the Queen as its nominal head, the Prime Minister and all other Ministers of the Crown both inside and outside the Cabinet. The more senior members of the civil service being those on whom the responsibility of executing policy largely falls are also usually comprehended within the phrase.

'The judiciary' may be limited to judges in the House of Lords, the Court of Appeal, the High Court and the Crown Court but judges in county courts and stipendiary magistrates are commonly thought of as also included. Lay magistrates – justices of the peace – are often excluded in common parlance though with little logic.

Many groups remain. Members and officers of local authorities are deeply involved in the executive function. So also are members and officers of public corporations such as the boards of nationalized industries and social service bodies. Members of administrative tribunals perform functions largely indistinguishable from those performed by the judiciary. The list could be extended and it must be a matter of choice and convenience whether a particular group shall be understood to fall within one of the three principal groups or should form a separate group of its own.

Public political power is thus in one sense widely distributed. But there is also a hierarchy of power and the distribution of functions amongst, for example, local authorities, nationalized industries, administrative tribunals, and the Monopolies Commission does not mean that the central Government departments operating under Ministers of the Crown are emasculated. The methods of control and influence which Ministers have at their disposal for effecting their policies are adequate and, despite the undoubted power and authority exercised by, say, the chairman of the National Coal Board, the chairman and Director General of the Greater London Council and the Chief National Insurance Commissioner, it is a poor Government that cannot get most of its way most of the time.

Governments also control the parliamentary and therefore the legislative machine. If they wish to acquire new powers, they possess the means to do so. The Government is the Government because it has a majority in the House of Commons and normally can, one way or another, control the House of Lords. A bill introduced by a Minister into Parliament will become an Act of Parliament. Certainly this is not a universal truth. Many political pressures may be exerted on a Government and the unpopularity of a proposal may be so great that a Government may be obliged significantly to amend or even to withdraw it. But a Government is entitled to demand loyalty from its supporters in Parliament and, save in the most unusual circumstances, will obtain it.

The very considerable strength which Governments of the United Kingdom can draw on, their powers to make new laws, their control of the administrative machine both central and local, make vitally important an examination of the way in which those who control that group we have called the Executive come to be appointed, and the nature and extent of their authority to govern.

What is meant by saying that a Government has or has not 'authority' to govern? When, in a country, there is a violent transfer of power at the highest governmental level, perhaps by a *coup d'état*, the question for the Governments of other countries is whether they will recognize the new group in power as the new Government.

Sometimes a distinction is made between *de jure* and *de facto* recognition. *De facto* recognition means that the new group is acknowledged as exercising effective political control; but it does not imply that the new group is the *legal* government. If that legality is acknowledged then the recognition is said to be *de jure*. The idea of 'authority' to govern may embrace one or both of these recognitions. When Germany forced the Government of France to capitulate in 1940, it could hardly be denied that, in practical terms, Germany had authority to govern France. The German rulers had the power to require Frenchmen to do as they wished. Yet it could be denied that Germany had the legal authority to govern France because conquest by arms does not of itself confer that authority. Similarly, Ian Smith's rebellion has provided Rhodesia with a *de facto* but not, under English law, a *de jure* Government.

If, at a general election, a Labour Government is defeated and the Conservative party is successful, then, after certain formalities have been observed, a Conservative Government takes over political power. That new Government is recognized by everyone as having legal authority to govern. This is because such a transfer of power is, as we say, constitutional and, in that sense, legal. In our constitution there is no document which lays down the principle that power may be properly so transferred from one group to another. But an unwritten constitution is still a constitution. Such transference of power is 'the set-up'. It is one of the basic rules which all political parties accept. It is how the game is played. And we speak of the law of the constitution as including these basic rules. So we say that the transference has been 'lawful' because it follows the recognized practice.

Yet this is a misleading identification of 'law' and 'practice' for we shall see that there are many important constitutional practices which are denied this legal status; that the distinction between law and practice is regarded by many writers as fundamental; and that the Courts themselves recognize this distinction.

'Law' in this context is therefore a word used in two different ways. First, there are some, very few, practices which are so fundamental to the working of the constitution that they are recognized as providing the absolutely basic framework. One such practice is that a political party which wins a general election with an overall majority becomes the Government. It is true that if a Government were defeated at a general election but did not resign and instead continued to act as the Government, it would soon find itself in many difficulties. It would not, for example, be able to pass the necessary financial legislation through Parliament. So it could not collect any money in taxes and would be unable to do those things which Governments are expected to do. But the reason why Governments which are so defeated at general elections resign is not because of these difficulties. They resign because they choose to play the game according to the rules. Similarly, many of the practices which apply to the actions of the Queen are of this kind. She does invite the leader of the party with an overall majority after a general election to form a Government; she does assent to a Bill which has been passed by both Houses of Parliament. And again this is because she plays the game according to the recognized rules. We are not concerned with the question *why* defeated Governments or the Queen follow these practices. They will have very good political and other reasons for so doing. The fact is that they do follow them.

Now these fundamental practices are, as we have seen, sometimes called laws of the constitution. But they are not laws in the usual sense of rules imposed by bodies, like the legislature or the courts, having the recognized authority to make laws. It is indeed another of the fundamental practices that laws made by the legislature and common law rules developed by the courts are recognized as being made under authority and as being enforceable by other bodies. Such laws so made derive their authority from those institutions. But the fundamental practices derive their authority from nowhere; or, if you prefer, from the constitution itself, from the set-up. And to describe those practices as laws is therefore a special use of the word.

There is no way of avoiding the ultimate statement that in the end there is a political situation in which power is exercised – and no more. Those countries which have a written constitution reduce some of these fundamental practices to writing – although written constitutions normally contain much else besides. But the mere reduction of fundamental practices – whether new or old – to writing does not give them any greater political validity, does not make them more, or less, fundamental, does not even make them more, or less, permanent. It may be much easier to change an unwritten constitution than to change a written constitution (for the amendment of which, for instance, special instead of simple majorities may be needed) but to change the fundamental practices may be no easier. As it happens, fundamental practices in the United Kingdom, though they have changed quite considerably during the twentieth century, have changed less than the fundamental practices in most continental countries. This is because those countries, as a result of revolutions and civil and international wars, have gone through greater political upheaval.

So we come to an obvious but most important conclusion: that the fundamental practices which provide the framework for the government of a country are determined not by constitutional or legal events, not by the making or unmaking of constitutions or of laws, but by political happenings, within the country or outside it, which shift the load of power from one group to another. Most of the important so-called conventions are examples of the political relationship and the power relationship between one body and another. These include all those powers vested in the Queen which she habitually exercises on the advice of Ministers; relations between the Government and Parliament and between the two Houses; and the position of the Speaker. All these and many more are called conventions of the constitution by some writers. But there is little advantage in such nomenclature. They are no more than statements about political relationships at a particular point in history.

The intimate interrelation between government and law is seen again in the ideas expressed by 'the Rule of Law'.

Law is most commonly thought of as an instrument of social – and thence of individual – control. Laws are to be obeyed, they are constraints on behaviour and if we break laws we will be punished. And of course this is an important part of the truth. Law is however much more than a collection of rules telling us what we should not do. It also confers rights, including social benefits like money payments for those who are sick or unemployed; it places obligations on public authorities to provide schools and houses. And some of the constraints it imposes are on public authorities so that they are prevented from exercising power in certain ways or beyond certain limits. As most of the new laws are made by Acts of Parliament which originate in Government departments we have a situation in which the Government gives itself new powers but, as these powers are not at large but limited to specified purposes and to be exercised in specified ways, the Government sets the limits of its powers. Much of the argument that goes on in Parliament when new laws are being debated turns on questions about the extent, and so the limits, of the powers being sought by the Government.

It is dangerous to give wide discretionary powers to a Government for the powers may be abused, if not by that Government, then by its successor who will inherit those powers. But modern industrial society is complex and so are its problems. It is impossible to reduce all the powers that Governments must have to precise rules which will cover every situation. Discretionary power is inevitable. What has to be guarded against is the conferment of too much discretion. These are vague and unsatisfactory words. Moreover, political opinions will differ about the desirable extent of discretion.

It is against this background that the idea of the Rule of Law has its modern significance. A rule of laws and not of men is impossible in our society. Laws there must be to confer powers on men who rule and to limit their activity within the bounds of the laws. But those laws must also give them some freedom of action and of choice, some flexibility. Yet those who rule must be subject to the law.

It is this last principle that is crucial to the preservation of any measure of liberty and to the control of Governments. This is not to denigrate political checks on power, but such checks are greatly strengthened by the insistence that all governmental activity which encroaches on the rights of the individual must have a firm basis in rules of law. The whole position of the judiciary in relation to the executive rests on this same foundation. For without this principle it would be impossible to challenge governmental action in the courts. As it is, no person or body of persons is exempt from action in the courts on the ground of illegality and in such an action every governmental body and the Government itself must to avoid liability be able to point to some provision in the law if it wishes to claim a privileged position.

Finally, a general concept much referred to in the writings on law and politics is that called the sovereignty of Parliament. It is an idea not without its difficulties and ambiguities.

Sometimes it is spoken of as though what the writer means is that Parliament is the supreme governmental institution. And this is emphasized when the 'supremacy' of Parliament is used as a synonym for sovereignty. The suggestion is made that in some ultimate analysis the two Houses have a superior place in the hierarchy of power to that of the Government. Plausibility is added to this suggestion by claiming that the House of Commons is the elected body and that 'all power resides in the people' who delegate it to their representatives who in turn, through the legislative function, instruct the Government what to do.

This is called the liberal fallacy. It is a comforting doctrine for it gives to constitutional and political arrangements the appearance of a working democracy. But for several reasons it will not hold. First and historically, political power has never resided in the people but in different groups of rulers who by reason of their military or economic strength have been able to wield it. With the coming of the wide franchise, the method of appointing the political rulers has resulted in different groups having differing degrees of power and differing electoral bases for their power. The groups who control economic power – the wealth of the country – have also varied to some extent in their make-up but they have had no necessary and indissoluble connection with the political groups although in broad terms they have been able to affect very deeply the kinds of decisions which are made by politicians.

Again, the Government of the day does not come into existence through indirect election – that is, by the electorate choosing their representatives who then choose the political leaders. The voter normally votes for a party knowing that by so doing he is hoping directly to appoint to political power the leaders of that party. Governments are formed, after a general election, before the House of Commons assembles. And Governments exercise great control over the House, so that to suggest that the representatives of the people in any real sense choose the Government or instruct it is very far removed from reality.

If we must find a resting place for sovereignty, it is better returned whence it came – to the Crown. The sovereign is still the Queen – as a constitutional monarch no doubt, her Ministers exercising the powers she enjoys as well as the powers directly conferred on them by statute.

What then of 'Parliamentary sovereignty'? This is to be understood in the limited sense that any bill passed by the two Houses and assented to by the Queen becomes legally enforceable in the courts as a new Act. It means also that there are no legal limitations on what may be included in an Act and no other authority – such as a Supreme Court – which can declare any particular Act to be invalid. An inevitable consequence of the power of Parliament to make new laws by passing bills and of the absence of any legal restriction on this power is that no Act can be made unrepealable by Parliament.

Parliamentary sovereignty does not mean that only Parliament can legislate, for, apart from the creative function of the courts in developing the common law, the Queen herself has a limited power to legislate without parliamentary approval for dependent overseas territories and even for certain domestic purposes – for example, in relation to the Civil Service Commission.

The impact on the notion of sovereignty of the United Kingdom's membership of the European Community is two-fold. Whenever a country enters into a treaty or binds itself in any other way to an international obligation, its freedom of action is thereby voluntarily curtailed. But the Treaty of Rome is said to be special in that there is no method provided by the treaty for a country to leave the Community. This may be a distinction without a difference because any country is always in practical political terms able to break its treaty obligations – perhaps at a price. On the other hand, the Treaty of Rome is unusual in that it certainly presupposes continued membership for a considerable number of years and to renege on its obligations would be a political act having very considerable consequences. So it is, without doubt, more 'binding' than an ordinary treaty.

The other part of the impact is that the Council and the Commission are empowered under the Treaty to make regulations and directives which are binding on member states.[2] The sovereignty of Parliament is directly affected by this. For it means that no member State may by its own legislation opt out of its treaty obligations or make laws which conflict with its treaty obligations or with those regulations or directives. It is in the nature of any agreement between states which establishes a supra-national authority with legislative power that the absolute sovereignty of each state is thereby curtailed both in the political and in the legislative sphere. It may be therefore that for the first time in the history of Britain, for better or for worse, the Parliament at Westminster has accepted a curtailment of its legislative sovereignty as well as some of its freedom of political action. If so, this represents a revolutionary change. But perhaps it is worth noting that those countries who have been Community members for more than a decade seem to have survived with their national identities unimpaired.

The activity of governing and the operation of law are both complementary and other-limiting. They interact on each other, together producing the regulation of individuals and of society, separately resulting in a tension between groups of people and kinds of function. In some circumstances, the activity of governing dominates and the law hardly impinges at all; but in other circumstances the provisions of the law determine the whole structure of the activity and its direction. Diplomacy is an example of the first set of circumstances, the power to tax is an example of the second. Most activity, of course, falls within neither of these extremes and partakes of both executive discretion and specific legal provision in differing quantities.

2
Political Parties

The foundations of the present political system in the United Kingdom were laid in the middle years of the nineteenth century at a time when, for a number of different but connected reasons, the State began to impose regulatory requirements on private persons and corporate bodies. This period saw the growth of legislation to promote public health, to administer the poor law, to control hours and conditions of work in factories, to reform the police and the prisons. This same period saw the extensions of the franchise in 1832, 1867 and 1884. Parliamentary democracy came into being. And the main differences between the nature and structure of the two major political parties as they exist today are the result of the fact that the Conservative party had its origins in the period before these reforms took place, whereas the Labour party was the heir to those reforms.

As R. T. McKenzie says[1] these two parties, as they face each other in the House of Commons, are correctly called 'the Conservative Party' and 'the Parliamentary Labour Party'. For the Conservative party was at first a grouping of Members of Parliament on to whom was grafted a national organization for the gathering of support in the country for the return to Parliament of Conservative Members. But the Labour movement began outside Parliament. Subsequently the leaders of the movement, trade unionists and others, decided they should seek representation in the House of Commons, and these representatives quickly became transformed into a political party which adopted the style of the existing parties especially in entrusting to the party leaders in Parliament the leadership of the whole party. This predominance of the Parliamentary leaders in the Labour party is not easily reconcilable with the fact that they are historically the creatures of a popular movement; and the resulting tension is still important today.

PARTY STRUCTURE

Conservative Party

The official publication of the Party describing its organization begins with this diagram which is a simplified version of the structure.[2]

Structure of the Conservative Party Organization
showing advisory committees

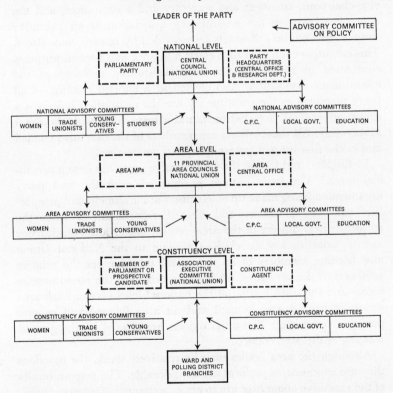

The national party is a union of Conservative and Unionist associations. Each is based on a parliamentary constituency and is autonomous in that it elects its own officers and committees, chooses its parliamentary and local government candidates, raises funds and normally employs its own agent. On these and other matters, it will be advised and assisted by the party's national and area organizations. Within each constituency, wards and polling districts are established by law and these are used as the bases on which branches of the constituency association are created. Within each branch there may be a further sub-division into units of streets or groups of houses – the ultimate grassroots for the organization of the party. Each branch raises funds to meet its own expenses and must pay contributions to the constituency association. Individuals normally join a branch, which makes them also members of the constituency association. Each branch elects a president, chairman, vice-chairman, treasurer and secretary and a committee, and the governing body of the constituency association is an executive council the members of which are provided by branch committees. This executive council in turn elects a finance and general purposes committee to make the necessary day-to-day decisions of the constituency association. Also elected at a general meeting of all party members in the constituency are the association officers – a chairman, several vice-chairmen, and a treasurer – with the agent as secretary. All these officers are members of the executive council and of the finance and general purposes committee.

In England and Wales, the Conservative party has eleven provincial areas.[3] The basic pattern is repeated, with the area party organization being made up of Members of Parliament and prospective candidates, officers and elected representatives from the constituencies, officers of the area central office, and constituency agents. Constituency associations affiliate to the National Union and become members of an area, and this signifies the relative weakness of the area level when compared with the constituencies below and the organization at the national level above. Each area generally has an area council and an area finance and general purposes committee. The usual officers are elected by the general meeting of the area council.

Although the area bodies may be relatively weak, the functions they are supposed to perform are considerable. The responsibilities of the executive committee are to act as a channel of intercommunication between constituencies within the area for the purposes of organizing mutual assistance and co-ordinating action; to advise the executive committee of the National Union of the views of the constituencies within the area; and to keep the chairman of the party organization in touch with constituency needs. The committee has the final responsibility for administering the funds of the provincial area.

The intention is that constituencies deal with the area office rather than directly with the Central Office which maintains a party headquarters in each area with a Central Office agent, who acts as secretary to the area council.

At the national level, under the Leader of the party, is the Central Council. This council consists of the members of the National Union Executive Committee (which includes the officers of the party organization) and the vice-presidents of the National Union; Members of both Houses of Parliament in receipt of the party whip and prospective Conservative candidates who have been officially selected by constituency associations; representatives from each constituency association, from central associations of divided boroughs, provincial area committees, national advisory committees, university graduates associations, the Society of Conservative Lawyers, Conservative clubs, the Commonwealth Council and Overseas Bureau and the party agents; and representatives from the party in Scotland and in Northern Ireland, together with their prospective candidates.

This means that the full membership of the Central Council is about 3,600. It holds a meeting in the spring when resolutions are debated; and has its annual general meeting in the autumn at the time of the Party Conference.

The Executive Committee of the party consists of the Leader of the party; the Leader of the party in the House of Lords; the party's chief whips in both Houses of Parliament and representatives of the 1922 Committee[4] and the Conservative peers; the senior officers of the party; the chairman of the party's advisory committee on Policy; representatives of advisory committees, graduates, Conservative clubs and party agents; and representatives from each area and from Scotland and Northern Ireland. The committee has power to co-opt up to fifteen members. This is a body of about 150 members. It meets eight or nine times a year, elects its own officers, including a chairman, and elects representatives to the party's Advisory Committee on Policy and other committees. The Executive Committee invites members of the Cabinet or shadow Cabinet to discussions on matters of political and party importance.

The annual Party Conference includes all the members of the Central Council and additional representatives from the constituencies who boost the possible attendance to some 5,600; the actual attendance is normally well over 3,000.

The selection of the Leader of the party is discussed below.[5] He appoints the chief officers of the party, who are the chairman, the deputy chairman, three vice-chairmen, and two treasurers. The functions of the chairman are officially described as being responsible to the Leader of the party for the state of the organization throughout the country, for making known the policy of the party and for keeping in touch with the views and feeling in the constituencies.[6] The three vice-chairmen give special attention to, respectively, the women's organization, the Young Conservatives and the candidates.

The Leader heads both the parliamentary party and the national party. The Advisory Committee on Policy consists of a chairman and deputy chairman, appointed by the Leader of the party, and fifteen others – seven consisting of Members of both Houses of Parliament (five selected by the Conservative Members' Committee and two selected by Conservative peers) and eight selected by the Executive Committee of the National Union from its own members, one of the eight being a Young Conservative. The Committee has power to co-opt up to six members. The Chairman and Deputy Chairman of the Party and the Director of the Conservative Political Centre are *ex officio* members.

Labour Party

The party has a number of sets of model rules on structure depending on whether the area is urban or rural.[7] The simplest structure is where the parliamentary constituency is a single borough or district. For this the diagram is:

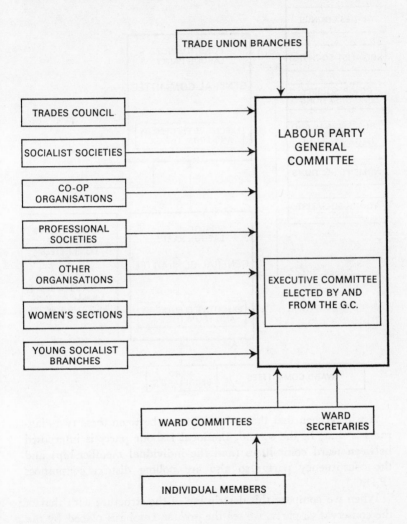

With this is to be contrasted the structure of a constituency party in a county area:

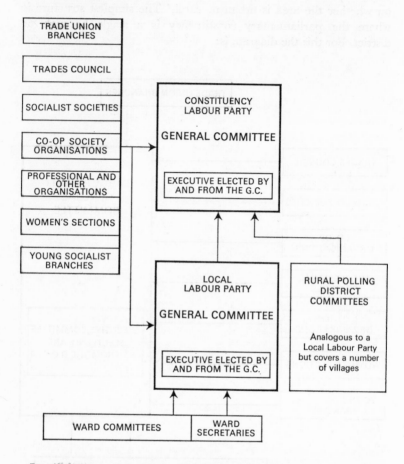

It will be seen that the main difference between these two diagrams is that, in the second, the local Labour party is interposed between ward committees (and the individual membership) and the constituency party; so also are polling district committees (P.D.C.).

When we compare this description of the structure with that of the conservative party, we see the greater emphasis placed by the Labour party on trade unions which, along with the other societies and organizations (the relative importance of which is over-emphasized in diagrams),[8] send representatives to the General Committee[9] of the constituency and of the local party.

Membership of the Labour party is reached by one of two routes or by both. An individual may join directly by accepting the constitution, principles, programme and policy of the national party and the rules of a constituency party.[10] Or he may join indirectly by being a member of an affiliated organization[11] of which by far the most important are the affiliated trade unions.

A significant difference in the Labour party, compared with the Conservative party, is that Labour party members do not meet together in an organizational body at the constituency but only at the ward or local party level. The General Committee is a body of delegates and the Executive (and any other) Committees are elected by and from the members of the General Committee. The rules of the constituency or local party determine representation and these rules, based on nationally drafted models, must be approved by the national party.

A constituency party will have as its most important officers a chairman; a secretary; an agent (who often acts as the secretary); and a treasurer. Others may include a publicity officer, a press officer, a literature secretary and a political education officer.

The Labour party, like the Conservatives, decided that some body was needed between the constituencies and the national organization and so established regional councils with an annual conference composed of delegates from the parties, the trade unions and other affiliated bodies. These delegates elect a regional executive committee and there may be other committees and sub-committees. The regional organizer normally acts as secretary to the Council. Eleven regional councils cover England, Wales and Scotland and, as in the Conservative Party, the regional organizer and his staff are responsible to the national party. We have seen that the regional bodies in the Conservative party are relatively unimportant in the party hierarchy. In the Labour Party they are even more so. McKenzie says it is 'difficult to understand how they succeed in holding the interest of those who attend their meetings'.[12]

At the national level, the Annual Conference is 'the fountain of authority',[13] declaring policy and electing the National Executive Committee. The Conference is composed of delegates from trade unions and other affiliated bodies (one delegate for each 5,000 members or part thereof); constituency parties (one delegate for each 5,000 members or part thereof) ;[14] one delegate for each central party;[15] and one delegate for each federation of constituency parties.[16] Members of the National Executive Committee, of the Parliamentary Labour party, endorsed Labour candidates, and the Secretary of the party are *ex officio* members of the Conference.

The National Executive Committee is divided into four divisions: twelve persons are nominated by trade unions and elected by their delegates at the Conference; one person is nominated by Socialist, Co-operative and Professional organizations and elected by their delegates; seven persons are nominated by federations, constituency and central parties and elected by their delegates; five women are nominated by all organizations and elected by the Conference as a whole. The Treasurer of the party is elected by the Conference. The Leader and Deputy Leader of the parliamentary party are *ex officio* members of the National Executive Committee. The Committee elects its chairman and vice-chairman from among its elected members.

The annual conference meets in the autumn for four and one-half days. Its potential membership, including *ex officio* members, is about 2,500 (less than half that of the Conservative Conference) but actual attendance is something over 1,000 (less than one-third of the Conservative attendance). The main reason for the shortfall at the Labour Conference is the non-appointment of many trade-union representatives. But those representative trade unionists who do attend can register the votes of all the Party members of their unions and the voting strength of the trade unions is about five-sixths of the total Conference vote.

We have seen that the National Executive Committee consists of twenty-eight persons.[17] Although the trade unionists nominate only twelve members, they cast the overwhelming votes for those elected by the whole Conference, that is, the five women and the Treasurer, although this does not mean that they will vote only for trade unionists for those six places.

The Labour party has a formal, written constitution which seeks to be comprehensive. So the constitution sets down the reason for the party's existence and the objects which nationally it tries to achieve. These are stated in Clause IV as being: to organize and maintain in Parliament and in the country a political Labour Party; to co-operate with the General Council of the Trades Union Congress, or other kindred organizations, in joint political or other action in harmony with the Party Constitution and Standing Orders; to give effect as far as may be practicable to the principles from time to time approved by the Party Conference; to secure for the workers by hand or by brain the full fruits of their industry and the most equitable distribution thereof that may be possible, upon the basis of the common ownership of the means of production, distribution, and exchange, and the best obtainable system of popular administration and control of each industry or service; generally to promote the political, social and economic emancipation of the people, and more particularly of those who depend directly upon their own exertions by hand or by brain for the means of life.

PARTY MEMBERSHIP

Any account of the structure of organizations like political parties tends to suggest a measure of efficiency and a scale of operations greater than exist in practice. Thus, for example, in rural areas the meeting of the local Labour party or of a polling district committee may consist of three or four people who may indeed operate only at the time of general elections. Similarly, in some parts of some industrial cities, the number of Conservatives gathered together for the purposes of the constituency party may be very small indeed. Press reports, based on handouts issued by the party, that a Member of Parliament or a nationally known politician addressed a party meeting may not reveal that his audience consisted of three local party officials, ten of the party faithful, and four members of the general public, including a 'spy' from the other party. When, during the campaign at the time of a general election, the cry goes out for volunteers, then many party supporters will appear to perform their menial duties. But between general elections, with only a mild surge of enthusiasm at the time of local elections, constituency parties are managed and the work is done by fewer, often far fewer, than fifty to one hundred people.

The total membership of the two main parties is difficult to assess accurately and claims made by the parties themselves are likely to be optimistic and to be revealed only when the figures are high. McKenzie refers to Conservative figures (for England and Wales) of about $2\frac{1}{4}$ million.[18] For the Labour party, he quotes figures of over six million but this includes some $5\frac{1}{2}$ million members of affiliated trade unions who are automatically Labour party members unless they choose not to be.[19] Such figures, as McKenzie points out, are almost meaningless if we are trying to assess the active membership – even on the widest definition of activity. If we consider a person active who attends six party meetings a year and does very little else except at the time of general elections, then there are perhaps at best 100 active members, on average, in each party in each constituency. On that basis each party would have 63,000 such members. On even the lowest claims of total party membership, such a number of activists does not amount to more than 2 per cent of the total. What is the importance of the active party membership on the working of the political system?[20] First, by working the party machine, the active members ensure that the party is financed, that subscriptions are obtained both to keep the party alive and to pay for the heavy expenses of running election campaigns. Secondly, the active members provide a body of unpaid labour without whose help the organization could not be sustained.

In return for this drudgery – as most of it is – what do the activists obtain? They first obtain the satisfaction of working for a political cause in which they believe. Of course this will include for some the pleasure of being important in their own eyes and in the eyes of others. If their party returns a Member to Parliament, they will be important to him and through him may meet others. A few of the activists will have political ambitions of their own. Some may covet honours. But for the great majority the satisfaction will be in the work itself. Secondly, active party members may exert a real influence over their Member particularly in matters which affect the constituency at large or which affect a considerable or an influential number of the electorate. No doubt a Member represents all his constituents and not only those who support him. But his interests and those of his supporters are likely to be close. He is expected to promote the activities on which his constituents depend. In a mining constituency, the National Union of Mineworkers will have been influential in his selection as candidate and in his election. The union's leaders will have his ear. So also the leaders of the National Farmers Union in a farming constituency will have the ear of 'their' Member. Thirdly, the active members select the parliamentary candidate.

THE SELECTION OF CANDIDATES

'The selection of parliamentary candidates is one of the least discussed and most recondite of the interlocking mysteries that make up the British system of government.' So wrote an American observer in 1965.[21] More recently, press publicity has increased, especially where safe party seats are known to be in the market. At any time, a number of former M.P.s (including former Ministers) or other public figures are understood to be seeking election to the House of Commons. And stories are carried in the newspapers of their endeavours to be adopted by this constituency and that. To fail consistently may become notorious and each failure tends to diminish the chance of adoption. But this is to anticipate.

Anyone seeking election to the House of Commons must, unless he intends to offer himself as independent of any party, be adopted by a local constituency political party as their 'prospective' candidate. If the seat is held by a Member of another party this may take place at any time between elections. If the seat is held by a Member of the same party, a new candidate will not be sought unless the sitting Member has announced his intention not to seek re-election or has resigned, died or lost favour with his local constituency party. This last contingency is rare.[22] Normally a sitting Member who wishes to seek re-election will be assured of his adoption.[23]

In the Conservative party the choice of candidate rests with each local association. But the National Union exerts some influence. In 1935 the Standing Advisory Committee on Candidates (S.A.C.C.) was set up and local associations are expected to consult this Committee before making their selections.

The Committee gives general guidance to local associations about the procedure to be adopted and the criteria to be looked for; it keeps a list of approved candidates which local associations are urged to consult; and it is empowered to withhold or withdraw approval from any locally adopted candidate. In practice the criteria are general and affect the selection hardly at all; there is little difficulty in an applicant finding a place on the list; and there have been very few examples of the Committee withholding or withdrawing approval. Moreover the Committee acts very largely on the advice of one man: a vice-chairman of the party organization known as the vice-chairman for candidatures.[24] Also influential in selection may be the area agent, who, although he advises the local associations, is employed by the Central Office and so may be instrumental in advancing the wishes of that office. It is usual for the chairman of the local association to visit the vice-chairman of the party organization to discuss possible candidates and the chairman may well return to his association bearing suggestions.

Despite all this machinery which enables the S.A.C.C., the vice-chairman of party organization, and the area agent to exert influence, the choice of prospective candidate remains very firmly with the local association, which is quick to resent any attempts to make it accept a candidate particularly favoured by central bodies. Moreover the local association will have received many applications directly and members of the local association will have suggestions to make. The competition is normally very real.

The number of applicants varies considerably – depending (naturally) on how desirable or 'safe' the seat is thought to be. A committee of the local association meets to prepare a short-list of applicants. This list contains no more than three or four names and is drawn up after the committee has interviewed perhaps four times that number. The executive council of the local association normally approves the recommended short-list and the selection conference is convened.

The selection conference is composed of the members of the executive council of the local association and usually numbers between thirty and one hundred members.[25] Each candidate makes a short speech to the conference and answers questions. Austin Ranney quoted this statement from a Central Office official:

What most associations want is a man of solid character. Not necessarily a brilliant man, you understand; in fact they may distrust a chap who seems too brilliant or flashy or glib. They want someone with the right sort of background, someone who looks and sounds right. They want someone they can count on to do the right thing, whether as a campaigner or a leader in association affairs or a Member of Parliament. They want someone who, by his business career, or his war record or his party service or his social standing, has proved that he is this kind of man.[26]

The conference selects by voting in a series of ballots until one person obtains a clear majority of votes cast. This is often done by eliminating after each ballot the person with the lowest number of votes.

The executive council then recommends to the whole local association the person selected and, save very rarely, the association accepts the recommendation without debate or question. The local association now rejoices in a prospective parliamentary candidate.

In the Labour Party the parts played by the central and by the local party organizations and the procedures adopted for the selection of candidates are, essentially, very similar to those just described for the Conservative party. The National Executive Committee of the party has an organization sub-committee which is concerned with candidatures. Austin Ranney lists the N.E.C.'s principal supervisory powers over local candidate selections as: authorizing the constituency Labour parties to select candidates; prescribing the selection procedures; setting the qualifications for candidatures; regulating local financial arrangements; and endorsing the selection of candidates.[27] The authority for the exercise of those powers derives in part directly from the constitution of the party and in part from Model Rules made under the constitution.

In the Labour party, headquarters keep two lists of approved candidates. List A consists of persons nominated by trade unions. List B consists of other persons. It is perhaps a little more difficult for a would-be Labour candidate to be placed on List B than it is for a Conservative would-be candidate to be placed on the list of approved candidates. And placement on List B does not necessarily ensure subsequent endorsement by the N.E.C.

In the Labour party, as in the Conservative party, headquarters use their influence to persuade local parties to adopt particular persons. There are notable examples of their success and also of their failure.[28]

Both in the exercise of the placement power and of the veto, the N.E.C is more prominent than similar bodies at headquarters of the Conservative party. But the scale of intervention is very small and Austin Ranney found for instance, some ten examples between 1945 and 1965 of Labour party headquarters denying to locally adopted candidates, on political grounds, the right to stand as official candidates.

In each constituency, it is the Executive Committee which draws up the short-list of candidates and the General Committee which, as a selection conference, makes the final choice.

Unlike the procedure in the Conservative party, a Labour candidate can be nominated only by an affiliated organization or local Labour party.[29] So the list of nominated Labour candidates is likely to be shorter than the comparable list of Conservative candidates. The short-list goes to the N.E.C. for approval and occasionally this approval is withheld in respect of particular persons whose political views the N.E.C. dislikes. The General Committee then approves the short-list, usually without amendment.

The selection conference in the Labour party is similar to that in the Conservative party, with short speeches and questions. After the voting, the name of the selected candidate goes to the N.E.C. for endorsement. There is no general gathering of the faithful in the constituency to adopt the nominee of the General Committee.

As Michael Rush says,[30] the two parties in selecting candidates pursue many common paths. In both a small constituency committee decides the short-list and a larger constituency body makes the selection after very similar procedures. So also, although in form local Conservative associations have more independence of the national party than have constituency Labour parties, in reality the extent of local autonomy in both is very similar and very considerable. Rush considers however that there are some 'important, perhaps fundamental, differences' between the parties.[31] The first is that constituency Labour parties must follow the nationally prescribed procedure and that under this no individual may apply for a vacancy but must be nominated by a party or affiliated organization. In the Conservative party there is no formal selection procedure and any individual may apply. Rush considers these and other similar differences in procedure to be important and concludes that the Labour party is more concerned with the democratic nature of the procedure and less with its efficiency while in the Conservative party the emphasis is the other way.

This generalization may or may not be valid but it is doubtful whether any of these or any other differences between the selection processes in the two parties can properly be designated as 'fundamental'. Above all, in both parties, the essential, crucial and close similarity lies in the amount of power exercised by the constituency parties and the very considerable difficulty which the central organizations have, except in the rarest cases, in even influencing the final selection.

THE INFLUENCE OF PARTY ON POLICY

A crucial question, much debated, is how far the Members of Parliament of each party, and particularly the leaders of each party, in and out of office, are, in political practice, influenced by, or have their policies determined by, party members in or out of Conference.

In its simplest formulation, one question is not difficult to answer. Of course, Members including their leaders in Parliament are influenced in their actions by the opinions of party members. They are influenced to some extent by all organs of public opinion and their supporters have a special right to be listened to. If parliamentarians disregard what they hear, they are more likely to make decisions which are highly unpopular or unworkable and so they will suffer in reputation and lose or fail to win power and office.

This must not be understood to mean primarily that parliamentarians and political leaders seek to act according to the wishes of the individual man in the street. Politicians are concerned with the powerful groups in a country, with industrial organizations, the large producing and financial companies, with trade unions, with professional bodies. They are also concerned with the effect of what they do on international trade and on international relations. But nevertheless, at the end of the day, it does lie with individual citizens, the mass of whom are not leaders of any of the opposing economic factions or firm adherents to any of them, to decide whether the Government shall or shall not continue to hold office. So regard must be had to the view of the general public and especially of those who are known supporters of the Government party. So also the opposition leaders must pay attention to public opinion and especially to the views of its known supporters. And for this purpose the views of party members are likely to reflect the views of those supporters.

How far does the largest organized group in the parties – the Party Conference – influence or determine the policies of the Leader and his parliamentary colleagues? The official publication of the Conservative party says that 'the Conference . . . debates resolutions submitted by constituency associations on policy and organization matters and provides the main forum for the expression of opinions by representatives of all sections of the party'.[32] These are cautious, even evasive, words for they tell us nothing about the extent to which the leadership is expected to pay attention to resolutions passed by the Conference. 'The Conference in recent years,' says McKenzie, 'has served primarily as a demonstration of party solidarity and as a source of stimulation to the constituency representatives who attend.'[33] The Leader does not appear until the conference is ended, when he addresses a mass meeting. Attacks on the leadership are rare. Occasionally what happens at the conference has an impact on party policy, as on the famous occasion in 1950 when the Chairman on behalf of the party leaders accepted the goal of building 300,000 houses a year. The resolutions which are passed are conveyed to the Leader. In practice, party members do not indulge in public recrimination when Conservative Governments appear to disregard what the conference has resolved.

The Labour Party because it has the advantage or disadvantage of a written constitution is more explicit. Clause V provides:

(1) The party Conference shall decide from time to time what specific proposals of legislative, financial or administrative reform shall be included in the party programme.

No proposal shall be included in the party programme unless it has been adopted by the party Conference by a majority of not less than two-thirds of the votes recorded on a card vote.

(2) The National Executive Committee and the Parliamentary Committee of the Parliamentary Labour Party shall decide which items from the party programme shall be included in the manifesto which shall be issued by the National Executive Committee prior to every general election. The Joint Meeting of the two Committees shall also define the attitude of the Party to the principal issues raised by the election which are not covered by the manifesto.

And then in Clause VI it provides:

(1) The work of the party shall be under the direction and control of the party Conference,[34] which shall itself be subject to the constitution and standing orders of the party. The party Conference shall meet regularly once in every year and also at such other times as it may be convened by the National Executive Committee.

So the party Conference decides what shall go into the party programme. And the N.E.C. and the Parliamentary Committee[35] decide what part of the programme shall go into the manifesto for a particular general election. In the early summer of 1973, the N.E.C. by a majority vote decided in favour of a policy for the State control of up to twenty-five unnamed leading manufacturing companies. The next day the Leader of the party (a member of both the N.E.C. and the Parliamentary Committee) issued a statement disagreeing with this policy and saying that the Parliamentary Committee would veto it – (presumably) if the party Conference adopted it. As the vote in the N.E.C. was less than half the membership of that body, it was not clear how many members of the N.E.C.

would support the proposal at the joint meeting of the two commit-tees. But, in any event, the constitution is itself not clear: does it give the right to one or other of the two committees to veto a proposal, as Mr Wilson assumed? Or does it envisage a vote at the joint meeting which might split the members of one or both commit-tees? Certainly there is the possibility under the constitution of a Labour Prime Minister being saddled with an election manifesto which in part he opposes. But, in political reality, the possibility is remote as a division amongst members at the joint meeting to settle the manifesto would be electorally most damaging.

From time to time party conferences pass resolutions which the leadership of the party would prefer they did not. But the most important principle is clear: neither a Labour Government nor a Conservative Government considers itself bound to adhere, in deciding its national policies, to resolutions passed by party con-ferences or indeed by any other organization, unless the policy has been enshrined in the election manifesto. And it is common know-ledge that promises in manifestoes are not invariably fulfilled. In opposition, the emphasis (at least) is different and resolutions passed at party conferences are strong pressures on the party leadership to adopt their purport as the party policy. Nevertheless, the leaders of the parliamentary parties backed up by their close associates (who in the Labour party normally include leading trade unionists) will get their way in almost all important situations. It is wholly significant that the biggest exception in recent years to this was when the Labour Government was forced to withdraw its proposals for the reform of industrial relations. For in this case the leaders of the parliamentary party, in the Cabinet, sought to implement a policy which was not merely disliked by the trade union leaders but, in their view, directly attacked the interest they represented. It was as though the parliamentary leaders had forgotten that the very heart of power in the Labour movement is the alliance between themselves and the leaders of the large unions.

It is remarkable how the organization of political parties in the United Kingdom has remained so unaffected by the provisions of the law. Statutes do affect some of their activities – especially their participation in elections – but their internal working is essentially uncontrolled by legal regulation. This is mainly because they operate as private organizations and so long as they do not infringe the rules of law applying to people generally there is no immediate reason why the law should seek to lay down rules for their conduct. Yet the functions they perform are of public significance; they spend a great deal of money; their influence, direct and indirect, pervades the whole political body. So the public interest in what they do is undeniable.

The political parties control the legislative process and no doubt they prefer to remain as they are, with no statute and no rules of law constraining them. So long as no major public scandal occurs, they are likely to be able to continue in their freedom from regulation.

However, the way the two parties conduct themselves is an example, at another level, of the difference between administrative flexibility and more formal quasi-legal structures. One may say that the Conservatives operate an unwritten constitution and the Labour party a written constitution. In real political terms, the power of the leaders in relation to other groups within their parties is very similar; but the greater apparent choice which the Conservative Leader has in choosing his shadow Cabinet and the more rigid constitutional objects and procedures for determining party policy which the Labour party must adhere to or seem to adhere to does make more likely the creation and disclosure of differences of opinion within the Labour party. The freedom from stated political object-ives enjoyed by the Conservatives enables the policy makers and tacticians in the party to put forward programmes to the electorate unconstrained by an explicit ideology. As with the Labour party, the Conservatives continue to serve the interests they represent but they do so without great publicity and so manage more successfully to avoid antagonizing others. This, together with their determined belief that it is better to be in office on any terms than out of office, accounts in part for their repeated success at the polls.

3
General Elections

The primary function of a general election is, of course, to choose the men and women who will be the members of the next Parliament. Since, however, the identity of the next Government depends on the composition of the House, an even more important function is to decide who will form the next Government, and because of this the campaign often takes on the character of a personal contest between the two rival party leaders.

It has sometimes been suggested that general elections have a third function: that of allowing the electorate to make a decision on questions of policy. According to the doctrine of mandate the party which wins the election should carry out the policies which it put to the voters in its election manifesto. It is also said that no fundamental changes should be made unless the Government obtains a mandate for them by putting them forward as party policy at an election. In practice, however, Governments frequently embark on the most important policy changes without any such mandate and it is not difficult for those with even a slight knowledge of contemporary events to point to cases in which election promises have been quietly forgotten once a party has come to power. The only constitutional significance of this doctrine, therefore, seems to be a vague and rather doubtful convention that major *constitutional* changes should not be undertaken without a mandate. Thus when the Liberals in 1910 wanted to take away the powers of the House of Lords to veto legislation passed by the Commons, a general election was specially held to obtain a mandate. Except in this kind of situation, however, the doctrine is no more than a convenient weapon with which to attack one's opponents in political debate.

Even if the doctrine of a mandate were accepted in its fullest sense, general elections would be a very imperfect means of allowing the voters to decide issues of policy. First of all it is the two parties which decide what the issues in the election are, and many important questions may be left out of the party manifestoes. Secondly, on many important issues both parties may have the same policies – both parties, for example, supported in principle British entry into the E.E.C. in the 1970 general election; and finally, even when the parties have different policies, a voter who favours the policy of one party on one issue may not support the policy of the same party on another issue.

This does not mean, however, that the electorate cannot influence Government policy. The parties choose their leaders and their policies; the electors merely choose between them. But because the parties are competing for the support of the electorate they choose their leaders and policies with an eye to their acceptability to the electorate. Each general election tends to be an inquest on the record of the Government in power, in which the electors accept or reject its request for another five years in office and, though between elections the Government has the constitutional freedom to choose its policies as it pleases, the fact that it must in due course face the electors puts limits on what it can do – there are some things the voters just will not stand – and provides an incentive for new policies that will win it popular support.

THE VOTING SYSTEM

The British electoral system is the product of history just as much as of principle.[1] A series of great reforms stretching from 1832 to 1948 has resulted in a system in which the slogan 'one man, one vote' is a reality; yet nevertheless in certain important ways each vote is not of equal value. For this reason, although the British system has been copied in most of the countries once ruled by Britain, it has not found much favour elsewhere and in most Continental countries electoral systems have been adopted which are aimed at reflecting more accurately the opinion of the electors.

The first principle of the British system is that of territorial representation. Each member of the House of Commons represents a particular local area and, under the modern system,[2] he is the only representative of that area. The second principle is that the candidate with the most votes in each constituency is elected even though, if there are more than two candidates, he might get a minority of the total number of votes cast. This is the 'first past the post' system or, more formally, the simple plurality system. This system has a number of important characteristics which affect the political process and the kind of government we get.[3]

First of all, as stated above, the successful candidate in a particular constituency may be elected on a minority of votes. Thus if there are three candidates standing and one receives 34 per cent of the votes and the other two get 33 per cent each, the first will be elected. This may be a somewhat unlikely result[4] but it quite often happens that the winning candidate gets under 50 per cent of the vote. When this occurs it could be said that that candidate does not truly 'represent' that constituency.

The second characteristic of the system is that the representation of the parties in the Commons does not accurately reflect their standing in the country. What normally happens is that the party with the most votes gains a disproportionately large number of seats while small parties are grossly under-represented. This can be seen from the following table[5] which compares the percentage of votes with the percentage of seats gained by each of the three major parties in the elections since the Second World War.

		1945	1950	1951	1955	1959	1964	1966	1970	1974
CON.	Votes%	39·6	43·5	48·0	49·7	49·3	43·4	41·9	46·4	38·1
	Seats%	32·8	47·7	51·3	54·8	57·9	48·3	40·1	52·4	46·6
LAB.	Votes%	48·0	46·1	48·8	46·4	43·9	44·1	48·1	42·9	37·2
	Seats%	61·4	50·4	47·2	44·0	41·0	50·3	57·8	45·6	47·4
LIB.	Votes%	9·0	9·1	2·6	2·7	5·9	11·2	8·5	7·5	19·5
	Seats%	1·9	1·4	1·0	0·9	0·9	1·4	1·9	1·0	2·2

It will be seen from this table that no party has ever obtained an overall majority of votes since the War (the nearest any party has got to this was the Conservative poll of 49·7 per cent in 1955) and yet, until 1974, there has always been a parliamentary majority – admittedly sometimes a fairly small one – for one party or the other. This tendency of the system to over-reward the most successful party and discourage small parties means that there is rarely any necessity for a coalition Government. The fact that the system favours strong, one-party government is generally regarded as one of its greatest virtues; yet it means that Parliament can only to a limited extent claim to reflect the opinion of the electorate.

It could be argued that a general election is a plebiscite to choose a Government rather than an attempt to produce an assembly that exactly mirrors the political opinion of the electorate at any given time, and therefore the defects mentioned previously are unimportant. However, it may happen that the system does not even fairly indicate who should form the next Government. The result in 1951 is a case in point. It will be seen from the table that in the election of that year the Conservatives got 48·0 per cent of the total vote as against 48·8 per cent for Labour; yet the Conservatives obtained a majority in Parliament and formed the next Government. Likewise in the election of February, 1974 the Conservatives won more votes than Labour but obtained 5 fewer seats. This defect in the system is caused by the fact that the support of one party may be less evenly spread throughout the country so that it may 'waste' a lot of votes by obtaining very heavy majorities in some seats and lose others by a comparatively small margin.

The last characteristic of the system that should be mentioned is that the result of a general election usually depends on the results of a small number of marginal constituencies. This means, first, that a small swing of opinion can produce a change of Government and, secondly, that individual voters in most constituencies are in one sense 'disenfranchised' since their vote is unlikely to have any influence on the result. Thus a voter in a safe seat for one party or the other knows that only in the most extraordinary circumstances will the sitting member fail to be returned. His vote can only affect the majority by which the seat is won: it is only in a marginal seat that it might affect the outcome.

CONSTITUENCIES

Fixing the boundaries of the constituencies is a job of great political importance since the way it is done can have a significant effect on the outcome of an election. Moreover, since constant shifts of population are occurring in different parts of the country, it is necessary for a redistribution of seats to take place at regular intervals if undue disparities in the size of constituencies are to be avoided. In view of this it is surprising that until 1944 there was no permanent machinery for keeping constituency boundaries under review. Before this, redistribution took place on an *ad hoc* basis at rather infrequent intervals in conjunction with other electoral reforms, and large differences in the size of constituencies were common.

The present legislation is the House of Commons (Redistribution of Seats) Acts, 1949 and 1958. This legislation established on a permanent basis four separate Boundary Commissions – for England, Scotland, Wales and Northern Ireland – to keep the distribution of seats under continuous review. Originally the commissions were required to undertake a general review every three to seven years (i.e. once during the life of each normal Parliament) but the parties objected to the organizational disruption caused by frequent changes, and the 1958 Act now provides that a general review is to take place not less than ten nor more than fifteen years from the last one.[6] Reports may, however, be made at any time concerning a particular constituency or group of constituencies.[7]

The Speaker of the House of Commons is *ex officio* chairman of each commission.[8] The rest of the English Commission consists of a High Court judge appointed by the Lord Chancellor (deputy chairman),[9] a member appointed by the Home Secretary, and another appointed by the Secretary of State for the Environment.[10] The appointments are made from persons who are not active in politics, and it is provided by the House of Commons Disqualification Act, 1957[11] that Boundary Commissioners are disqualified from membership of the House of Commons. The Registrar General for England and Wales and the Director General of Ordnance Survey[12] act as assessors for the commission.

The total number of constituencies for each part of the United Kingdom is given in the Act as follows:[13]

Great Britain ....Not substantially greater or less than 613
Scotland ....Not less than 71
Wales ....Not less than 35
Northern Ireland ...12

It will be seen that only Northern Ireland has a fixed number of seats. There is a minimum laid down for Scotland and Wales but the commissions for those countries may provide for a greater number than the minimum, and Wales, in fact, has one additional seat at present. The number of seats for England must not be substantially greater or less than the number obtained by subtracting the actual number of Scottish and Welsh seats from 613. This gives a target of 506 but this has been exceeded by the Commission. The present numbers after the election in February 1974[14] are:

England 516
Scotland 71
Wales 36

Total for Great Britain 623
Northern Ireland 12

U.K. total   635

Scotland and Wales have more seats relative to their population than England; Northern Ireland has fewer.

The rules that guide the commissions in their work are set out in the Acts.[15] The two most important are that local government units must be respected as far as practical (e.g. one county must not share a constituency with another) and that the electorates of each constituency must be as nearly equal as possible. When these principles conflict, as they quite often do, preference must be given to the first unless 'excessive disparity' in numbers results. The commissions may also take geographical considerations into account (e.g. the size, shape and accessibility of an area) and must also take into consideration the inconveniences that result from alterations in constituencies.[16] These rules are, of course, fairly elastic and it is also expressly laid down that the commissions are not obliged to give full effect to them in all circumstances.[17] The result is that the commissions have a fair measure of discretion.

Within the limits laid down by the Acts the timing of the reviews is a matter for the commissions[18] and they normally co-ordinate their work so that their Reports appear at the same time. When they decide to start a general review a public announcement must be made.[19] The commission first makes provisional recommendations and publishes them in local newspapers together with a notice that representations can be made within one month. The representations are then considered and in certain cases local inquiries are held.[20] If it is decided to amend the recommendations objectors are given the opportunity to make further representations. The final recommendations are then embodied in the Report and this is presented to the Home Secretary.[21]

Once the Home Secretary has received the Report he must lay

it before Parliament together with a draft Order in Council to give effect to it.[22] The Act provides that the draft Order may give effect to the Report 'with modifications' but in this case a statement giving the reasons for the changes must be laid before Parliament as well.[23] If the draft Order is approved by a resolution of each House the Home Secretary must submit it to the Queen in Council who makes an Order in Council in terms of the draft.[24] This Order will come into force on the date specified in it but will not apply before the next general election, i.e. by-elections will not be affected. The Act provides that the Order cannot be challenged in any legal proceedings.[25]

There have been several occasions on which attempts have been made to obtain the intervention of the courts in the redistribution process by seeking remedies against what was claimed to be unlawful action by a Boundary Commission or the Home Secretary. The first two arose out of the 1954 general revision. In *Hammersmith Borough Council* v. *Boundary Commission*[26] an application was made to obtain a mandatory injunction against the English Boundary Commission to require it to inform the Home Secretary that its Report was contrary to the provisions of the Act. The injunction was refused on the ground that it was improper for the Court to interfere. In *Harper* v. *Home Secretary*[27] an injunction was sought against the Home Secretary to prevent him from presenting a draft Order, which had been approved by Parliament, to Her Majesty in Council to be made into an Order in Council. It was claimed that the Report was not a 'Report' within the meaning of the Act because it did not comply with the rules. Since a draft Order can be presented to Parliament only to give effect to a 'Report', it was argued that there was no statutory authority for making the Order. (Since the Act prevents the courts from impugning the validity of an Order in Council[28] it was necessary that any proceedings should be brought before the Order was made.)

An interim injunction was granted by Roxburgh J. but it was lifted three days later by the Court of Appeal, which held, first, that the rules had not been broken and, secondly, that it was not the intention of Parliament in passing the Act that the courts should have the jurisdiction to decide whether particular decisions of the Commission were right or not. It was, however, expressly left open whether the courts would be able to grant redress if the Report were 'manifestly in complete disregard' of the provisions of the Act.[29]

The door was not, therefore, closed completely but it is unlikely that the courts will ever intervene effectively in a matter which concerns the composition of the House of Commons and is under the ultimate control of Parliament.[30]

Even greater controversy resulted from the 1969 Reports. This was caused by the fact that the Labour Government refused to implement the Reports, ostensibly on the ground that a radical reform of local government was planned, which would necessitate another revision of the constituencies in the near future. Most observers, however, thought that the real reason was that Labour stood to lose ten to twenty seats in the forthcoming general election if the Reports were implemented. The Government proposed that the constituencies should remain as they were except in the case of Greater London (where the reform of local government had already taken place) and a small number of very large constituencies. A bill was brought in to provide for this but it was drastically amended in the House of Lords and the Government had to drop it. Instead the Home Secretary introduced draft Orders into the Commons to give effect to the recommendations and then put the whips on to defeat them.[31] The letter of the law was thus complied with. The 1970 general election was therefore held on the basis of the 1954 distribution of constituencies, which meant that the variation in the size of the constituencies was in some cases quite considerable.[32] When a Conservative Government was returned after the general election the Reports were implemented in full.

The object of entrusting the redistribution of seats to independent commissions was to take the matter out of politics. The problem is that the matter has not really been taken 'out of politics' at all because the functions of the commissions are only advisory: the final decision rests with Parliament and, as has been seen, Governments are prepared to use their parliamentary majorities to enable them to get their own way. Since, moreover, the conflicting requirements of equality of size and respect for local government units make the commissions' task a difficult one, there is often some fairly plausible ground on which the Government can intervene. The jealousy with which Parliament protects its powers and privileges makes it unlikely that it will ever agree to give the final say to an independent body; yet if this is not done it is probable that further controversies will arise in the future.

THE RIGHT TO VOTE

The legal rules concerning the right to vote are based on the concept of universal adult franchise. Although the policy of the law is to give everyone the right to vote there are necessarily certain restrictions in practice.[33] First of all, no one can vote unless his name is on the electoral register for the constituency. These registers are prepared annually and are based on the circumstances existing on 10 October each year (the qualifying date). The new register comes into force on 16 February and applies to any election held during the following twelve months.[34]

The preparation of the register is the duty of the registration officer of the constituency who, in England and Wales, is the County or Town Clerk.[35] A form is usually sent to each household in the constituency requesting the names of all those entitled to be registered. If necessary a house-to-house inquiry is made as well. The registration officer then prepares a preliminary list which is published so that claims and objections can be made. Claims are made by persons who are not on the list and consider that they ought to be; objections are made by persons who are themselves on the list but object to other persons being registered.[36] Claims and objections are made to the registration officer and there is an appeal from his decision to the county court.[37] The decision of the Court of Appeal on appeal from the county court is final.[38] The next requirement is that one must be resident in the constituency on the qualifying date.[39] The only exceptions to this concern merchant seamen and service voters (members of the armed forces, civil servants stationed overseas, etc.), who may be registered in the constituency where they would have been resident but for their employment. They are entitled to vote by proxy or by post.[40] If a person is resident in the constituency on the qualifying date and is included in the register, he can vote during the period in which it is in force, even if he moves to another constituency. Persons in this situation are entitled to vote by post.[41]

The case of *Fox* v. *Stirk*[42] concerned the question whether a student at Bristol University who was living in a university residence was entitled to vote in the constituency where the university was situated instead of where his parents had their home. The Court of Appeal held that he could, even though he was not entitled to occupy his room in the residence during the whole of the year. Lord Denning, M.R. laid down the following propositions: First, it is possible for a person to be resident in two places – for example someone with a flat in London and a house in the country – and in such a case he would be entitled to be on the electoral register in both places though he could vote in only one of them.[43] Secondly, temporary presence is not residence: a weekend guest is not resident where he is visiting. Thirdly, temporary absence from a place does not deprive a person of his residence there, for example if he goes on holiday. The test of residence is the degree of permanence of the person's stay. A student living in lodgings in the university town would be resident there. If he lives with his parents during the vacation he can choose whether he wants to vote there or in the constituency where the university is.

The next requirement is that one should be free of any legal incapacity to vote both on the qualifying date and on the date of the poll. By common law a peer is not entitled to vote. It has been provided by statute that peeresses in their own right are also incapable.[44] The reason for this is, of course, that such persons are entitled to sit in the House of Lords and obtain their political representation in this way. Secondly, convicts cannot vote while they are in prison.[45] Thirdly, at common law insane persons cannot vote except during a lucid interval. Finally, persons who are guilty of corrupt or illegal practices at elections are under an incapacity to vote for the next five years.[46]

The next qualification is one of citizenship. It is usual for foreigners to be excluded from the franchise and this is the position in Britain; but the requirements are drawn in fairly wide terms: first, any British subject can vote, and this includes not only United Kingdom citizens but also citizens of every Commonwealth country; secondly, Irish citizens are also qualified.[47] It is necessary again that the qualification of citizenship exist both at the qualifying date and on the date when the election is held.

The last qualification is that one must have attained the age of 18. This qualification is only required to exist at the date of the poll and persons who are not 18 when the register is compiled, but who will turn 18 during the period when it will be in force, have their names on the register together with the date of their birthday: they can vote only if the election takes place after that date.[48]

QUALIFICATION OF CANDIDATES
The qualifications for candidates are in many respects similar to

those for voters. There is, however, no general provision setting out the qualifications; the law instead proceeds by disqualification. Thus aliens are disqualified; so only British subjects and citizens of the Republic of Ireland are eligible.[49] Persons under the age of twenty-one are also disqualified. This was laid down by section 7 of the Parliamentary Elections Act of 1695 and when the age of majority was lowered to eighteen by the Family Law Reform Act 1969 this provision was expressly preserved.[50] Thus a person can vote at eighteen but cannot be a candidate until twenty-one. Before the Reform Bill of 1832, however, some infants (including Charles James Fox) sat 'by connivance'.[51]

Lunacy is a disqualification at common law. Section 137 of the Mental Health Act 1959 now provides a procedure for vacating a seat held by a lunatic: the Speaker receives reports on the Member's health from two specialists; after further reports six months later, the seat becomes vacant.

Peers and peeresses in their own right, other than Irish peers (who do not sit in the House of Lords), are disqualified. The Peerage Act 1963, however, allows peers and peeresses to disclaim their peerages and once this is done the person concerned is eligible for election to the House of Commons.[52]

A bankrupt is also disqualified for election. The disqualification remains for five years after his discharge unless the adjudication of bankruptcy is annulled or he obtains from the court on his discharge a certificate to the effect that his bankruptcy was not caused by any misconduct on his part. If a sitting member goes bankrupt the court must certify this to the Speaker after six months (unless the disqualification is removed) and his seat then becomes vacant.[53]

It was provided by the Forfeiture Act 1870[54] that a person convicted of treason or felony who was sentenced to more than twelve months' imprisonment was disqualified for membership of the Commons while serving his sentence. However, since the category of offences known as felonies has been abolished,[55] the provisions of this Act now apply only to treason. A convict (other than one guilty of treason) can therefore stand for election to the Commons, although if he is elected he cannot sit or vote while in gaol. The House may also resolve to expel him. The position is the same where a sitting member is convicted of a crime: he will not automatically lose his seat (unless the offence is treason) but he will be unable to sit or vote while serving his sentence and he may be expelled by resolution of the House.[56]

Corrupt practices at elections may disqualify. A candidate who is reported personally guilty by an election court of a corrupt practice is not eligible, for five years, for election for any constituency; he is also disqualified for ten years for election to the constituency where the corrupt practice was committed. Ineligibility also flows from being reported guilty through agents of a corrupt practice, or personally guilty of an illegal practice.[57]

Clergymen are also disqualified. Under the House of Commons (Clergy Disqualification) Act 1801 all persons who have been ordained to the office of priest or deacon are ineligible. This applies to all episcopally ordained clergymen. However, when the Church of England was disestablished in Wales, the disability was lifted as regards Church of England clergy in Wales.[58] Section 9 of the Roman Catholic Relief Act 1829 disqualified all persons in Holy Orders in that Church. With one exception, however, clergymen who have not been ordained by a bishop (Nonconformists) are not disqualified: the exception applies to ministers of the Church of Scotland (Presbyterian), who were also disqualified by the Act of 1801.

There is no logic in these rules. The Church of England is of course represented through its Bishops in the House of Lords; it is also the established Church in England. The Church of Scotland is the established Church of Scotland, but it has no representation in the House of Lords. On the other hand the Roman Catholic Church, the Church of Ireland and the Episcopal Church of Scotland are neither established nor do they have representation in the House of Lords. It is unlikely, however, that the law will be changed: a select committee investigated the matter in the 1950s and decided that it was best to leave things as they were.[59]

Disqualification can also result from holding certain offices. The Act of Settlement 1700 said simply, comprehensively, but not altogether clearly:[60]

No person who has an Office or Place of Profit under the King, or receives a Pension from the Crown, shall be capable of serving as a Member of the House of Commons.

This provision was quickly replaced by other legislation but the 'office of profit' principle was maintained for the next 250 years.

The House of Commons Disqualification Act 1957 erases the rule by providing:[61]

Except as provided by this Act, a person shall not be disqualified for membership of the House of Commons by reason of his holding an office or place of profit under the Crown or any other office or place, and a person shall not be disqualified for appointment to or for holding any office or place by reason of his being a member of that House.

It does, however, list six classes of office holders who are disqualified.[62] These are:

1. The holders of certain judicial offices[63] (including judges of the High Court and Court of Appeal).
2. Civil servants, whether established or not and whether whole or part time.
3. Members of the regular armed forces.
4. Members of police forces in the United Kingdom.
5. Members of the legislature of any country outside the Commonwealth.
6. Holders of other offices listed in the Act.[64]

This list is a long one and includes the boards of nationalized industries, new town development corporations, the Lands Tribunal, the University Grants Committees, Governors of the B.B.C., Directors of Cable and Wireless Limited, Boundary Commissioners and many others no less diverse.

The Act also provides:[65]

Not more than ninety-one persons being the holders of offices specified in the Second Schedule to this Act (in this section referred to as Ministerial offices) shall be entitled to sit and vote in the House of Commons at any one time.

The Second Schedule lists fifty Ministerial Offices. (This includes Secretary of State and Minister of State which may be held by more than one person.) The schedule is amended from time to time as new Ministers are created or titles are changed.

The rationale of these provisions is complicated but most of the non-ministerial office holders are excluded because membership of the House would be incompatible with the political neutrality required by their offices. The reason for the limitation of ministerial office-holders is the desire to prevent the Government side of the House being entirely dominated by members of the Government (who are normally less independent than back-benchers). If, therefore, the Prime Minister wishes to create additional ministerial offices above the permitted number, he must either amend the law or grant peerages to the persons appointed.

Finally it should be mentioned that anyone who accepts the offices of bailiff or steward of the Chiltern Hundreds or the Manor of Northstead is automatically disqualified.[66] This is the traditional method of resignation from the House.

The way a dispute concerning the qualifications of an M.P. is settled normally depends on whether he was disqualified when he was elected or whether he became disqualified after election. If a candidate who is ineligible wishes to stand for election the returning officer cannot reject his nomination papers. He must be allowed to stand; but if he is elected the matter can be brought before an election court.[67] If the ground of his disqualification was known to the voters at the time of the election, the court may declare that the candidate who came second is duly elected; otherwise the election is declared void and another poll held.

If an M.P. becomes disqualified after election the matter will normally be dealt with by the House itself. The usual procedure is to refer the matter to a select committee.[68] If the disqualification results from the House of Commons Disqualification Act 1957, any person can apply to the Privy Council for a declaration that the member is disqualified.[69] A declaration will not, however, be given if the ground of the disqualification has ceased to exist by the time the case is brought before the Privy Council and the House has passed a resolution that the disqualification be disregarded.

Finally, there is one case – disqualification under the House of Commons (Clergy Disqualification) Act 1801 – in which the old procedure survives whereby a common informer (i.e. any member of the public) can sue the M.P. for a penalty of £500 for every day he sits in the House while disqualified.[70]

An interesting case which illustrates the way some of these procedures work is that of Anthony Wedgwood Benn. He was the heir to a peer (Lord Stansgate) and was an M.P. in 1960 when his father died. He claimed that he could renounce his peerage and remain an M.P. The House, however, ruled otherwise (it was before the passing of the Peerage Act 1963). A by-election was held to elect a new member and Mr Benn (or Lord Stansgate, as he should have been known) stood as a candidate and won. The election was then challenged by petition and the election court held that he was disqualified and, since the voters knew the facts when they cast their votes, his opponent was declared duly elected.[71] When the Peerage Act was passed in 1963 he immediately disclaimed his peerage and was later re-elected to Parliament.

THE ELECTION CAMPAIGN

The decision to call a general election rests with the Prime Minister.[72] When he decides to call the election the Queen issues a proclamation dissolving Parliament and summoning a new one. Writs are then sent out to the Returning Officers (who are usually Mayors or Sheriffs)[73] commanding them to hold an election in their constituencies. The Returning Officer announces the date by which nominations must close (eight days after the proclamation) and the date of the poll (nine days after the close of nominations).[74] The candidates deliver their nomination papers (signed by ten electors in the constituency), appoint their election agents,[75] pay their deposits of £150[76] and the campaign begins.

Even though the law still regards a general election simply as a set of individual elections held in each of the 630 constituencies, there is no doubt that today general elections are fought on national issues in a national campaign. The press conferences and speeches of the national leaders (which are extensively reported on T.V.) are much more important than the propaganda efforts of the individual candidates. House-to-house canvassing is, however, done on a constituency basis and is important not so much because it converts voters but because it enables the party to get the maximum number of its supporters to the polls. Election meetings are attended mainly by the faithful and their function is to provide inspiration to party workers so that they will not flag in their efforts.

The object of election law is to regulate the campaign so that it is fought fairly and honestly and nothing is done which might impair the free choice of the voters.[77] The law seeks to achieve this by creating special election offences, most of which are designated as either corrupt practices or illegal practices. The former are more serious and carry a maximum penalty of a year's imprisonment or a fine of £200 while the maximum penalty for the latter is a £100 fine.[78] A person who has been convicted of a corrupt or illegal practice can also be disqualified from voting or standing as a candidate in future elections.

In the earlier part of the nineteenth century bribery and corruption were very extensive and seats were bought and sold in the most cynical way. This was gradually eliminated by various reforms and today prosecutions for bribery,[79] treating[80] (for example, free beer for voters) and undue influence[81] (threats of temporal or spiritual injury) – all corrupt practices if done to influence voting – are virtually unknown. The main problems now concern the more mundane matters of limiting expenditure in elections and attempting to control that most potent form of mass communication and persuasion: television.

The purpose of setting limits to the amount of money that can be spent in elections is to prevent rich candidates and parties obtaining an unfair advantage and also, perhaps, because if parties and individuals had to rely too heavily on large sums of money from outside sources they might find that they were expected to give special favours to the donors if they did not want the source of funds to dry up. There are a number of ways in which the law tries to limit the money spent on electioneering. Thus it is an illegal practice for a candidate or agent to employ paid canvassers[82] or to pay any elector for the exhibition of posters (unless the elector is an advertising agent and the payment is made in the ordinary course of his business).[83] Secondly, section 63 of the Representation of the People Act 1949 provides that expenditure on advertising, holding meetings and certain other forms of publicity cannot be incurred 'with a view to promoting or procuring the election of a candidate at an election' by anyone except the candidate, his agent or someone authorized in writing by the agent. To spend money contrary to the section is a corrupt practice. Thirdly, section 64 puts a limit on all such expenditure[84] by a candidate and provides that if he knowingly exceeds the stipulated amount he is guilty of an illegal practice. This seems a simple and effective solution: anyone who spends money on behalf of a candidate without the agent's permission is guilty of an offence; and if the consent of the agent is obtained the money spent is included in the candidate's allowance.

The weakness of these provisions is that they relate only to expenditure on a constituency level and not to national publicity campaigns. This was illustrated in *R. v. Tronoh Mines Limited*[85] where a company which had placed an anti-socialist advertisement in *The Times* six days before the 1951 general election (without the consent of any candidate's agent) was found not guilty of contravening section 63. The Court held that the section relates only to promoting a particular candidate in a particular constituency and not to general political propaganda even if this assists all candidates of a particular party. Since the advertisement did not refer to any particular candidate or constituency, it did not contravene the section.

Section 63 also came before the courts after the 1964 general election. A number of Party Political Broadcasts had been transmitted by the BBC and ITA, and the leader of the Conservative Party, Sir Alec Douglas-Home, had appeared in one of them. After the election, a Communist candidate who had stood against him in the Kinross and West Perthshire constituency brought a petition before an Election Court to have the election declared void on the ground that the BBC and ITA had contravened section 63 by incurring expenses in presenting Sir Alec to the electors without the authority of his agent. He also claimed that Sir Alec or his agent had aided and abetted the commission of the offence. The court held that no breach of the law had taken place. Even though the broadcasts may have helped Sir Alec's campaign this was not the purpose of the television authorities in transmitting the broadcasts: the BBC and ITA had not incurred the expenses 'with a view to' promoting Sir Alec's election but in order to give information to the public.[86]

It will be apparent from the foregoing that the law has not been entirely successful in its efforts to limit election expenditure. There appears to be no legal limit on the amount that may be spent in national public relations and advertising campaigns so long as no reference is made to any specific constituency. It has often been said that this puts the Labour party at a disadvantage since it has less money to spend. It is true that the Conservatives usually have somewhat larger sums of money to spend in this way but it is extremely doubtful whether this has any marked effect on the outcome. The fact is that the publicity that is bought by such means as advertising in newspapers and on billboards[87] is far less important than the free publicity given to the two big parties and their leaders by the press and television. The speeches and public statements of the leaders are always fully reported and during the election campaign this coverage reaches – surpasses in the eyes of many – saturation point. Daily press conferences, speeches and party political broadcasts make the national leaders familiar figures on television and in the papers. Even before the beginning of the campaign, coverage is fairly full though here the party in Opposition is at something of a disadvantage.

The only legislation passed by the Labour Government of 1964–70 to deal with this issue was a provision in the Companies Act of 1967 requiring the directors of companies to disclose in their reports all sums above £50 given for political purposes (and who the recipients of the donations were).[88] Since most political donations from business go to the Conservatives it was hoped that publicity might make companies less ready to give money. The fact that nothing more radical than this was done suggests that the leaders of the Labour party are not dissatisfied with the existing position. The groups that do suffer from a lack of publicity are the smaller parties and independents, who do not get the large-scale coverage given to the big parties and who lack the resources to stage their own publicity campaigns. An effective limitation on election expenditure would, however, give little benefit to these groups because it would not affect the disparity in general coverage and would not make it any easier for them to buy publicity. A government subsidy for political parties might have some effect but if this were distributed on the basis of the representation of each party in Parliament or the number of candidates standing it would go mainly to the big parties. It is, of course, unlikely that any such subsidy will ever be forthcoming and it is probable that the present law will remain unchanged for some time to come.[89]

The law has taken a long time catching up with the development of television and it was not until 1969 that legislation was passed to regulate the use of television for electoral purposes. The way this was done is as follows. First, it is an illegal practice to make use of a foreign television or wireless transmitting station in order to influence voting at an election.[90] Secondly, it has been provided that when an election is pending it is unlawful to broadcast any item about the constituency from a U.K. television or wireless transmitting station if any candidate takes part and does not consent to the broadcast.[91] Thirdly, if the candidate's consent is given, he is guilty of an illegal practice if he takes part to promote his election and, either the broadcast is made before the close of nominations, or, if it is made after that time, is made without the consent of all the other candidates.[92]

The effect of this is to give each candidate a veto over any other candidate's appearing on a broadcast covered by these provisions. However, the law only covers the broadcasting of an 'item about a constituency' and would therefore not seem to cover general political broadcasts which do not refer to any specific constituency. Party political broadcasts and other television appearances by party leaders are consequently outside its scope. It also does not cover broadcasts about a particular constituency in which none of the candidates appears. It is unlikely, therefore, that these provisions will have a very significant effect on the election campaign and extra-legal methods will continue to provide the principal means by which the use of television is controlled.

When the votes have been counted it is the duty of the Returning Officer to declare elected the candidate with the greatest number of votes. He must endorse the election writ with the candidate's name and return it to the Clerk of the Crown. That candidate is then duly returned as the member for the constituency.[93]

The only way in which the result of an election can be questioned is by means of an election petition.[94] This may be presented by a candidate or voter in the constituency concerned to an Election Court, which in England and Wales consists of two judges of the Queen's Bench Division.[95] Witnesses are not excused from answering questions relating to election offences on the grounds that they may incriminate themselves but if they answer truthfully they are entitled to a certificate of indemnity which protects them from prosecution.[96] The Court certifies to the Speaker of the House of Commons what the result of the election was, i.e. the name of the candidate who was duly elected or that the election was void (in which case a new one must be held). If the two judges differ among themselves the member returned is deemed to be duly elected: an election result can be upset only if both judges agree.[97]

There are various grounds on which an election petition may be presented. The most important are as follows. First, if the successful candidate is guilty of any corrupt or illegal practice, either personally or by his agents, his election is void.[98] A candidate is guilty through his agent if any authorized agent of his commits such a practice, even if it is done without the knowledge and contrary to the express instructions of the candidate. An agent here means not only the officially appointed election agent but anyone authorized to work for the candidate in the election campaign, e.g. a canvasser.[99] Secondly, the election may be declared void if corrupt or illegal practices committed by anyone to promote the election of the winning candidate have prevailed so generally that they may reasonably be supposed to have affected the result.[100] It does not matter that the candidate and his agents were quite blameless. Both these rules may seem harsh since a candidate may be deprived of his victory through the actions of other people.[101] It is, however, his responsibility to appoint only reliable agents and if he gains votes as a result of such practices it would be wrong if he were allowed to take his seat.

Thirdly, an election may be declared void if the successful candidate is disqualified from sitting in Parliament, for example because he is a peer or was found guilty of corrupt or illegal practices in a previous election.[102] If, however, the ground of the disqualification was known to the electors when they voted, the court may, instead of declaring the election void, declare that the candidate with the next highest number of votes is duly elected.[103]

Election petitions were fairly common in the past but are very rare today. One reason seems to be that there is a tacit understanding between the main parties that they will not dispute elections won by the other side.[104] The heavy expenses involved may be another factor.[105]

4
The Government

THE QUEEN

'Elizabeth the Second, by the Grace of God of the United Kingdom
of Great Britain and Northern Ireland and of Her other Realms and
Territories, Queen, Head of the Commonwealth, Defender of the
Faith.'

She is the only supreme head of the realm, of the executive arm
of government, and is the fount of justice. But neither she nor
persons claiming authority under her are above the law, though
there are special laws which affect her.[1] The Queen cannot be said,
in similar terms to those used for the executive and the judiciary, to
be head of the legislature for, as we have seen,[2] that sovereignty she
exercises in Parliament.[3] So, when Ministers or other public
authorities exercise powers conferred on them by Act of Parliament
(which is indeed their main source of power) these are not the
Queen's powers but their own. On the other side of that coin,
almost all of the powers which the Queen enjoys as head of the
executive and head of the judiciary are exercised, not by her, but
by others in her name. Nevertheless this legal supremacy and
political insulation of the Queen is a useful device for it enables the
Government and the judiciary to keep their distance from one
another (when they choose) as neither is dependent on the other for
its authority.

In another sense, however, the Queen is not politically insulated
but politically involved. It would be possible for the sovereign to be
only a figurehead of the State and to be no more knowledgeable of
the affairs of the Government than any onlooker close to the scene.
But the Queen is more than a figurehead. She is kept in close touch
with the affairs of State by her Prime Minister whom normally she

sees at least once a week, and she is entitled to receive State papers. Her views on affairs when she chooses to give them to the Prime Minister will be taken into account. The person who becomes the sovereign is likely, because of birth and upbringing, to be on the right in political opinion. Moreover she is surrounded by people of like persuasion. The sovereign is also a person of considerable personal wealth, apart from the income which she draws from the State.[4] Again, the royal family have a personal and social magnetism and their recognition is much sought after by many men and women (including those in positions of political and economic power). The influence of the Queen's court is not to be underrated, especially in a country where the chances of political success in the Conservative party, and to some extent in the Liberal and even the Labour parties are enhanced by social acceptability.

Statute law has interposed itself into the conventional rules and the traditional characteristics which shape the monarchy. The Act of Settlement 1700 determines the line of succession and limits it to Protestants. The Royal Marriages Act 1772 is assumed to require the Queen's assent to the marriage of certain of her relatives. The Regency Acts 1937 to 1953 provide for the circumstances of the sovereign's infancy, ill health or absence from the country which may require others to exercise the sovereign's powers. But essentially the Queen's position in the political life of the State is the result of historical development which is continuing and which would cease only were a republic to be declared.

THE GOVERNING PARTY AND THE PRIME MINISTER

Chief among the Queen's Ministers is the Prime Minister. He has more political power than any other person in the country. It is possible that others – or other groups – have more economic power, more social influence, than he has. But no one can challenge his pre-eminence in the political world. He appoints all Ministers and may dismiss any. His voice is the strongest in Cabinet and in the constituencies. His appearance on television, his speechmaking, have more influence than those of any other person. He exerts great patronage and can dispense many favours, especially honours, which are very widely and assiduously sought after even by men and women whom one would have thought were so well known for their accomplishments that further public recognition was unnecessary. He has only one weakness compared with other very important people. Those others will often derive their importance from positions – in industry, in society, in the arts or in administration – which are effectively permanent. The Prime Minister holds office until the next general election when his power is put wholly at risk. It may be renewed for a further term, or it may be lost, probably for ever. But, while in office, his influence in domestic affairs is probably greater than that of any other head of government in Western Europe and North America.

How in these days does he come to this position? First, he must have been a member of the Conservative or of the Labour party since his youth. And he must have been a member of the House of Commons for many years. He must, in keen competition with many of his contemporaries within his party, have shown ability in the House of Commons and surefootedness in those slippery places where his seniors fought with one another. He should, at certain points in his career, either have thrown in his lot with one of those seniors who then went from success to success; or, at the very least, he should have avoided close identification with others who failed.[5] He must have been picked out for junior office at an early age and have incurred the minimum possible displeasure from those of his contemporaries who were passed over at the same time. And when he came to the top and into contest for the leadership of the party it must have been at a time when his particular qualities were thought to be preferable for reasons which might have had nothing whatever to do with himself.[6] Obviously, then, he must also have luck.

For almost fifty years now, the leader of the party having most seats in the House of Commons has been the Prime Minister of the day. And only three times during that period (in 1924, 1929–31 and 1974) did the Government not have an overall majority.

Until 1965, the Conservative party had no formal procedure for deciding who should be its leader. But in that year a set of rules was adopted and Mr Heath was the first leader elected under those rules. They provide that the leader shall be elected by a ballot, conducted amongst all the Conservative Members of the House of Commons, under the control of the chairman of the 1922 Committee.[7] Candidates must be proposed and seconded in writing (the names of the proposers and seconders not being disclosed) and the consent of the candidates obtained. A meeting is then called and each voter at the meeting receives a ballot paper and may vote for one candidate. If a candidate receives both an overall majority and 15 per cent more votes than any other candidate, he is elected. If no candidate is elected, a second ballot is held, not less than two nor more than four days later, after new nominations. On this second ballot any candidate receiving an overall majority is elected. If no candidate is elected, the three candidates who received the most votes on the second ballot go forward to the third and final ballot. On this occasion each voter gives a first preference to one of the three, and a second preference to another. The scrutineers add the number of first preferences and eliminate the candidate with the fewest votes. Then the second preferences of those who gave first preference votes to the third candidate are distributed amongst the two remaining candidates and the candidate with the most votes is elected. He is then 'presented for election' as party leader to the party meeting which consists of all Conservative M.P.s and peers and approved Conservative candidates and other non-Parliamentary members of the executive of the Conservative and Unionist Associations.

In the Labour party, the procedure is simpler and less formal. If the election is contested, the Parliamentary Committee devises the timetable for approval by the parliamentary party. If on the first ballot, a candidate receives more than 50 per cent of the votes cast, he is elected. If not, then the candidate with the lowest number of votes is eliminated and a second ballot is held.[8] As in the Conservative party, only Labour M.P.s in the Commons may vote.

Under neither of these procedures, therefore, are the rank-and-file members of the parties given an effective voice in the selection of the Leader. All is left to the elected M.P.s. Since the Leader is to be either the Prime Minister or the Leader of the Opposition and so the most important person so far as those M.P.s are concerned, this is to some extent understandable. But he is the leader of 'the party' not merely of the party in Parliament and it would be equally, if not more, logical if representatives of the constituency organizations were enabled to participate. On the other hand, this might make a considerable change in the Labour party if, as would seem inevitable, the trade union membership were also to be entitled to vote. So also it is possible that neither Sir Alec Douglas-Home nor Mr Heath was the first favourite of the constituency members at the time they became Prime Minister.

It is now accepted that each party will always nominate its Leader. If the Leader dies or resigns, the party will select another. If at a general election the governing party is defeated, then the Queen will ask the leader of the successful party to be Prime Minister and to form a Government. Does any power or discretion remain in the Queen? If a Government were re-elected at a general election with the largest number of seats but with less than an overall majority – always a possibility so long as the Liberal or any other third party remains capable of winning seats – and if that Government failed to persuade the third party to support it in the lobbies, then the Government might resign.* If so, the Queen would ask the Leader of the second party if he could form a Government and the third party might decide to support the second party and give it a majority in the House. But suppose the Government, re-elected without an overall majority, immediately asked the Queen for a dissolution and for another general election before it had been discovered whether the second party could obtain the support of the third party, could the Queen refuse to grant the dissolution? It seems to us that she could and that, in those circumstances, she should not grant a dissolution until she was sure that no combination of parties or of members could result in a Government with a majority of seats in the House.

If therefore we say that the Queen has no choice between rival claimants for the leadership of a party because both parties operate mechanisms to resolve that rivalry, this does not disentitle the Queen from trying to find a coalition which could serve her as a Government and she is not obliged to dissolve Parliament until it is clear that that is the only way out of the deadlock. For a new election may not resolve the deadlock and may even tighten it.

In the first half of this century there were twelve general elections (counting 1900 but not 1950); on two occasions the Government had no overall majority and on only one other occasion was the majority less than 100. In the seven elections from 1950 to 1974, on no occasion did the majority exceed 100, on four of these occasions it was 31 or less, and on one occasion (1974) there was no overall majority.

* If, as in February 1974, the Government party obtained fewer seats than the principal Opposition party, it might still be able to command a majority in the House of Commons and to continue as the Government if a sufficient number of members of other parties or groups were willing to support it.

In 1900 the Conservative party obtained 51·1 per cent of the votes cast; in 1931, 55·2 per cent; and in 1935 53·7 per cent. Since then no party has received 50 per cent. Whenever the two principal parties are separated by only a few seats, a third party or group of parties may hold the balance and a coalition may result.

MINISTERS AND THE CABINET

The immediate task of a new Prime Minister is to appoint other Ministers, first to fill the posts he intends to have in his Cabinet, then to appoint Ministers acting as heads of other departments or of sub-departments, and finally to appoint junior Ministers. It is often said that some posts must be Cabinet posts, and that some people (the most important in the Parliamentary party) must be in the Cabinet. But the Prime Minister is under no legal obligation to continue the same style of Cabinet as has been common, except in wartime, for many years. He could decide to have a Cabinet of any number, large or small. Thus he could turn the Cabinet into a small central policy-making body of himself and three or four others. Or he could appoint a Cabinet of forty or fifty and operate through a system of committees and sub-committees. He can in a word do as he likes with the machinery of government.[9] But if he remains conventional, then he will end with a cabinet of about twenty members.

In mid-1973 Mr Heath's Government contained fourteen principal departments. These, in order of the seniority of the Cabinet Ministers in charge, were the Civil Service Department (headed by the Prime Minister), the Foreign and Commonwealth Office, the Treasury,[10] the Northern Ireland Office, Defence, the Home Department, Health and Social Security, Environment, Education and Science, Scotland, Trade and Industry, Employment, Agriculture Fisheries and Food. Without responsibility for principal departments but in the Cabinet were the Lord Chancellor, the Lord President of the Council and Leader of the House of Commons, the Chancellor of the Duchy of Lancaster, the Lord Privy Seal and Leader of the House of Lords, and the Secretary of State for Wales; also in the Cabinet but within the Department of Trade and Industry was the Minister for Trade and Consumer Affairs.[11]

This made a cabinet of nineteen members of whom sixteen were in the House of Commons and three in the House of Lords.

In mid-1973 there were twenty-eight Ministers not in the Cabinet, all but one[12] of whom were departmental Ministers whose chiefs were in the Cabinet. Twenty-one were in the Commons and seven in the Lords. There were also the four Law Officers (the Attorney-General, the Solicitor-General, the Lord Advocate and the Solicitor General for Scotland); all were in the Commons.

Finally there were the junior Ministers. If the head of a department is designated Secretary of State then junior Ministers are called Under-Secretaries of State. If the head is designated Minister then junior Ministers are Parliamentary Secretaries. In Mr Heath's Government there were twenty-six such Ministers. To these must be added ten whips and assistant whips; and thirteen members of the Royal Household.

Mr Heath was thus responsible for the appointment of eighteen Cabinet Ministers, twenty-eight Ministers not in the Cabinet, four Law Officers, and forty-nine junior Ministers and others – ninety-nine people in all.

The first and most senior appointments the Prime Minister makes must be entirely personal decisions. Only he can decide who shall be his Home and Foreign Secretaries, his Chancellor of the Exchequer. In practice, at the beginning of a new Government, his choice will be limited to a small group of senior members of the party. Later when reshuffles occur the Prime Minister may promote more junior Ministers to high office because he believes in their ability – promotion certainly does not go by seniority alone. When the first appointments have been made, the Prime Minister will be able, if he wishes, to consult with those he has appointed when he considers other cabinet posts. And in filling the ranks of departmental Ministers not in the Cabinet, the head of the department will obviously be influential – as he will be even more when junior appointments are made.

But the importance of the Prime Minister's power to hire and fire Ministers can hardly be exaggerated. He is capable, especially at times when he considers the reputation of the Government to be at stake, of large-scale changes. In modern times the most famous occasion was Mr Macmillan's 'night of the long knives' when in July 1962 he dismissed seven members of his Cabinet.

The group of senior Ministers who form the Cabinet concentrate a great deal of political power in their hands. To do its business the Cabinet establishes committees (the details of which are never revealed openly during the currency of a Government) especially for those matters which because of their nature – for example the planning of the legislative programme of the Government – must be dealt with at a supra-departmental level. But committees are also set up from time to time to consider special matters; and other committees – as on defence, economic policy, home affairs and the social services – have been appointed, continued for a few years and then either been abandoned or replaced.[13] Though it may not be given the formal status of a committee, some kind of inner Cabinet, headed by the Prime Minister and consisting of some of his most senior colleagues, seems commonly to be used. With Cabinets having twenty or so members it is almost inevitable that a smaller body should be created even if its purpose is only to enable the Prime Minister to discuss questions to which an answer must fairly quickly be found. Other Cabinet Ministers may be added from time to time and for special reasons to this inner body.

Important arguments concern the relationship of the Prime Minister to the Cabinet and to the departments. The relationship used to be summed up by saying that the Prime Minister was *primus inter pares*, the first among equals. Connected with this was an image of the Cabinet as a body drawing into itself the threads from all the departments and exercising a general supervisory role reviewing the work of the departments and considering the most important of the policy decisions made by Ministers in charge of departments. For the performance of such functions, the most appropriate and natural position for the Prime Minister to adopt would be that of chairman.

But it is doubtful if the Cabinet ever worked in this way. An opposite view emphasizes the power of the Prime Minister and suggests that political power essentially lies in his direct relationships with individual Ministers in charge of departments. This view inevitably diminishes the importance of the Cabinet because it implies that many of the questions which might otherwise be discussed and answered by the Cabinet are dealt with by the Prime Minister. So it enhances his importance.

One thing is certain: the style and the way of doing business varies from one Prime Minister to another and from one Cabinet to another, and indeed may vary at different times during the existence of one Cabinet, particularly if the Prime Minister has never held that office before. It is also clear that the extent to which the Cabinet deals with matters which fall wholly within one department's jurisdiction is small; and that many of the problems that arise between departments are dealt with by inter-departmental committees and, where necessary, by committees of the Cabinet rather than by the Cabinet itself. On the other hand, any issue which begins to assume national dimensions, which is well publicized, and which may affect the general reputation of the Government will find its way on to the Cabinet agenda.

The Prime Minister controls that agenda in the sense that he can decide what goes on to it. But the inference is often made that he can also keep items off it. This almost certainly over-formalizes the question. The picture of a Prime Minister refusing to allow a matter to be put on the agenda although several members wish it to be discussed is unrealistic. No member can insist that an item be discussed but also no Prime Minister would persist in his refusal to admit an item once it was clear that a number of Cabinet members wanted to express views on the matter.

The Cabinet Office has as its civil service head the Secretary to the Cabinet, an influential and important appointment. It is the function of the secretariat to attend to the business of the Cabinet and its committees and to see that Cabinet decisions are put into effect.

Much has been written about the collective and individual responsibilities of Ministers. And sometimes the responsibilities of Cabinet Ministers are especially talked of. Several different ideas are involved in these matters and must be distinguished.

First, every Minister, whether or not in the Cabinet, is accountable to Parliament. This means that he is expected to answer criticisms of his work as a Minister and of his department. No Minister can be forced to do so – for example, he is not obliged to answer even a formal Parliamentary Question.[14] A refusal to answer on the ground that to do so would be contrary to the national or public interest or to national security may be acceptable to Members or at least to Members on the Minister's own side of the House. But if the Minister answers inadequately or ineptly, or shows by his answer that he does not fully understand the matter, then his reputation as Minister will suffer, his chances of promotion will be diminished, and he may in due course be dropped by the Prime Minister from his team.

This notion of accountability carries its own limitations. In particular, Ministers are accountable only for decisions and actions which fall within their area of activity. If decisions or actions are, by statute, vested in some other body, such as a local authority or a nationalized industry, then Ministers cannot be held accountable and will suggest that the criticism should be directed elsewhere.[15]

Secondly, a Minister is usually accountable for every decision or action taken by civil servants within his department. Of course, he will directly know about only a small fraction of what goes on in the department and of what is done in his name and on his behalf. Much of what is done will flow from the general policy of the department which the Minister will have either initiated or accepted. But mistakes will be made both in the interpretation of policy and by its unwise or insensitive implementation. For these the Minister will not seek to evade accountability. More difficult is the situation where the fault is attributable to gross mismanagement or even deliberate wrongdoing by civil servants. Such cases are rare, but where they occur the Minister will still be accountable although he will not be adjudged blameworthy unless it appears that the general administration of the department is less efficient than it should be and that this has contributed to the fault. If the fault is very serious, the Minister may resign. Those civil servants directly involved may be dismissed or may resign or may be moved to other work; in this latter case, their personal reputation will suffer and their future careers in the service may be severely impeded.

Thirdly, Ministers are said to be collectively responsible. This is often elevated by writers to the level of a 'doctrine' but is in truth little more than a political practice which is commonplace and inevitable. Ordinarily, Ministers form the governmental team, all being appointed by the Prime Minister from one political party. A Cabinet Minister deals with his own area of policy and does not normally have much to do with the area of other Ministers. Certainly no Cabinet Minister would be likely to make public statements which impinged on the work of another Minister's department. On a few important issues, policy is determined by the Cabinet after discussion. Collective responsibility means that Cabinet decisions bind all Cabinet Ministers, even if they argued in the opposite direction in Cabinet. But this is to say no more than that a Cabinet Minister who finds himself in a minority must either accept the majority view or resign. The team must not be weakened by some of its members making clear in public that they disapprove of the Government's policy. And obviously what is true for Cabinet Ministers is even more true for other Ministers. If they do not like what the team is doing, they must either keep quiet or leave. In a political world where the Opposition are anxious to reveal disagreement or disputes within ministerial ranks, no other principle of political action is workable.

THE ORGANIZATION OF CENTRAL GOVERNMENT

Immediately before its defeat in the general election of 1970, the Labour Government was operating through seventeen major departments (including the Scottish Office but excluding the Lord Chancellor's Department). Each department had its group of Ministers with as many as six in the Ministry of Defence, the Foreign and Commonwealth Office, the Ministry of Technology and the Treasury (excluding the whips) and as few as two in small departments like Posts and Telecommunications, and Public Building and Works.

Within a few months of taking office, the Conservative Government undertook some reorganization. The emphasis was on the 'grouping of functions together in departments with a wide span, so as to provide a series of fields of unified policy'.[16] This was a further step in a development which had been proceeding for some time under the Labour Government. It was said to offer the following advantages:

1. A capacity within such unified departments to propose and implement a single strategy for clearly defined and accepted objectives.

2. A capacity to explore and resolve conflicts both in policy formulation and executive decision within the line of management rather than by interdepartmental compromise.

3. A capacity to manage and control larger resource-consuming programmes, in terms both of formulation and administration, within departmental boundaries, making possible in turn more effective delegation of executive tasks.

4. The easier application of analytic techniques within large and self-contained blocks of work and expenditure.

5. More direct identification to the community of the Ministers and departments responsible for defined functions, programmes and

policies, more open communication between Government and the public about these, and better opportunities to discuss and challenge them.

6. A capacity to contribute more effectively to the formulation and development of the Government's overall strategy.

There was a reordering of responsibility for functions between the departments dealing with trade and industry, aviation supply, the environment, overseas aid, the personal social services, and education and the urban programme in Wales.

Previously, responsibility for general industrial policy and administration (other than employment and manpower questions, including industrial relations) was divided between the Board of Trade and the Ministry of Technology. The Conservative Government set up a unified Department of Trade and Industry. This was based on the functions of the Board of Trade (including the Board's civil aviation responsibilities) and of the Ministry of Technology; responsibility for government policy towards monopolies, mergers and restrictive practices was also transferred from the former Department of Employment and Productivity. The Minister at the head of this very large department is entitled Secretary of State for Trade and Industry and President of the Board of Trade. In mid-1973 there were in the department four other principal Ministers – for trade and consumer affairs, for industrial development, for industry, and for aerospace and shipping – and four under-secretaries of state. The objective of the department was said to be 'to assist British industry and commerce to improve their economic and technological strength and competitiveness'.[17] The department is also responsible for the nationalized industries of electricity, gas, coal, atomic energy, steel, airlines and airports.

A second very large Department was created – that of the Environment. This combines under a secretary of state the Ministries of Housing and Local Government, of Public Building and Works, and of Transport. It embraces housing, town and country planning, the construction industries, the preservation of amenity, the control of pollution and much else. Under the Secretary of State, there are three principal Ministers – for transport industries, for local government and development, and for housing and construction – and four under-secretaries of state.

The personal social services – welfare, child care and personal health – were integrated at the local level by the Local Authority Social Services Act 1970 which received the Royal Assent on the day Parliament was prorogued for the general election. The Labour Government had had a Secretary of State for the Social Services and his department was continued by the Conservative Government but enlarged by the transference from the Home Office of responsibility for child care.

The functions of the Ministry of Overseas Development were transferred to the Foreign and Commonwealth Office where a Minister is responsible, under the Foreign Secretary.

The Conservative Government thus operated through fourteen major departments, seven departments having been amalgamated into two, but with the Northern Ireland Office as a new creation.

The senior officers in a Government department are headed by the Permanent Secretary[18] under whom the department is divided into branches. The Permanent Secretary is directly responsible for finance, often also for establishment and organization, and for some particular areas of the work of the department. The next rank in seniority below the Permanent Secretary is that of Deputy Secretary of whom there will be several, each responsible for a number of branches. Each branch is headed by an under-secretary who will have beneath him a number of assistant secretaries. As an example the chart on the next page shows the structure of the Department of Education and Science early in 1973.

The Secretary of State and the parliamentary under-secretaries of state are Ministers. So also is the Paymaster-General who is shown in the chart because he happens to bear responsibility for the arts, which fall within the scope of this department. Amongst those appearing in the chart are some with specific professional qualifications. Of these the most senior (in this department) is the Legal Adviser with the rank of a Deputy Secretary. At under-secretary level are the Chief Architect, the Accountant General, the Medical Adviser and the Director of Statistics. Most of those shown as assistant secretaries in the Architects and Building branch are architects or quantity surveyors. Also at that level are assistant lawyers, accountants, scientists, medical officers, and statisticians. Excepting the ranks of the inspectorate, the chart includes some twenty-seven such 'specialists'. In addition there are about seventy 'generalists'. These hundred or so men and women, under their political masters, are responsible for making the most important

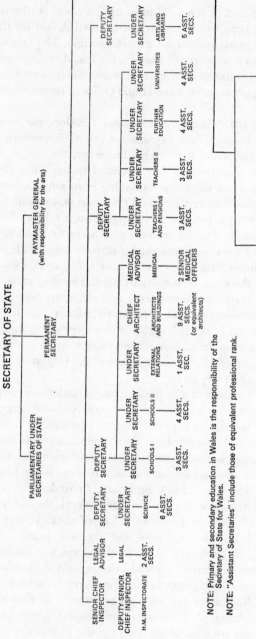

SECRETARY OF STATE

PARLIAMENTARY UNDER SECRETARIES OF STATE

PAYMASTER GENERAL (with responsibility for the arts)

PERMANENT SECRETARY

SENIOR CHIEF INSPECTOR
DEPUTY SENIOR CHIEF INSPECTOR
H.M. INSPECTORATE

LEGAL ADVISOR
LEGAL
2 ASST. SECS.

DEPUTY SECRETARY

UNDER SECRETARY
SCHOOLS I
3 ASST. SECS.

UNDER SECRETARY
SCHOOLS II
4 ASST. SECS.

UNDER SECRETARY
SCIENCE
6 ASST. SECS.

UNDER SECRETARY
EXTERNAL RELATIONS
1 ASST. SEC.

CHIEF ARCHITECT
ARCHITECTS AND BUILDINGS
9 ASST. SECS. (or equivalent architects)

MEDICAL ADVISOR
MEDICAL
2 SENIOR MEDICAL OFFICERS

DEPUTY SECRETARY

UNDER SECRETARY
TEACHERS I AND PENSIONS
3 ASST. SECS.

UNDER SECRETARY
TEACHERS II
3 ASST. SECS.

UNDER SECRETARY
FURTHER EDUCATION
4 ASST. SECS.

UNDER SECRETARY
UNIVERSITIES
4 ASST. SECS.

DEPUTY SECRETARY

UNDER SECRETARY
ARTS AND LIBRARIES
5 ASST. SECS.

ACCOUNTANT GENERAL
FINANCE
5 ASST. SECS.

UNDER SECRETARY
ESTABLISHMENTS AND ORGANISATIONS
7 ASST. SECS.

UNDER SECRETARY
PLANNING AND PROGRAMMES
1 ASST. SEC.

DIRECTOR OF STATISTICS
STATISTICS
4 ASST. SECS.

DIRECTOR
SCIENCE MUSEUM

DIRECTOR
VICTORIA AND ALBERT MUSEUM

SECRETARY FOR WELSH EDUCATION

UNDER SECRETARY
1 ASST. SEC.

H.M. INSPECTORATE (WALES)

NOTE: Primary and secondary education in Wales is the responsibility of the Secretary of State for Wales.

NOTE: "Assistant Secretaries" include those of equivalent professional rank.

administrative decisions affecting the course of education. There are of course many influential advisory and other bodies like the University Grants Committee, the teachers' unions, and the gatherings of administrative heads of universities and polytechnics. And other, different, pressures are exerted from other professional bodies and from local education authorities and their associations.

Nevertheless most of the important administrative decisions are made at one or other of the levels shown in the chart. By whom any particular decision is taken depends partly on the 'size' of the problem involved but also on many political factors including the personalities concerned, the extent to which the department (and so the Minister) are vulnerable on the issue, and the degree to which other departments are involved. Frequently the only person who can decide whether the matter should be passed up higher is the person who at that time has the problem in front of him. But also it is understood that certain classes of decision are taken at certain levels.

In this context, Government departments operate in ways very similar to other large organizations with the usual advantages and perils which flow from encouraging relatively junior members of the organization to take responsibility; and the usual advantages and perils which result when senior members insist on detailed oversight of the work of others. At what level any particular decision should be taken is finally a matter of judgment. Given the large number of decisions which are required and the great differences in their quality, a hierarchical structure is inevitable. But styles of Ministers and of senior civil servants are various and it must not be assumed that, because the structure is hierarchical, the system is necessarily rigid. The form of the chart does not mean, for example, that the Permanent Secretary is insulated from under-secretaries or assistant secretaries by the intervening deputy secretary. Moreover, branches operate more as teams and not, as the chart might be taken to indicate, as groups of individuals linked by their position in a chain of command.

Some idea of the dimensions of the different public services and of their relation to each other can be seen from the following table, taken from the annual review of public expenditure, published in December 1972.[19]

Looking at the 1972–3 column we see that the largest single item is social security representing 17·9 per cent of the whole. Education

PUBLIC EXPENDITURE 1972-3 and 1976-7

£ million at 1972-3 outturn prices
(including the relative price effect)

	1972-3	1976-7	Average annual growth rate per cent
Defence and external relations:			
1. Defence Budget	3,003	3,304	2·4
2. Other military defence	61	98	12·6
3. Overseas aid	275	324	4·2
4. EEC and other overseas services	205	362	1·2
Commerce and industry:			
5. Agriculture, fisheries and forestry	582	479	—4·7
6. Research Councils, etc.	141	137	—0·7
7. Trade, industry and employment	1,670	1,070	—5·5
Nationalized industries:			
8. Nationalized industries capital expenditure	1,811	2,184	4·8
Environmental services:			
9. Roads	1,013	1,256	5·5
10. Surface transport	287	238	—4·6
11. Housing	1,415	1,241	—3·2
12. Miscellaneous local sevices	1,257	1,456	3·7
13. Law and order	847	1,079	6·2
14. Arts	41	50	5·1
Social services:			
15. Education and libraries	3,569	4,331	5·0
16. Health and personal social services	2,917	3,525	4·8
17. Social security	5,050	5,325	1·3
Other services:			
18. Financial administration	446	354	—5·6
19. Common services	326	403	5·4
20. Miscellaneous services	101	114	3·1
21. Northern Ireland	711	715	0·1
Total programmes	25,728	28,045	2·5
22. Debt interest	2,350	2,225	—1·4
23. Contingency reserve	—	700	
24. Shortfall	—200	—200	
25. Price adjustments	6	—331	
Total	27,885	30,439	2·5

and libraries took 12·9 per cent, the defence budget 10·7 per cent, health and personal social services 10·4 per cent. The social services taken together total £11,536 million or 41·1 per cent. In terms of estimated growth from 1972–3 to 1976–7, against an overall growth rate of 2·5 per cent, it can be seen that education and health and personal social services are expected to grow at twice the average – and indeed the social security figure is unrealistically low for 1976–7 as it does not take into account any further changes in the level of benefits.[20] The defence budget figure is about the average growth rate. Other significant changes are the increases in expenditure on roads, law and order, and the nationalized industries capital expenditure. The only major decrease was estimated for trade, industry and employment but 5·5 per cent excludes investment grants and this item is perhaps the most dubious in the whole table.

While the figures for 1972–3 are likely to be accurate estimates, those for 1976–7 are more statements of intentions or, often, reflections of changes in the size and age of the population. Different Governments, different policies, different assessments, different expectations, all operate to affect the development of different services. Or, as the Treasury statement puts it:

Looking at the programmes in the second half of the period, where expansion occurs it reflects familiar and accepted considerations: increases in the number of people entitled to benefits or other social services; improvements in standards, within the limits of the resources which can be made available; and in some cases new services of high social or economic priority.[21]

It is impossible in an elementary introduction to attempt a description of the detailed administration which Government departments undertake and which is so closely linked with expenditure by local authorities.[22] One indication of the dimension of these undertakings is that whereas consumers' expenditure as a part of the gross national product in 1971 amounted to £34,504 million, public authorities' current expenditure on goods and services totalled £10,278 million of which the central government accounted for £6,183 million and local authorities £4,095 million.[23] So out of a combined total of £44,782 million, the central Government departments and local authorities were responsible for 22·9 per cent.

The central departments, together with other public bodies (including local authorities) are responsible for providing a wide range of services and for exercising considerable powers of regulation. Almost all governmental activities require special powers over and above those exercisable by private individuals: powers to tax, to acquire land compulsorily, to enter private property, to control the use of land, to force landlords to keep houses in proper repair, to regulate trade, to maintain an army, to provide schools and universities, to finance agriculture, and so on, some functions being very large and expensive, others being small but important to those affected.

Almost all these functions, because of the need for special powers, require to be supported by legislation. The authority to take action is contained in Acts of Parliament so that when an official of a Government department wishes to enter my land, or to acquire it, or in any other way to infringe my rights, he must be able to show me (and, if there is a dispute about his action, to persuade the courts) that a statute or statutory instrument[24] entitles him to do so. Of all the activities of Departments, only the conduct of foreign affairs needs little or no statutory backing and that is because individual rights are not directly affected by diplomacy, by treaties, by conferences. If as a consequence of this activity, it is necessary to impinge on individual rights (as may be, for example, under the treaties concerned with entry into the European Community) then special legislation is necessary. But this is exceptional.

The law therefore, in the form of statutes and statutory instruments, provides the authority for the effective exercise of the administrative process. On the other hand, very little of the structure of the central government, of the political relationships, of the power of the Prime Minister or of the Cabinet derives from parliamentary enactment. Thus there is nothing in the law to prevent the political parties changing the way in which they choose their leaders – as did the Conservative party in the mid 1960s – and nothing in the law to prevent their adopting a method of selection that is either random, or arbitrary, or dictatorial. Yet the person chosen may well be the next Prime Minister. This is not to say that the law should intervene, that a statute should prescribe how the election of party leaders should be conducted, as statutes do for the election of Members of Parliament and local councillors. Even less is it suggested that the written law is a suitable way in which to seek to determine more subtle and changing political relationships. But, compared with the constitutions of other countries, the United Kingdom is remarkable in the extent to which so little of the framework of government derives from formal provisions set out in Acts of Parliament.

5
The Civil Service

INTRODUCTION

Civil servants are usually defined as 'servants of the Crown, other than holders of political or judicial office, who are employed in a civil capacity and whose remuneration is paid wholly and directly out of monies voted by Parliament'.[1] This excludes Ministers, judges, the employees of nationalized industries (including the Post Office, which was formerly a Government department), the police, the armed forces and local authority employees. The civil service consists of approximately 700,000 people, about 2·7 per cent of the total working population of the country. This figure is made up of 210,000 industrial workers (e.g. in Royal Ordnance Factories and Royal Naval Dockyards) and 490,000 non-industrial civil servants. The non-industrial civil servants work in almost a hundred different departments and public bodies varying in size from departments like the Ministry of Defence with its 112,000 employees to the Historical Manuscripts Commission with sixteen. About 70 per cent of civil servants are employed outside London but most of the top civil servants are in the headquarters of their departments in Whitehall or near by.[2]

The foundation of the modern civil service took place in the middle of the last century. Before this the various Government departments and public offices were organized quite separately from each other and there was no concept of a unified corps of public servants. There were no common principles of recruitment, organization or control; admission and promotion were usually on the basis of nepotism and political patronage; pay was not necessarily related to work done, and lethargy and inefficiency pervaded many departments. The starting point of reform was the Northcote–

Trevelyan Report (1854) which drew inspiration from the Indian Civil Service. The Report proposed that patronage should be abolished and that recruitment to all branches of the service should be on the basis of competitive examinations conducted by an independent central board. It also made proposals to encourage promotion on merit and emphasized that the service should be viewed as a unified whole. These proposals were gradually put into effect and, together with subsequent reforms, created a unified career service, immune from personal or political influence, which is characterized today by a spirit of disinterested public service, integrity and political neutrality.

The most recent report on the civil service is the Fulton Report (1968).[3] This criticized the civil service ideal of the intelligent all-rounder and called instead for greater professionalism and specialist expertise. One of its most important recommendations was that the system of classes should be abolished. This system was actually the result of the Northcote–Trevelyan reforms and has had a very important influence on the organization of the civil service. The original idea was that a distinction should be made between intellectual and routine work with graduates recruited for the former and non-graduates for the latter. The result of this was that there were separate career 'ladders' for persons with different entry qualifications. As the system developed a large number of classes came into existence. Some of these were linked to specialist qualifications (e.g. lawyers or scientists); others were general. The three most important general classes were (in descending order of status) the Administrative Class, the Executive Class and the Clerical Class. Members of the administrative class were recruited almost entirely from graduates and they held the most important posts in the service. Members of the executive class held many of the middle-ranking jobs and members of the clerical class filled the posts concerned with routine work. Some of the specialists were also divided into classes: thus scientists were divided into three classes – the scientific officer class, the experimental officer class and the scientific assistant class.

In 1969 there were 147 classes which contained 100 or more persons.[4] Most jobs were allocated to a particular class and each class had its own qualifications for entry and its own pay scale. Classes were sub-divided into grades and most civil servants spent their entire career within one class, moving up the ladder in that class. (It was possible to move to a different class but this was not very common.) There was, of course, considerable overlap between the pay scales of different classes but some offered much better career prospects than others. Thus a young man in a fairly senior class might be earning more than an older man in a lower class.

The Fulton Report criticized this system on the ground that it led to inflexibility and inefficiency. They therefore recommended that classes should be abolished and that civil servants should be organized in a uniformly graded structure in which there were an appropriate number of different pay levels matching different levels of skill and responsibility. Under this system people would still enter the service at different levels depending on their qualifications but the way to the top would be open (at least in theory) to everyone in the service. This proposal was accepted by the Government and a job evaluation programme was started. It will, of course, take some years for the full implementation of these recommendations but the first step was taken when the administrative, executive and clerical classes were merged on 1 January 1971. A unified grading system at under-secretary levels and above (i.e. grades in all classes with salaries of £6,000 or more) was also introduced.

Another recommendation of the Fulton Report was that the function of managing the civil service, which had previously been carried out by the Treasury, should be transferred to a new department. This was also accepted by the Government and the Civil Service Department was created in November 1968.[5] It is responsible for personnel management, the promotion of administrative and managerial efficiency, and terms of service. The Prime Minister is in charge of the department but much of the day-to-day responsibility is delegated to a senior Minister. The department has also been given the job of restructuring the civil service in the light of the Fulton Report, and a Structure Review Division has been established to examine the implications of a unified grading structure and to develop job evaluation techniques. The permanent head of the Civil Service Department has been designated Head of the Home Civil Service.

Responsibility for senior appointments in the civil service is vested in the Prime Minister. All promotions to the level of deputy secretary and above are considered by the Senior Appointments Selection Committee,[6] which is chaired by the Head of the Home Civil Sevicce and advises the Prime Minister. The duty of civil servants is to serve all Governments and Ministers impartially, and normally changes of Government do not involve changes in the personnel at the top of the civil service. Occasionally, however, Ministers bring in outside experts who are known to them personally to serve as their advisers. These appointments are, of course, temporary and they normally do not continue after a change of Minister.

RECRUITMENT

When patronage was finally abolished in 1870 the method of recruitment that was adopted was selection on the basis of examinations held by the Civil Service Commission. The examinations were of an academic nature and were in the subjects normally studied at schools and universities. No preference was given to subjects that might be relevant to the work of the service since the examinations were intended to be a test of general ability. They were set at various levels for entry into different classes of the civil service and the examinations for entry into the administrative class were at university honours degree level. The merits of this system were its complete impartiality and the high intellectual standards that were maintained. Today, however, the development of the national educational system has made it no longer necessary for the civil service to set academic examinations of its own and selection is now usually on the basis of ordinary academic or professional qualifications (e.g. G.C.E. or degree results) and an interview. The only examinations at present conducted by the Civil Service Commission (which is now part of the Civil Service Department) are aptitude tests and certain general examinations, for example essays or papers on the use and comprehension of English.

Direct entry for graduates at the level of Assistant Principal is now on the basis of a series of tests and interviews. Most top civil servants of the future will probably be recruited in this way, though some will work their way up from lower grades and others may be appointed at a higher level after successful careers in industry or other fields. Direct entry on this basis is open to all those with first- or second-class degrees (or a third-class plus a graduate degree). The first stage of the procedure is a qualifying examination consisting of an essay, an English paper and a general paper. Those who pass this go on to the next stage which consists of various tests lasting two days. Candidates are divided into groups of five or six and they do exercises which are intended to test not only their intellectual ability but also personal qualities such as their ability to get on with people. Those who do best in these tests go on to the final stage which is an interview before the Final Selection Board, which makes its decision on the basis of the candidates' educational qualifications and the results of the qualifying examination and the tests. It will be seen that this is a very thorough system and only a small proportion of candidates are successful. Its advantage over the old system of academic examinations is that it attempts to give due weight to the non-academic qualities that are relevant to administrative work.[7]

STAFF ASSOCIATIONS

There is no law to prevent civil servants belonging to trade unions and they are in fact encouraged by their departments to join the various staff associations which represent different categories of staff. There are a large number of different associations ranging in size from organizations like the Civil Service Clerical Association with 145,000 members and the Institution of Professional Civil Servants with 57,000, to small groups with only a few hundred members representing fairly specialized categories of staff.[8] A number of these associations have, however, joined a federal body called the Civil Service Alliance.

The Trades Disputes Act of 1927, which was passed after the General Strike, prohibited civil servants from joining any trade union which was affiliated to an outside body or which had any political objectives, but this was repealed in 1946 and there is today nothing to prevent a staff association joining the T.U.C. or being affiliated to the Labour party. The Industrial Relations Act 1971 applies to the Crown, and civil servants benefit from the various provisions in it designed to protect the right to join a trade union, although there are certain limitations on the remedies that can be obtained against the Crown.[9] The associations which are considered to be representative of a given category of staff are officially recognized as representing that category and this gives them the right to negotiate on behalf of the staff they represent and to go to arbitration.

Consultations and negotiations between the two sides are given a formal framework by the Whitley Council system. There is a National Whitley Council and there are also departmental Whitley councils in almost every department. A Whitley council consists of two sides, the official side and the staff side. The official side represents the Government and normally consists of top civil servants. The staff side represents the associations and its members are appointed by the associations concerned; they are normally civil servants or full-time association officials. The chair in a Whitley council is always taken by a member of the official side. Decisions are not taken by vote but by agreement between the two sides and the constitution of the National Whitley Council provides that decisions 'shall be reported to the Cabinet, and thereupon shall become operative'.[10] This means that the Government is bound by decisions of the council; but since the official side will only negotiate within the framework of policies already accepted by the Government there is no danger of the Cabinet being bound by a decision which is contrary to Government policy.

Whitley councils can consider any matter relating to the conditions of service of the staff concerned and this includes pay, recruitment, tenure, promotion, discipline, superannuation and hours of work. However, only the general principles can be discussed: individual cases of, for example, discipline or promotion cannot be negotiated. In view of the fact that the members of the official side are themselves senior civil servants, the Whitley machinery is not suitable for negotiating the pay and conditions of service of the highest grades. Since 1957 a body called the Standing Advisory Committee on Salaries of the Higher Civil Service, whose members are appointed by the Prime Minister from persons outside the civil service, has had the task of advising the Government on these matters.

If an agreed settlement cannot be reached through the Whitley machinery there are several courses of action which the associations can take. They may try to bring pressure through Parliament: there are usually a number of M.P.s who are, or have been, connected with one of the staff associations and who will raise the matter through parliamentary channels. There is no law to prevent civil servants from going on strike but until recently strikes have been rare. The normal course of action is to go to arbitration. This is provided for in the Civil Service National Whitley Council Arbitration Agreement of 1925, as amended,[11] and under it any recognized staff association can go to arbitration provided the matter in dispute is arbitrable. The Agreement defines what matters are arbitrable and they include pay (except for the highest grades), weekly hours of work and annual leave. Certain general matters such as super-annuation, and all matters concerning individual civil servants, are not arbitrable. If there is a dispute as to whether a matter is arbitrable the official view prevails. The Government can also refuse 'on grounds of policy' to go to arbitration, but this right, which is justified on the ground of the Government's overriding responsibility to Parliament, is rarely exercised.

Arbitration takes place before the Civil Service Arbitration Tribunal which consists of a chairman and two other members selected by the chairman from panels representing the two sides. The chairman and the members of the two panels are appointed by the Government after appropriate consultations. Civil servants and officials of the associations are excluded from appointment. Each side presents its case to the tribunal which then gives its decision. The three members of the tribunal almost always agree on the decision but where this is not possible the chairman gives the award himself. The decisions are binding on the Government 'subject to the overriding authority of Parliament'.[12]

INTERNAL REGULATION AND DISCIPLINE

The Crown has power under the Prerogative to regulate and control the civil service. Under Article 5 of the Civil Service Order in Council 1969, which was made under the Prerogative, the Minister for the Civil Service is empowered to make regulations and give instructions to control the home civil service. The most important of these are contained in Estacode, which is a code of general civil service regulations distributed within the service. In addition, each department is empowered to make its own regulations and issue its own instructions, provided these do not conflict with anything contained in Estacode. Departments normally compile staff manuals which contain the regulations and instructions for the department.

There is thus a code of 'law' for the civil service which is enforced by internal disciplinary proceedings. It is not certain how far the courts would be prepared to recognize this civil service 'law' but since it now seems to have been established that a civil servant can bring legal proceedings to recover back pay,[13] the courts would have to recognize at least those regulations which lay down the scales of pay. This would probably be done on the basis that the regulations form part of a contract between the Crown and the civil servant. The theory is that if the civil servant continues in the employment of the Crown after he has been informed of a change in the regulations he is taken to have consented to them. This is rather an unrealistic approach but it is hard to see on what other basis a civil servant could be given a legal right to his pay.[14]

Most of the detailed rules governing the conduct of civil servants are laid down in the departmental staff manuals but certain general principles are set out in Estacode. These are that civil servants must give their undivided allegiance to the State; that they must not use their official positions to further their private interests; that they must not bring discredit on the service through their private activities; that they must not give even the appearance of dishonesty; and that civil servants who advise Ministers and carry out their policies must not take part in any public controversy that might cast doubts on their impartiality.[15]

In addition to these general principles Estacode contains a number of rules on specific topics. These rules contain far greater restrictions than would ever apply in the case of someone in private employment and they cover aspects of the civil servant's private life as well as what he does during office hours. Thus civil servants are restricted as regards the outside activities and part-time work they are allowed to do and there are also rules limiting the employment that may be taken by senior civil servants for two years after they have retired or resigned from the service.[16] Permission must be obtained before a civil servant can publish a book or appear on a radio or T.V. broadcast if the subject of the book or broadcast is concerned with Government work.

Any invention made by a civil servant belongs to the Crown, though in certain cases the Crown may give the civil servant a monetary award or allow him to exploit the invention commercially himself. These rules are, of course, made in the public interest and there is normally consultation with the staff associations before they are made.

If a civil servant breaks any of the regulations he is liable to be subject to disciplinary proceedings. The penalties which can be imposed include a reprimand, loss of increments, a fine, downgrading or dismissal without pension. The decision to punish a civil servant is taken by one of his superiors in the department. In serious cases the civil servant is given certain procedural rights. First of all he is informed in writing of the charge against him and is told of the facts which are alleged to support it. He is then given time to submit a written reply. If there is a dispute as to the facts, he is given the right to present his case orally before a more senior officer in his department. In doing this he has a right to the assistance of a friend or colleague, who may be a representative of a staff association.

If the decision is against the civil servant, he has a right of appeal to the head of his department or, in the case of a decision to dismiss him, to an independent Appeal Board (provided he has been a civil servant for at least two years). The Appeal Board consists of three persons: a permanent chairman and two members, one drawn from a panel nominated by the official side and one from a panel nominated by the staff side. The civil servant first submits his case in writing to the board and later has the right to appear before it in person. If he so desires, he may be assisted by a friend. His department submits a statement containing the relevant facts and the reasons for its decision; a copy of this must be given to the civil servant, who is entitled to have access to all relevant papers (subject to security considerations). If the board decides that the decision to dismiss him was unfair, it will recommend that he should not be dismissed or that he should be paid compensation. A recommendation against his dismissal can, however, be rejected by the head of his department; but in this case the board can decide to award him compensation. A recommendation by the board that compensation be paid is binding on the department.

POLITICAL ACTIVITIES

The duty to serve Governments and Ministers impartially has resulted in the imposition of certain restrictions on the political activities of civil servants. In theory, of course, it might be possible for a civil servant to remain totally impartial in his official work and at the same time carry on party political activity in his free time, but it is doubtful whether it would be possible in practice for a man to isolate his official from his private views to such an extent. Even if this were possible, public confidence would suffer if there were even the appearance of political bias.[17] For these reasons there are special rules in Estacode limiting the political activities that civil servants are permitted to undertake.

Two factors are taken into account by the rules:[18] first, the status and work of the civil servant concerned and, secondly, the level of politics in which he wishes to engage. The rules relate only to public political activities (every civil servant has the right to vote in elections and to discuss politics in private) and these are divided into two categories: national and local politics. National political activities include adoption as a parliamentary candidate, holding office in party organizations if the office is related mainly to politics at a national level, public speaking or writing on national political issues, and canvassing for parliamentary candidates. Local political activities are the same things done in relation to local government politics – for example, standing for election to a local council or canvassing in local government elections.

Civil servants are classified into three groups for the purpose of these rules. The first group is the politically free, who include all industrial staff and minor and manipulative grades. Members of this group, who have no influence on the formation and implementation of policy, are free to engage in any form of political activity. If they wish to stand for Parliament, however, they have to resign their posts before the election – civil servants are disqualified by law from membership of the House of Commons[19] – but they are entitled to be reinstated if they are not elected.

Secondly, there is the intermediate group, which includes typists, clerks and other white-collar workers. They are entitled to engage in any form of political activity, except standing for Parliament, provided they first obtain the permission of their departments. In deciding whether to grant permission the department will consider the extent to which the person concerned takes decisions involving individual members of the public. Certain categories of civil servants within the intermediate group are given standing permission *en bloc*; civil servants in other categories, however, have to apply individually.

The third group is the politically restricted group, which consists mainly of those concerned with the formation and execution of policy – in the past, the administrative and executive classes. They may not engage in national politics but may apply for permission to take part in local politics.

These rules were formulated after consultation with the staff associations and they have been carefully drawn to ensure that the restrictions on the rights of civil servants are kept to a minimum. There does not in fact seem to be any evidence that the more senior civil servants, who form the politically restricted group, have any desire to engage publicly in politics and these restrictions could be regarded as the price which must be paid for the influence which they have on policy formation within the civil service.

SECURITY

The object of the security procedures in the civil service is to prevent civil servants whose loyalty is suspect from gaining access to secret information.[20] There are two procedures designed to achieve this end – the 'purge procedure' and 'positive vetting'. The purge procedure is applied to civil servants whose reliability is suspect and is intended to give them an opportunity to clear themselves before action is taken. Positive vetting is the name given to the security check given automatically to all civil servants concerned with exceptionally secret work and in this case there is no formal procedure to allow them to answer any accusations made against them.

There are of course many reasons why a person might decide to pass on information to a foreign intelligence service – he might, for example, do it for money or because he is being blackmailed – but the purge procedure is aimed mainly at detecting persons with Communist sympathies or associations who might become spies for ideological reasons.[21] The procedure was introduced in 1948[22] and it appears to have been most frequently used during the Cold War period when there were a number of cases of highly placed diplomats and civil servants who became Soviet agents from ideological motives.

The way the purge procedure works today is as follows. The persons to whom it applies are those who are employed in work which is 'vital to the security of the State'[23] and the Minister in charge of each department decides what posts are covered by this description. It is important to note that the purge procedure is limited to those posts where it is necessary: there is no general loyalty test for civil servants as such. The procedure starts with the Minister responsible for the department to which the civil servant in question belongs. He makes a decision, normally on the basis of information supplied by the Security Service, whether there is a *prima facie* reason to doubt the reliability of the civil servant. If the Minister decides there is a *prima facie* case the civil servant will be informed and will be given the details of the allegations against him except in so far as this might endanger secret sources of information.

If the civil servant denies the allegations he is given fourteen days to make written representations to the Minister. The Minister will then reconsider his *prima facie* ruling in the light of what the civil servant has to say. If he adheres to his original decision the civil servant is given seven days to decide whether he wants his case to go before the Three Advisers. The Three Advisers are usually retired civil servants and normally one of them is someone who has been associated with one of the civil service staff associations. Their function is to consider the facts and advise the Minister, who retains the final decision.

The Three Advisers must decide whether there are reasonable grounds for supposing that the civil servant 'is or recently has been a member of the British Communist Party or of a Fascist organization or . . . in such a way as to raise legitimate doubts about his reliability, is or recently has been sympathetic to Communism or Fascism or associated with Communists[24] or Communist sympathizers or is susceptible to Communist pressure'.[25] It will be seen from this that not only are the civil servant's own political beliefs in issue but also those of persons with whom he associates. Thus, for example, a person might be considered a security risk because his wife is a Communist. 'Character defects' (e.g. drunkenness, drug addiction or homosexuality) are considered if there is also evidence of Communist sympathies or associations since they might expose the civil servant to blackmail. If the civil servant wants his case to go before the Three Advisers he is allowed to make oral representations before them and he can bring witnesses to testify on his behalf. He is permitted to have a friend with him – who may be a representative of a staff association – but if he does this he may be asked to appear a second time without the friend so that he can be questioned in private. All the evidence against the civil servant will be put before the Three Advisers but he himself will be excluded from the proceedings where this is necessary to safeguard sources.

The Three Advisers are required to give their opinion on the case and the grounds for the conclusions they reach. If they are in doubt they must give their assessment of the evidence. The Minister considers their report and then makes the final decision. Before the Minister decides what action to take, however, the civil servant is given yet another chance to make representations. A civil servant who is found to be a security risk is posted to non-secret work in his department or, if this is not possible, in another department. If there is no alternative employment available in Government service he is given the option of resigning or being dismissed.[26] However, before this decision is taken the civil servant's staff association is given the opportunity to suggest alternative work that he might do.

The positive vetting procedure is an even more intensive process used in the case of persons whose work is especially secret. It applies to those who have regular access to the most highly classified defence information and the more highly classified categories of atomic information as well as to all persons of the grade of under-secretary or above. The procedure involves four stages. First, a check is made with the Security Service to see whether there is any adverse information on the person concerned; secondly he is asked to fill in a security questionnaire (for example about any associations he might have had with Communists); then he is asked to give the names of two referees; and finally a field investigation is made into his character and circumstances by the Security Service. There is no appeal to the Three Advisers in this procedure.

These procedures are the result of an attempt to balance the demands of security with the rights of the individual. Inevitably, in view of the great harm that could be done by a successful spy, any doubts must be resolved against the individual. It must also be admitted that the purge procedure falls a long way short of what natural justice normally demands when serious accusations are made.[27] In particular, the fact that the full case against the civil servant may not be disclosed and that he may not be able to cross-examine his accusers represents a substantial derogation from fair procedure. Indeed the whole idea of putting a man's beliefs on trial (or those of his friends and associates) is repugnant. However, the various spy cases that have come to light show that the danger is a real one; consequently there seems to be no option but to use procedures such as these. In fact it seems that the Government has used these procedures very sparingly in practice. This is shown by the following Table which gives the number of people involved in the purge procedure during the thirteen years from 1948 to 1961:[28]

	Industrials	Non-Industrials
Transferred to non-secret work	20	63
Dismissed	17	7
Resigned	14	10
Reinstated	12	20
	63	100

Thus, in spite of the spy mania that has affected some countries, there has been no wholesale purge in the British civil service.

THE LEGAL RIGHTS OF CIVIL SERVANTS

At common law civil servants have no security of tenure and they can be dismissed at any time by the Crown without notice.[29] This applies even if it was agreed at the time of the appointment that the civil servant would be employed for a fixed term. A good illustration of this is the case of *Dunn* v. *The Queen*.[30] Dunn claimed that he had been appointed to the post of consular agent in the Niger Protectorate for a term of three years by the High Commissioner, Sir Claude McDonald. He had been dismissed before the end of the period and he brought a petition of right for damages, but it was held by the Court that, even if there was a contract between him and the Crown, it contained an implied term that the Crown could dismiss him at pleasure and any express term to the contrary was void.

Having failed in his petition of right, Dunn then sued the man who appointed him (Sir Claude McDonald) for damages for breach of warranty of authority.[31] Dunn argued that McDonald had held himself out as having the authority to engage him for a period of three years when in fact McDonald had no power to do this, since he could not exclude the right of the Crown to dismiss Dunn at pleasure. This action also failed, on the ground that no action lies against a public servant in respect of a contract made by him on behalf of the Crown. So Dunn obtained no remedy in the courts for his dismissal.

The rule that the power of the Crown to dismiss at pleasure cannot be abrogated by a term of the contract of employment has been affirmed in subsequent cases[32] and it has also been held that contractual terms providing for a period of notice to be given to a civil servant[33] or stipulating that he would be granted a hearing before dismissal[34] are void since they also limit the power of the Crown to dismiss at pleasure. The only doubt that has been cast on these rules comes from a dictum of the Privy Council in the case of *Reilly* v. *The King*.[35] The Privy Council said:[36]

If the terms of the contract definitely prescribe a term and expressly provide for a power to determine 'for cause' it appears necessarily to follow that any implication of a power to dismiss at pleasure is excluded. This appears to follow from the reasoning of the Board in *Gould* v. *Stuart*.

At first sight this seems to contradict the law laid down in the previous cases but the terms of the appointment in *Reilly*'s case were not set out in a contract but were laid down by statute and the same was true in the case of *Gould* v. *Stuart*[37] which was cited by the Board as authority for their dictum. It is therefore possible that the Board intended their words to apply only where the terms of the appointment are in a statute, though it must be admitted that the language used does not support this interpretation. However this may be, the statement was clearly *obiter* and has not been followed in subsequent cases.[38] Thus in a recent case the Privy Council has restated the traditional rule as follows:[39]

It is now well established in British constitutional theory . . . that any appointment as a Crown servant, however subordinate, is terminable at will unless it is expressly otherwise provided by legislation. . . .

Although it is clear, therefore, that any contractual term giving security of tenure is void, the precise legal reason for this has never been settled. A new civil servant is normally appointed on behalf of the Crown by a more senior civil servant and one theory is that an undertaking giving security of tenure does not bind the Crown because the civil servant making the appointment does not have the authority to give such an undertaking on behalf of the Crown.[40] It is a principle of the law of agency that generally speaking a person acting on behalf of another cannot bind the latter except to the extent that he has been authorized to do so and the same rule applies to a civil servant acting on behalf of the Crown. The extent to which a civil servant is authorized to act on behalf of the Crown depends on the circumstances[41] but it is assumed that there is a general rule that no civil servant has authority to appoint another civil servant except on the terms that he is dismissable at pleasure.

If this theory is correct it would seem to follow that where the appointment is made directly by the Crown – by Letters Patent, for example – a term giving security of tenure would be valid, since the Crown itself can hardly lack authority to agree to such a term. This certainly seems to have been the position in the past when the Crown appointed persons to hold office *quamdiu se bene gesserint* (during good behaviour)[42] and this was how judges obtained security of tenure until the matter was put on a statutory basis by section 3 of the Act of Settlement, 1700.[43] Modern authority is, however, divided on the matter[44] and it is therefore uncertain whether the Crown still has the power to divest itself of its right to dismiss its servants at pleasure.

The alternative theory is that a term providing for security of tenure is void because it is contrary to public policy. If this were correct it might seem to open the way for argument that in certain cases it would be in the public interest for security of tenure to be granted. This argument was put forward in *Terrell* v. *Secretary of State for the Colonies*,[45] a case concerning the question whether a colonial judge could be dismissed at pleasure by the Crown. Counsel for the judge argued that public policy was the basis of the rule and that, since it was in the public interest that judges should have security of tenure, the rule did not apply to them. But this was rejected by the court. Lord Goddard C.J. held that once a doctrine has become a rule of law the court must apply it without inquiring into its origin.

The common law position of civil servants has, however, been significantly altered by the Industrial Relations Act 1971 which applies to the Crown, subject to certain limitations.[46] Under sections 22 and 106 civil servants have the right to present a complaint to an industrial tribunal if they have been unfairly dismissed. If this is proved, the tribunal may in certain circumstances recommend that the civil servant be reinstated; otherwise compensation up to a maximum of two years' pay or £4,160 (whichever is the less) may be awarded. Although most civil servants will be covered by these provisions, certain categories will be excluded;[47] moreover in the case of top civil servants the amount of compensation obtainable is low. However, it is unlikely that the Crown would refuse to accept a recommendation of reinstatement and there is no doubt that the Act has made a substantial improvement in the legal position of civil servants even though it does not remove all their common law disabilities.

Even though a civil servant has no common law protection against dismissal it does not necessarily follow that he has no legal right to the salary he has earned by work already done. The question of a civil servant's right to salary already earned has been the subject of conflicting decisions and it is only recently that it has been settled.[48] It seems clear that members of the armed forces cannot sue for their pay[49] and in some cases the same rule has been applied to civil servants.[50] Thus in the Scottish case of *Mulvenna* v. *The Admiralty*[51] Lord Blackburn said:

... this qualification must be read, as an implied condition, into every contract between the Crown and a public servant, with the effect that, in the terms of their contract, they have no right to their remuneration which can be enforced in a civil court of justice ...

This view of the law was followed in the English case of *Lucas* v. *Lucas*.[52] In this case the wife of an Indian civil servant sought to attach her husband's salary for maintenance but it was held that the husband himself could not maintain an action for his salary and therefore it was not a debt 'owing or accruing'[53] to him and could not be attached.

There have, on the other hand, been a number of cases in which the decision has been based on the assumption that a civil servant does have a legal right to his pay, though in most of these the point was not properly argued.[54] Thus in *Sutton* v. *Attorney-General*[55] a Post Office employee[56] successfully obtained damages for breach of contract in a petition of right. The facts were that the Postmaster-General had published a circular in 1914 which offered Post Office employees enlisting as telegraphists in the armed forces full civilian pay in addition to their military pay. Sutton enlisted on the basis of this offer and served for several years. During this time the pay of civilian telegraphists was increased but this increase was not applied to those who had enlisted. The applicant petitioned for the extra pay and it was held by the House of Lords that he was entitled to it; but the main point at issue was the meaning of the circular and it was not argued that, as a civil servant, Sutton had no legal right at all to his pay.

The matter has, however, now been settled by the decision of the Privy Council in *Kodeeswaran* v. *Attorney-General of Ceylon*[57] in which it was decided, after full argument, that there is no rule of law to prevent a civil servant from bringing legal proceedings to recover pay for services already performed. Although this case was decided on the basis of the law of Ceylon, the Privy Council made clear that they considered the position to be the same in English law. The dictum in *Mulvenna* v. *The Admiralty* quoted above was stated to be wrong. The correct position, in the opinion of the Privy Council, is as follows:[58]

A right to terminate a contract of service at will coupled with a right to enter into a fresh contract of service may in effect enable the Crown to change the terms of employment in futuro if the true inference to be drawn from the communication of the intended change to the servant and his continuing to serve thereafter is that his existing contract has been terminated by the Crown and a fresh contract entered into on the revised terms. But this cannot affect any right to salary already earned under the terms of his existing contract before its termination.

Until the Superannuation Act 1972 came into force a civil servant had no legal right to his pension and the final decision always rested with the Treasury.[59] Now, however, the 1972 Act makes provision for the determination by the courts of questions of law – though it is still possible for the Minister to provide that questions of fact will be decided by himself.[60]

In the discussion up to now it has been assumed that the relationship between a civil servant and the Crown is based on contract. It is not, however, entirely certain that this is so and it has been suggested that the relationship is based on status[61] or appointment to an office. Thus Lord Goddard C.J. said in 1956:[62]

... an established civil servant is appointed to an office and is a public officer, remunerated by moneys provided by Parliament, so that his employment depends not on a contract with the Crown but on appointment by the Crown, though there may be, as indicated in *Reilly*'s case, exceptional cases, as, for instance, an engagement for a definite period, where there is a contractual element in or collateral to his employment ...

Lord Goddard suggested that the basis on which a civil servant could recover his salary was a *quantum meruit*; but this was not the basis on which the House of Lords proceeded in *Sutton* v. *Attorney-General*:[63] this case was clearly decided on the assumption that there was a contract. Most of the cases have in fact taken it for granted that the relationship is contractual and the language of contract is almost always used to describe the legal position.[64]

Lord Goddard did, of course, accept that there may be a contractual element in exceptional cases. In *Reilly*'s case, to which he refers, the matter is, however, put a little differently. What the Privy Council said was:[65]

... in some offices at least it is difficult to negative some contractual relations, whether it be as to salary or terms of employment, on the one hand, and duty to serve faithfully and with reasonable care and skill on the other.[66]

This was said in response to the opinion of the Exchequer Court in Canada, where the appeal originated, that there was no element of contract. There is no reason to believe that the Privy Council necessarily regarded a contractual relationship as the exception rather than the rule.[67] In *Riordan* v. *War Office*[68] Lord Diplock refused to commit himself on the point but thought that the relationship was sufficiently analogous, at least, to a contractual one to make it proper for him to construe the regulations which governed the rights of the civil servant as if they were a contract. Thus, though the matter cannot be regarded as finally settled, it seems probable that the relationship is contractual in the case of most civil servants though there are probably some exceptions.[69]

Even before the Industrial Relations Act was passed civil servants were not in the precarious position which phrases such as 'dismissal at pleasure' might suggest. It is well known that in practice civil servants have for a long time had much greater security than almost any other class of employee.[70] But the basis of this security – which is considered desirable in order to safeguard the political neutrality of the civil service – has always been the internal rules and procedures of the service. These internal safeguards provide more effective protection in most cases than could be obtained by recourse to the courts and this is borne out by the fact that the civil servants' staff associations have never shown any desire for a change in the law.[71] Now that civil servants also have the rights provided by the Industrial Relations Act their position is even stronger and the only category who might be insufficiently protected are part-time and temporary civil servants, who may in some cases be excluded from the provisions of the Act relating to unfair dismissal.[72] Some change in the law might be desirable to allow them to bring an action if they are dismissed in breach of their contracts.[73]

POWERS

Powers are not normally conferred by law directly on civil servants.[74] Instead they advise Ministers how powers conferred on them (and on the Crown) should be exercised. They also often take decisions in the name of the Minister without referring to him. Thus many powers conferred by statute on a Minister are actually exercised by civil servants: it would be quite impossible for the Minister personally to take all the decisions which have to be made in his name but he will take political responsibility for what is done. The courts recognize this and the exercise of a power given by law to a Minister will not normally be invalid because the decision to exercise it was in fact taken by an official.[75] Thus in the case of *Carltona* v. *Commissioners of Works*[76] it was provided by legislation[77] as follows:

A competent authority, if it appears to that authority to be necessary or expedient so to do in the interests of the public safety, the defence of the realm, or the efficient prosecution of the war, or for maintaining supplies and services essential to the life of the country may take possession of any land.

In this case some land had been requisitioned under this power but there was no evidence that the Minister of Works, who was the 'competent authority' referred to, had considered the matter personally at all. All that the owner of the land received was a letter on Ministry of Works notepaper which was signed by a civil servant and stated that 'the department have come to the conclusion that it is essential, in the national interest, to take possession of the above premises occupied by you.'

The court, however, held that it did not matter that the Minister had not personally considered whether the requisition of the land was 'necessary or expedient . . . in the interests of the public safety'. Lord Greene M.R. said:[78]

In the administration of government in this country the functions which are given to Ministers (and constitutionally properly given to Ministers because they are constitutionally responsible) are functions so multifarious that no Minister could ever personally attend to them. To take the example of the present case no doubt there have been thousands of requisitions in this country by individual Ministries. It cannot be supposed that this regulation meant that, in each case, the Minister in person should direct his mind to the matter. The duties imposed upon Ministers and the powers given to Ministers are normally exercised under the authority of Ministers by responsible officials of the department. Public business could not be carried on if that were not the case.

THE CIVIL SERVICE AND POLITICAL POWER

The duty of civil servants to serve different Governments and Ministers impartially has been emphasized. This duty is very largely fulfilled in the sense that civil servants will not seek to frustrate the policies of a Minister because they disagree with the political beliefs that lie behind those policies; but will seek to promote those policies when the Minister has finalized and clarified them.

This practice of impartiality in the implementation of ministerial policies sometimes leads, wrongly, to the idea that civil servants do not or should not take an active role in policy formation but merely act as neuter agents of ministerial will. Civil servants, however, especially the more senior, have usually worked for many years in the same department, have seen many policies tried, have lived year after year with problems which do not greatly change over periods of time. Foreign affairs, international trade, education, the administration of justice, race relations – all these and similar matters, while they may vary in national importance from time to time and while the difficulties of each change in emphasis and shape, continuously give rise to the same kind of questions to which answers must be found.

Inevitably, therefore, civil servants acquire much experience and much expertise. But this is not all. They also with their colleagues in the same department tend to come to a common opinion of the way policies should develop in the years ahead. They may, of course, differ amongst themselves. But in the major sectors of a department's work there will generally exist, especially among the more senior officials, a civil service view. This may be a source of great strength to a Minister, because it will have been argued over by people who know their job and their subject. But it carries obvious dangers. Civil servants have direct access to much more information than a Minister and most of his information must come indirectly through them. It is therefore not difficult for them to present arguments based on facts and findings which are effectively irrefutable without evidence which the Minister does not possess. This is not to say that civil servants deliberately present only that which is favourable to themselves – although it is said, perhaps with more truth, that they are sometimes reluctant to present the Minister with facts which *he* may find politically unpalatable.

Occasionally incidents are revealed which show that Ministers have been misled by civil servants, possibly because of an excess of zeal or conviction of the rightness of the view taken. What must be recognized is that civil servants play a central part in the process of decision-making within a department and that the system works best when a strong and able Minister is served by strong and able civil servants, all of whom are acting honestly and fairly. If the quality of any of the major participants is poor, or any of them is idle or fundamentally uninterested in what is to be done – and these are more likely to be defects of Ministers than of civil servants – then the system works badly.

Every Government in an industrialized society requires a considerable bureaucracy of public servants. Inevitably they come to exercise power, more or less, according to their degree of permanence, their security of tenure in office, and their relationship with Ministers and other persons and institutions in the political structure. In Britain, we are fortunate that few of our public servants are corrupt and many are men and women of great ability and integrity. But, like all who exercise power, they need to be kept under scrutiny. The responsibility falls largely on Ministers, not least because the practice which shields individual civil servants behind a veil of anonymity makes public criticism difficult. Some commentators urge that this anonymity is too comprehensive for present-day conditions. Its advantages and disadvantages are nicely balanced.

6
Local Authorities and Public Corporations

LOCAL GOVERNMENT IN ENGLAND AND WALES
The administration of many public functions is carried out by local authorities. Some functions – like national defence – are obviously unsuited for local administration. Others – like the planning of motorways – so transcend local boundaries that they would be difficult to administer locally. Others again – like national insurance – while they could fall within the field of local administration have, as a matter of history, always been managed by Government departments. So today some public functions fall wholly within the sphere of the central Government, but for others, while the departments exercise varying degrees of control, the administration is largely in the hands of local authorities.

In this context, 'administration' does not mean simply the putting into effect of policy decisions taken elsewhere. Certain major decisions will normally be reserved to the central departments but local authorities also take decisions of importance which may properly be called decisions of policy.

The major public functions in which local authorities participate include education, town and country planning, housing, the building and maintenance of highways, public transport, environmental health, police and fire forces, and many personal social services.

Structure and Functions of Local Authorities
The structure of local authorities was reformed in the late nineteenth century and this resulted (after some changes during the next eighty years) in this pattern for England and Wales (outside Greater London):

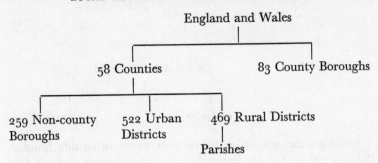

In broad terms, the county boroughs were the big cities, the non-county boroughs and urban districts were the townships, and rural districts were the remaining countryside. There were many anomalies, some non-county boroughs (for example) having larger populations than some county boroughs. But the most important defect was the existence of many county boroughs with populations below 200,000.[1]

In the county boroughs, all local government functions were the responsibility of the city councils. Over the remainder of the country, functions were divided, some (like education, planning, police and fire forces, major highways and personal social services) being the responsibility of the counties; and others (like housing, minor highways and environmental health) being the responsibility of the second tier (non-county boroughs, urban and rural districts). It was an important principle of local government outside the county boroughs that the counties did not exercise powers over the second-tier authorities. In other words, the counties did not in any sense supervise the powers exercised by the second-tier authorities who were, for their functions, their own masters. So also, with only two important exceptions, the counties in the exercise of their powers did not use the second-tier authorities as servants or agents. The two exceptions were planning and education where, to a limited extent, the counties delegated some part of their functions to the second-tier authorities.

In Greater London, the structure was reformed in 1963 and the pattern is:

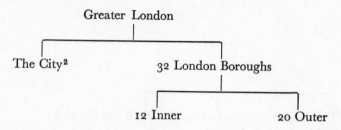

Although this resembles the two-tier structure outside London, the City and the London Boroughs have rather more of the important functions and the Greater London Council rather fewer. Education in the inner London Boroughs is administered by a single Inner London Education Authority; each of the outer London Boroughs administers education in its area.

A Royal Commission (chairman: Lord Redcliffe-Maud) reported in 1969 on the structure and functions of local government in England (outside London).[3] Separate inquiries were made for Wales. The Labour Government decided to adopt a modified version of the Royal Commission's recommendations but lost office in 1970 and the reform eventually enacted in the Local Government Act 1972 by the Conservative Government[4] departed considerably from those recommendations.

Answering their own question 'What is Wrong?' the Royal Commission emphasized first that local government areas no longer corresponded to the pattern of life and work, that town and country were interdependent and that the areas should be redrawn to recognize this.[5] Secondly, the Royal Commission were of the opinion that the fragmentation of England into so many county boroughs and counties had made impossible the proper planning of development and transportation. Similarly they found the division of responsibility between counties and the second-tier authorities a great weakness partly because counties had no general development powers, in particular no house-building powers; and partly because housing was the responsibility of the second tier while the personal social services (personal health, welfare and children's services) were the responsibility of the counties. Thirdly, and consequential on the first two defects, no single authority in the counties was responsible for 'thinking about the totality of related services and their adequacy for local needs'.

The Royal Commission also accepted the criticism that many

local authorities were too small in terms of area, population and resources; that a clarification of the local government system was needed to make it more understandable by the public; and that a reformed local government structure would improve the relations between central departments and local authorities and enable the departments to reduce the number of controls.

For these and other reasons, the Royal Commission recommended that, with the exception of some areas, the system should be one based on 'unitary' authorities: that is, for each area of local government – and the fifty-eight such areas they proposed for England were large and embraced cities and the surrounding countryside – there should be only one local authority (as was the system for county boroughs). But the exceptional areas were those of the greatest concentrations of populations: the conurbations of Merseyside; south-east Lancashire and north-east and central Cheshire (centred on Manchester) and the West Midlands (centred on Birmingham). For these three areas, the Royal Commission recommended twenty second-tier authorities which would exercise some of the functions exercised by the unitary authorities elsewhere, the remaining functions being the responsibility of a separate authority for each of the three conurbations.

Not surprisingly this radical solution was strongly opposed in some quarters but the Labour Government, as we have said, accepted it in principle while proposing to modify it in some details. The Conservative Government, however, reverted to a two-tier system for the whole country and the pattern which is provided for under the Local Government Act 1972 (still excluding Greater London) is:[6]

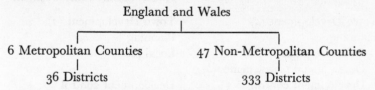

England and Wales

| 6 Metropolitan Counties | 47 Non-Metropolitan Counties |
| 36 Districts | 333 Districts |

The metropolitan counties are those of greater Manchester, Merseyside, South Yorkshire (centred on Sheffield), Tyneside, West Midlands (centred on Birmingham), and West Yorkshire (centred on Leeds). These are conurbations but in the Act the boundaries are drawn more tightly around the built-up areas than under the previous proposals. The districts in the metropolitan counties have many of the functions of non-metropolitan counties.

Under the system before the Act of 1972, there were 141 top-tier authorities responsible for the more important functions (58 counties and 83 county boroughs) and 1,250 second-tier authorities (259 non-county boroughs, 522 urban districts and 469 rural districts). Under the Act there are 53 top-tier authorities (6 metropolitan counties and 47 non-metropolitan counties) and 369 second-tier districts. But if we count the 36 metropolitan districts as authorities exercising the more as well as the less important functions we have a total of 89 major authorities to compare with the 141 major authorities before the Act; and 369 authorities responsible for less important functions to compare with 1,250 before the Act.[7]

The allocation of functions between counties and districts from 1st April 1974 has been summarized thus:[8]

County Councils (outside Metropolitan Areas) and Metropolitan District Councils

> Education
> Youth Employment
> Personal social services
> Libraries

All County Councils	*All District Councils*
Museums and art galleries (*a*)	Museums and art galleries (*a*)
Housing	Housing
Certain reserve powers	Provision
	Management
	Slum clearance
	House and area improvement
Town Development (*a*)	Town Development (*a*)
Planning	Planning
Structure plans	Local plans
Development plan schemes (*b*)	
Development control	Development control
	Advertisement control
Derelict land (*a*)	Derelict land (*a*)
National parks	
Country parks (*a*)	Country parks (*a*)
Conservation areas (*a*)	Conservation areas (*a*)
Building preservation notices	Building preservation notices
(*a*)	(*a*)

	Listed building control
Tree preservation (a)	Tree preservation (a)
Acquisition and disposal of land for planning purposes, development or redevelopment (a)	Acquisition and disposal of land for planning purposes, development or redevelopment (a)

Footpaths and Bridleways	Footpaths and Bridleways
Surveys	
Creation, diversion and extinguishment Orders (a)	Creation, diversion and extinguishment Orders (a)
Maintenance	
Protection (a)	Protection (a)
Signposting	

Transportation	Transportation
Transport planning	
Highways	
Traffic	
All parking	Off-street parking
Public transport	Public transport undertakings (c)
Road safety	
Highway lighting	
Footway lighting (a)	Footway lighting (a)

Environmental Health	Environmental Health
Animal diseases	Food safety and hygiene
	Communicable disease
	Slaughterhouses
	Offices, shops & railways premises
	Factories
	Home safety
	Water and sewerage

Refuse disposal	Refuse collection
Consumer protection (e.g. weights & measures, trade descriptions explosives, food and drugs).	Clean air
	Building regulations
	Coast protection
	Cemeteries and crematoria

Police	Markets and fairs
Fire	Bye-laws
Swimming baths (a)	Swimming baths (a)
Physical training and recreation (a)	Physical training and recreation (a)
Parks and open spaces (a)	Parks and open spaces (a)
Smallholdings	Allotments
	Local licensing
Airports (a)	Airports (a)

Under the Act of 1972 the name of 'principal councils' is given to councils of counties, metropolitan and non-metropolitan districts, Greater London, and the London boroughs (this excludes the City of London and parishes). Every county and district has a council consisting of a chairman, a vice-chairman, and councillors; the chairman and vice-chairman being elected annually by the council from among the councillors. Councillors are elected by the general electorate of the area for four years. County councillors retire together every fourth year. One-third of metropolitan district councillors retire in each of the years between county council elections. Non-metropolitan district councils, once established, may choose between all members of the council retiring together every fourth year and one-third of the members retiring each year. All councillors may stand for re-election.[9]

In England, the parishes will continue in rural areas, though with some boundary changes and with new parishes being created out of sub-divisions. In addition, however, the Act envisages the creation of new parishes to take the place of some of the boroughs and urban districts which cease to exist and become absorbed into the new and larger districts. This will enable townships to retain individuality as local government units, to exercise limited powers and to influence the decisions of the new districts. In Wales there will be about 1,000 'communities', being former rural parishes or parts of parishes, and former boroughs or urban districts.[10]

Each of the 11,000 or so parishes and communities has a 'meeting' of the local government electors. But their powers are, save for the smallest, vested in the elected parish or community council.

Parishes and communities have powers in relation to car and cycle parks, footway lighting, rights of way, public footpaths and bridleways, seats and shelters, public conveniences, drainage, wash-

houses and launderettes, litter, allotments, entertainments, ceme-
teries and crematoria and other functions. They also have the right
to be consulted about planning applications. There is no general
limit to the amount they may spend on their functions. And they may
spend annually the product of a 2p rate for anything which in the
council's opinion is in the interest of the inhabitants and for other
similar purposes.[11]

A person is qualified for election if he is a British subject or a
citizen of the Republic of Ireland, is over 21 years of age, and is
either a local government elector for the area or has certain other
property or residential qualifications. He is disqualified if he is
employed by the local authority, or is bankrupt or has within five
years been surcharged by a district auditor to an amount exceeding
£500, or within five years has been sentenced to imprisonment for
a period of not less than three months, or has offended against
certain electoral laws.[12]

Local government elections are fought on a party basis but often
with a considerable number of candidates who stand independently
and without party support. Most of the 'independents' are drawn
from the Conservative and Liberal end of the political spectrum.
Parties seek to obtain majority control of local councils so that they
may dominate the committees and, within the area of discretion
left to them, put into effect the policies they prefer. The differences
between policies can be significant, particularly in educational and
housing matters.

In April, May and June 1973 elections were held for the new
authorities in anticipation of April 1974 when the reorganization
came into operation.

The parties winning control in these elections are shown in this table:

	Con.	Ind.	Con. with Ind.	Lib.	Lab.	Dem. Lab.	None	Total
Metropolitan Counties	–	–	–	–	6	–	–	6
Non-Metropolitan Counties	13	5	5	–	11	–	13	47
Metropolitan Districts	5	–	–	–	26	–	5	36
Non-Metropolitan Districts	60	–	83	1	90	1	98	333
Total	78	5	88	1	133	1	116	422

These figures show the usual phenomenon in voting in the United Kingdom of Labour strength in the cities and the Conservative strength in the more rural areas. The number of councils where no party holds control is much higher than under the former system.

In addition Labour won control of the Greater London Council in 1973 winning fifty-eight seats to the Conservatives thirty-two; the Liberals gained two seats.

Although the Liberal party won control in only one local authority, they won over 1,000 seats and this represented a considerable advance over their more recent record.

A local authority may arrange for the discharge of any of its functions by a committee, a sub-committee or an officer of the authority, or by any other local authority.[13] In practice, in the larger authorities, almost all except the most formal acts and decisions are normally taken by committees to which are delegated the powers of the council of the local authority. Persons who are not elected members of the authority may be co-opted on to committees (other than the finance committee), but although this is quite commonly done (especially by education committees) co-opted persons do not much influence the decisions taken. Serving each committee which is responsible for a function (for example, education or health or planning etc.) there is a chief officer, employed by the authority. He is the administrative head of a department which will contain many other, more junior, officers.

Every major function is administered under the authority of Acts of Parliament. So we have Education Acts, Town and Country Planning Acts, Public Health Acts, Housing Acts and very many others. These Acts give local authorities the powers they need to provide the services. The Acts, with more or less precision, spell out the powers of Ministers as well as of local authorities and the relationships between them. Local authorities must be enabled to buy goods, to acquire land (compulsorily if need be), to employ staff; also to inspect private property, to regulate activities, and to execute works of all kinds.

Finance

All this needs money, so local authorities are enabled to tax those who live in their area. The tax is by means of the local rate. Each unit of occupation (such as a house and garden, or a flat, or a factory) is given, by the Inland Revenue, a rateable value based, rather remotely, on the rent at which the property might reasonably be expected to let on an annual basis.[14] Each local authority knows what is the total of the rateable value in its area.

At the beginning of every calendar year, each local authority estimates how much it will spend on providing its services. Then it estimates how much income it is likely to receive from sources other than its own taxes. By far the largest income from those other sources will be grants given by the central Government. When the authority has subtracted that other income from the estimated expenditure, it knows how much it has to raise through its own taxes.

Let us suppose that the total rateable value of a local authority is £90 million. If, after the arithmetic indicated above, the authority finds that it must raise £45 million for a particular year from its local taxes, then it will levy a rate of 50 pence in each pound of rateable value. If therefore the house and garden which I occupy have a rateable value of £300, I will be liable to pay tax of £150 for that year to the local authority.

This rating system is simple and cheap in its application. The rate is levied on occupiers, not owners; thus in rented accommodation the tenant, not the landlord, is the person taxed. But it has some serious disadvantages. First, as it is levied only on occupiers, many wage- or other income-earners in the house are not liable to pay. Secondly, it is based on the size and desirability of the unit of accommodation. So a man with a large family who occupies a large house may pay more than another who has a higher income and no family and so occupies a smaller house. In this sense, the rating system is said to be not progressive (where the higher the income the higher the rate of tax) but often regressive.

The regressive nature of rating in England and Wales is shown clearly by the following table which relates to 1963–4.[15]

Household income group

	Under £312	£312– under £520	£520– under £780	£780– under £1040	£1040– under £1560	£1560 and over	All
% of household in each group	10·1	9·9	12·9	18·5	26·8	21·8	100·0
Average household income	236·3	410·8	662·5	909·9	1280·5	2333·5	1168·7
Average disposable income[16]	234·3	396·3	607·4	821·9	1142·4	1957·8	1025·2
Average 1963–4 rates	19·2	24·7	25·2	26·0	30·9	42·9	30·2
Rates as % of household income	8·1	6·0	3·8	2·9	2·4	1·8	2·6
Rates as % of disposable income	8·2	6·2	4·1	3·2	2·7	2·2	2·9

So the lower the income, whether household income or disposable income, the higher the proportion of income taken by rates. In the lowest income group, rates took 8·1 per cent of household income and 8·2 per cent of disposable income; in the highest income group, rates took 1·8 per cent of household income and 2·2 per cent of disposable income.

This situation is to some extent affected by statutory provisions,[17] which entitle poorer tenants to claim rate rebates which reduce the amount of rates for which they would ordinarily be liable. But for a variety of reasons – including that of personal pride – by no means all those so entitled claim the rebate. Moreover, in 1973, rateable values were revised (upwards) and although the rate in the pound levied was reduced as a result, there is evidence to suggest that the values of smaller properties increased more than those of larger properties so that the regressive nature of the rating system was strengthened.

All local authorities make their separate estimates of income and expenditure for each financial year and so arrive at the amount which must be raised by local taxation to cover their spending. But only district and London borough councils levy the rate and collect payment. Counties, the Greater London Council, parishes and communities precept on district councils.[18] This means that they inform district councils, in terms of so many pence in each pound of rateable value, how much district councils should levy on their behalf. So a district council must add to its own rate that required by the precepting authorities, collect the whole, and pay over to those authorities the amounts due to them.

Some local government statistics for England and Wales for 1969–70 were as follows:

£ thousands	Rate fund services	Housing and trading services	Super-annuation & special funds	Total
Expenditure	4,049,605	1,088,338	495,739	5,633,682
Income				
Rates	1,515,184	–	–	1,515,184
Government grants				
Rate support grants	1,610,938	–	–	1,610,938
For specific services	202,902	139,660	–	342,562
Licences	1,431	–	–	1,431
Special funds	–	–	495,739	495,739
Sales	83,824	58,795	–	142,619
Fees and charges	324,295	728,299	–	1,052,594
Other income	311,031	155,942	–	466,973
Fall in balances	–	5,642	–	5,642
Total	4,049,605	1,088,338	495,739	5,633,682

From these figures it can be seen that on rate fund services (that is virtually all services except housing) over three-quarters of the expenditure is met by rates and Government grants with the latter contributing a little more than the former. On housing and the small amount of trading services the large amount of £728·3 million (being nearly three-quarters of the total income) represents principally the rents paid by tenants of local authorities. The biggest single item in the fees and charges on rate fund services is £118·9 million being fees paid towards education services (mostly in the further education sector).

Rate support grants are given by the Central Government to local authorities as block payments not earmarked for particular services.[19] The Government, after talking with the representatives of local authorities acting through the local authority associations, of which the most important are the Association of Metropolitan Authorities and the Association of County Councils,[20] and with the Greater London Council, decide what amount to adopt as the estimated relevant expenditure of local authorities for the next, or the next two, financial years. The Government then decide what percentage of that amount to pay by way of grant. From the resulting amount, the grants for specific services are subtracted and the remainder is distributed amongst local authorities in accordance with a formula which reflects most strongly the population of the authority and the number of school-children.

For 1973–4, the figures were:

		£m.
Estimated relevant expenditure by local authorities		5,216
Total Government grant at 60% of above		3,130
Government grant for specific services	255	
Rate support grant	2,875	

By far the largest single item in the total of £5216 million[21] was for education which took £2623 million, the next largest being highways at £433 million. The percentage (for 1973–4 fixed at 60) has in recent years been increasing annually. The largest single item in the figure of £255 million (where the Government make grants for specific services) was for the police at £140 million, the next largest being house improvement grants at £25 million. Altogether nineteen services received specific grants; these were mostly of small amounts and fourteen services received less than £10 million each.

The great bulk of grant money is therefore distributed through the rate support grant, and forms, as we have seen, between one-half and one-third of the total income (apart from that derived from housing and trading services) of local authorities.

The accounts of all local authorities must be audited either by a district auditor or by a professionally qualified auditor. District auditors are appointed by the Secretary of State with the consent of the Minister for the Civil Service. Each local authority, except the Greater London Council and the London boroughs, has power to choose whether to have its accounts audited by professional or district audit. The accounts of the Greater London Council and of the London boroughs are required to be audited by district auditors. Any interested person may inspect the accounts at the time of an audit. Any local government elector, or his representative, may question the auditor about the accounts and, if the audit is conducted by a district auditor, may make objections to any of the accounts. Further, if the audit is by a professional auditor, any local government elector may ask the Secretary of State to direct a district auditor to hold an extraordinary audit.

Where it appears to a district auditor that any item of account is contrary to law, he may apply to a court for a declaration that this is so, unless the item has been sanctioned by the Secretary of State. If the court makes such a declaration, it may order any person responsible for the unlawful expenditure to repay it in whole or in part; and if such expenditure exceeds £2,000 and the person responsible is a member of a local authority, the court may order him to be disqualified for membership for a specified period. Any objector to the accounts may require the district auditor to state the reasons for any decision not to apply to the court for a declaration and may appeal to the court against that decision. Where a sum is lost by wilful misconduct the district auditor can certify that an equivalent sum is due to the authority from the person responsible.[22]

Elected members of local authorities are entitled to receive attendance allowances; non-elected members may receive financial loss allowances. Travelling and subsistence allowances are also payable, as are allowances for attending conferences.[23]

Local government finance is always being examined and proposals for its reform abound. Especially popular are ideas for replacing or supplementing the rating system. But nothing much happens.

Associated with the reform of structure, promises have been recently made for new financial legislation, but it is doubtful whether this will introduce any radical reforms. In July 1971 the Government published a Green Paper on the future shape of local government finance.[24] Green Papers are supposed to put forward the Government's present but not final views on a matter so as to stimulate and focus discussion. This paper consisted mainly of a list of possible additional sources of local revenue and some proposals for the improvement of the rating scheme, making clear that the Government did not intend to reform the system drastically. Rates and government grants will remain the basis of local government revenue for the foreseeable future.

The additional sources of local revenue discussed in the Green Paper were a local income tax, a local sales tax or value-added tax, a local employment or payroll tax, motor fuel duty, and motor vehicle duties. Ways of increasing the yield of rates which were discussed included super-rating (the levy on the rateable value of non-domestic properties of a higher rate poundage than on domestic properties), surcharge on the rates for earning non-householders, site value rating, the rating of agriculture,[25] and local lotteries.

Relations with Central Departments

Although local authorities derive their powers directly from statute and so are legally enabled to act by the conferment of direct authority, their relations with central government departments shape and affect every important decision they make. Ministers and civil servants seem often to regard them as administrative agents for the implementation of policy decisions taken in Whitehall. Local authorities, on their part, while recognizing that national policies must inevitably lay down the general lines within which they work, are highly sensitive to detailed directives which suggest the ways in which these national policies should be put into effect.

Much lip-service is paid to the concept of partnership between central and local authorities but conflicts continually arise which cannot be resolved except by the process of argument followed by Ministerial decision. In the end the Government holds most of the big sticks and carrots though local authorities do have the advantage that it is they who are the operators of Governmental policy and by their enthusiasm or their lack of it can affect the speed with which that policy becomes action and, to some extent also, the quality of that action.

Almost every Government statement about the attitude of Ministers to local authorities insists that those authorities must be made more free of the constraints hitherto imposed by the central departments. But local authorities have come to regard these statements with some cynicism. Two paragraphs from the report of the Royal Commission on Local Government in England[26] in 1969 accurately reflect the reality. In the chapter on local government finance the report states:

531. The local authorities must accept their role as partners with national Government in the provision of services; they must conform to current national policies and recognize the necessary limits to their fiscal freedom; they must be allies of the Government in long- and short-term economic management. Part of their income must take the form of central grants and their investment expenditure must be broadly subject to control.

532. But the central Government for its part ought, we think, to recognize that a reasonable measure of financial independence is an essential element in local democracy, that there is positive virtue in variety . . . and that each central control weakens the sense of local responsibility.

In the first of these paragraphs, a number of propositions for local authorities is laid down which they *must* accept. And the sum of those propositions makes them subject to a very considerable degree of control and of conformity with Government intentions. The language of the second paragraph is significantly different. The imperative is gone and is replaced by 'ought, we think'. This attitude of the Royal Commission would not be dissented from by many, except those in the local authorities who see a much more positive role for themselves.

The argument about the extent of central control and its desirability or otherwise is too often conducted in highly emotional tones and it is suggested by some that democracy and responsiveness to the needs of men and women are attainable only at the grassroots level and, by others, that those in Whitehall know best. The approach should surely be to decide which questions are most efficiently decided at which level. And here 'efficiently' should mean providing the best service to those who need it.

Certain considerations require some decisions to be made centrally. Resources of labour and materials are always limited and their distribution must, by one means or another, be to some extent controlled. For many services – education is the most obvious example – the quality must not differ too greatly in different parts of the country or, to put this another way, certain minimum standards must be insisted on. Poorer local authorities need more financial help and this may be supplied in part by the richer authorities.

The most important single power which the central Government exercises over local authorities flows from the general economic responsibility which Governments have assumed for the control of capital investment in the public sector. Today the Government is expected to plan over a period of years how much capital investment shall be embarked on by central departments, local authorities, nationalized industries and all other bodies within the Government's area of control. This includes, for local authorities, how large, for example, the school-building programme will be. Thus, after much consultation and discussion and argument in Cabinet and Cabinet committees, the Secretary of State for Education and Science will emerge with an allocation representing so many million pounds worth of school building for a financial year. In the meantime each local authority will have submitted its own requirements for new schools and these in total will far exceed the amount which the Secretary of State has to distribute. So the Secretary of State has to decide how much each local education authority is to receive. It must be understood that what is being decided is not the distribution of *money* but how much school-building each local authority may embark on.

For the maintenance of minimum standards, some Government departments employ their own inspectors – for schools, for the police, for children's services – whose function is not only to inspect but also to advise. Some powers of local authorities are, by statute, not exercisable without specific Government approval, such as the compulsory acquisition of land[27] and from some other decisions, such as the refusal to grant permission to develop land[28] in a particular case, appeal lies to the central department.

If a local authority fails, wholly or in large part, to perform any statutory duty, Ministers are often empowered, after inquiry, to declare that the authority is in default and to transfer the functions either to another local authority or to a Government department. Under the Housing Finance Act 1972[29] the Secretary of State is empowered in such cases to appoint a Housing Commissioner to discharge the functions. In these cases all expenditure incurred falls on the defaulting authority.

So also grants may be withheld. For example, the Local Government Act 1966[30] empowers Ministers to reduce rate support grants if satisfied that a local authority has failed to achieve or maintain a reasonable standard in the discharge of its functions. The local authority has an opportunity to make representations and the approval of the House of Commons must be obtained before the grant can be reduced.

An important form of control is exercised through the machinery for the audit of local authority accounts which has been discussed above.

These formal means of control – default, reduction of grant, surcharge – are seldom used though their importance as deterrents to misbehaviour should not be underestimated. But in day-to-day administration and in the making by local authorities of decisions, the real influence of the central departments is exerted informally by civil servants on local government officers and on councillors. Relationships between the departments and local authorities are generally amicable but long before the last resort the departments have adequate powers to persuade local authorities to fall in with Governmental policy. Whether or not the reorganization of local government will result in substantial changes in the relationship remains to be seen. But it seems unlikely.

Officers

A general power is given to local authorities to appoint such officers as they think necessary for the proper discharge of their functions. They hold office 'on such reasonable terms and conditions, including conditions as to remuneration' as the appointing authority think fit.[31] Under certain statutes, some officers must be appointed – for example chief education officers[32] and directors of social services[33] – and special qualifications may be prescribed by the appropriate Minister.

The general words about terms and conditions quoted above

may give the impression of a personal contractual relationship between an officer and the authority who appoints him. But this would be misleading. Local government officers are strongly 'unionized' and negotiations on terms and conditions of service are conducted between representative members of local authorities (as employers) and union representatives. It must be remembered also that although many officers perform administrative functions, servicing the councils and committees directly, many more are employed to provide services directly to the public and these include schoolteachers, welfare workers, child care officers, firemen, engineers and others. Many professions and trades are involved and, to perhaps a greater extent than is true of civil servants, the quality of life for urban and rural dwellers is determined by the skills of these officers.

The Future of Local Government

Some years must elapse before we can judge the success or failure of the new reorganization. But it has one apparent major defect for which there is one possible, though partial, remedy.

Conflict has long existed between the demands, on the one hand, for local government to be close to the people and for units to be as small as is politically possible and, on the other, for efficient services which often require larger units. The Royal Commission and the Labour Government in 1969 and 1970 leant strongly in favour of the latter. But the Conservative Government and the Act of 1972 preserved, though on a much reduced scale, second-tier authorities outside as well as inside the metropolitan counties. It is accepted on all sides that the major functions of local government must be vested in large authorities and this means the counties in non-metropolitan areas. What then is left for the district councils in those areas and can it be enough to satisfy those authorities and to make them worthwhile units? As we have seen, these councils are the principal housing authorities, have some planning powers, and are responsible for environmental health. Their other functions, though numerous, are not of great importance.

When it is remembered that many of the new district councils were formerly county boroughs exercising all local government functions, it will be realised that the reorganization is likely to cause much frustration.

The remedy referred to lies in the power contained in sections

101 and 102 of the Act of 1972 whereby a local authority may arrange for the discharge by another local authority of any of the first authority's functions. This remedy is not simple nor is it complete. But it does enable the transition of power to be eased by reducing its scope, in a flexible way, varying from area to area. So far the remedy has proved difficult to implement. The non-metropolitan counties have not shown themselves very willing to use the district councils as their delegates or agents; and in any event, it is not easy to spell out the relationship that is to exist between the larger and the smaller authorities under such an arrangement.

The fear remains that district councils in non-metropolitan areas may wither through lack of proper powers and adequate functions.

The finance of local government, so long the factor determining the health or sickness of the system, awaits[34] promised reforms. There are, however, no signs that anything radical is likely to be proposed which would give local authorities independent sources of revenue of worthwhile richness. So local authorities will continue to be constrained within the Government-controlled grants, on one side, and an inequitable method of local taxation on the other.

Local government has never lacked its supporters, its prophets and its martyrs. The future of local government will continue to be often and loudly debated. But neither Ministers nor civil servants are at all anxious to hand down to local authorities any greater range of decision-making on matters affecting policy. However, it may be that the new authorities will be able more unitedly to confront the central departments.[35]

OTHER PUBLIC CORPORATIONS

A corporation is in law a legal person and is a device for enabling certain groups of individual persons who have joined together for a common purpose to express their identity. The corporation, being a legal person, exists separately from those individuals who are its members and this has certain advantages of a practical kind. For example, an individual person may own land or have some other interest in land short of ownership. So also two or more people may share an interest in land. If one person holding a shared interest wishes to abandon it or if he dies, then special arrangements may have to be made to ensure that the interest passes to those remaining; and similarly if those in the group wish to add other members. But when a number of people come together and form themselves into a corporation, that corporate body can continue to hold the legal interest although the individuals change. Private companies are formed in this way.

In public affairs, townships from the fifteenth century formed themselves into corporations as boroughs and came to acquire five essential characteristics: the right of perpetual succession; the power to sue and be sued 'as a whole and by the corporate name'; the power to hold lands; the right to use a common seal; and the power of making by-laws.[36]

Today all local authorities except parish and community 'meetings' are corporations. So also are many Government departments, including those created by Act of Parliament. The Crown itself – the body which sues and is sued on behalf of Government departments – is a corporation.

But in addition to these, there are many other bodies, very divergent in purpose and function, which are corporations and which play an important part in the administration of public affairs. We can list, as examples, the Atomic Energy Authority, British European Airways and British Overseas Airways Corporation, the British Railways Board, the British Steel Corporation, the British Waterways Board, the Charity Commission, the Civil Aviation Authority, the Electricity Council, the Central Electricity Generating Board and the twelve Area Electricity Boards, the Post Office, the Gaming Board, the Gas Council and the Area Gas Boards, the fifteen Regional Hospital Boards, the Independent Broadcasting Authority, the London Transport Executive, the National Bus Company, the National Freight Corporation, the National Coal Board and the Thames Conservancy.

The corporations managing airways, transport, steel, electricity, gas and coal are all nationalized industries. Although they differ in detail from one another, they have many principal characteristics in common. Their function is to supply goods or services and to charge the consumer directly for what he uses. He either buys his ticket or pays for the commodity at a fixed price. The price is fixed at a level which will enable the corporation at least to cover its costs – and this is required by the Acts of Parliament creating each of these corporations. The aim is that the corporation shall be self-financing and shall not cost the Government or the taxpayer anything. For many of these corporations this aim is realized. But some from time to time, and some frequently, fail to break even and accumulate deficits which the Government has to meet by one means or another. British Railways – like the railways of most countries – often has to be subsidized; so occasionally do airway corporations; and the National Coal Board.

A second type of corporation is exemplified by the Regional Hospital Boards. But these are being replaced, under the National Health Service Reorganization Act 1973, by Regional and Area Health Authorities or Area Health Authorities (Teaching) which will be responsible not only for hospital services but also for personal health services previously administered by local authorities. The essential difference between the corporations managing the health services (under both the old and the new provisions) and those managing nationalized industries is that the health services are financed in very large part by public funds and few charges are made to the individual user of these services.

Other public corporations perform a wide variety of functions. Thus the Independent Broadcasting Authority has the duty of providing broadcasting services through the programme companies under contract with the Authority, and it also exercises general supervision over the programmes. The programme companies pay a rent to the Authority and a levy to the national Exchequer but finance themselves out of advertising revenue.[37] The Thames Conservancy is responsible for the drainage of the river, the navigation and licensing of boats, the prevention of pollution and other functions. It finances itself primarily by precepting on local authorities and also from fees paid by users of the river. The list of differing examples could be continued.

What follows is an outline of some of the characteristics of public corporations. Not every characteristic is wholly true of every corporation referred to.

Each corporation consists of a body of persons normally appointed by the appropriate Minister,[38] sometimes after consultation with other organizations or interests. The number of such persons ranges from less than ten to twenty or so, some being employed part-time, others full-time. The chairman and full-time members of the nationalized industries are well paid. Thus the chairman of the British Railways Board gets £22,500 a year and full-time members have salaries ranging from £12,000 to £17,000. The chairman of the British Steel Corporation is paid £25,000 and full-time members get between £15,000 and £24,000.

The appropriate Minister can dismiss members but they are normally appointed for a term of years and the usual practice is for the Minister not to reappoint at the end of the term if he is dissatisfied. Nevertheless, there have been dismissals or forced resignations after what looked like clashes of personalities or of policies.[39]

The relationship between Ministers and public corporations varies. But for the nationalized industries which, as we have seen, enjoy a considerable measure of financial independence, Ministers' powers are restricted by statute. The provision which in formal terms indicates the nature of the relationship states that the Minister may give to the corporation directions of a general character as to the exercise and performance by the corporation of its functions in relation to matters appearing to the Minister to affect the national interest. No doubt this is imprecise – how general is general? – and leaves to the Minister the determination of what affects the national interest, and what that interest is. Nevertheless it does put the corporation and the Minister at some distance from each other. Other provisions, such as those which specifically require nationalized industries, when they are framing programmes of reorganization or development, to act on lines approved by the Minister, and those which give the Minister special powers in relation to training, education and research, by the very fact that they spell out what Ministers can do imply what they cannot do.

We may contrast these provisions with the whole structure of the Acts which have governed and will govern the national health service. The Act of 1973 vests in the Minister himself the power to provide the necessary services; and then empowers him to direct Regional Health Authorities to exercise on his behalf such of his functions as are specified in the directions. The Regional Authorities may then direct Area Health Authorities[40] similarly. It is clear that Regional and Area Health Authorities are merely the instrument of the Minister and have no effective statutory powers or duties of their own.

The limited statutory powers of the Ministers to control the corporations administering nationalized industries and the subservient position of some other corporations, such as the Regional and Area Health Authorities, result in different degrees of ministerial responsibility and so different degrees of ministerial accountability to Parliament. The phrase often used in relation to nationalized industries is that the Minister has no responsibility for matters of 'day-to-day' administration. And this means, in its turn, that Ministers will not hold themselves accountable to Parliament for such matters. If therefore a Member of Parliament puts down a Question to a Minister about the day-to-day administration of a nationalized industry, the Minister will normally refuse to answer and refer the Member to the corporation. Indeed, as the lines of ministerial responsibility have become clearer, the Clerks in the House of Commons (acting under the Speaker) will no longer accept such Questions. When the House is debating a matter which concerns a nationalized industry, the rules are not so strict, but nevertheless Ministers will not accept that they are accountable for those decisions and actions of nationalized industries over which they have no statutory power.

This does not end the problem. For it is well known that in practice, whatever the statute may imply about the limits of direct Ministerial power, Ministers are in close and frequent touch with the chairmen of nationalized industries and may discuss many matters, perhaps at the request of the chairmen, which fall within the corporations' sphere of action. So the influence of Ministers is much wider than their area of responsibility and accountability. This has caused some concern amongst Members of Parliament who see in it also some confusion of function which could be dangerous and lead to inefficiency. The dilemma is real, for merely to extend the area of accountability to make it accord with the reality of ministerial influence would inevitably lead to a reduction in the real autonomy which the corporations enjoy and which it was the intention of the statutes to preserve. So the solution is not easy to find and has not been found.

The principal instrument of parliamentary control is the Select Committee on Nationalized Industries. Its terms of reference are to examine the reports and accounts of the nationalized industries, and of the Independent Broadcasting Authority, Cable and Wireless Ltd and the Horserace Totalizator Board, and to examine some but not all of the activities of the Bank of England. The Select Committee has fourteen members, with power to work through sub-committees. Its practice is to select one or more of the corporations in each parliamentary session, or a more general topic, for examination. Thus in December 1972, one sub-committee was to examine first the British Steel Corporation and then the National Freight Corporation, and another sub-committee was to inquire into the procedures followed in coming to decisions on major capital investments by the nationalized industries.[41] The Select Committee and its sub-committees work through the study of written evidence submitted by the industries, the related Government departments, and other bodies and persons, and by oral examination. They also have power to appoint persons with specialist knowledge for the purpose of particular inquiries, either to supply information which is not readily available or to elucidate matters of complexity.

The Select Committee publishes its reports and the evidence received, both written and oral. And from time to time the House of Commons uses these reports and the annual reports of the corporations to provide information and the framework for a debate on one or more of the industries. This Select Committee is considered to provide a valuable means of oversight by the House.

Quite different is the position of the Minister in relation to those corporations which are little more, in statutory form, than extensions of himself. Here also the form and the reality diverge, but in an opposite sense. The new Health Authorities, like the former Regional Hospital Boards, act on behalf of the Minister and exercise, as we have seen, his powers. It follows that for all their actions the Minister is accountable. The paradox is that in this field of medical care, with its inevitable emphasis on personal relationships, it is impossible for a Minister to be in any real terms responsible for more than a fraction of what goes on. Yet for the conditions in any hospital, for the efficiency of any ambulance service, for the quality of any personal health services, it seems that he is accountable to Parliament.

The statutes creating the nationalized industries set up various consultative and consumer councils the function of which is to receive complaints and to bring them to the attention of the corporations. As democratic devices, they have been failures. Under the National Health Service Reorganization Act 1973, there are to be appointed Health Service Commissioners to investigate complaints against National Health Service authorities. The list of matters not subject to investigation is not inconsiderable and the effectiveness of this device is clearly questionable. But events must be allowed to prove or disprove the value of these Commissioners.

To speak of 'the nationalized industries' conceals the very considerable differences in scale and importance that exist amongst them. The capital expenditure of the separate groups of corporations gives some indication of these.[42]

NATIONALIZED INDUSTRIES CAPITAL EXPENDITURE

£ million

	1971-2 pro-visional outturn	1972-3 estimate	1973-4 estimate	1974-5 estimate	1975-6 estimate	1976-7 estimate
At 1972 Survey Prices						
Expenditure on fixed assets:						
National Coal Board ..	72·0	86·0	90·0	94·0	79	67
Electricity Council and Boards	417·0	443·0	454·0	482·0	504	566
North of Scotland Hydro-Electric Board ..	16·2	18·6	17·3	22·1	43	49
South of Scotland Electricity Board ..	76·4	83·6	65·0	54·4	50	57
Gas Council and Boards	157·7	136·6	183·0	182·6	157	135
Total fuel	739·3	767·8	809·3	835·1	833	874
British Steel Corporation	248·0	259·0	305·0	330·0	315	360
Post Office	540·3	589·9	636·7	662·3	662	670
British Overseas Airways Corporation	59·1	31·1	36·4	64·5	112	75
British European Airways	59·5	39·0	34·4	87·9	73	44
British Airports Authority	10·9	14·0	25·5	25·4	15	16
Total airways and airports	129·5	84·1	96·3	178·7	200	135
British Railways Board	62·5	70·0	71·3	70·1	88	111
British Transport Docks Board	11·1	15·2	9·5	10·0	13	13
British Waterways Board	0·9	1·3	1·0	1·1	1	1
Transport Holding Company	0·5	0·4	—	—	—	—
National Freight Corporation	15·8	15·4	24·1	24·1	23	23
National Bus Company	14·1	17·3	14·9	13·3	13	13
Scottish Transport Group	3·0	5·0	4·7	3·5	3	3
Total surface transport industries	107·9	124·6	125·5	122·1	141	164
Total expenditure on fixed assets	1765·0	1825·4	1972·8	2128·2	2151	2203

Looking at the provisional outturn for 1971–2 we can see that the fuel corporations incur the largest amount (41·4 per cent) of the total expenditure, followed by the Post Office (31·2 per cent), the British Steel Corporation (14·0 per cent), airways and airports (7·3 per cent), and the transport industries (6·1 per cent). The estimates over the following years appear to show a rise and then a sharp decline for the coal and gas industries but elsewhere generally an increase in expenditure overall. The increase is sharper during the earlier years 'arising from the increased demand for tele-communications, the purchase of new aircraft by the state airlines, the modernization of the steel industry, and the acceleration of projects including electricity power stations'.[43]

The figures inevitably conceal almost as much as they reveal. Thus the Treasury explain that because of the ongoing review of the coal industry's problems, highlighted by the miners' strike in early 1972, 'it is not possible to give substantive estimates for mining investment'.[44] Investment in electricity generation has to be determined against forecasts of peak demand many years ahead as major power stations require at least five years for construction.[45] Again, the network of pipelines for gas as at present planned is nearing completion.[46] The arguments and public discussion which centre around the building and purchase of Concorde on the one hand, and the building of the third London airport on the other, indicate both how difficult it is to make forecasts of capital invest-ment for this industry and how far ahead purchases must be planned. Long-term policy for the railways is known to be under review and water reorganization affects the Waterways Board. These and other changes are either reflected in the figures or serve to place question marks against them.

A different indication of the relative size of the nationalized industries is shown by the number of persons they employ.[47] As would be expected, the Post Office heads the list with 416,000 followed by the National Coal Board with 354,000, the British Railways Board with 264,000, and the British Steel Corporation with 230,000. Three industries (the North of Scotland Hydro-Electric Board, the British Airports Authority and the British Waterways Board) employed fewer than 5,000 persons.

LOCAL AUTHORITIES AND PUBLIC CORPORATIONS AS STATUTORY BODIES

It was not until the closing years of the last century that Acts of Parliament interposed to reorganize local government, though there had been important reforms from the time of the Municipal Corporations Act of 1835. For 500 or more years, boroughs have existed on the grant of royal charters which require no kind of parliamentary approval. Boroughs indeed acquired many statutory powers, but not until the nineteenth century were these of great importance. From the time of the reorganization of the 1880s and 1890s, however, statute law has dominated their structure, as well as their membership, powers, elections, appointment of officers, financing, conduct of meetings and almost every other aspect of their working. The boroughs are said to retain certain 'prerogative' powers and to possess the attributes (where possible) of 'natural' persons. But this is remote stuff. Essentially 'the law' dominates although of course discretionary powers exist within the legal framework. If this dominance were not so, the independence of local authorities from the central departments would be less than it is. At least the local authority associations can today require the departments to quote statutory chapter and verse when they claim the right to exercise control over local authorities. For statutes which affect local authorities confer legal powers on them *directly* and not as agents of the departments. And it is through this direct conferment that local authorities derive that measure of autonomy they enjoy.

As we have seen, some public corporations like the new health authorities, although they are created by statute, derive their powers through the Minister for whom they act as agents. Nationalized industries, in contrast, have many important powers conferred directly on them by statute. In this they are very similar to local authorities, the principal difference being that the powers of the appropriate Ministers in relation to the industries are spelt out with much more precision than is usual in statutes conferring powers on local authorities.

Despite this similarity in statutory provision and legal relationship, the willingness (almost enthusiasm) of local authorities to challenge the departments, if they seem to be overstepping the boundary of the division of powers, is not shared by the nationalized industries. No doubt there are demarcation disputes but only very rarely does the chairman of an industry publicly complain of Ministerial interference and, as we have seen, the practical working relationship between chairman and Minister is normally very close. We have here, therefore, an interesting and important example of how similar legal relationships, provided for by statute, conceal significant differences in political relationships. The reasons for the differences are two. First, local authorities are not newly created bodies and even if they have existed in their modern form (present reorganization is not here significant) only for eighty or so years, the tradition of local government is very long. And that tradition has been one of suspicion of the central power. Nationalized industries, in contrast, have existed in their present form for less than thirty years and were created by the central departments, by national politicians. Secondly, local authorities are elected bodies, not appointed by Ministers. They have a separate allegiance, another point of reference. This is further emphasized, in their relations to the central departments, if the party political make-up of the council of an authority differs from that of the Government; and it will be little diminished if that make-up is the same as the Government's.

And so, as one would expect when considering such bodies as public corporations, local authorities and Governments, politics determines the nature of their relationships, largely overriding the differences and the similarities in the statutory provisions which govern them.

7
The Police

Although the office of constable is very ancient – its history goes back to the Middle Ages and even earlier – organized police forces are comparatively recent in origin. In the eighteenth century the office of magistrate at Bow Street was held by the Fielding brothers (first by Henry, the novelist, and then by his blind half-brother, John) and they organized a body of men who came to be known as Bow Street Runners. The Fielding brothers did a great deal to make the public aware of the need for a properly organized police force to deal with the crime and violence which flourished during this period, but there was strong opposition to the introduction of a police force on the Continental model because it was feared that it might undermine traditional liberties and pave the way for despotism. This is illustrated by the fact that the word 'police', which first came into the language from French at about this time, had a rather sinister connotation, as the phrase 'police state' has today. Eventually, however, the rising tide of lawlessness made change inevitable and in 1829 Sir Robert[1] Peel, who was then Home Secretary, managed to get Parliament to pass the Metropolitan Police Act, which established the Metropolitan Police Force, the first of the modern police forces in England. In the years that followed police forces were created in the boroughs and counties outside London until the whole country was covered.

Unlike many countries, Britain still has no national police force. The country is policed by a network of separate local forces, though the central Government has obtained various powers which enable it to co-ordinate police activities and lay down uniform standards. It has often been argued that the creation of a national police force would increase efficiency and make it easier to fight crime. It would also produce a more satisfactory career structure for policemen, enable available manpower to be used where it is most needed, and bring about greater uniformity of practice in law enforcement throughout the country. In spite of these advantages, however, the 1962 Royal Commission, the most recent body to investigate the structure of the police, decided not to recommend the creation of a national force.[2]

The reason why they favoured the continuance of local forces was not that a national force would lead to a police state – many European democracies such as Belgium, Denmark and Sweden have national police forces without endangering their system of government – but because they felt that partnership between central and local Government in the administration of public services was of great value because it brought local people into the administrative process. They considered that this fostered a sense of civic responsibility and encouraged the police to take account of local conditions.

The system of local police forces has therefore been retained but special steps have been taken to avoid its disadvantages. Very small forces have been eliminated through a programme of amalgamations. This took place under Section 21 of the Police Act 1964, which provides for two or more police authorities to submit an amalgamation scheme to the Home Secretary for his approval. If approved, the scheme establishes a combined police force and police authority for the area concerned. If the Home Secretary considers that two or more forces ought to be amalgamated and the police authorities concerned are unwilling to agree, he has the power to impose an amalgamation scheme of his own. In this case, however, the police authorities can require the Home Secretary to hold a local inquiry before reaching a final decision.[3] These powers have been used to great effect: in 1961 there were 123 provincial forces in England and Wales; by 1970 these had been reduced to 45.[4]

The Act also provides for collaboration agreements between different forces[5] and the giving of aid by one force to another.[6] Collaboration agreements relate to the joint discharge of certain police functions or the sharing of premises or equipment. Aid usually consists of the loan of men to reinforce a police force which is faced with an emergency. In both cases the Home Secretary has power to direct what action should be taken if the forces concerned do not make satisfactory arrangements between themselves. Finally, the Home Secretary has power to provide a number of central services.[7] These include a police college, forensic science laboratories and wireless depots. He also promotes research programmes.

The provincial forces in England and Wales are governed by the Police Act 1964 (as amended). Besides these, there are the two London forces, the Metropolitan Police Force and the City of London Police.[8] The Metropolitan Police Force is the largest in England and its detective division, known as Scotland Yard, is world famous. The City Police is responsible for the City of London – approximately one square mile in the middle of the Metropolitan Police District – and has developed specialized ability to deal with company fraud and other financial crimes. These forces are to some extent in a special position and there are special Acts which apply to them.[9] There is also separate legislation for Scotland[10] and Northern Ireland.[11] The discussion in this chapter will be concerned mainly with the provincial forces in England and Wales but the Metropolitan Police Force will also be considered.

ORGANIZATION

The organization of the police outside London is based on a tri-partite structure. The three centres of authority are the chief constable of each force, the police authority for each force and the Home Office. There is a distribution of powers among these three authorities and each acts to some degree as a check on the others. The result is that there is a balance between central and local control and between the powers of the professionals inside the force and the laymen outside it.

The chief constable of each force is appointed by the police authority with the approval of the Home Secretary.[12] There is also a deputy chief constable (who commands the force in the absence of the chief constable) and there may be one or more assistant chief constables.[13] Appointments to these ranks are made by the police authority, again with the approval of the Home Secretary, and after consultation with the chief constable.[14] The force is under the direction and control of the chief constable[15] and he makes appointments and promotions to all ranks below that of assistant chief constable.[16] He is also the disciplinary authority for these ranks.[17]

There are two kinds of police force: county forces and combined forces created under amalgamation schemes.[18] The police authority for a county force is a committee of the council known as the police committee[19] and the authority for a combined force is a body corporate known by such name as is prescribed in the amalgamation scheme.[20] The composition of both these police authorities is as follows: two-thirds of the members of the authority are councillors chosen by the local authority (or authorities) and one-third are chosen by local magistrates from among their own number.[21]

The police authority has the duty of maintaining an efficient police force for the area[22] and to do this it has the power to provide such buildings, vehicles and equipment as may be required for police purposes.[23] It also appoints the senior members of the force,[24] decides on the number of persons of each rank which is to constitute the establishment of the force[25] and acts as the disciplinary authority for senior officers.[26] All these powers are exercised subject to the approval of the Home Secretary. The chief constable submits an annual report to the authority on the policing of the area.[27] The authority can also ask him to submit a special report on any matter specified by them, but if the chief constable considers that the report would contain information which in the public interest ought not to be disclosed, or which is not needed for the discharge of the police authority's functions, he can ask the authority to refer the matter to the Home Secretary, who then decides whether the report should be made.

The police authority has the power, provided the approval of the Home Secretary is given, to require the chief constable to retire in the interests of efficiency – i.e. because he is not doing his job properly.[28] The chief constable has the right to make representations to both the police authority and the Home Secretary before a final decision is made and, if representations are made, the Home Secretary may order an inquiry to be held into the question. If the police authority is unwilling to exercise this power the Home Secretary can force it to do so; but in such a case he *must* order an inquiry to be held.[29] This power is important because it enables a police authority (or, if it fails to act, the Home Secretary) to get rid of a chief constable who is no longer up to the mark.

The cost of running a police force is met out of the local police fund.[30] The local authority is responsible for providing the money and no payment can be made out of the fund without its consent.[31] The Home Secretary, however, has the power to make a grant for police expenses from central Government funds and at present this covers 50 per cent of expenditure.[32] He can, however, withhold the grant if he considers that the force is not efficiently run.

The Home Secretary has extensive powers designed to allow him to supervise police authorities in the exercise of their functions. Many of their powers can only be exercised with his approval and in some cases he can require the authority to act even if it does not wish to do so. There are also many important matters which are decided centrally by the Home Secretary and embodied in regulations applicable to all forces.[33] These are matters where uniformity throughout the country is desirable. They include pay and conditions of service, qualifications for appointment and promotion, the code of disciplinary offences, disciplinary procedure, and the ranks in the force. These regulations are made by statutory instrument which is subject to annulment by resolution of either House of Parliament.[34]

The Home Secretary sees the annual reports made by chief constables and he also has the power to ask a chief constable for a report on any matter connected with the policing of his area.[35] He appoints a number of inspectors known as Her Majesty's Inspectors of Constabulary who inspect the various forces and report to him.[36] The chief inspector of constabulary produces an annual report which is laid before Parliament and published.[36] These powers enable the Home Secretary to keep himself fully informed on the way in which the police forces are operating.

A good illustration of the way central and local government work together is the appointment of a chief constable.[37] The normal procedure for this is as follows. First, the vacancy is advertised. Then a list of applicants is drawn up by the police authority and sent to the Home Office. It is examined by officials there and the inspectors of constabulary are consulted. The Home Office inform the police authority whether there are any applicants whose appointment might not be approved by the Home Secretary and which applicants are considered particularly well qualified. The police authority may request a meeting at the Home Office to discuss the matter further. Then the police authority makes the appointment and approval is automatic unless the person appointed was someone whom the Home Office had already stated to be unsuitable. There are two requirements which the Home Office insist must be fulfilled by all applicants: approval will not be granted unless the person appointed is a professional police officer whose previous career has been in the police in this country; and he must have had experience at a senior level in some other force than the one in which the appointment is made.

There is a greater degree of central control in police matters than in most other local government services and the Home Secretary has ample powers to ensure that the police forces are efficiently run. For this reason many of the drawbacks of a system of local forces are avoided. In fact, if the Home Secretary used his powers to the full – his ultimate weapon is the threat of withholding the annual police grant – there would be little scope for local initiative. In practice, however, the Home Secretary normally refrains from using his powers to this extent and local autonomy is retained within the limits set by the Home Office.[38]

The Metropolitan Police force is in a special position. The police authority for the Metropolitan Police is the Home Secretary, who consequently has much greater powers over this force than he has over the provincial forces. The chief officer of the force is the Commissioner of Police of the Metropolis, who is appointed by the Crown on the advice of the Home Secretary. There are also five Assistant Commissioners appointed in the same manner. The Commissioner and the Assistant Commissioners hold office during the pleasure of the Crown and can therefore be removed by the Crown on the advice of the Home Secretary.[39] Even though there is no local control over the Metropolitan Police, part of the cost of the force is borne by the local rates. There is also a Home Office grant.

Policemen are not allowed to join trade unions[40] but there are special organizations to represent their interests. The largest of these is the Police Federation, which represents all ranks below superintendent.[41] The constitution of the Police Federation is laid down by the Home Secretary[42] and there is a statutory provision that it must not affiliate with any outside organization without the authorization of the Home Secretary.[43] There are also separate organizations for superintendents and for the ranks above superintendent.

Pay and other negotiable conditions of service are considered by the Police Council for the U.K.[44] This body is modelled on the civil service Whitley councils and consists of a staff side and an official side. The staff side is made up of representatives of the Police Federation and the other police organizations. The official side includes representatives of the police authorities and the Home

Office.[45] The two sides negotiate on the questions brought before them and try to reach an agreed settlement. If this is not possible, there is provision for arbitration. Although the Government is not bound to accept the recommendations of the Council there is a convention that it will do so in all save the most exceptional cases.[46] Non-negotiable matters are not considered by the Police Council, but before the Home Secretary makes regulations on these matters he is obliged to consult another body called the Police Advisory Board for England and Wales.[47]

These arrangements are the outcome of a struggle by the police to obtain collective bargaining rights.[48] This started in 1913 when a clandestine trade union was formed called the National Union of Police and Prison Officers. This union organized a strike of London police in 1918 which was very effective and resulted in a large pay increase. The Government, however, refused to grant recognition to the police union. They proposed instead the setting up of the Police Federation and Police Council. This was unacceptable to the police union and a second strike was called in 1919. But the Government's proposals had sapped the support of the union and the strike soon collapsed. All those who took part in it were dismissed and never reinstated. The present system, therefore, represents a compromise which aims at giving the police the right to bargain over most matters which affect them without giving them the right to strike.

STATUS AND CONTROL

The legal status of a police constable has been considered by the courts in a number of cases. The most important of these is *Fisher* v. *Oldham Corporation*.[49] In this case the Oldham police had arrested the wrong man by mistake and he brought an action for damages against the Oldham corporation. This raised the question whether the corporation was legally responsible for the acts of the local police, which in turn depended on whether a relationship of master and servant existed between the local authority and the force. The plaintiff claimed that it did: he maintained that the corporation through their watch committee were the employers of the police and that the police were in law their servants. This was rejected by the court. The police, it was held, are not the servants of the local authority; a policeman is the holder of an office recognized by the law – the office of constable – and he is an officer of the Crown.[50]

The question of control over the police is more difficult. It is best to start off by considering the different aspects of police activity over which control might be exercised.[51] First, there is the enforcement of the law in individual cases. Examples of this are whether X should be arrested, Y prosecuted, or the affairs of Z investigated. Secondly, there are administrative matters: the type of equipment to be used, the size of the establishment of the force or the kind of buildings that are necessary. Thirdly, there are general policies of law enforcement. Examples of these are whether the police should operate speed traps; whether a policy should be adopted not to prosecute in certain classes of case; the way the force should be deployed to protect persons wishing to work during a strike in which there have been threats of violence; the tactics used to deal with riots; whether students occupying university buildings should be evicted; or whether resources should be concentrated against particular kinds of crime.

There is little doubt that questions falling within the first category are for the police alone to decide. These matters involve the professional judgment of the police: is there reason to suspect that the person in question is guilty of an offence? The police should act in a completely impartial way in deciding this question and ought not to be subject to any outside pressure. It is also clear that matters in the second category – administration – fall within the jurisdiction of the police authority (subject to the overriding control of the Home Office) though considerable weight will normally be given to the views of the chief constable.[52] The position with regard to the third category, however, is more controversial.

It is laid down in the Police Act 1964 that each provincial force is under the control of the chief constable;[53] but is the chief constable himself subject to any control? The Police Act grants various powers to the police authority and the Home Secretary but it says nothing about the general control of the force. The usual view is that the chief constable is not legally subject to any outside control as regards general policies of law enforcement. Thus Mr Henry Brooke, then Home Secretary, said in the Commons in 1963 when the Police Bill was being debated:

The chain of command does not, under the present law, go beyond the chief constable and the Bill does not propose to extend it. The chief constable, therefore, will not be subject to the orders or directions of higher authority in relation to the deployment of his men or the action to be taken in individual cases.[54]

A similar statement had been made a few years earlier in the House of Lords[55] and this was also the view of the Committee on Police Conditions of Service.[56]

The position with regard to the Metropolitan Police is rather different. The force is under the command of the Commissioner[57] but it has long been thought that the Home Secretary is entitled in law to give him directions with regard to general policies of law enforcement and successive Home Secretaries have been prepared to answer questions in the House on the actions of the Metropolitan Police even though they have disclaimed such responsibility in the case of the provincial forces.[58] The legal basis for this power is said to be section 1 of the Metropolitan Police Act 1829. This reads:

It shall be lawful for his Majesty to cause a new police office to be established in the city of Westminster, and . . . to appoint two fit persons as justices of the peace . . . to execute the duties of a justice of the peace at the said office . . . together with such other duties as shall be herein-after specified, *or as shall from time to time be directed by one of his Majesty's principal secretaries of state,* for the more efficient administration of the police within the limits herein-after mentioned . . .[59]

It could be argued that the words in italics empower the Home Secretary to give orders to the Commissioner (the two justices of the peace mentioned in the statute were subsequently called Commissioners of Police of the Metropolis[60] and later reduced to one),[61] but it could also be maintained that the section merely allows the Home Secretary to give the Commissioner additional duties, not to give directions on the way in which he is to carry out those he already has.[62]

The leading case on the subject is *R. v. Commissioner of Police of the Metropolis, ex parte Blackburn.*[63] The facts were these. In April 1966 a policy decision was taken by the Metropolitan Police to stop sending men into licensed gaming clubs for the purpose of detecting offences under the Betting, Gaming and Lotteries Act 1963. The effect of this was that the law on gaming was no longer enforced in London. Blackburn was a private citizen who was concerned about what was happening. He wrote to the Commissioner of Police to ask for his assistance in enforcing the law. In reply he was told that there were difficulties in enforcing the Act,[64] that the way in which police manpower was used was a matter for the

Commissioner's discretion and that there were higher priorities for the deployment of manpower than the enforcement of the gaming law.

Blackburn then turned to the courts and moved for an order of mandamus directed to the Commissioner to require him to reverse his policy decision. The application failed in the Divisional Court and by the time the case came to the Court of Appeal the Metropolitan Police had issued a statement that they intended to enforce the law. There was consequently no need for the Court of Appeal to decide whether the order should be made, but they had some interesting things to say on the legal position of the police.

The fullest discussion is found in the judgment of Lord Denning M.R. It is worth reproducing his words at length:[65]

I hold it to be the duty of the Commissioner of Police of the Metropolis, as it is of every chief constable, to enforce the law of the land. He must take steps so to post his men that crimes may be detected; and that honest citizens may go about their affairs in peace. He must decide whether or no suspected persons are to be prosecuted; and, if need be, bring the prosecution or see that it is brought. But in all these things he is not the servant of anyone, save of the law itself. No Minister of the Crown can tell him that he must, or must not, keep observation on this place or that; or that he must, or must not, prosecute this man or that one. Nor can any police authority tell him so. The responsibility for law enforcement lies on him. He is answerable to the law and to the law alone. That appears sufficiently from *Fisher* v. *Oldham Corporation*,[66] and *Attorney-General for New South Wales* v. *Perpetual Trustee Co. Ltd.*[67]

Although the chief officers of police are answerable to the law, there are many fields in which they have a discretion with which the law will not interfere. For instance, it is for the Commissioner of Police of the Metropolis, or the chief constable, as the case may be, to decide in any particular case whether inquiries should be pursued, or whether an arrest should be made or a prosecution brought. It must be for him to decide on the disposition of his force and the concentration of his resources on any particular crime or area. No court can or should give him direction on such a matter. He can also make policy decisions and give effect to them, as, for instance, was often done when prosecutions were not brought for attempted suicide. But there are some policy decisions with which, I think, the courts in a case can, if necessary, interfere. Suppose a chief constable were to issue a directive to his men that no person should be prosecuted for stealing any goods less than £100 in value. I should have thought that the court could countermand it. He would be failing in his duty to enforce the law.

It is interesting to note that Lord Denning made no distinction between the Metropolitan Police and the provincial forces; nor did he make any mention of the Metropolitan Police Act 1829.[68] He clearly thought that the chief officers of both the Metropolitan Police and the provincial forces were independent in questions of law enforcement both as regards individual cases and general policies. The only possible means of control was by the court.

Whatever the legal position may be, however, it is likely that in practice the commanders of all police forces would listen very carefully to any views expressed by their police authority or by the Home Secretary, even if such views were expressed in the form of advice rather than command. The Royal Commission on the Police went so far as to say that if a chief constable were persistently to disregard advice from the police authority or the Home Secretary his fitness for office would be in question.[69] However, it is unclear to what extent attempts are in fact made either by police authorities or the Home Office to influence police policy, though it is probable that police autonomy is greater in the provinces than in London.

The lack of any legal duty on the part of chief officers of police – at least in the provinces – to submit to outside control over policies of law enforcement has been criticized on the ground that the formation of policy – whether in law enforcement or anything else – involves a choice between conflicting interests and this should be decided by elected bodies rather than by senior policemen.[70] The solution which has been proposed is to give police authorities the right to issue instructions to the police on these matters.

This proposal is superficially attractive but in fact has many disadvantages. It is probable that police authorities in the provinces, two-thirds of whose members are local councillors, would be less impartial than chief constables, especially where politics or local interests were involved. If the proposal were put into effect it is likely that there would be considerable variations in police policies between different areas, depending on the political composition of the police authority. The attitude of the police to demonstrations, for example, would be very different in an area with a left-wing majority on the council than where conservatives were in control and it might even vary depending on the political objectives of the demonstrators.

The problem of local variations would not exist if full control were given to the Home Secretary and this solution would be preferable to local control since the actions of the Home Secretary could be criticized in Parliament. However, the danger of political bias would still exist. One could imagine that a Conservative Home Secretary, backed by a Conservative majority in the House, might instruct the police to take much stronger measures against violent picketing than would a Labour Home Secretary. One cannot help feeling that it would be wrong if police policies were altered whenever a new Government came to power. Democratic control over the police should be limited to Parliament's power to change the law: the administration of the law should be as impartial as possible. If changes are to be made it might be better to strengthen the independence of chief officers of police from government control and to give the courts greater powers in cases where it is claimed that the police have acted improperly.

COMPLAINTS AGAINST THE POLICE

The problem of how the police themselves are to be policed has given rise to continuing controversy. The present procedure is based on the idea that the police should discipline themselves, but there are a number of external checks. If a member of the public has a complaint against the police – whether because they have failed to take some action they should have taken or because they have exceeded their authority – he has the choice of either lodging his complaint with the police or taking legal action himself by bringing a private prosecution or a civil action.

A criminal prosecution will only be possible if the policeman concerned has committed a crime, such as assault or false imprisonment, and if he can be personally identified. If he has committed a tort – assault and false imprisonment are also torts – it will be possible to bring a civil action for damages. The proceedings may be brought against the individual policeman concerned and also against the chief constable, who is liable for the torts committed by constables under his direction and control in the performance or purported performance of their functions in the same way as a master is liable for the torts committed by his servants in the course of their employment.[71] This is not because there is a common law relationship of master and servant between a chief constable and his men but is the result of section 48 of the Police Act 1964, which provides that any damages awarded against the chief constable are to be paid out of the police fund. The advantage of this provision, besides ensuring that the plaintiff will recover any damages awarded, is that it does not matter if the identity of the policeman concerned cannot be established.

The disadvantage of bringing legal proceedings is that it may be difficult for the plaintiff to prove his case in court, especially if there are no witnesses. If, on the other hand, a complaint is made it will be investigated by the police who will gather the necessary evidence. The result may be a criminal prosecution brought by the police or disciplinary proceedings. There is a code of discipline[72] which applies to all policemen and this lays down a number of disciplinary offences. Some of these are defined in such wide terms that almost any improper conduct could be brought within their scope. Thus there is an offence of discreditable conduct which includes any act reasonably likely to bring discredit on the reputation of the police service. Other offences include disobedience to orders, neglect of duty, falsehood (which includes the making of a false statement or the destruction of any official document) and corrupt or improper practices.

The disciplinary machinery[73] can be brought into operation either by a complaint from a member of the public or a report from another member of the force. All complaints from the public must be recorded and investigated.[74] The investigation will normally be carried out by an officer with the rank of superintendent or above and he will not normally be from the same division or branch as the person under investigation. Sometimes someone from another force will be brought in and this must be done if the Home Secretary so directs.[75]

The policeman whose conduct is under investigation will be informed in writing by the investigating officer of the allegations against him. He will also be told that he may make a statement to the investigating officer or to the chief constable but that he is not obliged to do so and that any statement may be used in disciplinary proceedings. When he has completed his inquiries the investigating officer makes a report to the chief constable. If there is any possibility that a crime may have been committed the chief constable must send the report to the Director of Public Prosecutions who will decide whether to bring criminal charges.[76] If the chief constable is satisfied that no criminal offence has been committed, he must decide whether to charge the policeman with a disciplinary offence.

If a disciplinary charge is brought there is a hearing before the chief constable in the presence of the accused. The case against the accused is presented by a member of the force and the accused is entitled to choose another member of the force to conduct his defence. Where the proceedings arose out of a complaint from a member of the public, the complainant is allowed to attend the hearings while the witnesses are being examined and he may ask the chief constable to put questions to the witnesses. In certain cases he may be allowed to have a friend or relative with him. When the hearing is concluded the chief constable gives his decision. If the offence is proved the punishments that may be imposed are: dismissal, forced resignation, reduction in rank, reduction in pay, a fine, a reprimand or a caution.[77]

Where the charge is against a senior officer (the chief constable, deputy chief constable or an assistant chief constable) the procedure is different.[78] In this case the disciplinary authority is the police authority. The hearing is conducted before a tribunal consisting of a single person selected and appointed by the police authority from a list of persons nominated by the Lord Chancellor. The police authority also appoints one or more assessors who are selected by the authority with the approval of the tribunal. One of them must be a present or past chief officer of police from a different force.

At the hearing the case against the accused is presented by a barrister or solicitor and the accused is also entitled to be legally represented. After the hearing the tribunal prepares a report stating whether the charges are proved and what punishment is recommended. This report is submitted to the police authority,[79] which makes the final decision. Dismissal is again the most severe penalty. A copy of the report and the decision of the police authority are sent to the Home Secretary.

Any policeman (whether a senior or a subordinate officer) found guilty of a disciplinary offence can appeal to the Home Secretary.[80] Unless the Home Secretary considers that the appeal can be decided without taking evidence he will appoint a tribunal consisting of one or more persons to hold an inquiry. Both the appellant and the respondent (the disciplinary authority) are entitled to be present at the inquiry and they may be represented by counsel. The inquiry is normally held in private but the complainant (if a member of the public) has the same right to be present and to put questions as in the initial hearing. The inquiry is conducted by way of a rehearing of the charge. The tribunal draws up a report stating what offences they find to be proved and whether they consider the punishment imposed to be just and proper. The report is presented to the Home Secretary who takes the final decision. He has power to allow or dismiss the appeal and to vary the punishment.

The total number of complaints in 1971 against the police in provincial forces in England and Wales was 7,939.[81] Many of these (23 per cent) were subsequently withdrawn and only 11 per cent were substantiated. Dissatisfaction with the way in which the complaint was handled was registered by 2 per cent of complainants. There were 1,117 cases (14 per cent) in which a report was sent to the Director of Public Prosecutions and there were 52 convictions of police officers as a result. Forty-two of these convictions related to traffic offences. There were 654 policemen charged with disciplinary offences – in the majority of cases the proceedings resulted from reports by supervisory officers rather than from complaints by members of the public – and charges were proved against 596 officers. This is equivalent to 7·9 offenders in every thousand policemen.[82] In 89 cases the officer concerned was dismissed or required to resign. There were 35 appeals to the Home Secretary but in no case was a tribunal appointed.[83]

These figures appear to be fairly satisfactory. However, many people feel that it is wrong that the investigation of complaints should be in the hands of the police themselves: they would like to see some outside body brought into the procedure.[84] It is felt that this would lead to greater confidence in the way complaints are dealt with and benefit the police by showing unjustified accusations to be groundless.

There are various ways in which this could be done. A review board could be set up which would receive complaints from the public and investigate them. Or the recording and investigation of complaints could be left in the hands of the police but some outside authority – perhaps the Parliamentary Commissioner for Administration – could be brought in where complainants are dissatisfied with the way the police have dealt with the complaint.[85]

There are, however, already a number of external safeguards in the system. The Director of Public Prosecutions normally makes the decision whether a criminal charge should be brought against policemen whose conduct has been subject to investigation following a complaint; and it is the duty of the police authorities and the inspectors of constabulary to keep themselves informed on the way complaints are handled.[86] If necessary the police authority can call for a report from the chief constable. The Home Secretary has even wider powers: he can order the chief constable to make a report; he can direct the chief constable to bring in an officer from another force to investigate a complaint; or he can order a local inquiry to be held.[87] Local inquiries are conducted by a person appointed by the Home Secretary and are normally used where there are allegations of widespread corruption or inefficiency in a force or if serious complaints are made against senior officers.

In spite of these safeguards there is still some disquiet. A Home Office working party was set up to consider the question and it reported to the Home Secretary in 1971. The report was not made public but the Home Secretary answered questions on it in the House of Commons.[88] At that time the Government appeared to have ruled out the inclusion of an independent element in the disciplinary process on the ground that in a disciplined force discipline must remain in the hands of the commander. Subsequently, however, there appears to have been a change of policy and at the beginning of 1973 the Home Secretary announced that he was considering an *ex post facto* review on ombudsman lines.[89]

It is not yet clear what form this will take but any attempt to introduce an independent element could cause difficulties. The Home Secretary seemed to feel that the investigation into a complaint had to be undertaken by a police officer. This might not be acceptable to some critics but, since the investigation could be carried out effectively only by someone with experience in criminal investigation work, it is hard to see who other than a policeman (or ex-policeman) could do the job. A second difficulty is that if the function of the ombudsman is merely to review the proceedings after they have taken place (which is the solution at present favoured by the Home Office), it would not be possible to take further disciplinary action if the ombudsman concluded that a policeman had been wrongfully acquitted. To do so would be to make him face double jeopardy. In these circumstances the complainant is likely to get little satisfaction from an appeal to the ombudsman.

8
Police Powers

ARREST

The law of arrest is important from the political standpoint because it defines the extent to which the police[1] may interfere with the freedom of the individual. It is also important from the legal point of view because various questions of civil and criminal liability depend on the lawfulness or unlawfulness of the arrest. If the arrest is lawful the arrested person will be guilty of the crime and tort of assault (as well as various statutory offences) if he uses force to resist; the policeman, on the other hand, is entitled to use such reasonable force as may be necessary to make the arrest.[2] Once the arrest is made, the arrested person will be guilty of an offence if he escapes from custody. If, on the other hand, the arrest is unlawful, the policeman will be guilty of the tort and crime of false imprisonment; if he uses force to effect the arrest he will be guilty of assault. Moreover, the arrested person is legally entitled to use reasonable force to protect his liberty and he will not be guilty of any offence if he resists arrest or escapes from custody.

The result of this is that if the suspect resists arrest and there is a scuffle in which both sides use force, the question whether it is the suspect or the policeman who is guilty of assault will depend on whether the arrest was lawful. This is illustrated by the case of *Kenlin* v. *Gardiner*.[3] Here some police officers in plain clothes saw two boys acting suspiciously.[4] One of the officers produced his warrant card and said 'We are police officers, here is my warrant card . . .' and started to question the boys. The boys, however, did not believe that they were genuine policemen and tried to run away. A policeman caught hold of the arm of each of the boys, and a struggle ensued in which the policemen were punched and kicked. The boys were charged with the offence of assaulting a police constable in the execution of his duty[5] and were convicted by the juvenile court justices. On appeal, however, it was held that no lawful arrest had taken place[6] and the policeman consequently had no right to take hold of the boys. It followed from this that the boys were legally entitled to resist and, since they had not used unreasonable force, they were not guilty of any offence. The conviction was quashed.

It is, of course, extremely unwise in practice to resist an arrest that one believes to be unlawful. Apart from any question of a moral duty to assist the police, the law of arrest is so complicated that one can never be entirely confident that the police have no power to make the arrest. It is therefore better to 'go quietly' and if necessary vindicate one's rights by legal action at a later date.

The English rule that a person is justified in using reasonable force to resist an unlawful arrest contrasts with that in many other countries where it is an offence for a citizen to resist even an unlawful arrest on the part of the police.[7] Although the English rule is superficially attractive in that it emphasizes the rights of the citizen, its effect in practice might be to encourage violence against the police. One cannot blame a man for struggling to prevent his capture by persons whom he thinks are trying to kidnap him – as the boys in *Kenlin* v. *Gardiner* apparently thought – but if he knows that he is being arrested by a policeman resistance is less justifiable. One might think that he ought to go peacefully and subsequently bring legal proceedings to vindicate his rights. Under the present law a suspect who thinks that he is being arrested unlawfully might be tempted to bash the policeman and run.

What exactly constitutes an arrest? This question can be important if, for example, a prisoner is charged with escaping from custody or a policeman is sued for false imprisonment. In each case the defence may be raised that an arrest was never made. The law is that an arrest can be effected by words alone provided that the intention to make an arrest is clearly conveyed to the person arrested and he acquiesces in the arrest. If he does not submit, it seems that the officer must also touch him physically. As soon as this is done he is legally under arrest, even if he immediately succeeds in freeing himself from the officer's grasp.[8]

Difficulty can arise in practice if the officer uses words that are ambiguous. Thus 'I must ask you to accompany me to the station' could be either a request or a command. In the former case there is no arrest and the suspect is legally entitled to run away. The tone of voice and the circumstances will normally make clear what is intended but it is advisable for policemen to use words that can leave no doubt that an arrest is being made.[9] A potential suspect would be wise to ascertain his position by asking whether he is being arrested.

It is important to note in this context that the police have no right to detain a suspect for questioning. There is no halfway house between arrest and freedom and if the police are not lawfully entitled to make an arrest the suspect is free to leave the police station. In practice the police do not always make this clear to persons who are 'helping them with their inquiries' and there seems to be a tendency to trade on suspects' ignorance of the law by asking them to come to the station to answer questions and not telling them they are free to refuse.

When are the police entitled to make an arrest? If there is no warrant there are only three classes of case in which an arrest can be made. These are: first, if the person arrested is suspected of having committed an arrestable offence (defined below); secondly, if he has committed a breach of the peace in the presence of the person making the arrest; thirdly, if the case comes within one of the many statutes that give a power of arrest in specified circumstances. If the case does not fall into any of these categories (and many do not) there is no power of arrest unless a warrant is obtained.

Under the common law there was a general power to arrest anyone suspected of having committed a felony. When the concept of felony was abolished by the Criminal Law Act 1967 a new concept, that of an arrestable offence, was created as a substitute. This is defined in section 2(1) of the Criminal Law Act as any statutory offence for which the maximum penalty on a first conviction is at least five years, any offence for which the penalty is fixed by law (e.g. murder and treason) or any attempt to commit either of the foregoing.

The Criminal Law Act specifies four cases in which a person may be arrested for an arrestable offence. Two of these apply only where the arrest is made by a constable but the other two apply also to an arrest by a private citizen. The relevant provisions are contained in sub-sections (2) to (5) of section 2 of the statute. They read as follows:

(2) Any person may arrest without warrant anyone who is, or whom he, with reasonable cause, suspects to be, in the act of committing an arrestable offence.

(3) Where an arrestable offence has been committed, any person may arrest without warrant anyone who is, or whom he, with reasonable cause, suspects to be, guilty of the offence.

(4) Where a constable, with reasonable cause, suspects that an arrestable offence has been committed, he may arrest without warrant anyone whom he, with reasonable cause, suspects to be guilty of the offence.

(5) A constable may arrest without warrant any person who is, or whom he, with reasonable cause, suspects to be, about to commit an arrestable offence.

It is important to note that these provisions permit the arrest to be made on mere suspicion, provided there is reasonable cause for that suspicion. This is entirely proper. It would be quite wrong if an acquittal at the trial had the effect of making the arrest unlawful. On the other hand, it would be equally wrong if the police could make an arrest without anything concrete against the person arrested. The requirement that there must be reasonable cause makes this unlikely.

In sub-sections (2), (3) and (5) it is sufficient if *either* the person arrested is in fact guilty *or* if the person making the arrest suspects him, with reasonable cause, to be guilty. This deals with the problem of so-called 'second-sight', i.e. where the arrester has no reasonable cause for his suspicion but it proves to be well-founded. The only exception to this is sub-section (4); but if the suspect is actually guilty the constable will always be covered by sub-section (3).

There are various ways in which the powers of a constable are wider than those of a private citizen. Under sub-section (2) a private citizen or a constable can arrest someone who is caught in the act. But a constable can, under sub-section (5), also arrest a person who is *about* to commit an arrestable offence. This power is denied to the private citizen. There is an even more important difference between sub-sections (3) and (4). The former, which applies to both constables and private citizens, authorizes an arrest only when the crime has actually been committed by someone – though not necessarily by the person arrested. Thus if no crime was in fact committed the arrest will not be authorized by this provision. This is not the case under sub-section (4), which applies only to a constable.

An example will make this clearer. Assume that a private citizen sees a person breaking into a car and driving it away. The next day he recognizes the person concerned and arrests him. If it turns out that he was breaking into his own car (because he had lost the keys) the arrest will be unlawful since no offence would have been committed. If a constable had made the arrest, however, he could have relied on sub-section (4), which protects him so long as he *suspected* (with reasonable cause) that the offence had been committed. For this reason it is risky for a private person to make an arrest unless he catches the suspect in the act. In the above example if the suspect had been arrested as he was breaking into the car, the private person making the arrest would have been able to rely on sub-section (2), under which reasonable suspicion is sufficient. The arrest would then have been lawful.

The power to arrest for a breach of the peace is still based on the common law. An arrest under this power can be made either by a policeman or a private citizen but the arrest is lawful only if the breach of the peace was committed in the presence of the person making the arrest or if he had reasonable grounds for fearing that it was about to be committed in his presence. Any act of violence against a person, even if he is not seriously hurt, is a breach of the peace and would justify an arrest. It has been said[10] that if two persons are fighting, an onlooker can arrest both of them: he is not required to decide who started it. A threat of violence could also justify an arrest if the person making the arrest reasonably feared that the threat would be carried out. It is not clear whether the concept of a breach of the peace extends beyond this, for example whether it covers violence to property.[11] Of course, a threat of force against property might give rise to a reasonable fear that a fight might ensue and this would justify an arrest.

It seems probable that a reasonable, but mistaken, suspicion that a breach of the peace is being, or is about to be, committed would justify arrest.[12] The power is, however, fairly limited in view of the requirement that the breach of the peace must be committed in the presence of the person making the arrest. Thus if a policeman arrives on the scene after the fight is over he cannot make an arrest under this power. A bystander can, however, make the arrest and give the culprit into the charge of the policeman. Another restriction is that the arrest must be made while the breach of the peace is continuing or immediately after it has ceased. Where the arrest is made for a threatened breach of the peace, the arrester must have reasonable grounds for believing that it is about to be committed. If the culprit runs away and a chase ensues, the arrest will be valid even if he is not caught for some hours provided the pursuit is kept up.

In addition to the general powers of arrest for arrestable offences and breaches of the peace there is also a miscellaneous collection of more specific statutory powers. The number of statutes granting such powers is large – there are said to be over seventy – and most of them are restricted to particular offences.[13] Many of them are in local statutes, that is statutes which apply only in a particular town or city.

A warrant can be issued for the arrest of someone suspected of any offence, though a summons will normally be issued instead if the offence is not serious.[14] Under the Magistrates' Courts Act 1952[15] a warrant may be issued by a magistrate if an information is laid before him that a person is suspected of having committed an offence. (An information is a statement that the suspect is believed to have committed the offence specified. It must be in writing and substantiated on oath.) The warrant must state the name (or description) of the person to be arrested and must specify the charge.[16] A warrant can be issued to a private person but normally it is issued only to the police.

Once the warrant has been obtained the police can arrest the person named in it. Under the common law the person making the arrest had to have the warrant in his possession at the time of the arrest. This has now been changed by section 102(4) of the Magistrates' Courts Act which provides that a warrant to arrest a person charged with an offence may be executed by a constable (but not by a private person) even though it is not in his possession at the time. However, if the arrested person demands to see the warrant it must be shown to him as soon as practicable. At first sight this rule might seem wrong; but a moment's consideration will show that it is very necessary. If the warrant is issued for the arrest of a man who is at large, all policemen in the area will be told to keep a lookout for him. Road-blocks may even be set up. In this situation the policeman who eventually makes the arrest is unlikely to be the one who has the warrant in his possession.

When an arrest is made (either with or without a warrant) the suspect must be told why he is being arrested. Failure to do this makes the arrest unlawful.[17] The only exceptions to this rule are, first, where the reason for the arrest is obvious (e.g. where the suspect is caught red-handed) and, secondly, where the suspect makes it impossible for the officer to tell him why he is being arrested (e.g. where he attacks the officer or runs away). It is not necessary that the suspect should be told what crime he is to be charged with but he must be told what act of his is the basis of the crime. Thus it will be sufficient if he is told, 'I am arresting you for killing Jones': he need not be informed whether he will be charged with murder or manslaughter.

This rule was of importance in the case of *Gelberg* v. *Miller*.[18] The facts were that a motorist had parked his car outside a restaurant in central London while he had a meal. It was a no-parking zone and a policeman asked him to move it. He refused to do this until he had finished his meal and took out the rotor arm from the engine to prevent the police from moving it. He also refused to give his name and address. The policeman then told him that he was arresting him for obstructing him in the execution of his duty by refusing to move the car and refusing to give his name and address. He took hold of his left arm to signify that an arrest was being made. The motorist was subsequently charged with a parking offence under the London (Waiting and Loading) (Restrictions) Regulations 1958 and with obstructing a constable in the execution of his duty.[19] He was found guilty on both charges. However, the police do not have the power to arrest for either of these offences (nor did his refusal to give his name and address constitute a ground for arrest); so he claimed that the arrest was unlawful and brought criminal proceedings against the policeman for assault (taking hold of his arm).

The court acquitted the policeman on the following grounds. Under section 54(6) of the Metropolitan Police Act 1839 it was an offence wilfully to obstruct the thoroughfare within the Metropolitan Police District. This provision also gave a policeman the power to arrest anyone committing this offence within his view. The court held that the motorist's action constituted obstruction of the thoroughfare within the terms of the statute and consequently the policeman had a power of arrest. The arrest was therefore lawful even though the motorist was not charged with an offence under the section and the policeman did not appear to have the section in mind when he made the arrest. The court held that the rule concerning the giving of reasons was complied with since the motorist had been told that one of the reasons for his arrest was his refusal to move the car. It did not matter that the arrest was made in terms of a different offence, that of obstructing a policeman. All that mattered, in the court's opinion, was that the suspect knew what he had done wrong.

It seems fairly clear from this case that arresting someone on a 'holding charge' is not unlawful. (This is the practice of arresting a person on a fairly minor charge while investigations into a more serious offence are taking place.) So long as the 'holding charge' is a genuine one and constitutes a lawful ground of arrest, it does not matter that he is subsequently charged with a more serious offence.[20]

It has already been pointed out that the police have no powers to detain someone for questioning: no one can be made to go to a police station to answer questions, nor, in fact, is he obliged to answer questions at all. Apart from a few special instances under statute, the police have no power to require that a person give his name and address. This is illustrated by the case of *Rice* v. *Connolly*[21] in which a policeman saw a man acting suspiciously at night and asked him for his name and address. The man refused and was then charged with obstructing the policeman in the execution of his duty. This is an offence under section 51(3) of the Police Act 1964 which provides: 'Any person who . . . wilfully obstructs a constable in the execution of his duty . . . shall be guilty of an offence . . .' The court held that the prevention and detection of crime were part of a constable's duty and the defendant's refusal to give his name and address made it more difficult for the policeman to carry out his duty and consequently obstructed him. However, an obstruction is only an offence if it is done 'wilfully' and the court held that this meant not only that it must be done intentionally but also that it must be done without lawful excuse. Since the defendant was lawfully entitled to withhold his name and address, he was not guilty of an offence. (The position might have been different if he had given a false name and address.)

A person who has not been arrested cannot be compelled to attend an identity parade; nor can he be forced to allow his fingerprints to be taken. There is, however, provision under the Magistrate's Courts Act 1952[22] for a person who has been arrested and charged with an offence before a magistrate's court to have his fingerprints taken, provided an order is obtained from the court. If he is subsequently acquitted the fingerprints must be destroyed.

It can hardly be maintained that police powers of arrest are excessive; on the contrary, there are some situations where the administration of justice could be hampered because they are insufficient. Say a policeman catches a man committing a non-arrestable offence which does not involve a breach of the peace or come within any statutory power of arrest. He cannot arrest him; he cannot require him to give his name and address; he cannot make him come to the station. The policeman could go off to the nearest magistrate to obtain a warrant but by the time that was done the culprit would have disappeared. All the policeman can do is to follow him in the hope of somehow discovering his identity.

This is a serious gap in the law since there are many offences for which there is no power of arrest without warrant. A good example is the offence of obstructing a policeman in the execution of his duty. This is not an arrestable offence and unless on the facts a breach of the peace is involved there is no power of arrest.[23] One solution to this problem would be to provide by statute that if a policeman suspects, with reasonable cause, that a person is guilty of *any* offence, he would have the right to ask for his name and address. If he failed to comply, or if the policeman suspected, with reasonable cause, that the name and address were false, he would be entitled to arrest him.[24] A reform on these lines would give the police the powers they need without exposing the citizen to unjustified harassment.

ENTRY, SEARCH AND SEIZURE

There are a number of separate problems to be considered here. First, when may the police enter private premises in order to conduct a search? Secondly, when may they search a person? Thirdly, what articles may they detain after a search? Unlawful entry on to private property constitutes the tort of trespass; the occupier is entitled to use reasonable force to expel the trespasser and if the latter retaliates he will be guilty of the tort and crime of assault. On the other hand if the policeman is entitled to enter the premises, anyone who uses force to eject him will be guilty of assault. Likewise, an unlawful search of the person constitutes assault and the person searched is entitled to use reasonable force to resist. If, on the other hand, the search is lawful, the position is reversed: the policeman is entitled to use reasonable force and resistance is assault. Finally, if a policeman takes goods without lawful justification, he is guilty of the tort of trespass to the goods (a separate tort from trespass to the land) and if he refuses to return them he will be liable for the tort of detinue or conversion. The owner can obtain damages from the police and a court order for the return of the goods. Similar rules apply concerning the use of force to take or to resist the taking of the goods.

The first question to consider is search in connection with a lawful arrest. The police can enter premises to make an arrest and they can search the premises in order to find their man. In the case of an arrestable offence this is provided by section 2(6) of the Criminal Law Act 1967, which reads:

For the purpose of arresting a person under any power conferred by this section a constable may enter (if need be, by force) and search any place where that person is or where the constable, with reasonable cause, suspects him to be.

Three points should be noted concerning this section: first, it only applies to a policeman and not to a private citizen; secondly, the entry is lawful even if the wanted man is not there, provided that the constable had reasonable cause to suspect that he was; thirdly, it seems clear that the power to search granted by the section refers only to a search for the wanted man, not for articles that might be used in evidence against him. The section applies only to an arrest for an arrestable offence but the law is similar in the case of an arrest under a warrant.[25] Although the constable has the right to use force to enter the building, he must not do so until the occupier has had the opportunity to open the door. The occupier should, therefore, be told by the policeman why he requires entry.[26]

When a lawful arrest is made the police are entitled to seize articles or documents in the possession or control of the suspect that could be used in evidence against him.[27] They are entitled to search his person and they can also take from him any weapon or article that he could use to harm himself or others. It is not clear to what extent the police may search the premises where the arrest is made. They could probably do so if the premises were occupied by the suspect (e.g. if he lived there) since in this case articles on the premises would normally be in his possession and control.[28]

The two most difficult questions are whether the police can search the premises where the arrest took place if they were not occupied by the person arrested and whether the police can seize articles which are evidence against a person other than the person arrested. Both these questions came before the court in the case of *Elias* v. *Pasmore*.[29]

The facts in this case were that the police arrested a man called Hannington at the headquarters of the National Unemployed Workers' Movement. Hannington, an official of the movement, was not the occupier of the premises. The premises were searched and documents taken which were not in Hannington's possession or control. The police also took a document found on Hannington.

None of these documents provided evidence against Hannington but some of them did provide evidence against another man, Elias, the chairman of the movement, who was subsequently tried and convicted on charges of inciting Hannington and others to commit sedition. The court held that the police were justified in taking the document in Hannington's possession (which was used in evidence against Elias). As far as the documents not in his possession were concerned the court held that the seizure of those documents containing evidence against Elias was 'excused'. The seizure of the other documents was illegal.

This case laid down the following propositions: first, the police may take all articles in the possession or control of the person arrested which may be or are material on a charge against him *or against any other person*; secondly, the police, having lawfully entered the premises where the arrest is made, are 'excused' if they take articles found on the premises which are *not in the possession or control of the person arrested* if these articles are evidence of a crime committed by *anyone*.[30]

This case has not, however, escaped criticism[31] and it is uncertain whether it fully represents the law. In *Ghani* v. *Jones*[32] Lord Denning thought that the court went too far in saying that documents could be seized if they were evidence against anyone. He seemed to think that the documents must be evidence either of a crime committed by the person arrested or by someone in association with him. This was in fact the case in *Elias* v. *Pasmore* since the offence with which Elias was charged was that of inciting Hannington to commit sedition. However, there seems no reason why this limitation should be put upon the police (must they ignore evidence of a murder just because it is not connected with the person arrested?) and it seems to be contradicted by what Lord Denning said in a later passage.[33]

The next question to consider is the extent of police powers where they have obtained a warrant. Under the common law a search warrant could be obtained only to search for stolen goods but these powers have been increased to a considerable extent by statute. There is not, however, any general statutory power to obtain a warrant to search for evidence of a crime. Instead there are a number of different statutes which give such a power in respect of specific offences. The wording of these statutes is not always the same but the provisions of section 26(1) of the Theft Act 1968 may serve as an example:

If it is made to appear by information on oath before a justice of the peace that there is reasonable cause to believe that any person has in his custody or possession or on his premises any stolen goods, the justice may grant a warrant to search for and seize the same; but no warrant to search for stolen goods shall be addressed to a person other than a constable except under the authority of an enactment expressly so providing.

Although the number of similar powers is large, there are some surprising omissions. For example, the police have no power to obtain a search warrant in a murder case and therefore have no statutory power to enter premises to search for the body or murder weapon.

Once the police have gained entry under a search warrant, what goods can they seize? This question arose in *Chic Fashions (West Wales) Ltd* v. *Jones*.[34] In this case the police obtained a warrant to enter certain shops owned by Chic Fashions in order to search for stolen clothes. The warrant specified the clothes as having been stolen from a certain manufacturer. When the police entered the shop they found no clothes from that manufacturer but they found other clothes, not specified in the warrant, which they believed on reasonable grounds to be stolen. It was later established that they were not stolen and the owner of the shop sued the police for damages for trespass to the clothes. The Court of Appeal held that the action of the police was justified. Lord Denning M. R. said:[35]

In my opinion, when a constable enters a house by virtue of a search warrant for stolen goods, he may seize not only the goods which he reasonably believes to be covered by the warrant, but also any other goods which he believes on reasonable grounds to have been stolen and to be material evidence on a charge of stealing or receiving against the person in possession of them or anyone associated with him.

This principle is quite justifiable as far as it goes but it leaves unanswered two important questions: can the police seize goods which are evidence of quite a different crime (e.g. blackmail or arson) and can they seize goods which are evidence against another person?

Common sense would suggest that the police should not be prevented from seizing goods which are evidence of a crime merely because they obtained entry to the premises under a warrant for a different crime and this was held to be the law in the case of *Garfinkel* v. *Metropolitan Police Commissioner*.[36] In this case the police had entered premises with a search warrant issued under the Explosive Substances Acts which authorized them to search for explosives.

They did not find any; but they found and seized some documents which they had reason to believe were evidence of a conspiracy to pervert the course of justice. The occupier of the house applied to the court for the return of the documents (mainly posters and leaflets) but this was refused by the court which upheld the action of the police.

Whether the police can seize goods in the possession of a person who is not implicated in any way in the crime is more difficult. In the *Chic Fashions* case one judge (Salmon L. J.) inclined to the view that the police could not take stolen goods if the person in possession of them came by them quite innocently.[37] However, the case of *Ghani* v. *Jones* (discussed below) suggests that they can be taken if the person in possession of them is quite unreasonable in his refusal to hand them over.

Since the *Chic Fashions* case was decided the law relating to stolen goods has been altered and under section 26(3) of the Theft Act 1968 a policeman acting under a warrant to search for stolen goods is empowered to seize 'any goods he believes to be stolen goods'. This provision does not say that his belief must be reasonable nor does it require that the person in possession of the goods must be implicated in any way. In these respects it goes further than the *Chic Fashions* case. However, that case is still important with regard to search warrants issued under other statutes.

There are also some statutes which entitle the police to search premises without a warrant. These are fairly restricted in scope. For example, section 9(2) of the Official Secrets Act 1911 provides that a superintendent of police can issue a written authority to search premises if it appears to him that the case is 'one of great emergency'; and section 26(2) of the Theft Act 1968 allows a superintendent to give such authority if the premises in question are occupied by someone convicted within the preceding five years of receiving stolen goods. There are also some provisions under which no written authority at all is needed but these relate mostly to licensed premises.[38]

The right to search the person of a suspect where no arrest is made likewise depends on a collection of miscellaneous powers. Most of these powers are only local in application. The best known is section 66 of the Metropolitan Police Act 1839 which gives a constable the right to stop and search anyone if he has reason to suspect that he has stolen property on him. (There is a similar power to stop and search vehicles.) This provision applies only in London but similar statutes have been enacted for a number of provincial cities. The number of general (i.e. non-local) provisions of this sort is limited. The two most important are the Firearms Act 1968 and the Misuse of Drugs Act 1971. Section 47(3) of the Firearms Act 1968 empowers a constable to search anyone whom he reasonably suspects of having a firearm in a public place; and section 23(2) of the Misuse of Drugs Act allows a constable to search anyone whom he reasonably suspects of being in possession of drugs. [39]

It will be seen from this brief survey that police powers of search and seizure under statute are very limited. [40] The question must now be considered whether there is any general common law power to take property which is evidence of a crime. A good example was put forward by Lord Denning in *Ghani* v. *Jones*. [41] After the great train robbers had committed their crime they spent some time in hiding on a farm. While they were there they gave a cat some milk out of a saucer and left fingerprints on the saucer. Could the owner of the farm, who was not implicated in the crime, have refused the police permission to examine the saucer? At the time no arrests had been made and the police had no warrant, so the case would not have been covered by any of the powers discussed so far. Lord Denning had no hesitation in saying that the farmer would have had no justification in refusing permission. But what principle would cover such a case?

In *Ghani* v. *Jones* [42] Lord Denning attempted to formulate such a principle. He said that when no one has been arrested or charged, the following requisites must be satisfied in order to justify taking an article:

First: The police must have reasonable grounds for believing that a serious offence has been committed – so serious that it is of the first importance that the offenders should be caught and brought to justice.

Second: The police officers must have reasonable grounds for believing that the article in question is either the fruit of the crime (as in the case of stolen goods) or is the instrument by which the crime was committed (as in the case of the axe used by the murderer) or is material evidence to prove the commission of the crime (as in the case of the car used by a bank raider or the saucer used by a train robber).

Third: The police officers must have reasonable grounds to believe that the person in possession of it has himself committed the crime, or is implicated in it, or is accessory to it, or at any rate his refusal must be quite unreasonable.

Fourth: The police must not keep the article, nor prevent its removal, for any longer than is reasonably necessary to complete their investigations or preserve it for evidence. If a copy will suffice, it should be made and the original returned. As soon as the case is over, or it is decided not to go on with it, the article should be returned.

Finally: the lawfulness of the conduct of the police must be judged at the time, and not by what happens afterwards.

This appears to give the police a general power in the case of serious crime to take an article that might be material evidence from a person either if he is implicated in the crime or if his refusal to give it up is 'quite unreasonable'. It is unclear how serious the offence must be (would all arrestable offences be serious enough?) or when a refusal would be 'quite unreasonable'; however, it is obviously desirable that some such general power should be recognized by the law.

Ghani v. *Jones* did not deal with the problem of entry to premises in order to conduct a search but it is likely that the courts will evolve a similar principle. If the police had a right to take the saucer used by the great train robbers, it would have been absurd if the farmer could have prevented them from going on to his land to get it. Another problem that the courts have still to deal with is whether a search which is initially unjustified would be validated (or excused) if incriminating articles are found. This problem is similar to that of 'second sight' in the law of arrest (where the police arrest without any reasonable grounds but it turns out that the person was guilty) and common sense would answer it in the same way.[43]

The fact that an article or document has been illegally obtained by the police (for example, by means of an illegal search) does not prevent its being used in evidence in criminal proceedings.[44] In America a different rule prevails[45] but it seems irrational to allow a criminal to go free in order to punish the police for conducting an illegal search. The right solution, surely, is the British one: use the evidence against the accused and then allow him to bring proceedings against the police afterwards.

It is clear from what has been said that the law is in need of reform. It is vague and complicated where it should be clear and straightforward. It is also obvious that the police have insufficient powers to do their job and it seems that they are expected to break the law where necessary. This is a quite unsatisfactory state of affairs and the powers of the police ought to be increased. At the same time, however, measures should be taken to ensure that these powers are used reasonably. There are various forms that such safeguards might take. It is important not only to keep a check on police action in individual cases but also to look at the general pattern of police searches to ensure that minority groups are not harassed. The warrant procedure, though it may have its uses, does not meet this need. What is required is a procedure whereby all police searches in any area are recorded with sufficient details to indicate whether the action was justified. The records should be scrutinized by an independent authority, possibly the local police authority but preferably a police ombudsman (if one is ever appointed). If it appeared from these records that searches were made with insufficient evidence or that a disproportionate number of searches were made of premises occupied, for example, by black people, action could be taken to change police policy. Disciplinary charges should, of course, be brought where individual policemen are shown to have abused their powers.

INTERCEPTION OF COMMUNICATIONS

This section is concerned with the power of the police, the security services and other public authorities to intercept letters, parcels and telegrams, to record their contents and, if necessary, to detain them. It is also concerned with the power to tap telephones and record conversations. Communications are intercepted in Britain (as in almost all other countries) but there are strict limits on the practice. It is only done for the purpose of safeguarding State security or investigating crime and a warrant must always be obtained from the Home Secretary (or the Secretary of State for Scotland).

The warrant is signed by the Home Secretary, who must give personal consideration to the matter. It states the name and address of the person whose mail is to be opened or the number of the telephone to be tapped. Most warrants are issued to the police (usually the Metropolitan Force), the Board of Customs and Excise or the Security Service. The police normally apply for warrants in cases where they want to break up dangerous gangs, to catch wanted men on the run, or to detect receivers of stolen property. The Customs apply for them mainly in cases of large-scale smuggling, especially exchange control evasion (currency smuggling). The Security Service applies for them in cases of spying, sabotage, subversion and terrorism.

The conditions that must be fulfilled before a warrant will be granted to the police or customs are, first, that the offence must be really serious; secondly, the case must be one where normal methods of investigation are unlikely to be successful; and finally, there must be good reason to think that an interception would result in a conviction. A crime is regarded as sufficiently serious to justify the issue of a warrant if a man with no previous record could normally expect a sentence of at least three years for it or, in the case of a customs offence, if it involves a substantial and continuing fraud which would seriously damage the revenue or the economy of the country if it went unchecked. At one time warrants were issued to prevent the illegal transmission of lottery tickets or obscene publications, but this is not done today as these offences are no longer regarded as sufficiently serious.

The rules are slightly different where the application is made by the Security Service. In this case the warrant will be granted if there is major subversive or espionage activity that is likely to damage the national interest and if the material that is likely to be obtained by interception will be of direct use to the Security Service in carrying out its tasks. The rule that interception will be used only if no other means of investigation are available applies as well. Less emphasis, however, is laid on the need to obtain convictions.

In all cases very careful safeguards operate to prevent abuse and there is a regular review of all warrants in force. When interception is no longer necessary the warrant is cancelled immediately. The material obtained through interception is not normally used in court proceedings, although there is no rule of evidence that necessarily excludes it. It would not be passed on to any private person outside the public service and the number of officials with access to it is strictly limited.[46] A number of very important cases have been solved by the police through this method and some major spies have been uncovered. The number of warrants issued is normally a few hundred each year for opening mail and a similar number for telephone tapping; clearly this power is used only in very special cases.[47]

The interception of letters has been a recognized practice ever since the postal services began. It has been said, in fact, that one of the reasons why carrying mails was originally made a Crown monopoly was to facilitate it.[48] When the Post Office began to operate telegraph and telephone services the practice was extended to these means of communication. It can hardly be denied, therefore, that interception is a well-established practice. Nevertheless, there is considerable dispute as to the legal foundation for it. It has been suggested that it is based on a prerogative power though the evidence for the existence of such a power is not strong. It is quite possible, however, that the Government has no need to rely on such a power.

Telephone tapping does not appear to involve a breach of the rights of the subscriber. It is normally done by means of a recording device in one of the telephone centres. All calls to the number to be tapped are recorded and the recording is passed on to the authority to whom the warrant was given. They select and transcribe only those parts of the recording that are relevant to the investigation in hand; all material not selected is destroyed.

Letters are intercepted while they are in the possession of the Post Office. The letter is normally extracted from the envelope, copied, and then sent on its way. It is doubtful whether this involves any breach of the law.[49]

If one turns to the criminal law the position seems to be the same. Section 88 of the Post Office Act 1953 makes it an offence for a Post Office employee to open a postal packet contrary to his duty; but there is a proviso which reads:

... nothing in this section shall extend ... to the opening, detaining or delaying of a postal packet ... in obedience to an express warrant in writing under the hand of a Secretary of State.

There are also a number of statutes[50] which make it an offence for a Post Office employee to intercept a telegram or a telephone message or to disclose its contents if it is contrary to his duty to do so; but the Post Office Act 1969[51] provides a similar exception in the case where a warrant has been obtained.

It is, therefore, doubtful whether, even in the absence of a special power, there is any breach of the law involved in interception. Even if there were a breach, however, there is little chance that a legal remedy could be obtained. The first problem is that interception is carried out in secret and the person concerned does not know that his communications are being interfered with. The second difficulty is that section 29 of the Post Office Act 1969 provides that no proceedings in tort may be brought against the Post Office or any of its employees for any loss caused by anything done in relation to anything in the post.[52] Thirdly, in the case of letters at least, an action for breach of contract is unlikely to be successful because the transmission of letters does not appear to be based on contract.[53]

It is obvious that no State can afford not to intercept communications; it is equally clear that these methods should be subject to the strictest control and used only in the most serious cases. In Britain these critera seem to be met. A committee of Privy Councillors who were appointed to inquire into the interception of communications reported in 1957:[54]

As a result of our review of the use and result of the power to intercept communications, we are satisfied that all the officers and officials concerned are scrupulous and conscientious in the use and exercise of the power to intercept communications. We are satisfied that interception is highly selective and that it is used only where there is good reason to believe that a serious offence or security interest is involved. We are satisfied that the number of people with access to material obtained by interception, either in its original or in its selected form, is kept to an absolute minimum. We are further satisfied that interception of communications has proved very effective in the detection of major crimes, customs frauds on a large scale and serious dangers to the security of the State.

The main criticism that can be made against the present system is that it might be thought undesirable to give powers of this nature to a Minister: a High Court judge might be a more appropriate person to issue the warrant. This point was considered by the committee but they concluded that in practice little would be served by making such a change.[55] However, since interception is carried out in secret, it is not normally possible to know whether the Government has abused its powers. For this reason some sort of external check on the issue of warrants would be desirable. In the absence of such a check, Parliament should always be ready to follow up any signs of abuse.

DEMONSTRATIONS AND PROTESTS
The right to take part in peaceful marches and meetings – the right of assembly – is an important aspect of civil liberty because it is a means whereby ordinary people can publicize their grievances and express their feelings. It is a means of communication open to those who lack ready access to the press and television. Freedom of assembly, however, inevitably presents problems because of its impact on individuals and on society. Assemblies of people can threaten or intimidate; or, however innocently, may unduly interfere with the rights of other citizens to go about the streets or to seek peace and quiet in parks and open spaces. If there are rival

assemblies, considerable dangers to person or property may arise if they come into conflict with each other.

In such cases the law empowers the police to take preventive action as well as to arrest persons who have broken the law. This in turn presents many difficulties. The police have to decide when to intervene and to what extent. If they are over-zealous they will infringe the rights of those who are assembling or demonstrating. If they fail to intervene at the right time persons may be injured or property damaged. These are the most important issues in this branch of the law. The best way to consider them is to examine the main kinds of demonstration in order to see what breaches of the law might occur. The powers of the police in each situation can then be discussed.

The first problem facing the organizer of a public meeting is to find a place to hold it. If it is to be held indoors a hall must be found. This may not be easy if the meeting is controversial and even a local authority is not obliged to allow halls owned by it to be used for meetings.[56]

It might be thought that this problem could be overcome by holding the meeting in the open air. This is not necessarily so: the use of parks and other open spaces is usually regulated by local Acts of Parliament or by-laws and these often provide that permission must be obtained before a meeting can be held. This is true even in the case of Hyde Park and Trafalgar Square: the common belief that there is an absolute right to hold a meeting in these places is fallacious.

Trafalgar Square is governed by The Trafalgar Square Regulations 1952[57] and paragraph 3 of these provides:

Within the Square the following acts are prohibited unless the written permission of the Minister has first been obtained:

. . . .

(4) organizing, conducting or taking part in any assembly, parade or procession;

(5) making or giving a public speech or address . . .

In Hyde Park anyone can stand up and make a speech at speakers' corner (officially known as the 'public speaking area') but if it is desired to hold an organized meeting or procession permission must be obtained.[58] In both cases applications are made to the Department of the Environment: permission will normally be granted unless there is a likelihood of disorder.

Another possibility is to hold the meeting in the street. But it is almost bound to cause an obstruction (either partial or total) and this is an offence under section 121 of the Highway Act 1959 (considered in more detail below).

One can conclude from this that in almost every case permission must be obtained from someone before a public meeting of any size can be held.

A procession differs from a meeting in that it is a moving body of people. The legal position is different in two respects: first, a procession is less likely to be an obstruction of the highway; secondly, there are specific powers to regulate or ban processions which do not apply to meetings.

The most important such power is found in section 3 of the Public Order Act 1936. Under this the chief officer of police in any area has the power to impose conditions on a public procession if he has reasonable grounds for apprehending that it may occasion serious public disorder. The conditions may only be such as appear to him necessary to preserve public order: the most normal would concern the route to be taken so as to avoid areas where trouble might occur.

It is also provided that if the chief officer of police is of opinion that the power to impose conditions is insufficient to prevent serious public disorder, he may apply to the local council for an order prohibiting all public processions (or a specified class of public procession) within the area for a period of up to three months. The council may then make the order, provided the consent of the Home Secretary is obtained. In London the order is made by the Metropolitan Police Commissioner (or the Commissioner of the City Police) after obtaining the Home Secretary's consent: the local authority is not involved.

It is an offence for anyone knowingly to fail to comply with a condition, to organize or assist in organizing a procession in contravention of a ban, or to incite anyone to take part in such a procession.

A fairly wide meaning is given to the word 'organize' in this context as is shown by the case of *Flockhart* v. *Robinson*.[59] At the time of this case the Metropolitan Police Commissioner had (with the consent of the Home Secretary) made an order banning all processions of a political character in the Metropolitan Police District. There was no ban in the City of London and the Union Movement had held a lawful march there. Later a group of about 150 members gathered at Hyde Park Corner and met the defendant, a senior official in the Movement. He then walked off along Piccadilly with the others following him in loose formation. Later, however, they formed themselves into a compact body and marched in close formation behind him. Political slogans were shouted. All this occurred spontaneously and without any previous arrangement. The defendant, however, led them and signalled to them to stop or turn and they obeyed his directions. Clearly they had become a public procession of a political character and, as they were in the Metropolitan Police District, they were breaking the ban.

The defendant was charged with organizing a procession contrary to the ban. He admitted that the procession was illegal but denied that he organized it since he did not plan it in advance. The court, however, held that 'organizing' a procession includes directing it and indicating the route. Lord Goddard C. J. said:[60]

The question here is whether there was evidence that the defendant organized this procession. 'Organized' is not a term of art. When a person organizes a procession, what does he do? A procession is not a mere body of persons: it is a body of persons moving along a route. Therefore the person who organizes the route is the person who organizes the procession.

The defendant was found guilty.

In addition to the Public Order Act there are various local Acts of Parliament and by-laws which contain similar provisions. For example, section 52 of the Metropolitan Police Act 1839 gives the Metropolitan Commissioner of Police the power to make regulations to prevent the obstruction of the streets within the Metropolitan Police District and any person who, after being informed of them, wilfully disregards them is guilty of an offence.[61] This power can be used to regulate processions.

One of the most common charges against demonstrators is that of an offence arising out of the obstruction of the highway. They might be charged with public nuisance; or with an offence under section 121 of the Highways Act 1959; or possibly with an offence under a by-law or local Act of Parliament.

The common law offence of public nuisance has been defined as:

... an act not warranted by law or an omission to discharge a legal duty which act or omission obstructs or causes inconvenience or damage to the public in the exercise of rights common to all His Majesty's subjects.[62]

Obstruction of the highway could obviously come within this definition.

Section 121 of the Highways Act 1959 provides that if a person 'without lawful authority or excuse, in any way wilfully obstructs the free passage along a highway' he is guilty of an offence.

Public nuisance is a more serious charge than an offence under section 121: in the former case there is no limit to the size of the fine or the length of imprisonment that may be imposed; in the latter case the maximum penalty is a fine of £50.[63]

Two points should be made about what constitutes obstruction. First, it is not necessary that the highway be completely blocked so that persons or cars cannot get by;[64] nor need it be proved that anyone was in fact obstructed. Secondly, not every *de facto* obstruction will be an offence: it must be shown that the accused was using the highway in an unreasonable way. This is the case both in a prosecution for public nuisance[65] or for an offence under the Highways Act.[66] What is a reasonable user is a question of fact that would depend on the circumstances of each case but a procession would be more likely to be regarded as reasonable than a meeting.

A good example of the way the law operates is the case of *Arrowsmith* v. *Jenkins*.[67] Miss Pat Arrowsmith, a well-known campaigner for nuclear disarmament, was charged under the Highways Act. She had addressed a meeting in a street for about half an hour and the highway was obstructed by the crowd. It was completely blocked for only about five minutes and she had requested the crowd to move closer to her to allow vehicles to pass. The place in question was apparently one where meetings were often held and no prosecutions had been brought in the past. In spite of this, however, she was found guilty: the fact that she had no desire to obstruct the highway and that she thought that she was entitled to hold the meeting did not avail her.

Another provision of great importance is section 5 of the Public Order Act 1936 (as substituted by section 7 of the Race Relations Act 1965). This provides:

Any person who in any public place or at any public meeting —
(a) uses threatening, abusive or insulting words or behaviour, or
(b) distributes or displays any writing, sign or visible representation which is threatening, abusive or insulting,
with intent to provoke a breach of the peace or whereby a breach of the peace is likely to be occasioned, shall be guilty of an offence.

The maximum penalty for this offence, if tried on indictment, is twelve months' imprisonment and/or a fine of £500.[68]

The following points should be noted about this provision. First, it applies only in a public place or at a public meeting. The definition of the phrase 'public place' was extended by section 33 of the Criminal Justice Act 1972. The new definition reads:

'Public place' includes any highway and any other premises or place to which at the material time the public have or are permitted to have access, whether on payment or otherwise.

This could include a sports ground, a theatre, a railway station[69] or a hall, so long as the public have access to it. It is no longer necessary that the place in question be out of doors. A public meeting is defined in the Public Order Act[69A] and includes a meeting (held in any place) which the public *or any section of the public* are permitted to attend, whether on payment or otherwise. A meeting open to only a section of the public would therefore be a public meeting, even though the place where it was held would not necessarily be a public place.

Secondly, the provision applies to either words or behaviour. It must, however, be proved that the words or behaviour were threatening or abusive or insulting. The House of Lords has refused to define these words and stated that they must be given their normal meaning. This was in the case of *Brutus* v. *Cozens*[70] in which an anti-apartheid demonstrator had jumped on to the court at Wimbledon and disrupted a match in which a South African was playing. The magistrates' court had dismissed a charge against him under section 5 of the Public Order Act on the ground that, though his conduct may have been annoying to the spectators, it was not insulting. The House of Lords refused to interfere with this decision. They rejected the view of the Divisional Court[71] that conduct evidencing a disrespect for the rights of others so as to cause their resentment is insulting behaviour.

The third point is that the prosecution must prove *either* that the accused intended to provoke a breach of the peace *or* that a breach of the peace was likely to be occasioned. In neither case is it necessary to prove that a breach of the peace actually occurred (though the prosecution's task will be much easier if it did) and under the second alternative (which is the one normally relied on by prosecutors) it is no defence that the accused did not want to cause disorder. The vital factor in this case is the mood of the crowd at the time. This is shown by the case of *Jordan* v. *Burgoyne*[72] which arose out of a National Socialist meeting held in 1962 in Trafalgar square. Among the crowd of over two thousand there were a group of opponents of the National Socialist Movement, including Jews, C.N.D. supporters and Communists. They appeared to have come with the intention of breaking up the meeting and made frequent attempts to attack the platform which was protected by a line of police. In the course of his speech the accused (Jordan) said:

... more and more people every day ... are opening their eyes and coming to say with us: Hitler was right. They are coming to say that our real enemies, the people we should have fought, were not Hitler and the National Socialists of Germany but world Jewry and its associates in this country.

At this point complete disorder occurred and the police had to end the meeting. Jordan was subsequently convicted of using insulting words whereby a breach of the peace was likely to be occasioned. It was argued that the people who caused the disorder were deliberate trouble-makers and ordinary reasonable people would not have been provoked to violence by the words. But the Divisional Court held that a speaker must 'take his audience as he finds them': the question is not whether a reasonable audience would have been provoked, but whether the particular audience in question would have reacted – and this is so even if they came there with the deliberate intention of breaking up the meeting.

Section 5 of the Public Order Act undoubtedly limits freedom of speech. The justification for it is the maintenance of public order. The main safeguard for the speaker is that no matter how much disorder results he cannot be convicted unless his words or behaviour are 'threatening, abusive or insulting'. This requirement prevents his guilt depending entirely on the reaction of his audience: the doctrine that a speaker must 'take his audience as he finds them' does not apply here. Nevertheless these three words can be subject to very different interpretations and in the end a great deal depends on the magistrate or jury hearing the case.[73] Sometimes magistrates give a wide meaning to these words: for example, in one case a protest group who held a match under an American flag outside the U.S. embassy in a demonstration against the war in Vietnam were convicted of insulting behaviour under the Act.[74]

Other charges[75] that might be brought against a speaker at a public meeting are: incitement to racial hatred,[76] inciting disaffection among members of the armed forces[77] or the police,[78] and sedition.[79] Other offences with which demonstrators may be charged are: being in possession of an offensive weapon,[80] malicious damage to property,[81] and assaulting a policeman in the execution of his duty.[82] It should also be mentioned that it is an offence under section 1 of the Public Order Act 1936 to wear a political uniform at a public meeting or in a public place; and section 2 makes it an offence to organize and train a body of men to use force for a political objective. (Both those provisions were originally intended to deal with the Fascists in the Thirties.)

Something should also be said about the crimes of unlawful assembly, rout and riot. These are all common law offences and there is some doubt about their exact scope. It seems fairly clear, however, that a demonstration would be an unlawful assembly if it consisted of at least three persons who had a common purpose and were assembled together in such a manner as to give reasonably courageous persons in the vicinity reasonable grounds for apprehending a breach of the peace. Any member of the assembly who shared in the common purpose (which might be legal or illegal) would be guilty of the offence. If members of an unlawful assembly begin to execute their common purpose, and use violent means to do so, they will be guilty of riot (sometimes called riotous assembly); rout appears to be the offence committed if an unlawful assembly is turning into a riot but has not quite got there.

Prosecutions against demonstrators for these offences are not very common but where they are successful fairly heavy sentences can result. When a group of Cambridge students took part in a violent protest against a dinner to encourage tourism in Greece (held at the Garden House Hotel in Cambridge) they were convicted of riot and some of them were sent to prison for periods of up to fifteen months.[83]

It will be apparent from what has been said that there is a wide range of offences that might be committed in the course of a demonstration. Even demonstrators who desire to keep within the law may find that they have committed an offence. In these circumstances a great deal depends on the discretion of the police. Offences of a minor nature may often be overlooked if the demonstrators are trying to abide by the law. If a prosecution is brought the police will have to decide whether to bring a serious charge or a minor one.[84] For example, the accused may be brought before a magistrate on a

charge of obstructing the highway; or he may be charged on indictment with public nuisance or unlawful assembly: the decision of the
police as to the charge could mean the difference between a small
fine and going to prison.

The power of arrest is obviously important in dealing with demonstrations. The law of arrest has already been considered and it will be
remembered that a policeman (or a private citizen) can arrest anyone who is committing a breach of the peace in his presence or whom
he believes, on reasonable grounds, to be about to do so. This power
will be used whenever disorder breaks out. Where there is no breach
of the peace the police will normally rely on specific powers of arrest
given by statute.[85] For example there is a power of arrest for a breach
of section 5 of the Public Order Act (threatening, abusive or insulting
words or behaviour) and section 1 (wearing a political uniform).[86]
The Act does not, however, give a power of arrest for a breach of an
order banning marches under section 3, though there is a power of
arrest for breaking a ban imposed under The Metropolitan Police
Act 1839.[87] There is a power of arrest for carrying a weapon in a
public place[88] and for obstructing the Highway;[89] but there is no
power of arrest for obstructing a policeman (unless there is a breach
of the peace).

In addition to making arrests the police also have the power to
take preventive action to preserve the peace, even if this involves
the use of force against persons who have not committed any offence.
The basic rule here is one of *necessity*: the police have a duty to prevent disorder and they are entitled to use reasonable force if they
have reasonable grounds for believing that no other means will serve
to prevent an outbreak of violence (or to put an end to one). In
extreme situations, when severe rioting has broken out, it may even
be justified to open fire. In all cases, however, the minimum necessary force must be used. An Irish judge has put the matter as follows:[90]

A constable, by his very appointment, is by law charged with the solemn
duty of seeing that the peace is preserved. The law has not ventured to
lay down what precise measures shall be adopted by him in every state of
facts which calls for his interference. But it has done far better; it has announced to him, and to the public over whom he is placed, that he is not
only at liberty, but is bound, to see that the peace is preserved, and that he
is to do everything that is necessary for that purpose, neither more nor less.

This rule, which is part of the common law, applies to soldiers no less
than to policemen (and could even apply to a private citizen). If,

however, unjustified or excessive force is used the person responsible will be civilly and criminally liable for the consequences.

The common law rule on the preservation of the peace has now been supplemented by statute. Section 3 of the Criminal Law Act 1967 provides that 'a person may use such force as is reasonable in the circumstances in the prevention of crime'. This provision does not expressly say that force may be used only when there is no other means available but in most cases this would probably be implicit in the phrase 'reasonable in the circumstances'.

The preventive power of the police can operate before any disorder has occurred or crime been committed. One example of it is the right which the police have to attend a public meeting, even if it is held on private premises, if they have reasonable grounds for believing that incitement to violence or a breach of the peace will occur if they are not present.[91]

They can also disperse gatherings or marches if this is necessary to preserve order. It appears that if those concerned refuse to disperse, they can be charged with obstructing a constable in the exercise of his duty.[92] The leading case on this is *Duncan* v. *Jones* which arose out of a meeting held in 1934. Mrs Duncan and about thirty others had gathered outside a training centre for the unemployed to hold a protest meeting. A similar meeting the previous year had caused a disturbance in the centre. A policeman therefore told Mrs Duncan that she could not hold her meeting outside the centre but could, if she wished, hold it in another street about 175 yards away. She insisted on holding the meeting outside the centre. So she was arrested and charged with obstructing a constable in the execution of his duty. The magistrate convicted her and fined her 40 shillings. His decision was upheld on appeal.[93]

The most difficult problems arise where there is a counter-demonstration or a dispute between rival factions. It sometimes happens that one group is holding a lawful march or meeting and another group threatens to attack them. In these circumstances the first duty of the police is to protect the lawful group and to arrest the members of the attacking group.[94] If, however, they lack the manpower to do this, they may tell the lawful group to disperse. If they refuse to do so, the police may use their preventive power to disperse them by force. Charges may even be brought against them for obstructing a policeman, unlawful assembly, or some similar offence.

The Irish case of *Humphries* v. *Connor*[95] (decided in 1864) is a good example of the use of the preventive power. The plaintiff in this case was a woman who walked down the street wearing an orange lily (a party emblem). This caused a hostile crowd to gather and there was a danger that a breach of the peace might occur. The defendant, a policeman, requested her to remove the lily and, when she refused, he (gently) took it from her. She subsequently brought an action against him for assault but the court held that his action was justified under the preventive power even though the plaintiff had done nothing illegal in wearing the lily.

In another Irish case, *O'Kelly* v. *Harvey*,[96] the court held that a Justice of the Peace was justified in using (minimum) force to disperse a lawful meeting which was threatened by a rival group. This was also an action for assault and the court held that necessity would be a good defence. Law L. C. said:[97]

The question then seems to be reduced to this: assuming the plaintiff and others assembled with him to be doing nothing unlawful, but yet that there were reasonable grounds for the defendant believing as he did that there would be a breach of the peace if they continued so assembled, and that there was no other way in which the breach of the peace could be avoided but by stopping and dispersing the plaintiff's meeting – was the defendant justified in taking the necessary steps to stop and disperse it? In my opinion he was so justified . . .

Both these Irish cases were examples of the preventive power. The next two cases concern prosecutions. The case of *Beatty* v. *Gillbanks*[98] (decided in 1882) concerned the Salvation Army, who were in the habit of parading through the streets of towns with a band in order to collect a crowd for a meeting. The activities of the Salvationists were often unpopular and a rival organization, called the Skeleton Army, had been formed to oppose them. Disorder frequently resulted when Salvation Army marches were attacked. This had occurred on several occasions in Weston-super-Mare and two local magistrates therefore issued a notice directing all persons to refrain from assembling to the disturbance of the peace. (This notice did not constitute a ban on marches since the magistrates had no legal power to do this.) The Salvationists, however, held their procession as usual and, when they refused to disperse, were arrested and charged with unlawful assembly. The magistrates found them guilty and ordered them to find sureties to keep the peace for twelve months or else go to prison for three months. It was held on appeal, however, that since the march was entirely lawful, and the Salvationists themselves had no intention of using violence, the conviction could not stand. The order was therefore discharged. Field J rejected the view that 'persons acting lawfully are to be held responsible and punished merely because other persons are thereby induced to act unlawfully and create a disturbance.'

A different result, however, was reached in the case of *Wise* v. *Dunning*.[99] Wise was a Protestant 'crusader' who used to hold meetings in Liverpool at which he frequently insulted the Catholic faith. There were many Catholics in the area and violence often resulted from Wise's speeches. On several occasions he was saved only by police protection. He was finally brought before a magistrate and bound over for twelve months in the sum of £100 with two sureties of fifty pounds each to keep the peace and be of good behaviour. Wise also appealed but the order was confirmed by the Divisional Court.

Before discussing these cases a word should be said about binding-over. This is a power possessed by all justices of the peace. Its origin is obscure but it seems to be based partly on the common law and partly on the Justices of the Peace Act 1361.[100] A binding-over order requires the person bound over to enter into a recognizance to keep the peace and/or be of good behaviour for a specified period. It may also require him to find one or more sureties to guarantee his conduct. A recognizance is an undertaking to pay the Crown a specified sum of money if he fails to abide by the order during the period in question. The order will also specify the amount that the sureties must pay if there is a breach of the order. If the person bound over refuses to enter into the recognizance or is unable to find sureties willing to guarantee his conduct, he can be sent to prison for a period up to six months.[101]

A binding-over order is an exercise in preventive justice and has the advantage that it may induce the person bound over to keep within the law. However, its use is not restricted to the case where the person concerned has been convicted of an offence (in which case it may be in lieu of, or in addition to, a sentence). It can also be made where the person concerned has been neither charged with, nor convicted of, any offence at all. It is sufficient if there is reason to believe that he might commit an offence in the future. For example if a big demonstration is planned the organizers may be brought before a magistrate and bound over to keep the peace. If they are required to find sureties and are unable to do so, they may be sent to prison. This seems unjust. Another objection is that it is not entirely clear exactly what 'being of good behaviour' entails.[102]

Some of the problems concerned with these orders are illustrated by the cases of *Beatty* v. *Gillbanks* and *Wise* v. *Dunning* (discussed above). In the former Beatty was charged with unlawful assembly. He was convicted by the magistrates and was bound over instead of being sentenced. Wise, on the other hand, was not charged with any offence but was bound over as a preventive measure. Neither Beatty nor Wise, however, had themselves committed any act of violence: in both cases it was their opponents who had done that. Why, then, was Beatty's order set aside but not Wise's? (Even if Beatty was not guilty of unlawful assembly this would not in itself prevent the order being made.) The answer usually given is that Wise's activities were provocative and insulting while Beatty's were not. This is a fair distinction. If Wise had carried out his 'crusade' today he would probably have been convicted under section 5 of the Public Order Act 1936 (threatening, abusive or insulting words or behaviour). His case was heard before the Public Order Act was passed but there was a similar provision in a local Act in force at the time (the Liverpool Improvement Act 1842). It was, however, unfortunate that he was not charged under this Act. If he had been, there could have been no possible objection to the case.

The next problem is to reconcile *Beatty* v. *Gillbanks* with *Duncan* v. *Jones* (discussed earlier). The principle laid down in *Beatty* v. *Gillbanks* was that an otherwise lawful act does not become unlawful because another person is likely to commit a breach of the peace if it occurs.[103] Beatty was asked not to hold his march because it might lead to a breach of the peace; a similar request was made to Mrs Duncan: why was the latter convicted but not the former? There are two possible answers to this question. First, Beatty was charged with unlawful assembly while Mrs Duncan was charged with obstructing a policeman. This prompts the question whether Beatty would have been convicted if he had been charged with obstructing a policeman.[104] It seems fairly clear that at the time he would not have been: *Duncan* v. *Jones* seems to have been a new interpretation of the law and previously the general view seems to have been that a charge of obstructing the police could not be brought in these circumstances.[105]

This does not mean, however, that Beatty would today be convicted of obstructing a policeman. The second distinction between the two cases is that in *Duncan's* case the breach of the peace, if it had occurred, would have come from the accused's supporters who would have been inflamed by her speech; in *Beatty's* case trouble would have come from his opponents. This does not seem to be an unreasonable distinction to make since it is far more acceptable to hold a person responsible for the acts of his followers than for those of his opponents.

Ultimately, however, the question comes down to this: is it desirable that the police should have the power to ban meetings on the spot if they fear a breach of the peace and use the offence of obstructing a policeman as a sanction if their ban is flouted? The dangers to freedom of assembly in such a power are obvious. Yet if one accepts the doctrine of necessity and the preventive power that is based upon it, it is hard to deny that the police should have the power to ban meetings if there is no other way to prevent violence. The decision in *Duncan* v. *Jones* seems, however, to go further than this since there was no finding by the court that there was *no other way* except dispersing the meeting to prevent the violence that was feared. An extra squad of police might have been sufficient.

Many people would probably feel that it would be putting too great a burden on the police to require them to show that dispersing the meeting was the only way of preventing a breach of the peace. However, even if this were accepted in a case such as *Duncan* v. *Jones*, the test of strict necessity should be applied in those cases where the threat comes from a hostile group. Otherwise it would be too easy for such a group to get their opponents' meetings stopped by the police.

Finally, something should be said about two situations in which the issues are somewhat different from those in a normal demonstration. These are picketing and 'sit-ins'.

Picketing might be regarded as a demonstration in the course of an industrial dispute. The normal law applies to picketing in the same way as to other assemblies but there are two statutory provisions which apply specifically to picketing. The first is section 7 of the Conspiracy and Protection of Property Act 1875, which creates offences relevant to picketing, and the second is section 134 of the Industrial Relations Act 1971, which gives protection to pickets so long as they remain within its scope.

Section 7 of the Conspiracy and Protection of Property Act 1875[106] provides:

Every person who, with a view to compel any other person to abstain from doing or to do any act which such other person has a legal right to do or abstain from doing, wrongfully and without legal authority —

1. Uses violence to or intimidates such other person or his wife or children, or injures his property; or,
2. Persistently follows such other person about from place to place; or,
3. Hides any tools, clothes, or other property owned or used by such other person, or deprives him of or hinders him in the use thereof; or,
4. Watches or besets the house or other place where such other person resides, or works, or carries on business, or happens to be, or the approach to such house or place; or,
5. Follows such other person with two or more other persons in a disorderly manner in or through any street or road,

shall, on conviction thereof by a court of summary jurisdiction, or on indictment as herein-after mentioned, be liable either to pay a penalty not exceeding twenty pounds, or to be imprisoned for a term not exceeding three months, with or without hard labour . . .

Paragraph 1 of this would apply to pickets who resort to violence or threats of violence (intimidation) against persons remaining at work. Paragraph 4 might appear to make all picketing illegal since watching and besetting the place where a person works is more or less exactly what picketing involves. However, whether this is so depends on the meaning of the words 'wrongfully and without legal authority' at the beginning of the section. It could be argued that what these words mean is that watching and besetting, or any of the other activities mentioned in the section, are offences only if they are done in circumstances where they would, apart from the statute, be unlawful at least in the sense of being a civil wrong (e.g. a trespass).[107]

The position is, however, remedied by section 134 of the Industrial Relations Act 1971. This replaces section 2 of the Trade Disputes Act 1906 which in turn replaced a similar provision in section 7 of the Conspiracy and Protection of Property Act 1875. Section 134 of the Industrial Relations Act reads:

(1) The provisions of this section shall have effect where one or more persons (in this section referred to as 'pickets'), in contemplation or furtherance of an industrial dispute, attend at or near —
(a) a place where a person works or carries on business, or
(b) any other place where a person happens to be, not being a place where he resides,

and do so only for the purpose of peacefully obtaining information from him or peacefully communicating information to him or peacefully persuading him to work or not to work.

(2) In the circumstances specified in the preceding subsection, the attendance of the pickets at that place for that purpose —

(a) shall not of itself constitute an offence under section 7 of the Conspiracy and Protection of Property Act 1875 (penalty for intimidation or annoyance by violence or otherwise) or under any other enactment or rule of law, and

(b) shall not of itself constitute a tort.

The importance of this provision is that, so long as the pickets remain within its scope, they are immune from the provisions of both section 7 of the Conspiracy and Protection of Property Act and also from any other laws which might affect them. The scope of the provision is, however, limited: it applies only to such acts as are reasonably necessary to achieve the purpose stated in the Act (peaceful persuasion) and anything going beyond this will not be protected. In particular pickets have no right to force persons entering the place of work to listen to what they have to say by blocking their way.

Thus in the recent case of *Broome* v. *D.P.P.*[108] pickets during a building strike stood in the roadway in front of a lorry when the driver was trying to deliver materials to a site so they could try to persuade him not to make the delivery. Their action was entirely peaceful and the driver was delayed for only about nine minutes; yet it was held that the pickets could be convicted of obstructing the highway contrary to section 121 of the Highways Act 1959. They were not protected by the Industrial Relations Act.

In a previous case, *Tynan* v. *Balmer*,[109] the pickets had walked round and round in a circle in a service road leading to a factory. The service road was a public highway and their action had the effect of blocking it. There was again no violence. A policeman asked the leader of the pickets to stop the manoeuvre; when he refused he was charged with obstructing a policeman in the execution of his duty. He was convicted. It was held that the action of the pickets constituted the common law offence of nuisance (discussed above[110]) since it was an unreasonable user of the highway. The policeman was therefore acting in the course of his duty in asking them to stop. They were again outside the protection of section 2 of the Trade Disputes Act 1906 (the forerunner of section 134 of the Industrial Relations Act).

Another case which shows the extent of police powers is *Pidding-ton* v. *Bates*.[111] This concerned a small factory with only twenty-four workers of whom eight did not join the strike. There were two entrances to the factory and the policeman on duty told the strikers that two pickets at each entrance were enough. Piddington refused to accept this and pushed (gently) past the policeman to join the two pickets already outside the back entrance and was (gently) arrested. He was charged with obstructing a policeman and his conviction was upheld on appeal. The court held that there was sufficient evidence to justify the policeman's apprehension that a breach of the peace was likely to occur unless the number of pickets was reduced. The policeman was therefore entitled to take action under his preventive power and a refusal to obey his directions was consequently an offence.

This case is similar to *Duncan* v. *Jones* and the remarks made when that case was discussed apply here too. Again there was no suggestion that a reduction in the number of pickets was the only way in which a breach of the peace could be avoided. Although Lord Parker C. J. was careful to say that it must be proved that facts existed from which the policeman could reasonably have concluded that a breach of the peace was a real possibility, he seemed to take the view that once this was established the policeman had a fairly wide discretion as to what action he should take. Lord Parker said:[112]

The real criticism, I think, is this: 'Well, to say that only two pickets should be allowed is purely arbitrary. Why two? Why not three? Where do you draw the line?' For my part, I think that a police officer charged with the duty of preserving the Queen's peace must be left to take such steps as, on the evidence before him, he thinks are proper. I am far from saying that there should be any rule that only two pickets should be allowed at any particular door. There, one gets into an arbitrary area, but, so far as this case is concerned, I cannot see that there was anything wrong in the action of this respondent.

Lord Parker had previously said that what influenced him in his decision was the question of numbers. There were only eight persons working and eighteen people arrived to picket. This was more than were needed for peaceful persuasion and the decision is therefore justifiable on the facts. But it does put great reliance on police discretion.

'Sit-ins' and other kinds of 'direct action' differ from the assemblies previously discussed in that they are deliberately intended to inconvenience, annoy or thwart those against whom they are directed and they often involve a conscious defiance of the law.

The exact legal position will, of course, depend on the facts of the individual case but normally persons 'sitting in' will be guilty of the civil tort of trespass. The effect of this is that the lawful occupier of the premises can use reasonable force to eject them (provided he does not act contrary to the Forcible Entry Acts) and he can call upon other persons, including the police, to help him. The police, however, are not obliged to help and in the case of private premises they seem to have a policy of not doing so unless a court order has been obtained. The normal remedy of the lawful occupier is, therefore, to obtain a court order to eject the trespassers. This will be enforced by the sheriff, if necessary with the help of the police.

If demonstrators use force to enter a building they will be guilty of an offence under the Forcible Entry Acts.[113] It should be noted that forcible entry is an offence even if it is committed by the lawful occupier. Consequently, if he has been shut out and cannot gain entry peacefully, he should go to the courts instead of trying to vindicate his rights himself. It is also an offence (forcible detainer) for an unlawful occupier to use force to remain in possession of property, even if his original entry was not forcible. It is not necessary in either case that violence should actually be used: a threat of violence is sufficient. Thus in one case squatters entered a house peacefully and then made preparations (including the manufacture of petrol bombs) to use force to resist eviction: they were found guilty of forcible detainer.[114]

If the demonstrators carry out their protest in such a way that other persons (either inside or outside the building) reasonably fear a breach of the peace, they will be guilty of unlawful assembly. A conspiracy (i.e. an agreement between two or more persons) to trespass is a criminal offence if it involves invading the public domain (such as an embassy or public building) or if it involves (and is intended to involve) the infliction of more than purely nominal damage. This would necessarily be the case where the intention is to exclude the lawful occupier or to prevent him from enjoying his property.[115] It would seem that most 'sit-ins' are covered by this. In addition it is possible that persons taking part in a 'sit-in' would be guilty of an offence under section 7, paragraph 4 of the Conspiracy and Protection of Property Act 1875 (discussed above).[116]

From what has been said it is clear that the police do not lack adequate powers to deal with demonstrators and protesters. If they used these powers to the full freedom of assembly would be seriously jeopardized. It may be thought unsatisfactory that freedom should depend on the discretion of the police but holding the balance between the often-conflicting rights of individuals and the power of the State has always been difficult. The way the police exercise their discretion and the extent to which the courts support them depend in the long run on the state of public opinion: this is the final determinant of the extent of civil liberty in Britain.

9
The Judiciary and the Administration of Justice

The administration of justice is one of the basic functions of the State. In most developed societies there is a special body of people, the judiciary, to fulfil this function though there may also be a role, as in Britain, for a non-professional and even a popular element. Deciding disputes between private citizens and enforcing the criminal law are the traditional functions of the judiciary; but it may also have the task of adjudicating between the citizen and the State. In some countries, such as France, this is done by a special system of tribunals but in Britain it comes within the jurisdiction of the ordinary courts.

The areas in which the courts are most obviously adjudicating between the citizen and the State are in the field of administrative law – governmental liability and judicial review of administrative action – but many civil and criminal cases are in fact concerned with the limits of State power and hence with the rights of the citizen *vis-à-vis* the State. Cases concerning police powers are the best, but by no means the only, example of this.

In spite of this, however, the British courts are probably less concerned with distinctly *political* matters than are the courts of some other countries, such as the United States. In Britain, as a result of the doctrine of parliamentary sovereignty, the courts lack the power to determine the validity of Acts of Parliament (though this may change one day as a result of joining the European Community). Also, since Parliament can in theory pass any Act it pleases, the Government can secure the passage of a statute to change the law in its favour (if necessarily, retrospectively), to remove certain questions from the jurisdiction of the courts (or stipulate that the courts must decide them on the basis of a certificate from a

Minister), or even to overrule a decision given by the courts against the Government.[1]

As a result of this the decisions of the courts are of less political importance to the Government than in countries with fairly rigid constitutions. The really big questions concerning government powers – the issues on which the Government cannot afford to lose – do not normally come before the courts. Although this means that the courts in Britain are less able to check excesses or even unconstitutionality on the part of the Government, it has the advantage that there is less political pressure on the courts and less reason for the Government to attempt to interfere with their workings.

In spite of the reduced political role of the courts in Britain, it is still of the greatest importance for the judiciary to be independent of the Government. This is the one aspect of the doctrine of the separation of powers that is accepted in the British constitution. The reasons for this are obvious: the principles of the rule of law and of equality before the law demand that justice should be administered impartially – 'without fear or favour' – and this would be jeopardized if the courts were, as is the case in most one-party regimes, subject to pressure by the Government.

The independence of the judiciary in Britain today is widely recognized and it is probably for this reason that the Government sometimes entrusts to members of the judiciary the extra-judicial task of conducting inquiries into events of political significance. When wild rumours are flying and confidence in some aspect of public life is at stake, it is advantageous for the Government to turn to that branch of the State whose integrity is most respected and appoint a judge to inquire into the facts and reassure public opinion. (Of course, if the Government feels that the facts might *not* be reassuring, it is unlikely to adopt this course.)

The reports produced by judges on these questions are widely accepted and usually do restore public confidence in the political system; but there may be a price to pay in that those who have a political interest in the outcome of the inquiry may be tempted to attack the impartiality of the judge concerned if the result is not to their liking. The effect of this might be a slight lowering of public esteem for the judiciary itself. In fact there are some questions on which partizan prejudice is likely to be so strong that a report by a judge is bound to be rejected by one side or the other. In such a situation the credibility of the judge will suffer in the eyes of some section of the community. For this reason judicial inquiries should be used sparingly.

THE COURT SYSTEM

To a large extent the court system in England and Wales is based on a division between civil and criminal courts. Less important criminal cases are tried in the magistrates' courts (summary procedure) and the more important ones are tried on indictment in the Crown Court. Trials on indictment are with a jury; summary trials are not. Civil cases go either to the county courts (if the sum in dispute is not very great) or to the High Court. There are three divisions in the High Court: the Queen's Bench Division (mainly for Common Law matters), the Chancery Division (mainly for Equity cases) and the Family Division (which hears matters such as divorce and custody). The Admiralty Court (shipping cases) and the Commercial Court (commercial cases) are part of the Queen's Bench Division. The Court of Appeal (which has a Civil and a Criminal Division) and the House of Lords are concerned only with hearing appeals. The Court of Appeal, the High Court and the Crown Court together make up the Supreme Court. There are also a number of specialized courts such as the Restrictive Practices Court (monopolies and competition) and the National Industrial Relations Court (labour disputes), and numerous tribunals.[2] Scotland and Northern Ireland have separate court systems.

A variety of judges sit in these courts. Magistrates' courts are staffed by justices of the peace and stipendiary magistrates. The justices are very numerous; they are part-time, unpaid and do not have to be legally qualified. The stipendiary magistrates are few in number and are found only in large cities (mainly London). They are full-time, paid and legally qualified. They normally sit alone; justices sit in a bench of between two and seven and are advised on points of law by their clerk, who is legally qualified and is normally full-time.

The Crown Court is staffed by High Court judges, Circuit judges and Recorders. Circuit judges are full-time salaried judges. Only persons who are barristers of at least ten years' standing or Recorders of at least five years' standing may be apointed. Recorders are part-time and salaried. To be qualified for appointment a person must be a barrister or solicitor of at least ten years' standing. (Since solicitors are eligible for appointment as Recorders, and Recorders are eligible for appointment as Circuit judges, it is possible for a solicitor to become a Circuit judge; none has yet done so.) The more serious cases usually come before a High Court judge. The judges in the Crown Court normally sit with a jury but when hearing appeals from a magistrates' court they sit with two to four justices of the peace.

County courts are staffed by Circuit judges. The High Court judges are as follows. The Lord Chief Justice presides over the Queen's Bench Division; the Lord Chancellor is nominally president of the Chancery Court but he never sits (there is also a Vice-Chancellor who does sit); the President of the Family Division presides over that division. The other High Court judges are called Puisne (pronounced 'puny') judges. High Court judges must be barristers of at least ten years' standing. They normally sit alone (juries are rare in civil cases) but for certain purposes a Divisional Court, consisting of two or more judges, is formed. The Divisional Court of the Queen's Bench Division has important functions in administrative law and issues writs of habeas corpus and orders of mandamus, certiorari and prohibition.[3]

The Court of Appeal consists of the Master of the Rolls (who presides), the Lords Justices of Appeal and a number of *ex officio* members, including the Lord Chief Justice, who often sits in the Criminal Division. A Lord Justice of Appeal must be a barrister of at least fifteen years' standing unless he is promoted from the High Court. The Court normally sits with a bench of three.

The following are entitled to hear appeals in the House of Lords: the Lord Chancellor, Lords of Appeal in Ordinary and peers who hold, or have held, high judicial office.[4] By convention lay peers do not take part in these proceedings. At least three members must sit when an appeal is heard but normally five (and occasionally more) are present. Lords of Appeal in Ordinary are life peers appointed under the Appellate Jurisdiction Act 1876; they must have held high judicial office for at least two years or be barristers or advocates of at least fifteen years' standing.[5] Normally at least two of them are Scots lawyers. Civil and criminal appeals from Northern Ireland and civil (but not criminal) appeals from Scotland are also heard by the House of Lords.

THE BASIC COURT SYSTEM IN ENGLAND AND WALES

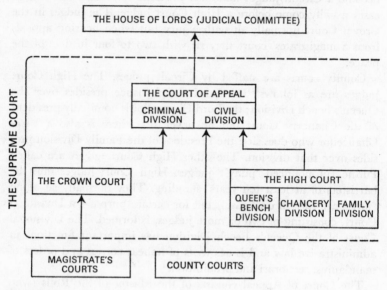

NOTES:

1 This table does not show any of the specialized courts or tribunals.

2 The system of appeals is more complicated than indicated by the arrows. In particular, appeals (by way of case stated) can also go from magistrates' courts to the Divisional Court of the Queen's Bench (and thence, with leave, to the House of Lords); and in certain cases appeals from the High Court can go direct to the House of Lords.

THE JUDICIARY IN ENGLAND AND WALES

	Number
Lord Chancellor	1
Lords of Appeal in Ordinary	10
Master of the Rolls	1
Lords Justices of Appeal	14
Lord Chief Justice	1
President of the Family Division	1

Puisne Judges of the High Court:

Queen's Bench Division	44
Chancery Division	11
Family Division	16
Circuit Judges	233
Recorders (part-time)	297
Stipendiary Magistrates	50 (39 are in London)
Justices of the Peace (part-time)	19,000 (approx.)

NOTES

1 The members of specialized courts and tribunals are not included.
2 The figures for the number of judges (except the J.P.s) are taken from the *Law List* for 1973. The number of judges actually appointed may be less than the statutory maximum.

THE INDEPENDENCE OF THE JUDICIARY

The importance of judicial independence has already been stressed. No Government in Britain would put pressure on a judge to decide a case in a particular way. However, direct control is not the only point to consider. There is also the question of the way in which judges are appointed to, and removed from, office and certain other matters which could affect judicial independence in practice.

Any discussion of the judiciary must start with the Lord Chancellor. He is the living refutation of the doctrine of separation of powers in England. The Lord Chancellor is a Government Minister, chosen by the Prime Minister and normally a member of the Cabinet. In the past some Lord Chancellors have not been career politicians, but this is not usual and a recent holder of the office, Lord Hailsham, has for many years been a prominent member of his party and was once in the running for the leadership. As a member of the executive he fulfils the role of a Minister of Justice and has important administrative functions connected with the judiciary. He is also responsible for law reform. To carry out these duties he has a small department (the Lord Chancellor's Department) staffed by civil servants.

Besides being a member of the Government he is also a judge. From time to time he sits in, and presides over, the judicial committee of the House of Lords and, though most Lord Chancellors might feel reluctant to sit in a case which directly affected the political standing of the Government, he might well hear a case in which issues of civil liberty were raised. For example, in the case of *Kamara* v. *D.P.P.*,[6] in which it was held that demonstrators who occupy a public building can be convicted of conspiracy to trespass, the main judgment of the House of Lords was given by the Lord Chancellor.

Finally, the Lord Chancellor is also a member of the legislature: he acts as Speaker of the House of Lords, where he sits on the Woolsack. He therefore combines executive, judicial and legislative roles.

It is of no importance that the Lord Chancellor is a member of both the executive and the legislature – all Ministers are. His judicial functions, however, are clearly contrary to the concept of judicial independence: when sitting as a judge he cannot be independent of the Government since he is part of it. He is, of course, always in a minority in the House of Lords (a minimum of three judges always sit on the judicial committee) and one assumes that he puts all party-political considerations out of his mind when acting judicially; nevertheless the judicial role of the Lord Chancellor is something which lawyers from other countries always find rather surprising and it would be better if he did not sit in cases concerning political disputes.

The method of judicial selection used in Britain is that of executive appointment and the members of the Government who choose new judges are the Lord Chancellor and the Prime Minister. Puisne judges of the High Court, Circuit judges, Recorders, stipendiary magistrates and justices of the peace are all appointed by, or on the advice of, the Lord Chancellor. The other judges are appointed on the advice of the Prime Minister.

This system is hardly ideal from the point of view of judicial independence. A better system would be to create a judicial service commission, as is found in some Commonwealth countries,[7] which would decide on new appointments. The members of such a body would themselves have security of tenure and steps could be taken to ensure their impartiality. In Jamaica, for example, the composition of the Judicial Service Commission is: the Chief Justice, the President of the Court of Appeal, the Chairman of the Public Service Commission (a similar impartial body concerned with the civil service), and three other members (appointed by the Prime Minister after consultation with the Leader of the Opposition) of whom one must be a judge or former judge, one chosen from a short-list drawn up by the Bar Council and one from a similar list compiled by the Council of the Law Society (these last two must not be practising lawyers).

How does the British system work in practice? Until the last few decades party political considerations did play a part in judicial appointments and former law officers or other M.P.s in the governing party stood a much better chance of becoming judges than persons outside politics. Today, however, this appears no longer to be the case and legal ability, as measured by success at the bar, is the governing consideration.

The only exception to this is the appointment of justices of the peace. These appointments are made by the Lord Chancellor who obtains advice (which he does not have to follow) from local advisory committees. The composition of these committees is kept secret (to prevent lobbying by persons seeking appointment) but the three main political parties are usually strongly represented. An attempt is made to keep a fair balance between the supporters of the three parties when appointments to the bench are made and for this reason the politics of candidates for appointment are taken into consideration. There is no reason why members of a political party should be excluded from the local bench but the present system could make political activity too important a factor. Appointment as a J.P. is sometimes used as a reward for faithful service to the local party and party loyalty is sometimes regarded as more important than ability. This seems wrong. In any event too few non-political persons are made magistrates.

One fact that promotes the independence of the superior judiciary is that they are all drawn from the bar after successful careers as barristers, a profession which tends to foster self-confidence and independence of mind. In this respect Britain is different from Continental countries where a young man will choose the judiciary as a career as soon as he finishes his university studies. He will undergo a period of training and then be appointed to the equivalent of a magistrates' court (where he will probably sit with two more experienced judges). In due course he will obtain promotion and may eventually be appointed to the highest court in the land. One might imagine that such a system would produce men with less independence of mind than the British system where judicial promotions are rare and there is little to be gained from attempting to curry favour with the Government.

English judges are well paid (puisne judges of the High Court, for example, get £15,750 per annum[8]) and their salaries are charged on the Consolidated Fund so that they do not come up for review in Parliament each year. Their salaries can be increased, but not reduced, by the Lord Chancellor with the consent of the Minister for the Civil Service.[9]

Judges are, of course, expected to abstain from political activity. They are disqualified for membership of the House of Commons but if they are peers (including Lords of Appeal in Ordinary) they can, and do, play a part in the work of the House of Lords. Today they avoid becoming involved in party political controversy but this has not always been the case. In the past it was not unknown for judges to hold office in the Government: for example Lord Cave, a Lord of Appeal in Ordinary, was Home Secretary for a few months in 1918/19.[10]

All superior court judges (except the Lord Chancellor) have security of tenure. Judges of the High Court and the Court of Appeal and Lords of Appeal in Ordinary hold office during good behaviour. They may be removed from office by the Queen on an address presented to her by both Houses of Parliament.[11] Circuit judges and Recorders may be removed from office by the Lord Chancellor for inability or misbehaviour.[12] Stipendiary magistrates and Justices of the Peace may also be removed from office by the Lord Chancellor:[13] strictly speaking, they do not have security of tenure but in practice they would not be removed without good reason.

In theory it would be more satisfactory if some kind of judicial procedure were used for the removal of judges (in some Commonwealth countries the final decision is referred to the Privy Council in London) but in practice there is no danger of abuse: the only U.K. judge removed from office since the Act of Settlement 1700 gave security of tenure was an Irish judge in 1830.

Something should also be said about the social background of judges. There is little doubt that by and large English judges come from a fairly narrow section of society. A recent study of the House of Lords[14] reports that almost all Lords of Appeal in Ordinary come from a solid middle-class background. Most went to public schools – Lord Denning M. R., a product of Andover Grammar School, is one of the exceptions – and then usually to Oxford or Cambridge.[15] The reason for this is that until recently the bar has been largely a middle-class preserve. This appears to be changing. It is also noticeable that women and coloured immigrants, two groups previously largely unrepresented in the profession, are becoming barristers in increasing numbers. These changes may be reflected in the composition of the judiciary in the future.

It is not easy to say to what extent judges ought to exclude their own values and attitudes from their decisions. One cannot expect a judge to be a mere computer without opinions or feelings of his own: this is both impossible and undesirable. The element of justice in the administration of the law must come from the personal feelings of the judge. Nor should one expect judges to take no account of policy. But when a judge's own values play too obvious a part in his decision he will be criticized by those who have different values: he will be accused of bias towards a particular group or prejudice towards particular ideas. This is especially likely to occur in cases which arouse strong feelings, for example those involving strikes, demonstrations, protests, racialism or terrorism. In such a case, a judge must follow the law; but this is often open-ended or uncertain. He may take public opinion into account; but he should not feel bound by it. In the end all one can ask is that he should do what he honestly believes to be right, while recognizing that his beliefs will inevitably be influenced by his upbringing, his education, and his social position.

JUDICIAL IMMUNITY AND CONTEMPT OF COURT

There are two important respects in which the law puts judges in a special position: they are immune from civil liability while acting in their judicial capacity and they have the power to punish litigants and members of the public for contempt. The purpose of these special rights, which were established by decisions of the judges themselves, is to promote the good administration of justice. As we shall see,[16] analogous rights exist for members of the two Houses of Parliament. These rights are known as 'parliamentary privilege' and they, too, are intended to promote the work of Parliament. They were established by decisions of the two Houses of Parliament but have been recognized by the courts.

Judicial Immunity

Judicial immunity is concerned with immunity from civil liability for acts done or words spoken by judicial officers in their capacity as such.[17] The basic rule is that there is no liability for acts done by a judicial officer as long as he is acting within his jurisdiction.[18] This rule applies to all persons exercising judicial powers, including magistrates and the members of tribunals. In the case of superior court judges the immunity exists even if it can be proved that the act was done maliciously; magistrates, however, are liable in at least some circumstances[19] if malice can be proved and it is probable that the same applies to the members of tribunals.

Generally speaking a judicial officer will not be protected as regards acts which are outside his jurisdiction. An exception to this applies where he was deprived of jurisdiction by the existence of some fact of which he was unaware.[20] Moreover, if a superior court makes a finding that it has jurisdiction, no other court or tribunal can challenge this finding; so it is impossible to establish that a superior court judge acted outside his jurisdiction. The reason for this is that a superior court has jurisdiction to determine its own jurisdiction.

The scope of judicial immunity is somewhat wider in the case of actions for libel or slander relating to statements made in the course of judicial proceedings. The privilege applies to statements made by judges, witnesses, parties, counsel and solicitors.[21] The privilege is absolute (i.e. it applies even if there is malice) in the case of superior courts, county courts, and other tribunals 'exercising functions equivalent to those of an established court of justice'.[22] Magistrates are absolutely privileged when they are exercising their summary jurisdiction[23] but not when they are exercising administrative functions such as licensing.[24] Some tribunals[25] also have absolute privilege; others[26] have mere qualified privilege (which gives immunity only if there is no malice).[27]

It will be seen from what has been said that a superior court judge has almost complete protection as regards everything he says or does while exercising his judicial functions. He cannot be sued even if he acts maliciously.[28] The justification normally given for this rule is that a judge cannot preserve the necessary detachment if he is constantly afraid of being sued, even if he knows that he is innocent of any misconduct. Whether such a rule is really justifiable might be open to doubt; but in practice the standard of judicial conduct is so high in Britain that the rule causes no injustice, though the habit that some judges have of moralizing can cause offence, especially since those whose conduct is criticized have little chance to answer back.

Contempt of Court

There are two kinds of contempt of court: civil contempt and criminal contempt. Civil contempt arises where someone refuses to obey an order given by a superior court – for example an injunction, an order of mandamus or a writ of habeas corpus. It is not normally of constitutional importance. A criminal contempt is committed by anyone who does anything which interferes with the administration of justice or brings the judiciary into disrepute. The superior courts have a common law power to punish persons guilty of contempt by imprisonment or a fine.[29] This power does not extend to inferior courts[30] or tribunals, but county courts have a limited power, granted by statute, to punish those who wilfully interrupt their proceedings or insult a judge.[31] Until recently there was no appeal from a decision adjudging a person to be guilty of contempt; but this has now been provided by section 13 of the Administration of Justice Act 1960.

One species of criminal contempt is that which arises when there is a breach of the *sub judice* rule. This rule applies while legal proceedings are imminent and prohibits any public comment that might prejudice their outcome. It is obvious that a criminal trial cannot be conducted fairly if newspaper or television comment is permitted that might prejudice the jury against the accused. In America it is common for friends and relatives of the accused to be interviewed on television while a murder trial is pending and to give their opinion on whether he is guilty. His background and character might also be subject to lurid comment. In England anything of this kind would be contempt of court and would be punished by the court hearing the case or, if the trial had not begun, by a Divisional Court of the Queen's Bench Division. In the latter case the Attorney-General will often initiate proceedings to bring the matter before the court. A party to the case can, therefore, either take action himself or complain to the Attorney-General.

The ban, which applies to both criminal and civil cases, begins when proceedings are imminent even if no charge has been brought or writ served; however, the person making the comment will have a defence if he can prove that he did not know, and had no reason to suspect, that proceedings were imminent.[32] The ban continues until the end of the proceedings but where an appeal is pending it applies less stringently.

The extent of the ban was subject to detailed consideration by the

House of Lords in the recent case of *Attorney-General* v. *Times News-papers Ltd.*[33] This arose out of the thalidomide tragedy. In 1958 a drug company called The Distillers Company Ltd started to manufacture and market thalidomide, a drug which was recommended as a sedative for pregnant women. It was subsequently discovered that it caused gross deformities in the unborn child and by 1961, when the drug was taken off the market, over 451 deformed children had been born. Parents of sixty-two children issued writs against Distillers within the three-year limitation period; these actions were settled. A further 266 obtained leave to issue writs after the expiry of the limitation period. The remaining 123 had issued no writs at all. Negotiations continued for a number of years but the actions which had been started were never brought to court. The reason for this long delay was that the advisers of the children were faced with two formidable legal obstacles. First, there was considerable doubt whether the law permitted a person to sue for injuries sustained before birth; secondly, Distillers would be liable only if it could be proved that they had been negligent. The result was that by 1972, when some of the children were ten years old, most of them had received no compensation.

The Sunday Times regarded this as a scandalous situation and started a campaign on behalf of the children. Their first article discussed the facts and suggested that, whatever Distillers' legal obligations might be, there was a moral obligation on them to provide generous compensation. The article called on them to recognize their moral responsibilities. Distillers complained to the Attorney-General about this article but he declined to take action. *The Sunday Times* then decided to publish a second article on whether Distillers had been negligent. Before publishing, however, the editor sent a copy to the Attorney-General who took immediate steps to obtain an injunction to prevent publication. The injunction was granted by the Divisional Court, set aside by the Court of Appeal, and restored by the unanimous decision of the House of Lords.

No one would quarrel with the proposition that comment should not be published if there is a serious risk that it might prejudice the outcome of the proceedings by influencing the judge, jury or witnesses. The House of Lords held, however, that even if this is not the case it is impermissible to make a comment that prejudges an issue in the case. It was on this ground that the injunction was granted. No satisfactory reasons were given why the public interest demanded this and the ruling could be unduly restrictive on the press. Say, for example, that the army of a foreign country were accused of massacring civilians. The truth of the allegations might become a national issue. Yet if a libel action were brought against the paper making the accusations, it seems that no paper could publish facts either supporting or disproving them.

It should also be mentioned that two out of the five judges thought that the first *Sunday Times* article was also a contempt; but the majority (Lords Reid, Cross and Morris) held that it is permissible to publish an article which brings moral pressure on a party not to insist on his legal rights provided that the article is fair and temperate and is published without any ulterior motive. It is also permissible to discuss general issues even if these have some bearing on a case; it is only the specific issues of the case that cannot be discussed.

Another species of criminal contempt is contempt in the face of the court. This occurs when anyone disrupts judicial proceedings or insults or assaults a judge in court. It sometimes happens that a disappointed litigant will vent his feelings on the judge hearing the case. Occasionally demonstrators will hold a protest in court. In all these cases the presiding judge has the power to pass instant sentence – of a fine or even imprisonment – without any separate proceedings. This power is defended as being necessary to maintain order in court but in exercising it the presiding judge is prosecutor, judge and victim rolled into one. It is a clear breach of the rule – assiduously imposed by the courts on other authorities – that no one should be a judge in his own cause. One can easily imagine that a judge who had just been insulted might lack due impartiality and might deal with the person responsible more harshly than would be warranted. Someone who disrupts court proceedings must be punished; but there is no reason why the powers of the presiding judge should not be limited to ordering the detention of the offender until such time as he can appear for trial before another judge.

The last species of criminal contempt to be considered is concerned with criticism of the courts. It is permissible for writers in newspapers or journals to criticize decisions of the courts and to suggest that they are wrong. There are, however, limits to such criticism and a writer who oversteps these limits can be brought before the courts and punished for contempt.

A case where this occurred was *R. v. Editor of the New Statesman*.[34]

In 1928 Dr Marie Stopes, the well-known advocate of birth-control, lost a libel action brought by the editor of the *Morning Post*. The judge in that case was Mr Justice Avory and many people thought that he had been biased against Marie Stopes because of her views. The *New Statesman* published an article on the case which contained the following statement:

The serious point in this case, however, is that an individual owning to such views as those of Dr Stopes cannot apparently hope for a fair hearing in a Court presided over by Mr Justice Avory – and there are so many Avorys.

The editor of the *New Statesman* was called before the King's Bench Divisional Court to show cause why he should not be imprisoned for contempt. His counsel argued that the article had not intended to assert that Mr Justice Avory was consciously biased but only that he had been unconsciously influenced by his dislike of Marie Stopes' views. He was nevertheless found guilty of contempt, although no punishment was imposed.[35]

The basis of the decision in this case was that, while it is in order to suggest that a judge was mistaken, it is not permissible to say that he was biased or unfair. The matter was put as follows by the Privy Council in a case in 1936:[36]

... no wrong is committed by any member of the public who exercises the ordinary right of criticizing, in good faith, in private or public, the public act done in the seat of justice. The path of criticism is a public way: the wrong headed are permitted to err therein: provided that members of the public abstain from imputing improper motives to those taking part in the administration of justice, and are genuinely exercising a right of criticism, and not acting in malice or attempting to impair the administration of justice, they are immune.

In other words, the critic's own motives must be pure and he must not attack the motives of the judge.

It appears that it is no defence to a charge of contempt to show that the criticism was justified. Even if the judge was in fact biased, it is probably contempt to say so. It would be extraordinary if no judge were ever biased in the sense that his personal values and attitudes influenced his decision; yet anyone who pointed out a case where this happened could be put in gaol.

There is, of course, a good reason why the courts should not allow the truth of the statement to be a defence: if they did, contempt proceedings would turn into a trial of the judge who was criticized. This would be highly embarrassing to the judges hearing the case and unfair to the judge criticized. Yet it seems wrong that a man should be punished for telling the truth about a matter of such great public importance as the administration of justice. Perhaps the answer would be to allow any criticism of judges – even an attack on their integrity – so long as the critic acts *bona fide*; he must honestly believe what he says and his motive must be simply that of righting a wrong: if he is actuated by personal animosity towards the judge or if he has any other ulterior motive (such as a desire to shake the public's confidence in the administration of justice in order to attain some political end) he would be guilty. A rule such as this would give full scope to legitimate criticism and at the same time give protection to the judiciary against malicious attacks.[35A]

PROSECUTIONS AND PARDONS

The general rule in England is that a criminal prosecution can be brought by anyone. The right of private prosecution is sometimes regarded as being of constitutional importance on the grounds that it enables the private citizen to enforce the law if the police fail to do so. There are various reasons, however, why this is not entirely realistic: first, in the case of a number of statutory offences a prosecution can be brought only with the consent of the Director of Public Prosecutions or, in some cases, the Attorney-General; secondly, the Director of Public Prosecutions has the power to take over any prosecution brought by somebody else (and, having done so, he can drop it); and thirdly, any prosecution on indictment can be stopped if the Attorney-General enters a *nolle prosequi*. There are also the important practical difficulties of gathering evidence (which may involve the use of scientific techniques) and meeting the legal costs, which may be very heavy.

In practice, therefore, private prosecutions are rare except in special cases such as shop-lifting, where large stores may have a policy of prosecuting offenders, and cruelty to animals, where organizations such as the RSPCA may take action. There are also a number of prosecutions undertaken by local authorities and Government departments, mainly for regulatory offences such as those concerned with factory safety or pollution control.

Normally, therefore, the decision to prosecute rests on the shoulders of the police, though, as will be seen below, they obtain advice from the Director of Public Prosecutions in important cases. The police are not obliged to prosecute in all cases where they have reason to believe that an offence has been committed. They have a discretion which will be exercised in accordance with what they believe to be the public interest. The probability of conviction will be the main factor but the gravity of the offence, the circumstances of the offender (e.g. his age or state of health) and whether it is his first offence will also be taken into account. The courts will not normally interfere with police discretion in individual cases but they may take action if a general policy is adopted which they regard as improper.[37]

If a prosecution is brought out of malice, the accused can bring an action in tort for malicious prosecution against the policeman (or other person) who brought the prosecution. Such an action can be brought only if the accused was acquitted and the accused must prove that the prosecutor was actuated by spite or some other improper motive and that he had no reasonable or probable cause for believing that the accused was guilty. Successful actions of this kind are rare.

In minor cases a policeman will often present the case in court but in more serious cases a solicitor will prosecute. Some police forces employ solicitors in private practice but others have a salaried prosecuting solicitor who, with his staff, conducts all prosecutions. In important cases a barrister will be briefed.

The office of Director of Public Prosecutions was created by the Prosecution of Offences Act 1879. The D.P.P. is a public official who acts under the direction of the Attorney-General. He has the power to institute or take over prosecutions in cases which he regards as important or difficult and to enable him to do this the police are required to notify him whenever certain specified offences are committed.[38] Prosecutions for offences under certain statutes may be instituted only by, or with the consent of, the D.P.P. He also gives advice on criminal proceedings to Government departments and the police. He functions both as an adviser and, to some extent, as a supervisor of the police and the existence of his office helps to promote uniformity of practice among the various police forces. His power to take over any prosecution[39] is also a check on private prosecutors.

The Attorney-General is a Government Minister. He is the chief legal adviser to the Government and he appears in court on behalf of the Government in important cases. He is assisted by the Solicitor-General who, like the Attorney-General, is a barrister. Under certain statutes, especially those of a political nature (e.g. the Official Secrets Acts) the consent of the Attorney-General is required before a prosecution can be brought. He can select the place of a trial on indictment and he has the power to stop any prosecution brought on indictment by entering a *nolle prosequi*. If he wishes to put a stop to summary proceedings he can instruct the D.P.P. to take over the proceedings and then ask the court for leave not to offer any evidence against the accused.

In exercising these powers the Attorney-General is entitled to consult with his political colleagues but the final decision is his alone and he is expected to exclude all party-political considerations from his mind. If he abused his powers – for example, by shielding party supporters from prosecution – the rule of law would be seriously undermined. Any suspicion that this was the case, however, would have the most serious consequences: in 1924, for example, the then Attorney-General was accused of bowing to pressure from his colleagues in the first Labour Government when he dropped a prosecution for sedition against the editor of a Communist newspaper, the *Workers' Weekly*. This led to the defeat of the Government in the House of Commons.

In Scotland a different system prevails. There prosecutions are taken entirely out of the hands of the police and vested in the Lord Advocate (the Scottish equivalent of the Attorney-General). Private persons normally have to obtain his consent if they wish to launch a prosecution; so in effect he has complete control of prosecutions in Scotland. He is assisted by the Solicitor-General for Scotland and by Crown Counsel. The latter are advocates who conduct most prosecutions in the High Court. The bulk of prosecutions in other courts are handled by the Procurators-Fiscal, who are appointed by the Lord Advocate and act under his supervision.

The Scottish system has various advantages. The decision to prosecute is taken out of the hands of the police. It is normally taken by the local Procurator-Fiscal who is legally trained and is probably able to view the case with greater detachment than the police officer who conducted the investigation. The control exercised by the Lord Advocate makes for greater uniformity of practice. It also benefits the police by taking a great deal of legal work off their shoulders and allowing them to concentrate on normal police work. Proposals have been made for the introduction of a similar system in

England.[40] This could be done by setting up a central prosecuting department under the D.P.P. which would take over most of the prosecution work done by the police. England is probably the only country in Western Europe in which the police are responsible for the conduct of prosecutions. It is time the English system was re-examined in the light of experience elsewhere.

The decision to grant a pardon is in some ways the reverse of a decision to prosecute. The granting of a pardon is a prerogative of the Crown but the Queen always acts on the advice of the Home Secretary. Before the Revolution of 1688 the King claimed two prerogatives: the suspending power and the dispensing power. The former was the power to suspend the operation of an Act of Parliament so that provisions creating criminal offences were inoperative. The dispensing power was the power to excuse a particular individual from obeying a statute. These powers were both used by James II, mainly with regard to statutes imposing disabilities on Roman Catholics, and were accepted by the courts to a certain extent. Parliament naturally considered that the existence of these powers undermined its authority and after the Revolution it was provided in the Bill of Rights 1689 that the suspending power was illegal and that the dispensing power was illegal 'as it hath been assumed and exercised of late'.

The power to grant a pardon might be regarded as an aspect of the dispensing power but it differs from the kind of dispensation prohibited by the Bill of Rights in that it is granted only after the wrongful act has been done and does not permit future transgressions. A pardon could probably be granted before the trial has taken place but in practice it is always granted afterwards.[41] In England there is no purely judicial procedure for reopening a criminal case after the time for appeal has expired. If, therefore, new evidence subsequently comes to light that establishes the innocence of the person convicted, the only way to rectify the matter is through executive action.

If the Home Secretary is in doubt as to whether a miscarriage of justice has occurred, he has the power under section 7 of the Criminal Appeal Act 1968 to refer the case to the Court of Appeal and it will then be treated as if it were an appeal. He can also refer an aspect of the case to the Court of Appeal for its opinion. These procedures enable the courts to consider a case of this kind but it might be better if it were possible, as it is in many other European countries, for the convicted person himself (or someone else on his behalf) to petition the courts to reopen the matter if new evidence comes to light which casts significant doubt on the conviction. It is not wholly desirable that this decision should rest with a Government Minister.

Even if a procedure of this kind were introduced, however, it would not be possible to abolish the power of pardon. There would still exist certain cases – no doubt fairly rare – in which it would be desirable to grant a pardon, not because of any doubt as to the guilt of the accused, but because of considerations (possibly of a political nature) which would make it undesirable that the law should be enforced in the normal way in the case in question. The power should of course be used for these purposes only in very special circumstances but it might be justified in certain cases, for example where considerations of international law or diplomacy entered the picture. Obviously it would be quite improper for the power to be used for party political advantage.

10
The House of Commons

GOVERNMENT AND PARLIAMENT

The central government of the United Kingdom of Great Britain and Northern Ireland is carried on by the Queen's Ministers. In the absence of a written constitutional document providing that this shall be so, it is impossible to say that this statement of political fact rests on legal authority. That does not mean that the authority of the Queen's Ministers is illegal but that it is extra-legal.

The Queen is the nominal head of the Government and her Ministers are those who exercise the substantial powers. When we speak of the Government as an institution, as a group of people, we usually mean the Queen's Ministers and perhaps the more senior civil servants under them who manage Government departments. Although many of these departments have offices in many parts of London, and outside London, the Ministers and their Departments are often referred to as Whitehall. This geographical statement is useful because it emphasizes the separation of the Government from Parliament whose geographical nickname is Westminster.

Two political facts are the key to an understanding of the working of the constitution of the United Kingdom. The first is this separateness of the Government from Parliament. Both are institutions. Each is composed of an ascertainable number of people whose names can be listed, though there can be some difference of opinion, deriving from slightly different definitions, as to who shall, on the margins, be included or excluded from the lists. But a list of names of those who are members of the Government and a list of names of those who are members of the two Houses of Parliament can be drawn up. The Government, we may say, consists of twenty or so Ministers in the Cabinet; about fifty-five Ministers (excluding whips and the members of the Royal Household) outside the Cabinet; and then we may include between twenty and fifty senior civil servants depending on whom we choose to call 'senior' for this purpose. The members of the two Houses of Parliament are similarly ascertainable for they consist of the 635 M.P.s elected from the constituencies and those 1,000 or so persons entitled to sit in the House of Lords, though we may prefer to restrict this latter figure to the 200–300 peers and others who actively participate.

The second political fact is that Ministers must in practice be members of one or other of the Houses. This partial overlapping of the membership of the two institutions often results in a confusion of the institutions themselves. This is not surprising when we remember that Ministers are not merely members of one or other House of Parliament but are, within the rules of procedure and the terms of party politics, accountable to Parliament. Yet at the same time Ministers, because of the majority which the Government has in the House of Commons, can control to a considerable extent how the time of the House is spent. But, again, the Government cannot exercise that control to the extent of avoiding or evading its duty to account, cannot stifle criticism in Parliament. For Her Majesty's Opposition can, unless it is very small in numbers, make the business of governing the country extremely difficult for the Government if determined to do so. And that determination is likely to be roused particularly if the Opposition feels that the Government is trying to deprive it of its traditional function.

For the separateness of Government and Parliament is not, of course, solely because each of these institutions is differently composed (though with overlapping membership). It is also because the function of each is different. It is the job of the Government to govern; to make political and policy decisions; to put those decisions into practical effect. And it is the job of the remaining members of the Houses of Parliament to scrutinize those decisions and that administration. Naturally, the criticism will come mainly from the Opposition, especially in the House of Commons; and the support for the Government will come from their own side. But all those who are not Ministers will scrutinize what Ministers are doing or proposing to do. And many suggestions will be made about how the job of governing could be better done. Nevertheless the decisions are for the Government, not for the members of the Houses, to make. Parliamentary government means government not by Parliament, but by a Government accountable to Parliament.

THE BUSINESS OF THE HOUSE OF COMMONS

No two Parliamentary sessions are the same. But inevitably there are similarities in the distribution of different kinds of business. The summary below is derived from the estimates made by Erskine May[1] and although the items will differ from session to session, these figures give an accurate general picture.

		Hours
A.	*Private Members' Time*	
	1 Discussion of bills	73
	2 Discussion of motions	31
B	*Government Time*	
	1 Address in reply to the Queen's Speech	35
	2 Government motions (excluding Supply)	110
	3 Opposition motions (excluding Supply)	5
	4 Adjournment motions (excluding Supply)	
	(1) Government time	29
	(2) Holiday adjournments	20
	(3) Daily adjournments	80
	(4) S.O. No. 9 adjournments	12
	5 Supply	
	(1) Opposition motions	80
	(2) Adjournment motions	52
	(3) Government motions	28
	(4) Select Committee reports	10
	6 Consolidated Fund Bills	40
	7 Government programme	
	(1) Government Bills	
	Second Reading	180
	Committee	140
	Report and Third Reading	205
	Consideration of Lords' amendments	35
	(2) Ways and Means, and Money resolutions	28
	(3) Government orders (affirmative procedure)	60
	(4) Government orders (negative procedure)	30
	8 Private Members' bills and motions in Government time	30
	9 Opposed private business	15
		1,328

These figures show the great predominance of Government time but it must be noted that the Opposition, apart from their right on any occasion to speak against a Government motion, do by convention determine what matters shall be discussed on a number of occasions. In addition to those nominated as Opposition motions, other opportunities include the address in reply to the Queen's Speech, many adjournment motions, part of the debates on the second reading of Consolidated Fund Bills, which is used to discuss special subjects, and most of the negative 'prayers' moved to Government orders.

The figures also show that some 560 hours (or a little less than half a session) are spent on debates on Government bills, reflecting this major legislative function of the House of Commons.

Much of the time of the House of Commons is in appearance devoted to financial matters. In the table set out above the hours spent on Supply, on Consolidated Fund Bills, and on money resolutions all seem to carry this implication. But the reality is quite other. The debates on Supply are almost wholly spent in considering topics of general interest where the opportunity arises for the Opposition to attack and the Government to defend some matters of policy. This is also true of the debates on Consolidated Fund Bills. Money resolutions attached to bills are rarely debated.

The most important debates relating to finance occur in Ways and Means when the Chancellor of the Exchequer makes his budget statement, which sets out the Government's proposals for taxation, and this is debated. These proposals reappear in the Finance Bill, with much administrative detail added. In recent years the debates in committee on the Finance Bill have been divided, some clauses being taken in committee of the whole House and other clauses being sent to a standing committee. This has made for closer scrutiny of the Bill and has given more opportunity for Members to seek amendments, especially for giving relief to particular categories of taxpayers. In the table, these hours on the floor of the House are concealed in the totals for Government bills, while the hours in committee are not shown.

The other principal opportunity for Members to consider financial matters in detail is in the Public Accounts and Expenditure Committees which are referred to elsewhere.[2]

PARTY ORGANIZATION IN THE HOUSE OF COMMONS[3]

When the Parliamentary Labour Party is in Opposition, it appoints four officers: the Leader, the deputy leader, the chief whip and the chairman. The executive authority of the Parliamentary party in Opposition is vested in the Parliamentary Committee which is composed of the four officers, twelve M.P.s, the leader and chief whip in the House of Lords, and one other Labour peer. We have seen how the party Leader is elected;[4] the other three officers are elected similarly. The twelve Commons Members of the Parliamentary Committee are elected by ballot, each Labour M.P. being entitled to vote for twelve Members.[5] Each member of the Parliamentary Committee is the official Opposition spokesman on a particular subject. The allocation of subjects is made by the Leader who can also appoint persons as spokesmen who are not members of the Committee.

When the Conservative party is in opposition, its Leader appoints his consultative committee from amongst Conservative M.P.s and there is no system of elections. He decides who shall be the spokesman on each subject.

The Labour party when in office sets up a liaison committee consisting of the chairman and vice-chairman of the parliamentary party, with the Leader of the House and the chief whip, both of whom are of course Ministers. The parliamentary Labour party meets regularly and Ministers attend on important occasions, though they resist strongly being forced into a position, by votes or otherwise, where they appear to be instructed by the Parliamentary party.

In the Conservative party, neither Ministers nor members of the consultative committee normally attend meetings of the backbenchers in the 1922 Committee but views expressed are transmitted to the Leader. The 1922 Committee has an executive which in 1973 numbered eighteen.

In and out of office, specialist and area groups work under the parliamentary parties. In 1973, the Conservatives had eighteen specialist groups – for agriculture, fisheries and food; arts and amenities; aviation supply; broadcasting and communications; consumer protection; defence; education; employment; finance; foreign and commonwealth affairs; health and social security; home affairs; housing and construction; industry; law; local government and development; trade; and transport. They also had seven area groups – for Greater London; the West Country; the North:West; the Scottish unionists; Northern Ireland; Yorkshire; and Wales and Monmouthshire. The Ulster unionists also formed a group. Similarly the parliamentary Labour party had twenty subject groups and eight area groups. Each of these groups has a chairman and one or more vice-chairmen. They exist to discuss the problems and policies of their particular interests; and directly and indirectly they influence policy-making. Inevitably their impact on the leadership of the party is likely to be greater when the party is in Opposition. But Ministers must also, at the lowest, have regard to the views expressed.

In this connection, we must also note that many Labour M.P.s are sponsored by trade unions.[6] In 1973 the National Union of Mine Workers sponsored nineteen M.P.s; the Transport and General Workers' Union sponsored eighteen; the Amalgamated Union of Engineering and Foundry Workers sponsored seventeen; the Co-operative Party sponsored fifteen (and six peers); and a further twenty-one unions sponsored a total of sixty-five other Members.

One of the duties of party whips, under the chief whip, is to ensure that party leaders are kept in touch with members of the parliamentary party, both as individuals and in their groups.

These sub-strata of organizations within the parliamentary parties are potentially of great importance. Attendance at group meetings varies considerably and, inevitably, some groups are more active than others. But their number and variety do reflect the extent to which party Members band together to further their different causes and interests, and correct the impression that the life of M.P.s is spent either in the division lobbies or in their constituencies. A great deal goes on in the palace of Westminster which only occasionally makes itself known to the outside world.

THE OFFICERS OF THE HOUSE OF COMMONS
The Speaker is described by Erskine May as having functions which fall into two main categories:[7] as the representative of the House in its relations with the Crown, the House of Lords, and other persons outside Parliament; and as the person who presides over the House. He is a Member of Parliament who if he stands for re-election while Speaker will not normally be opposed by the other main parties. He has very great powers when he presides over the House and enforces the observance of the rules for preserving order. He decides, subject

to certain conventions of the House, who shall speak. His interpretation of the rules of procedure are rarely challenged although the House may subsequently decide to change the rules. He can be criticized only on a substantive motion and is expected to act impartially between the parties and individuals in the House. He selects amendments during debate in the House, especially on the Report stage of bills, and he decides whether to allow the House to vote on the closure of debate and whether to stop a Member who is becoming repetitious or irrelevant or is otherwise out of order.

The Chairman of Ways and Means normally presides when the House is in committee and also acts as Deputy Speaker. He is also a Member and follows the same tradition of impartiality as the Speaker. He is helped by two Deputy Chairmen.

Each session the Speaker nominates a panel of temporary chairmen from Members. Their main function is to chair standing committees on bills and, when acting, must also do so impartially. But when not so acting, they take part in the ordinary political controversy of the House.

In addition there are several principal permanent officers who are not Members and who serve the House and its committees. The most senior is the Clerk of the House. There are two Clerks Assistant and other such officers include the Serjeant-at-Arms, the Counsel to the Speaker, some ten Principal Clerks and more than thirty other Clerks. The Library of the House has a staff of between thirty and forty. The Comptroller and Auditor General is referred to below.[8] And, in a unique position, is the Parliamentary Commissioner for Administration (also known as the Ombudsman).

Parliamentary Commissioner for Administration

The Parliamentary Commissioner is appointed by letters patent under the Parliamentary Commissioner Act 1967 for the purpose of conducting investigations. He holds office during good behaviour, can be dismissed only on an address from the two Houses and retires at 65 years of age. He is debarred from membership of the House of Commons.

He may investigate any action taken by or on behalf of a Government department or other authority to which the Act applies in any case where a written complaint has been made to a member of the House of Commons by a member of the public who claims to have sustained injustice in consequence of maladministration, and the complaint is referred to the Commissioner by a Member.

The Act excludes from the Commissioner's power of investigation many cases such as those where there is a right of appeal to a tribunal or where the ordinary courts provide a remedy. Matters not subject to investigation also include action taken in relation to foreign affairs, the hospital service,[9] most contractual and commercial transactions, personnel matters concerning the civil service, and the grant of honours, awards or privileges. The list of Government departments which fall within the scope of the Act is comprehensive of most bodies that could be so called. But local authorities and nationalized industries are not included.

The Commissioner takes evidence in private from the parties concerned and has power to obtain documents and other information from the departments, except Cabinet papers. At the close of his investigation he sends a report to the Member of Parliament and to the Department concerned. He also makes an annual report to Parliament.

The number of cases referred to the Commissioner between 1967 and 1972 declined from over 1,300 in 1967[10] to 548 in 1971 and rose to 573 in 1972. In each year about half the cases referred are found to be outside the jurisdiction of the Commissioner. It seems therefore as though the number of referred cases which the Commissioner is empowered to investigate may be settling down at about 300 or less each year. This is an unexpectedly small number.[11]

The House of Commons appoints a Select Committee to examine the Commissioner's reports. The Committee does not re-try the cases reported or review his findings but considers generally Members' use of the Commissioner and his scope and functions.

The Commissioner has not made any considerable impact on Government or on the House of Commons. This is in large part because the individual citizen does not often come into direct contact with the central departments but rather with local authorities; or where he does feel a grievance because of departmental action, means of review or appeal (as to a tribunal in national insurance and other social security cases) are often provided. The Commissioner's power to obtain documentary and other evidence from departments is nevertheless an important and, in the United Kingdom, a remarkable power. It is easy to imagine a set of circumstances where the use of the Commissioner could prove most valuable. As a champion of the small man, he has not been able to operate on a large scale. But on a major issue he may yet surprise us all.

GOVERNMENT AND OPPOSITION IN THE HOUSE OF COMMONS

The House of Commons makes its own rules – sometimes given formal statement in Standing Orders – for the conduct of its business. But the Government, through its majority, makes the important decisions on what these rules shall be.[12]

Before the public business of the House commences an hour (sometimes more) is set aside on the first four days of each week for Questions to Ministers[13] and certain other matters. The main sections of public business are classified by May as, first, the substantive motion, which is a 'self-contained proposal submitted for the approval of the House and drafted in such a way as to be capable of expressing a decision of the House'. Secondly, a motion for the adjournment of the House, which is a 'technical form devised for the purpose of enabling the House to discuss matters without recording a decision in terms'. Except under Standing Order No. 9, adjournment motions must be moved by Ministers. That Standing Order enables private Members to move the adjournment for the purpose of discussing a specific and important matter that should have urgent consideration; the Speaker must be satisfied that the matter is proper to be so discussed.[14] Thirdly, financial business, that is, relating directly to expenditure or taxation. Fourthly, the consideration of bills, that is legislative proposals of which the most important are bills introduced by Ministers and together forming the legislative programme of the Government for a Parliamentary session.

Usually, a Parliamentary session begins at the end of October. The House adjourns for a few weeks at Christmas and at Easter; and from the beginning of August until early in October. Then there is a very short recess before the new session begins.

Standing Orders provide that on Mondays, Tuesdays, Wednesdays, and Thursdays the House shall meet at 2.30 p.m. At 10 p.m. the business is interrupted and a Minister may move the adjournment. The private Member who has been successful in the ballot held fortnightly for this purpose may then initiate a half-hour debate on a subject of his choice. But certain categories of business are exempted from the interruption at 10 p.m. and, in any case, a Minister may move that business be proceeded with after 10 p.m., in which case the half-hour adjournment debate begins when the business is finally concluded). Late sittings or all-night sittings are common occurrences. On Fridays the House meets at 11 a.m. and normally adjourns at 4.30 p.m.[15]

The control exercised by the Government over the time of the House is based on Standing Order No. 6. This provides that government business shall have precedence at every sitting; except that private Members' notices of motions and bills shall have precedence on twenty Fridays in each session, and on four other days private Members' notices of motions shall have precedence until 7 p.m. This is supplemented by Standing Order No. 15 which provides:

The orders of the day shall be disposed of in the order in which they stand upon the paper; the right being reserved to Her Majesty's Ministers of arranging government business whether orders of the day or notices of motion in such order as they think fit.

These considerable controls which the Government exercises over the time of the House can be further extended by motions suspending the standing orders and, for example, reducing the time allotted to private Members or removing it altogether.

Most of these Government powers over the House are contained in Standing Orders. The rights of the Opposition to take time to criticize the Government mostly depend on the practice of the House. Each session is opened by the Queen's Speech in which Her Majesty (usually in person) reads a speech, prepared for her by the Government, which outlines the major legislative proposals of the Government, and refers to foreign and home policy in broad terms. This is immediately followed by a motion that an humble Address be presented to Her Majesty thanking her for her speech, and the Debate on the Address begins. Thus at the beginning of the session 1972–3, the debate took place on six consecutive days. After a general opening debate, the subjects chosen by the Opposition concerned industrial relations and unemployment; housing and land; prices and food; poverty; and the economic situation. In all, the debates lasted for over thirty-eight hours and on the last two matters the Opposition moved amendments and forced divisions. On all substantive Government motions, there will be debates. They may be motions to take note of reports from commissions or committees or Government statements of policy; for procedural changes; for guillotine orders.[16] Occasionally the Opposition will move a vote of censure on the Government. Adjournment motions may be moved to enable discussions to take place on a great variety of topics.

As in all debates it is the practice of the Speaker to call on Members alternately from the two sides of the House, the Opposition always has the opportunity to voice its criticisms. Standing Order No. 18 provides that twenty-nine days in each session, before August 5th, shall be allotted to 'the business of supply'. The importance of this lies in the practice that the choice of subjects to be debated rests with the Opposition. The legislative process is separately discussed below.[17]

Although the Opposition have relatively few 'rights' enshrined in standing orders, the practices and procedures of the House do enable criticism to be made. The Government respects the function of the Opposition and this not only because both sides are agreed in seeking to make the constitution work but also because the Opposition can, as already mentioned, by means of many devices, make the life of a Government difficult and embarrass the Government in the performance of its duties.

There is one other consideration. The Opposition may choose to obstruct Government business beyond the limits which the Government is willing to accept. And so there has grown up a number of procedures which enable Governments to frustrate this. The most usual method of obstruction is for the Opposition to seek to prolong debate and so to postpone the passing of resolutions which record the decisions of the House.

Standing Order No. 30 provides that at any time after a question has been proposed, a Member may claim to move 'that the Question be now put'. This is what is usually referred to as a closure motion. Whoever is in the chair must consider whether such a motion is an abuse of the rules of the House or an infringement of the rights of the minority. Thus if he considers that there has not yet been a debate of reasonable length and if it is clear that there are members who still wish to speak, he may refuse to accept the motion. Otherwise, he must put it forthwith and, if it is carried, the substantive question is immediately put. The closure motion can be put only when the Speaker or, in committee, the Chairman of Ways and Means or Deputy Chairman, or (on supply matters or on report of a bill) the Deputy Speaker, is in the chair. Further the motion will be carried only if not less than 100 Members vote in the majority in support of the motion.

The Opposition may seek to obstruct business by putting down a very large number of amendments, especially to bills. The chairman in committee, and the Speaker otherwise, is empowered by Standing Order No. 33 to select some amendments and disregard others. In practice the multiplication of amendments for the purpose of obstruction is not common.

Frequently when a bill is going through Parliament, and especially when it is being considered in committee or on report, an agreement is come to between Government and Opposition settling broadly how many sittings or how many hours will be spent on that stage of the bill. If such an agreement cannot be arrived at or if it breaks down, the Government may introduce a guillotine motion (which has to be approved by the whole House) which allocates a specified time to different stages of the bill and to different parts of the bill within committee and report stages. When at the pre-stated hour the guillotine falls, the remainder of the stage or part of the stage is not debated, although Government amendments go through. If the Opposition persist, there may be many divisions, especially in committee, and this is what is commonly taking place when it is reported that the House stayed up for much of the night 'tramping through divisions', as was the case on the Industrial Relations Bill in 1971.

Although for much of the time the relative strengths of Government and Opposition in the House result in a reasonable compromise being reached on the allocation of time, matters do arise on which the conflict between the two sides is acute. This happened recently as just mentioned, over the Industrial Relations Bill 1970–1; and again on the European Communities Bill 1971–2. In the end, so long as its majority holds together, the Government will have its way though, it may be, after a long struggle of attrition.

PARLIAMENTARY QUESTIONS
For a period of about an hour on Mondays, Tuesdays, Wednesdays and Thursdays, Ministers present themselves in the House of Commons to answer questions of which notice has been given by Members. If the Member does not indicate – by an asterisk – that he wishes the Question to be answered orally, a written answer will be given and recorded in *Hansard*. A Member may not ask more than

two Questions requiring oral answer on the same day. The rules of the House about Questions are strict and Questions may be ruled out of order though the ingenuity of Members in framing their Questions so as to keep them within the rules is considerable. Questions must relate to matters for which the Minister who is asked the Question is officially responsible.[18]

Ministers can refuse to answer Questions and the most common reason given by Ministers is that to answer would not be in the public or national interest. If a Question requiring an oral answer is not reached by the end of Question time, it will usually be answered in writing unless the Member indicates that he prefers the Question to be postponed.

Questions have broadly one of two purposes: the first is to obtain information; the second is designed to embarrass the Minister or the Government. This latter purpose relies heavily on the right of Members to ask supplementary Questions of which notice is not given and the content of which the Minister will be unaware. The officials in the Minister's department will seek to anticipate what the supplementaries may be about so that they can provide the Minister with the relevant information in advance.

Question time is often a true test of the Minister's adroitness and agility and is one of the ways in which the House enables a Minister to reveal these qualities or his lack of them. But it is doubtful whether the procedure tests much else and frequently the occasions are no more than entertainments in which the Member tries to trap the Minister with a difficult supplementary and the Minister tries to avoid giving the Member the kind of answer which reveals a weakness or a fault on the part of the Government.

THE LEGISLATIVE PROCESS

The law by which we are governed is derived from three principal sources: the rules of the common law; Acts of Parliament, and regulations of different kinds made under the authority of the Acts of Parliament; and regulations and directives made by the Council and the Commission under Treaties establishing the European Communities.

Rules of the common law are the accretion of principles laid down by judges in deciding disputes between private persons or institutions (including government institutions). The application of decided principle to new situations often restricts or enlarges the definition of these principles and so gives rise to modifications which are then the new principles. European community law is discussed elsewhere.[19] Here we deal with Acts of Parliament and regulations made thereunder.

ACTS OF PARLIAMENT

A distinction must be made at once between public Acts and private Acts. Public Acts are introduced as bills into one or other of the Houses of Parliament by a Member and deal with some aspect of public policy. Private Acts are promoted as bills by 'private' interests, most often by local authorities, and are for the limited benefit of those interests.[20]

A public bill introduced by a Minister is commonly called a Government bill and a public bill introduced by someone other than a Minister is commonly called a private Member's bill.

To a very large extent the making of new laws by way of Acts of Parliament is a function of the Government. Certainly the great majority of public bills which are passed and become Acts are introduced by Ministers. The following table shows the pattern in two recent sessions:[21]

	1970–1	*1971–2*
Government bills		
introduced	76	59
passed	76	59
Private Members' bills		
introduced	67	82
passed	13	17

Although it is unusual for Government bills to be defeated, it is by no means unheard of. In 1968–9 there were two such defeats.[22] One was the Parliament (No. 2) Bill which was designed to reform the House of Lords but was abandoned by the Government after being attacked in the House of Commons at great length by backbenchers of both sides. The other was the House of Commons (Redistribution of Seats) (No. 2) Bill which was dropped when the Opposition in the House of Lords refused to agree to the House of Commons' rejection of Lords' amendments. Also in this session the Government announced their intention to introduce an Industrial Relations bill but, under strong pressure from the Trades Union Congress, changed their mind.

These examples of Government defeats and withdrawal took place under the Labour administration. In 1972–3, the Conservative Government were threatened with defeat on their European Communities bill because of some defections amongst their own ranks, but with Liberal support and some defections from the Opposition benches, they carried the day.

We are dealing with the legislative process as one of the functions of Parliament but, on a wider view, that process, for Government bills, begins long before a bill is introduced into one or other of the Houses.

The Government's intention to introduce legislation may be expressed in its election manifesto for a general election. In that manifesto, each party puts forward its policy, much of which will require legislation before it can be put into effect.

Other, often unexpected, issues of policy will also arise during the course of a Government's years in office. Thus in 1970–1, the Conservative Government introduced bills on hijacking and on the purchase of Rolls-Royce. In 1971–2, a change in policy resulted in a bill to make grants to industry in certain regions; and in 1972–3 the Counter-Inflation (Temporary Provisions) Act was quickly passed to enable the Government to apply the first stage of its policy to control wages and prices. Royal Commissions, committees of inquiry, and the Law Commissions make reports to which the Government may decide to give legislative effect. Every year there are Finance bills which authorize the Government to raise taxes and Consolidation Fund and Appropriation bills to authorize expenditure.

The number of Government bills in a session is rarely less than fifty or more than eighty. But only a small number of these is of major importance. In 1971–2 the major measures (apart from annual financial legislation) were the European Communities Bill, the Housing Finance bill, the Housing (Financial Provisions) (Scotland) bill and the Local Government bill. Altogether, in an average session, fewer than twenty bills (including financial measures) form the vital part of the Government's legislative programme. The remainder consists of a large number of bills, often to amend previous legislation in order to deal with administrative difficulties which have arisen; to revise 'technical' law; and to consolidate earlier statutes. Many of these are far from unimportant but they concern the necessary, on-going business of government rather than, in any real sense, the political policy of particular Governments.

The House of Commons spends nearly half its time on the consideration of bills, and legislative committees of the House spend about as much time as the House itself. But the number of working days in a session is only about 160, so the number of bills a Government can expect to get through the House is limited. More bills are proposed by different Ministers for Government acceptance and for introduction into Parliament than can be dealt with and the Cabinet has to decide which shall be included in the legislative programme for each session.

A Government bill originates in a Government department and begins to take its shape – not yet as a bill but as memoranda or discussion papers of different kinds – as soon as it is clear that the bill will become part of the legislative programme for the next session of Parliament. Four major groups of people become involved in the process. The first group consists of the Ministers who will introduce the bill and see it through Parliament, and the civil servants under them; the second group consists of the Treasury and other Government departments which are or may be affected by the bill; the third group consists of the draftsmen who are to work on the bill – they are civil servants called Parliamentary Counsel who together operate as a separate unit servicing all Government departments; the fourth group are those institutions and organizations both public (like local authorities or nationalized industries) and private (like associations of companies or trade unions) whose interests are likely to be most affected by the provisions of the bill.

The first three of these groups are all within the Government machine and discussion between them is not likely to be restricted. But the fourth group, being outside this machine, is dealt with more at arm's length. The Department will tell those whom it chooses to consult within this fourth group what are the broad intentions of the Government, what is sought to be achieved by the bill then being put together, and what means are proposed. On particular matters, or when asked by the affected interests, the department may go into more detail, sometimes by putting forward alternatives and seeking the opinion of those interested on the various merits of the alternatives. Where, as is often the case, the co-operation of the affected interests is highly desirable in order to make the bill most effective in practice, something very like a bargain may be struck and undertakings may be given on both sides.

Finally, after meetings and conferences between those in the first three groups, the final draft of the bill will be agreed, and, at the time allotted to it in the Government's legislative programme, the bill will be introduced into Parliament and the second stage of the legislative process will begin.

For private Members' bills, the pre-Parliamentary stage may hardly exist except that there will inevitably have been discussions with outside groups which may be the effective sponsors of the bill. Private Members' bills are not part of the Government's legislative programme (though sometimes the Government may make some of their time available if they particularly favour the bill). If the bills are to pass, they must do so within the time allotted to private Members' bills. Because that time is strictly limited, Members ballot for the right to introduce bills and of those who are successful only those few drawn early in the ballot are likely to have enough time allotted to them to have a chance of getting their bills through Parliament.

We have seen that twenty Fridays are set aside for private Members' bills and motions.[23] Recently, sessional orders have distributed these twenty days between bills and motions; in 1970–1, for example twelve 'bill' days and eight 'motion' days were allotted.[24] A further division has to be made of 'bill' days.[25] At first the days are devoted to second readings of bills (so far as there is time) in accordance with the ballot order. Later, however, precedence is given to further proceedings on bills which have received a second reading, or have further advanced through the procedures.

Standing Order No. 89 provides (in part):

This House will receive no petition for any sum relating to public service or proceed upon any motion for a grant or charge upon the public revenue. . . . unless recommended from the Crown.

The effect of this on private Members' bills is that if the bill requires or authorizes public expenditure, the Government must be persuaded to agree and, under S.O. No. 90, to put forward a financial resolution. As it is unlikely that the Government will agree (unless they are positively in favour of the bill) few private Members' bills contain provisions which would incur expenditure.

In November 1972, the twenty Members successful in the ballot for 1972–3 presented their topics for legislation. The titles of the bills were: Penalties for Murder; Hallmarking; Export of Animals (Control); Heavy Commercial Vehicles (Controls and Regulations);

Anti-Discrimination; Employment of Children; Dangerous Drugs and Disabled Children; Elderly and Disabled Persons (Warning Devices); Domicile and Matrimonial Proceedings; Employment Agencies; Supplementary Allowances (Non-payment to Strikers); Police Acts (Amendment); Guardianship of Minors; Protection of Wrecks; Law Reform (Diligence) (Scotland); National Lottery; Transplant of Human Organs; Public Indecency; Heating for the Elderly; Cruelty to Animals Act 1876 (Amendment). Most of these bills would either make new regulations or amend the law, and so would be self-operating without the *necessary* intervention of the Government or other public authority and so without the necessary expenditure of public money. Some of these areas of activities are already the concern of Government (for example, employment of children, dangerous drugs, the police) and are unlikely to be subjected to piecemeal reform. Many are bills which the Members introducing them never expect to see enacted but which give those Members and their supporters an opportunity to further a campaign by forcing the Government to respond to the proposal for legislation.

The attitude of the Government to private Members' bills may vary considerably from bill to bill. On some they will be neutral, on some positively in favour, on some hostile. In the last two situations, they will seek to get their way by using all the pressures and powers available to them. Governments are chary of embarking on legislation which most closely affects private consciences – such as capital punishment, homosexuality, abortion, censorship, divorce, Sunday entertainment[26] – and tend to leave such matters to private members. They normally adopt an officially neutral attitude though sometimes making Government time available or offering drafting assistance.

Private bills,[27] as we have said, are promoted by private interests who deposit petitions. They are of limited effect (when promoted by a local authority they affect only those who are within the area of that authority) but may have considerable consequences within those limits. The Houses of Parliament deal with private bills in special ways which are summarized below.[28]

Public bills may be introduced into either House of Parliament. After a formal first reading, a day is set down for the bill's second reading when usually the Member in charge of the bill (who will be a Minister in the case of a Government bill) moves that the bill 'be now read a second time'. A debate follows at the end of which the question is put and agreed to or negatived, with or without a division. On a Government bill, the Opposition will have decided what their general attitude will be. They may object to it strongly in which case they will force a division against the motion for the second reading. They may occasionally welcome it unreservedly. Or they may accept it in part and indicate that they intend to try in committee to change the parts they do not like. Two types of amendments may be moved. The first is to propose to leave out the word 'now' and to add 'upon this day six (or three) months'. The effect of carrying this amendment is effectively to kill the bill. The second type is a 'reasoned' amendment which states that the House declines to give a second reading for certain reasons which are then stated. Again, the practical effect of passing such an amendment is to kill the bill. The Opposition may be content, however, merely to oppose the bill by speaking against it and then voting against the motion for second reading.

The debate on second reading is concerned with the general principles of the bill and the Member who moves the motion normally outlines its purposes and the ways it proposes to achieve those purposes. He may in so doing refer to the specific provisions in the more important clauses of the bill. After the second reading has been agreed to, the financial resolution (if any) [29] is approved, usually without debate.

Second reading debates in the House of Commons normally take place in the chamber but Standing Orders permit this stage to be sent 'upstairs' to a committee. Since any twenty Members can, by objecting, prevent this being done, the agreement of the Opposition is necessary and will be forthcoming only when the subject matter of the bill is wholly uncontroversial. Scottish bills may be sent for the equivalent of second reading to the Scottish Grand Committee unless ten Members object; this committal is usual.

Second reading debates are important because they focus attention both inside and outside Parliament on the contents of the bill, they give Ministers and others probably their first Parliamentary opportunity to speak, and they provide affected interests with another chance, through Members, of pressing their points of view. For private Members' bills they may be crucial as defeat will be total (for that session) and narrow victory will suggest that the way ahead is stony and hard. Votes on private Members' bills are highly unpredictable, depending so much on how many Members feel strongly enough about the issue, one way or the other, to attend the debate and vote. For Government bills, the situation is quite different. Unless the Government has no overall majority, or one so small that casual illness can destroy it, it will not be defeated in the House of Commons on the second reading of Government bills. Or if it were, then it would have deliberately courted defeat in the knowledge that some of its supporters would desert it. That might happen if the Government felt obliged to force its dissentient members into the open. But all that argues a party crisis of some magnitude – which *might* have happened on the European Communities Bill but did not because (and this would apply to other similar occasions) parties try very hard not to destroy themselves.

After second reading in the House of Commons, the bill goes to a committee. The rule now is[30] that it goes to a standing committee unless the House otherwise resolves. The ordinary alternative is to resolve that the bill goes to a committee of the whole House, though other possibilities are committal to a select committee or to a joint committee. It is also possible for the Member in charge of the bill to move that the bill be committed to a standing committee in respect of some of its provisions and to a committee of the whole House in respect of other provisions, and in recent years this has been the practice with the Finance Bill.

A committee of the whole House is what it sounds like – all the Members but under a chairman, not the Speaker. Standing committees consist of a chairman[31] and sixteen to fifty Members,[32] the two major political parties being represented in numbers reflecting their proportion in the House. This has meant a majority of few or none for the Government since 1970 – minor parties may be allowed one Member. A Committee of Selection decides who shall be Members but on a Government bill the whips on both sides make the effective recommendations. The Minister, or private Member, in charge of the bill, is a member of a standing committee.

The debates in committee centre around the amendments put down, mostly by the Opposition but also by the Minister or Member in charge. After discussion, amendments will be agreed to or negatived or withdrawn. And each clause, amended or not, must be put to the committee for agreement or disagreement. The chairman is entitled, as we have seen,[33] to select some amendments and not to select others but his practice of grouping a number of amendments together for discussion (although only one in the group will be moved) enables Members, in very large measure, to have the opportunity to say what they wish.

Debates in committee can be highly controversial and acrimonious or humdrum and good-humoured. Mostly this will depend on the subject matter of the bill. One which sharply divides the parties, like the Housing Finance Bill 1971–2 or the Industrial Relations Bill 1970–1, can lead to long sittings. Occasionally the atmosphere in committee can change quickly either because of some real or imagined change of mood or intention on the part of one or other side; or because of a major dispute between the parties which may have nothing to do with the bill but which suddenly affects the relationships between Members.

Every bill must be reported to the House when the committee stage is finished. If a bill was in committee of the whole House and is reported without amendment, it is not considered by the House on report. But if the bill was sent to a standing committee, or was amended in committee of the whole House, then opportunity must be given for it to be considered on report – and it is this consideration that is usually referred to, in a slightly confusing shorthand phrase, as the report stage.

During the report stage, which is in the chamber with all Members entitled to be present,[34] amendments may be tabled for debate. The Minister or Member in charge may well table many amendments at this stage, some of which will be in response to points made by Members in committee. All amendments moved by the Minister or Member in charge will be selected for debate but those put down by other Members may not. Usually the Opposition will be able to debate most of the issues they wish to raise.

The report stage is followed by the third reading which is often formal only and at which no amendments may be moved in the House of Commons.

In the House of Lords, the procedure is similar but with these important differences. First, the committee stage is often dispensed with, especially for Finance, Consolidated Fund and Appropriation bills; if a bill is committed, but on the day when it is to be considered it appears that no one wishes to speak or move an amendment, the order of commitment may be discharged. Secondly, unless (exceptionally) it is sent to a joint or select or public bill committee, the bill will be considered in committee of the whole House. Thirdly, amendments are allowed on third reading.

If the second House to receive a bill amends it, the amendments must go back to the first House for approval. Where the House of Lords amends a bill and the House of Commons rejects the Lords' amendments, the Lords will almost always agree to that rejection.[35]

The procedure on private bills is detailed and complex.[36] Here only a summary can be made. A private bill is founded on a petition made by the promoters of the bill. Before the bill is presented to Parliament, notice must be given to those affected by the bill who may then petition against it. In the House of Commons, the second reading of the bill is moved by the Chairman of Ways and Means.[37] If not then rejected, it is sent to a committee. As May says,[38] 'the expediency of a private bill, being mainly founded upon allegations of fact, which have not yet been proved, the House in agreeing to its second reading, affirms the principle of the bill conditionally, and subject to the proof of such allegations before the committee.'

If a private bill is not petitioned against, it is sent to a Committee on Unopposed Bills which consists of six members including the Chairman and Deputy Chairman of Ways and Means. If the bill is opposed it is sent to a committee of four Members of the House of Commons who must have no local or personal interest in the bill. Government departments affected by the bill may make reports to the House; if so, these stand referred to the committee on the bill.

A committee on unopposed bills must be satisfied by evidence produced by the promoters that the bill is desirable and necessary. Before committees on opposed bills, the promoters and the objectors appear, generally represented by counsel, and call witnesses, who are open to cross-examination.

The bill is reported to the House and, if amended in committee, is considered by the House (when it may be further amended). It is then read a third time.

In the House of Lords[39] opposed bills are sent to a select committee of five Lords where the procedure is similar to that in the House of Commons. Unopposed bills are examined by the Chairman of Committees.

SUBORDINATE LEGISLATION
Government bills are primarily designed either to regulate conduct by laying down what shall and shall not be done (with penalties of many different kinds being prescribed for failure to comply) or to empower Ministers, local and other public authorities to provide

services. Thus bills are required to regulate activity in the interests of health or good housing or the best use of land; and to provide schools or roads or electricity or national insurance payments or to give grants to industry.

A major bill will become an Act of Parliament which may extend to twenty or fifty or even a hundred pages of the statute book. But even so there may be more details to be provided for, some trivial but some substantial, and so Acts of Parliament often empower the Queen in Council or Ministers to make further laws within limits and for purposes laid down by those statutes. These laws may be termed orders or regulations or rules or schemes or some other such word. Because they are made under statutory authority they are collectively referred to as subordinate legislation; or as delegated legislation (meaning that Parliament has delegated its legislative function in these instances). The resulting orders or regulations or rules or whatever are known as statutory instruments and are subject to the provisions of the Statutory Instruments Act 1946.[40]

Thus under the Town and Country Planning Act 1971 planning permission (that is permission to develop land by, for example, building a house on it) is normally given by a local authority as an executive act. But section 24 provides:

(1) The Secretary of State shall by order (in this Act referred to as a 'development order') provide for the granting of planning permission.
(2) A development order may either —
    (a)   itself grant planning permission for development specified in the order, or for development of any class so specified . . .

Section 287(4) of the same Act provides that the power to make orders under section 24 'shall be exercisable by statutory instrument'.

A different use of subordinate legislation is exemplified by section 131 of this Act. The primary purpose of the section is to authorize the Secretary of State to set up a joint body for certain purposes if he wishes. Sub-section (3) provides —

Regulations under this Act may make such provision consequential upon or supplementary to the provisions of this section as appears to the Secretary of State to be necessary or expedient.

And section 287(2) provides that any power conferred by this Act to make regulations 'shall be exercisable by statutory instrument'.

Statutory instruments are general or local in character, a distinction similar to that used for public and private Acts. Every year about 2,000 instruments are made of which rather less than half are general. The consultation of interests which we noted as an important pre-Parliamentary stage for bills is frequently undertaken for the more important types of statutory instruments.

Statutory instruments are required by statute to be printed and put on sale.[41] In any proceedings against any person for an offence consisting of a contravention of a statutory instrument, it is a defence to prove that the instrument had not been published at the date of the alleged contravention unless it is proved that at that date reasonable steps had been taken to bring the purport of the instrument to the notice of the public or of persons likely to be affected by it or of the person charged.[42]

Statutes conferring powers on the Queen in Council or on Ministers to make subordinate legislation generally require that the instruments shall be laid before Parliament. When this is required, the statute most often provides also that instruments 'shall be subject to annulment in pursuance of a resolution of either House of Parliament' generally within forty days of their being laid; this is called the negative procedure. But not infrequently statutes provide that instruments or drafts of instruments shall not have effect until approved by resolutions of each House of Parliament, or shall cease to have effect unless so approved; this is called the affirmative procedure. An Act of Parliament may use one procedure for some instruments and another for other instruments.[43] Under the negative procedure, any Member may move the annulment but the initiative is with him and he may not be able to find Parliamentary time for this purpose. Under the affirmative procedure, a Minister will move the resolution to approve and he may then be opposed. In practice, because virtually all subordinate legislation is Government legislation, motions to annul are very rarely successful and motions to approve very rarely unsuccessful. But both procedures give opportunities for criticisms to be made and these may bear some fruit eventually.

An important House of Commons safeguard[44] is exercised by the Select Committee on Statutory Instruments. It may consider any general statutory instrument and may draw the attention of the House to any provision which imposes a charge on public revenues; is made under an enactment which excludes challenge in the courts; appears to make unusual or unexpected use of the powers conferred; purports to have retrospective effect not authorized by the statute under which it is made; has been withheld from publication or from being laid before Parliament by unjustifiable delay; has not been notified to the Speaker in accordance with section 4 of the Statutory Instruments Act 1946;[45] calls for elucidation of its form or purport; appears to be defective in its drafting. The Select Committee must, before reporting to the House, give an opportunity to the Government department concerned to explain what has happened. The Select Committee has been useful as a watchdog but its order of reference does not permit it to consider the merits or policy of any provision, although recently reforms have been suggested which would enable it to do so.

The House of Lords has a similar committee called the Special Orders Committee but this looks only at instruments subject to the affirmative procedure, so its scope is much smaller.

SELECT COMMITTEES OF THE HOUSE OF COMMONS

During the course of a session, the House of Commons appoints several Select Committees. In 1971–2, twenty-two were set up and under these there were nineteen sub-committees.[46] Altogether 250 out of the 630[47] Members served on these committees.

Six Committees are concerned with procedural matters connected with the running of the House: the Select Committees on Procedure and on Standing Orders; the Committee of Selection; the Business Committee and the Business Sub-Committee; and the Chairmen's Panel. Two are part of the legislative process, being the Joint[48] Committee on Consolidation etc., bills and Court of Referees on private bills. The Committee of Privileges examines and reports on alleged breaches of the privileges of Members.[49] A select committee is appointed to examine reports from the Parliamentary Commissioner for Administration,[50] and another examines public petitions presented to Parliament. The House of Commons (Services) Committee has referred to it a variety of ancillary matters relating to the House. Three of the most important select committees are those on expenditure, on public accounts, and on nationalized industries.[51] Three 'specialist' committees were appointed in 1971–2; on race relations and immigration on science and technology, and on Scottish affairs. The select committee on statutory instruments, has been discussed above.[52] Finally three select committees in 1971–2 were appointed to examine special problems which had arisen, concerned with the civil list (which makes provision for the royal family), delegated legislation (a joint committee with the House of Lords), and parliamentary questions.

The Committee of Public Accounts is appointed 'for the examination of the accounts showing the appropriation of the sums granted by Parliament to meet the public expenditure, and of such other accounts laid before Parliament as the committee may think fit'. Not more than fifteen Members are appointed to serve and five form a quorum. In 1971–2, the committee sat on thirty-one days and of the eleven who were members throughout the whole session (four were discharged and others added at different times) only six attended more than twenty sittings. The chairman, who is by tradition an Opposition Member, has considerable responsibility. The committee works with the assistance of the Comptroller and Auditor-General who is a public officer appointed under statute and removable only on an address from the two Houses. He and his staff continuously audit the accounts of Government departments and report to the committee not only the spending of money for a purpose other than that for which it was voted but also cases of extravagance or inefficiency. The reports of the committee carry considerable weight and are a valuable safeguard.

Until 1970 there was a Select Committee on Estimates which conducted inquiries into items of its choice appearing in the estimates for each financial year. From the beginning of 1971, this was replaced by the Select Committee on Expenditure. Its terms of reference are 'to consider any papers on public expenditure presented to this House and such of the estimates as may seem fit to the committee and in particular to consider how, if at all, the policies implied in the figures of expenditure and in the estimates may be carried out more economically'. It consists of forty-nine Members of whom nine are a quorum, and may appoint sub-committees each with a quorum of three. In 1971–2 the Committee appointed seven sub-committees one of which was a steering committee, another a public expenditure (general) sub-committee and the remaining five dealt with defence and external affairs, education and arts, employment and social services, environment and home office, and trade and industry. A large number of reports is made but it is too early to assess whether or not this new, and potentially important, committee is a success.

Some select committees are appointed under standing orders.[53] Others are appointed under sessional orders which are regularly renewed;[54] others may be appointed for special purposes as required;[55] the 'specialist' committees may be reappointed for a number of years but it is becoming the practice for other committees with different specialisms to be appointed as replacements for one or more of these committees. The House also sometimes appoints select committees to consider bills.

The House of Lords

COMPOSITION

Historically the House of Lords gave direct representation to the most powerful men in the land, the great landowners both temporal and spiritual. First and foremost they represented themselves (unlike the members of the Commons, who represented their constituents) though their interests might also in some cases be the interests of their tenants or of the regions from which they came. Even today, when the status of the House of Lords and its members has changed so much, peers are still not entitled to vote in parliamentary elections, presumably on the ground that they can represent themselves in the Upper House.[1]

There are four groups in the composition of the House of Lords. The Lords Spiritual constitute the first group. These are two archbishops and twenty-four bishops of the Church of England. The two archbishops (of Canterbury and York) and the Bishops of London, Durham and Winchester are entitled to sit *ex officio*. The remaining twenty-one seats are taken by those diocesan bishops in England who are most senior in terms of the length of time they have held their sees. Only the Bishop of Sodor and Man is excluded. When one of the Lords Spiritual resigns his see he also loses his right to sit in Parliament and, unless he is a member of the class who sit *ex officio* in the House, his place will be taken, not by the successor to his see, but by the most senior bishop who is not already a member of the House.

The Lords Spiritual were once a far more important element in the House than they are today and this was understandable in view of the importance of the Church both as landowner and as an element in the government of the country.[2] Originally all the bishops were entitled to sit in the House but in the nineteenth century when new bishoprics were created the present system was introduced in order that the number of bishops in the House should not be increased.[3] The greatest anomalies about the spiritual peers are that they represent only one church and only one part of the United Kingdom: they are all of the Church of England and their sees are all in England. In Scotland the established church is the Church of Scotland (Presbyterian) and in Wales and Northern Ireland there is no established church. Nevertheless there is no direct representation of other religions or any religion from other parts of the United Kingdom.[4]

The second group in the House is the hereditary peerage: dukes, marquises, earls, viscounts and barons. They fall into a number of classes. First, there are the hereditary peers of England: these are peerages created before the union with Scotland on 1 May 1707. Secondly, there are the hereditary peers of Scotland, who were also all created before the union. On the coming into force of the Treaty of Union both these groups of peers were entitled to equal rights in all respects except one: all the English peers were entitled to sit in the Lords but the Scottish peers were to elect sixteen of their number to sit in the House and the remainder were excluded. This state of affairs continued until the Peerage Act 1963[5] gave all peers of Scotland the right to sit.

Peers created between the union with Scotland and that with Ireland are peers of Great Britain and are all entitled to sit. Under the Union with Ireland Act 1800 the hereditary peers of Ireland were given the right to elect twenty-eight of their number who were entitled to sit in the House for life, but no elections have taken place since the independence of Southern Ireland and the last Irish peer died in 1961.[6] Since Irish peers are no longer represented in the Lords it was provided in the Peerage Act 1963 that they would no longer be disqualified from election to the Commons or from voting in parliamentary elections.[7]

Hereditary peerages created since 1 January 1801 are peerages of the United Kingdom. All such peers are entitled to sit.

Peeresses were traditionally excluded from the House[8] but this was changed by the Peerage Act 1963[9] which provided that women holding hereditary peerages in the peerages of England, Scotland, Great Britain or the United Kingdom should have the same right to sit in the House and be subject to the same disqualifications as regards membership of the Commons or voting in parliamentary elections as male peers.

The third group in the House is the Lords of Appeal in Ordinary. Since the House of Lords is also the highest appeal court in the country it is necessary that there should be a sufficient number of peers with the necessary judicial ability and experience to hear appeals. (By convention non-judicial peers do not take any part in the appellate work of the House). It was therefore provided by the Appellate Jurisdiction Acts 1876–1947 and the Administration of Justice Act 1968 that up to eleven Lords of Appeal in Ordinary could be appointed by the Crown on the recommendation of the Prime Minister. They hear appeals together with the other Law Lords[10] and receive salaries until they retire from their offices at the age of seventy-five. Lords of Appeal in Ordinary are barons for life and have the full rights of members of the House. They play a part in the non-judicial business of the House[11] and keep their seats in the House when they retire from their offices. Their right to sit does not descend to their heirs.

The fourth and most recent group in the House are the life peers and peeresses created under the Life Peerages Act 1958. (At common law the holder of a life peerage was not entitled to sit in the House.)[12] Life peers are entitled to the rank of baron and have the same rights as hereditary peers except that their peerage cannot be inherited by their heirs.

New peerages (including life peerages) are created by the Crown on the advice of the Prime Minister[13] and this power is politically valuable because it enables the Prime Minister to reward those who have supported him in the past as well as allowing him to bring men who are not M.P.s into the Government without having to find seats for them in the Commons. The kind of persons given peerages today are, first of all, politicians, many of whom were previously in the Commons, and secondly, eminent people outside politics. Successful industrialists and businessmen form the bulk of the latter but there are also people who have achieved prominence in the professions, the arts, social work, public service, science, academic life, the trade union movement and other fields. The result of this is that there is a wide representation of interests in the Lords and on some questions debates are better informed than in the Commons. Most of the non-political peers do not take any party whip but join the ranks of the cross-benchers.[14]

At common law it was impossible for a peer to disclaim his peerage so that an M.P. who succeeded to a peerage was permanently barred from the Commons; thus when Anthony Wedgwood Benn succeeded to a peerage and became Lord Stansgate his career in the Commons was cut short.[15] Partly as a result of his efforts, the Peerage Act 1963[16] was passed, providing for the disclaimer of peerage, and Wedgwood Benn was the first to take advantage of it. Other peers who have disclaimed their peerages include Sir Alec Douglas-Home (Lord Home) and Quintin Hogg (Lord Hailsham).[17]

The Act only applies to persons who succeed to peerages and thus excludes hereditary peers of first creation as well as life peers and Lords of Appeal in Ordinary. There is a strict time limit within which the disclaimer must be made: this is twelve months from the date on which the person succeeded to the peerage, or, in the case of someone who succeeded to a peerage when he was under the age of twenty-one, twelve months after he attains that age. (Persons who succeeded to peerages before the Act was passed had twelve months from the date when it came into effect to make their decision.) If a person is a member of the House of Commons when he succeeds to a peerage the time limit is restricted to one month but during this period he is not disqualified from being an M.P. (although he cannot sit or vote until he disclaims).[18]

The disclaimer of a peerage is irrevocable and divests the person concerned (and his wife, if married) of all titles, rights, offices, privileges and precedence attaching to it as well as relieving him from all obligations and disabilities of the peerage (including disqualification from membership of the Commons and voting in parliamentary elections). A person who has disclaimed a peerage cannot be given a new hereditary peerage at a later date but this does not prevent his being made a life peer under the Peerage Act 1963 or being made a Lord of Appeal in Ordinary.[19] Disclaimer has no effect on any property rights nor does it accelerate the succession to the peerage or affect its devolution on his death, i.e. the heir of the person disclaiming succeeds to it on the death of the person disclaiming, but not before.

The disqualifications for membership of the House of Lords are more restricted than for the House of Commons. As in the Commons, aliens,[20] persons under twenty-one years of age,[21] bankrupts[22] and persons convicted of treason are disqualified;[23] but the other disqualifications for membership in the Commons do not apply in the

Lords. Disputes relating to peerages and the right to sit in the House are decided by the Privileges Committee of the House of Lords. Its membership includes four Lords of Appeal in Ordinary and at least three of them must be present whenever it meets.[24] Unlike M.P.s, peers are not paid a salary but they are now given a tax-free allowance of £8.50 for each sitting they attend, together with their travelling expenses.

Peers who are unable to attend the sittings of the House are expected to apply for leave of absence.[25] This can be obtained at any time for either a session or for the remainder of the Parliament. The Lord Chancellor is required to write at the beginning of every session to all those who were previously granted leave of absence and those who did not attend any sittings in the previous session to ask them whether they wish to apply for leave of absence. This is granted automatically if no reply is received. Leave of absence can be ended on one month's notice but while it is in force a peer is expected not to attend, though there is no way in which he can be legally prevented from doing so. The importance of this is that it prevents a sudden descent of backwoodsmen (peers who do not normally attend) when a controversial matter is being discussed. In 1968 the number of peers who had leave of absence was 192; there were also eighty-one who had never applied for a writ of summons.[26]

The following table[27] shows the numerical composition of the House of Lords on 1 August 1968:

Lords Spiritual	26
Hereditary Peers by succession	736
Hereditary Peers of first creation	122
Lords of Appeal in Ordinary (serving and retired)	23
Life Peers	155
TOTAL	1062

It will be seen from this that the great bulk of the House is made up of hereditary peers by succession and that those members who owe their seats to their personal merit are in a clear minority. It is also interesting to note that the House has almost doubled in size since the year 1900 when it contained only 590 members. About one-third of the total number of peers do not attend at all and less than one-third can be said to attend regularly, i.e. one-third of the sittings.[28] Thus the working House is considerably smaller than the total numbers might suggest and average attendance in 1967–8 was about 230 daily. This figure indicates that attendance has been growing recently: in 1963 the corresponding figure was 140 and in 1955 it was 92. Not surprisingly the peers by succession are less interested in attending the House than those who were created peers. Thus although peers by succession constitute over two-thirds of the total membership of the House they make up less than half of those who attend regularly: less than 10 per cent of the peers by succession attend regularly; 47 per cent of the others do.

Just over half of the total number of peers are not in receipt of any party whip but the great bulk of these do not attend regularly. Conservative peers outnumber Labour peers overall by about three to one but among the regular attenders the gap is much narrower although there is still a preponderance of Conservatives. Peers in receipt of the Conservative whip do not, however, have an overall majority even in the 'working House', where they could be outvoted by a combination of opposition and crossbench peers. Most of the latter are, however, probably conservative in spirit so that the House of Lords will not often be hostile to the measures of a Conservative Government. This preponderance of Conservative peers stems from the hereditary element in the House: among the created peers Labour supporters outnumber Conservatives, though the crossbench peers are still the largest group.[29]

The overall picture one has of the House is, therefore, that of a potentially large body with a fairly small core of regular attenders. The political complexion of the House is conservative but independent peers are an important factor. The majority of the members are there by right of birth but they play a less active part in the affairs of the House than those who owe their position to their personal qualities. A body such as this is clearly unsuitable to decide the great political issues of the day but its greater independence from the dictates of the party whips as well as the general high quality of its membership suggests that it might have a valuable role to play with regard to the many issues of government which are outside the realm of party political controversy.

POWERS

Until the Parliament Act 1911 was passed every bill had to receive the assent of the Lords before it became law. The legislative powers of the Lords were equal to those of the Commons except that all financial legislation had to be introduced in the Commons; the

Lords had the power to reject it outright but could not amend it.[30] However, when the Lords in 1909 made use of this power – to reject the Finance Bill embodying Lloyd George's budget – the result was that the power was taken away from them.

The events which led to the passing of the Parliament Act 1911 illustrate the interaction between law and politics and show that even then the real powers of the Lords were much less than a purely legal analysis might lead one to believe. The story starts with the general election of 1906 when the Liberals obtained a large majority and embarked on a programme of radical social reform. The Lords, dominated then as now by Conservatives, opposed and obstructed their efforts. The crisis came with the rejection of the budget of 1909; the Government, led by Asquith, appealed to the people and, though they lost their outright majority in the general election of January 1910, they remained in power with the support of the Irish Nationalists and the Labour party. The Lords then gave way over the Finance Bill, which was duly passed, but this was not enough for the Liberals: they insisted on abolishing altogether the power of the Lords to veto legislation passed by the Lower House.

This could, of course, be done only by statute but the problem was that it was extremely unlikely that any bill designed to achieve this end would itself be passed by the Lords. The only solution was to ask the King to use his prerogative to create enough new peers of the right political persuasion to ensure the passage of the necessary legislation. Asquith approached the King (Edward VII) who was prepared, reluctantly, to do this provided that the Government first obtained a mandate in a general election. In May 1910 Edward VII died and was succeeded by George V who entered into a secret agreement with Asquith that he would create the necessary peers if the Liberals fought and won an election on this issue. The election was held in December, 1910 and resulted in little change in the state of the parties. The Parliament Bill, which had been first introduced in the previous parliament, was reintroduced and when the King's promise was made public the Lords gave way and passed the bill without any new peers actually being created.

The effect of the Parliament Act was to remove the power of veto and replace it with a power of delay. A basic distinction is drawn between money bills (traditionally the preserve of the Commons) and other bills. If a money bill is passed by the Commons and sent up to the Lords at least a month before the end of the session, the

Lords have one month to agree to it: if it is not passed by then it can obtain the royal assent and become law without the consent of the Lords.[31] This, of course, virtually eliminates the power of the Lords in the financial field. The term 'money bill' is defined at some length in the Act[32] but basically it means a bill concerned with taxation, public expenditure or certain related matters. The bill must, however, be concerned solely with these matters: if provisions of a different kind are tacked on to a bill dealing with finance, it ceases to be a money bill for the purposes of the Act.

If the bill is not a money bill the period of delay is longer. Originally the Parliament Act 1911 specified a delay of two years but this was reduced to one year by the Parliament Act 1949, which was itself passed under the provisions of the Parliament Act 1911. As the requirements are rather complicated it is useful to set out the words of the statute:[33]

2 (1) If any Public Bill (other than a Money Bill or a Bill containing any provision to extend the maximum duration of Parliament beyond five years) is passed by the House of Commons [in two successive sessions] (whether of the same Parliament or not), and, having been sent up to the House of Lords at least one month before the end of the session, is rejected by the House of Lords in each of those sessions, that Bill shall, on its rejection [for the second time] by the House of Lords, unless the House of Commons direct to the contrary, be presented to His Majesty and become an Act of Parliament on the Royal Assent being signified thereto, notwithstanding that the House of Lords have not consented to the Bill: Provided that this provision shall not take effect unless [one year has elapsed] between the date of the second reading in the first of those sessions of the Bill in the House of Commons and the date on which it passes the House of Commons [in the second of those sessions].

...

(3) A Bill shall be deemed to be rejected by the House of Lords if it is not passed by the House of Lords either without amendment or with such amendments only as may be agreed to by both Houses.

It will be seen that under this section a bill must be passed twice by the Commons (in different sessions) but on its rejection for a second time by the Lords it may be presented for the Royal Assent. The bill must be sent up to the Lords at least a month before the end of the session and if it is not passed by the end of the session it is considered to have been rejected. The effect of this is to reduce the powers of the Lords to the imposition of a delay of approximately a year and a month from the original second reading of the bill in the Commons.[34] However, as the bill would in any case take a certain length of time to pass through the stages in the Commons after the second reading (and to pass through the Lords if it were not rejected) a rejection by the Lords does not effectively delay the bill very long.

The Speaker of the House of Commons has an important role to play under the Parliament Acts. It is his duty to decide whether a bill is a money bill within the meaning of the Act and he must endorse a certificate to this effect on every such bill.[35] When a non-money bill is presented for the Royal Assent under the provisions of the Act the Speaker must also certify that the provisions of the Act have been complied with.[36] In both cases the Speaker's certificate is conclusive and cannot be challenged in any court.[37]

It is important to note that the Parliament Acts do not apply to all legislation and when they are not applicable the power of the Lords to veto remains intact. First, bills to extend the life of Parliament beyond five years are expressly excluded from section 2. (The maximum life of Parliament had previously been seven years[38] but this was reduced to five years by section 7 of the Parliament Act of 1911). Secondly, the Acts only apply to public bills; so private bills are excluded. Section 5 of the Act provides that provisional order bills are not to be treated as public bills; so they are excluded as well. Finally, since the Acts apply only to bills, delegated legislation is altogether excluded. Since, however, a bill to amend the Parliament Acts could be passed under the Parliament Acts, it would be possible to remove these restrictions by means of the Parliament Act procedure. Thus if the Government wanted to extend the life of Parliament beyond five years and this was opposed by the Lords, a bill could be passed to amend the Parliament Acts. This could become law without the Lords' consent after thirteen months and could provide, for example, that a bill to extend the life of Parliament could not be delayed for more than one month. The other possible procedure would be to ask the Queen to create sufficient new peers to overcome the opposition; but it is not clear that she would be obliged to accede to such a request in all circumstances: the promise made by George V to do this in 1910 was conditional on the holding of a general election to test public opinion on the issue.[39]

In the sixty years since it was passed, the Parliament Act has been used only three times: to pass the Welsh Church Act 1914 (to disestablish the Church of Wales), the Government of Ireland Act 1914 (which provided home rule for Ireland but was never put into effect) and the Parliament Act 1949. The reason for this is that the Lords have usually given way gracefully when the Commons have insisted on having their way.

WHAT THE HOUSE OF LORDS DOES

It is clear today (whatever may have been thought fifty years ago) that the House of Lords is fundamentally unsuitable to act as a check or curb on the power of the Government, first, because the majority of its members owe their seats to heredity alone and, secondly, because there is a permanent majority for the Conservative Party.[40] A largely hereditary body can hardly purport to represent public opinion and a body under the permanent control of one party will always be suspected of party bias. For these reasons any attempt by the Lords to thwart the will of the Government on a matter of importance would be unacceptable to public opinion and might well lead to the abolition of the House.

The delaying power cannot, moreover, be used as a means of appealing to public opinion over the heads of the Government because there is no way in which public opinion can effectively express itself except through the Commons. (Before 1911, of course, it was possible for the Lords to force an election by rejecting Government measures but it was precisely in order to put an end to this that the Parliament Act was passed.) What the delaying power can and should be used for is to make the Government reconsider measures which the House of Lords considers to be unsound; but if the Government insists on the bill in question being passed there is usually little point in the Lords using their power to delay its enactment.

It seems fairly clear that the Lords themselves do not consider that it is their function (save in most exceptional circumstances) to thwart the will of the Government. This is borne out if one looks at the occasions since 1911 on which the Lords have clashed with the Commons. There are only three cases[41] in which both sides have stuck to their guns to the bitter end and the Acts in question have become law under the provisions of the Parliament Act 1911. Before the Second World War (when the Lords were more assertive) there were a number of occasions[42] on which bills were rejected by the Lords and subsequently dropped by the Government; but outright rejection of bills hardly ever occurs these days.

One recent occasion when there was a clash between the two Houses was over the House of Commons (Redistribution of Seats) Bill 1969. This bill was introduced by the Labour Government to enable them to avoid putting into effect the recommendations of the Parliamentary Boundaries Commissions on the redistribution of seats. A wrecking amendment was carried in the Lords and the Government decided to drop the bill; but this was hardly a victory for the Lords as the Government were able to find other means of attaining their object.[43] The usual outcome of these clashes, however, is that the Lords give way after they have made their protest. One recent example of this was the Southern Rhodesia (United Nations Sanctions) Order 1968, a piece of subordinate legislation which allowed the Government to extend sanctions against Rhodesia. This was rejected by the Lords in a narrow vote in June 1968 but this action had no effect because a second order was subsequently assented to by the House. In spite of this, however, their action aroused tremendous controversy and nearly resulted in the Lords losing the power to reject such legislation.[44]

The main functions of the House of Lords are concerned with work which, though it lacks the political excitement of clashes over basic policy, is nevertheless very useful and important. The most important is the job of examining and revising bills sent up from the Commons. If a bill is contentious and meets determined opposition in the Commons, the Government might have to curtail debate on it with the result that some clauses will not be considered at all. In this situation the Lords' role is especially important, but even when this is not the case there is often a need for revision.

There are various reasons why amendments are moved in the Lords. First, the Government often moves amendments: these may represent second thoughts by the Government or concessions to opposition in the Commons or outside Parliament which could not have been put into effect until the bill reached the Lords. Amendments which are consequential on earlier amendments made in the Commons, improvements in the drafting and other technical amendments are also made by the Government. Secondly, amendments may be moved by peers in order to change the way the bill will operate: these may be accepted by the Government or a compromise may be reached which will result in an amendment moved by the Government. Amendments which are not accepted by the Government are usually withdrawn, though they may be pressed to a vote and occasionally the Government is defeated. If this happens the Government has to decide whether to insist on their original policy in which case the amendment will be rejected in the Commons and the Lords will almost invariably give way; or the Government may give way or try to reach a compromise. This sort of give and take is conditioned by two factors: the Government's desire not to delay the enactment of the measure and the Lords' appreciation of the dangers involved in pushing the Government too far.

Thus in the session of 1968–9, for example, forty-six bills were sent up to the Lords from the Commons. Sixteen of these were amended by the Lords and when the amended bills went back to the Commons the amendments were accepted in ten cases and rejected in the remaining six cases. In the cases of five of these bills the Lords gave way: the sixth was the House of Commons (Redistribution of Seats) Bill.[45]

An interesting example of the way the Lords can persuade the Government to change its mind arose in connection with the Foreign Compensation Act 1969. When the bill was going through the Commons the Government added an amendment preventing the courts from reviewing any determination made by the Commission. This amendment, which was made as a result of a decision of the House of Lords in its judicial capacity,[46] was severely criticized in legal circles and when the bill reached the Lords an amendment was carried against the Government. The Government then reconsidered its position and agreed to an alternative amendment which gave a right of appeal in certain situations to the Court of Appeal.[47] In this case informed public opinion probably influenced the Government but it was the Lords who secured the change.

Quite a number of bills are introduced first in the Lords with the result that they have already been carefully examined before they come to the Commons. This procedure is often adopted in the case of less controversial Government bills such as law reform measures and consolidation bills.[48] Thus in the session of 1969–70, fifteen Government bills were introduced in the Lords and nine of these reached the statute book. In the same session forty-eight Government bills were introduced in the Commons and twenty-nine of them became law. The number of Government bills that failed to reach the statute book in this session was unusually large but the proportion introduced in the Lords (just under a quarter) was fairly typical.[49]

The House of Lords also plays an important role with regard to non-Government bills. Two questions are involved: first, the introduction of bills in the House of Lords by private peers; and secondly, the Lords' handling of private Members' bills that come up from the Commons. Recently quite a number of private peers' bills have succeeded in becoming law. In the 1969–70 session, for example, out of thirteen bills introduced by private peers, five reached the statute book. This compares with ten private Members' bills in the Commons which were successful out of a total of eighty-five.[50]

Private Members' bills that get through the Commons and are sent up to the Lords are usually treated kindly. The Lords do, of course, have much more power in regard to private Members' bills because it is unlikely that the Parliament Act procedure would be used in this case. Moreover, in view of the shortage of time for private Members' bills in the Commons, a rejection by the Lords would probably prove fatal unless the Government decided to provide time for the bill in question.

One subject on which the Lords showed themselves to be as reactionary as they are often pictured by those committed to their abolition was capital punishment.[51] The saga starts in 1947 when Sydney Silverman moved a new clause to the Government's Criminal Justice Bill to provide for the abolition of the death penalty. The Government allowed a free vote on the clause though the Home Secretary and most of the members of the Government voted against it. The clause was, however, passed and was included in the bill when it went up to the Lords. There it was rejected by a large majority. The bill was then returned to the Commons and the Government moved a compromise clause which provided that capital punishment should be retained only for certain kinds of murder. The whips were put on and the clause carried. The bill returned to the Lords but this clause too was rejected. As the end of the session was near, there was a danger that the whole bill might be lost for the session and the Government therefore advised the Commons not to insist on the clause and the bill became law without it.

In 1956 a private Member's bill to abolish hanging was again passed by the Commons and rejected in the Lords. This time the Government introduced a compromise bill (along similar lines to the clause which had been defeated before) and this was introduced into the Commons as a Government bill in the following session. It was passed by both Houses and became law as the Homicide Act 1957.

This made a distinction between two kinds of murder, capital and non-capital, and abolished hanging in the case of the latter. The complete abolition of hanging for murder only came about in 1965 when the Murder (Abolition of Hanging) Bill became law. This started off as a private Member's bill in the Commons (introduced by Sydney Silverman) but was given time by the Government. By now there was an abolitionist majority in both Houses and the bill was passed by a large majority in the Lords. The Act provided that hanging would be abolished for a trial period of five years unless a motion to make it permanent was passed by both Houses before the end of that period. Such a motion was passed in 1970.

Thus although the Lords finally came round to reform they delayed the abolition of capital punishment for eighteen years. They had previously succeeded in delaying the abolition of corporal punishment for almost as long.[52] In recent times, however, the Lords seem to have become more 'progressive' on social and moral issues than the Commons. Thus they led the way when it came to reform of the law relating to homosexuality: it was only after two bills had passed the Lords but failed to get through the Commons that the successful bill was introduced in the Commons. They were also responsible for an amendment to the Immigration Act 1971 to protect the position of Commonwealth immigrants already in the UK; and in 1973 they were the champions of free contraceptives.

Other functions of the House of Lords are private legislation[53] – about half of all private bills are introduced in the Lords and they do as much work as the Commons – and the scrutiny of subordinate legislation.[54] The Parliament Acts do not apply in either of these fields and the Lords have equal powers with the Commons. Finally, the House also tries to keep a watch on the activities of Government departments – parliamentary questions can be asked in the Lords as well as in the Commons – and debates are frequently held on Government policy as well as more general matters, such as social and cultural questions. These debates are often useful in airing issues that the Commons would not normally consider.

REFORM

Discussions about House of Lords reform are always complicated by the fact that the connection of the House with the aristocracy brings an ideological element into the debate. For this reason attitudes at the two extremes of the political spectrum are often more emotional than rational: the Left favouring the abolition of the House because it dislikes social privilege and the Right coming to the support of the House because of its traditional associations. If, however, one looks at the matter from the point of view of the requirements of an efficient system of government, it seems clear that a second chamber of some sort is desirable to fulfil the revising and scrutinizing functions at present performed by the House of Lords; but there is no necessary reason why the members of such a chamber should be peers. It is also fairly clear that the functions of such a chamber should not extend beyond this; in particular it should not be the job of the chamber to act as a check on the Government. Even if the composition of the House were reformed so that the objections considered previously no longer applied, it would still be undesirable for the second chamber to interfere in major political issues. The modern constitution is based on the political accountability of the Government to the Commons and through them to the electorate and there is no place in this process for a second chamber.

What the second chamber should do is to assist and complement the Commons by doing things which lack of time or expert knowledge might prevent the latter from doing. If it is accepted that the major *political* questions must be decided by the Commons and that the task of the second chamber lies in the less glamorous field of technical and administrative matters – the mechanics rather than the objectives of government – it follows that the powers of the second chamber should be limited. It could be argued that the House's present powers of delay and veto should be entirely abolished: the House would then be able to recommend changes in legislation but would have no means – other than that of arousing public opinion – of putting pressure on the Government to accept its proposals. This, however, would be too extreme a solution. A completely 'toothless' Upper House would not attract people of ability and if the Government were able to ignore it completely it could not fulfil its proper role. The answer is to give it sufficient powers to make the Government think again – and to give way where fundamental policies are not at stake – but not to allow it seriously to obstruct the Government's programme.

The question of composition obviously depends to a considerable extent on the powers of the chamber. If it had no powers of importance it would not matter very much how it was composed, as long as it contained enough able members to carry on its work. If, however, the House is to retain significant powers it is desirable that its composition should be reformed so that no party has a permanent majority. In fact, it might be desirable to strengthen the non-party element so that the Government of the day could never rely on an automatic majority to put its measures through. Election would not be an appropriate means of choosing the members of a reformed Upper House and some form of appointment – preferably with safe-guards to prevent excessive political partizanship – is probably the answer.

This view was not accepted when the first Parliament Act was passed in 1911 and the preamble to that Act speaks of an intention to replace the House of Lords with a popular assembly. Nothing came of this, however, and by the time the second Parliament Act was passed the idea of an elected chamber had ceased to command support. When the Act was going through Parliament in 1948 an all-party conference was held to see whether any basis for agreement could be found on the way the House should be reformed. A number of meetings were held and though the conference broke down in the end over the powers that the House should have, in particular the length of time that a bill could be delayed, preliminary agreement was reached on the following proposals.[55]

(1) The Second Chamber should be complementary to and not a rival to the Lower House, and, with this end in view, the reform of the House of Lords should be based on a modification of its existing constitution as opposed to the establishment of a Second Chamber of a completely new type based on some system of election.

(2) The revised constitution of the House of Lords should be such as to secure as far as practicable that a permanent majority is not assured for any one political party.

(3) The present right to attend and vote based solely on heredity should not by itself constitute a qualification for admission to a reformed Second Chamber.

(4) Members of the Second Chamber should be styled 'Lords of Parliament' and would be appointed on grounds of personal distinction or public service. They might be drawn either from Hereditary Peers, or from commoners who would be created Life Peers.

(5) Women should be capable of being appointed Lords of Parliament in like manner as men.

(6) Provision should be made for the inclusion in the Second Chamber of certain descendants of the Sovereign, certain Lords Spiritual and the Law Lords.

(7) In order that persons without private means should not be excluded, some remuneration would be payable to members of the Second Chamber.

(8) Peers who were not Lords of Parliament should be entitled to stand for election to the House of Commons, and also to vote at elections in the same manner as other citizens.

(9) Some provision should be made for the disqualificaton of a member of the Second Chamber who neglects, or becomes no longer able or fitted, to perform his duties as such.

These proposals show a fair measure of agreement between the parties but after the breakdown of the conference the Government made no attempt to go ahead with reform on their own.

The next twenty years saw the introduction of minor reforms – life peerages, the right to disclaim a peerage and the right of female peers to sit in the House – but it was only in 1967, when Labour was again in power, that another all-party committee was set up. This committee held a long series of meetings and it was near agreement when the Lords rejected an Order in Council to extend sanctions against Rhodesia.[56] The Government then broke off the talks and went ahead with its own plans of reform (though it is thought that they were similar to what had been agreed on in the committee). A White Paper[57] was published in November 1968 setting out the Government proposals and this was debated and approved in both Houses though, significantly, support for it was much stronger in the Lords than in the Commons. A bill[58] was introduced in the Commons in December 1968 and, though there was a three-line whip on the Government side and support from the Opposition front bench, it came under attack from the left (who thought it did not go far enough) and the right (who thought it went too far). This unusual alliance proved too much for the bill in the end, and though it passed its second reading by 285 votes to 135, it was abandoned by the Government in April 1969 in order to provide time for legislation on industrial relations.

The principles on which the bill was based were those of the 1948 agreed statement but there were a number of new ideas especially in matters of detail. Perhaps the greatest innovation was the provision that the membership of the House would be divided into two classes, voting and non-voting peers. The latter would be entitled to speak and move motions but not to vote. Succession to a peerage would cease to be a qualification for membership but as a transitional measure existing peers by succession would be qualified as non-voting peers for their lifetimes. Persons succeeding to peerages in the future would have no automatic right to membership.

Non-voting peers would consist of the existing peers by succession and those created peers who did not meet the requirements of voting membership. Voting peers would be created peers who made a declaration that they wished to be voting peers. They would be expected to attend regularly and would lose their voting rights if they failed to attend at least a third of the sittings of the House. (Ministers and certain other peers would be exempt from this requirement.) Provision was also made for a retiring age of 72 for voting peers, though this would not have taken effect immediately. The Lords Spiritual were to be progressively reduced from twenty-six to sixteen but they and the Lords of Appeal in Ordinary would be qualified to be voting peers. A peer by succession could become qualified to be a voting peer if he was given a life peerage in addition to his existing peerage and it was stated in the White Paper that this would be done in the case of quite a number of existing peers by succession so that they could continue to play a full part in the work of the House. It was the Government's intention that sufficient new life peers would be created at the beginning of each new Parliament to give the Government a majority over the Opposition parties but not over the Opposition and crossbench peers together. The White Paper spoke of paying voting peers 'at a rate which would reflect their responsibilities and duties' but the Prime Minister said in debate that this would be deferred.[59] It was also provided that the delaying powers of the House would be reduced to six months from the date when the bill was disagreed to by the Lords and that there would be no power to delay or reject subordinate legislation.

If these proposals had been put into effect the Government might have been prepared to consider procedural changes which would have allowed the Lords to take on more work. If some sort of division of labour between the two Houses could be introduced, the Commons would be freed to concentrate on those things which they alone can do and the overall efficiency of Parliament would be increased. A number of suggestions for changes of this kind which could have been considered by Parliament were put forward in the White Paper.[60] One was that non-controversial bills, such as law reform measures, which were introduced and thoroughly discussed in the Lords could either go through the Commons under a specially accelerated procedure or could be considered by a joint committee of the two Houses. A joint committee of the two Houses might also be set up to scrutinize subordinate legislation that came before Parliament and similar provisions might be made in the case of private legislation. It has even been suggested by one writer[61] that the Lords could take on the function of investigating the machinery of government and could exercise a supervisory role over administrative tribunals: it might in fact develop in some ways along the lines of the French Conseil d'Etat.

The main objection to the Labour Government's proposals was that they would have increased the powers of patronage of the Prime Minister and the Leader of the Opposition (who would have been consulted by the Prime Minister when members of the Opposition were made peers). One problem is that up to now the impetus for reform has always come from actual or threatened obstruction of Government measures by the Lords and this has not created the best atmosphere for a detached consideration of the problems involved. If the next time that reform is considered it is done in the context of a general review of procedure in both Houses with the aim of increasing the efficiency and usefulness of Parliament as a whole it might be possible to produce a viable solution.

12
Parliamentary Privilege

Parliamentary privilege is the name given to the special rights and immunities enjoyed by members of the two Houses of Parliament and to the powers and immunities of each House in its corporate capacity. The basis of parliamentary privilege is the law of Parliament, an ancient body of customary law which regulates many aspects of parliamentary activities. There are two aspects to parliamentary privilege. First, there is the power of each House to punish persons for contempt of Parliament. Any action which impedes the effectiveness of the House could constitute contempt and the House has the power to punish both its own members and any member of the public. Secondly, there are certain immunities from the ordinary law enjoyed by Members of Parliament (and by each House in its corporate capacity) which are recognized by the ordinary courts. To this extent, therefore, the law of Parliament is also administered by the ordinary courts. The purpose of these immunities is to enable Parliament to do its work more effectively.

Although the law of Parliament is common to both Houses of Parliament, the Commons and the Lords enjoy their privileges separately and each House exercises its powers to punish for contempt independently of the other. Certain differences do exist between the privileges of the two Houses but in regard to most questions they are the same and the discussion that follows will focus on the privileges of the Commons.

THE PENAL JURISDICTION OF THE HOUSE
The House uses its penal powers to punish persons whom it finds guilty of contempt of Parliament. Any action which impedes the House or its members in fulfilling their functions could be held to be

a contempt. The House is the sole judge of what is a contempt – there is no appeal from the decision of the House – and since there is no code defining what constitutes a contempt and since the House is not bound by its previous decisions, the law of contempt is rather elastic. This elasticity means that the limits of the law of contempt are uncertain but it could be defended on the ground that the House must be free to meet any new threat that might arise in the future.

The term 'breach of privilege' is often used as a synonym of 'contempt' but strictly speaking it should be reserved for those actions which are contrary to the legal immunities of M.P.s and the House.[1] Thus, bringing an action, or even threatening to bring an action, against a Member of Parliament in respect of words spoken in the course of Parliamentary proceedings, or arresting a member contrary to his immunity from civil arrest would constitute a breach of privilege. (It might also constitute a contempt if the House chose to treat it as such.) Where these legal immunities are not involved it is more accurate to speak of a contempt rather than a breach of privilege; but since the Committee of Privileges frequently uses the two terms interchangeably the distinction between them has become blurred.

The present practice in privilege cases is as follows.[2] The complaint is normally brought by an M.P. who raises the matter in the Chamber immediately before the commencement of public business. If a document is involved, for example a newspaper article, this must be produced. The Speaker then announces that he will consider whether a *prima facie* breach of privilege has been established. The Speaker considers the matter and announces his decision the following day. If he decides that there is no *prima facie* breach or that the member waited too long before raising the matter – there is a rule that a complaint must be raised at the earliest possible opportunity – it is still open to a member to place a motion on the Order Paper that the complaint be referred to the Committee of Privileges, but the motion normally has little prospect of discussion.

If the Speaker decides that a *prima facie* case has been made out, a motion relating to the case will normally take precedence over the Orders of the Day. The motion is usually moved by the Leader of the House that the matter be referred to the Committee of Privileges, though the House has the power to deal with the matter directly. The Committee of Privileges is a committee of the House appointed at the beginning of each session. It consists of fifteen experienced

M.P.s and the chairman is normally a member of the Government. It does not consist entirely of lawyers but it is customary for one of the law officers to sit on it.

The committee has power to summon witnesses and it hears evidence on the facts of the case. The accused is usually allowed to speak in his defence – though he has no right to this[3] – but he is usually not allowed to be represented by counsel. The committee then decides whether a breach of privilege has been established and reports its opinion to the House. The House is not obliged to accept the report of the committee and in one recent case it did not do so.[4] If the House decides that a breach was committed it then decides on the punishment.

The punishments that can be imposed are as follows.[5] First, the House has the power to imprison the person concerned. The person is detained in the custody of the Serjeant-at-Arms or sent to one of H.M.'s prisons. The House does not imprison for any specified length of time – the Commons probably does not have this power[6] – but the person is kept in prison until the House decides to release him. He must be released when the parliamentary session is over but the House can, if it wishes, commit him again to prison when the new session begins.

The House of Commons – unlike the House of Lords[7] – has no power to impose a fine and the only other punishment that can be imposed on members of the public is an admonishment or reprimand. When this is done the person concerned is summoned to the Bar of the House (he no longer has to kneel) and is reprimanded by the Speaker. If the person is a member of the House, two additional punishments are available: suspension from the House for a certain period of time and expulsion. If a member is expelled a by-election is held, but there is nothing to prevent him from standing again and taking his seat in the House if elected.[8]

It will be seen from this that the House has quite formidable powers for dealing with those whom it finds guilty of contempt; but in practice these powers are rarely used, at least in relation to outsiders. Thus the last time that anyone was imprisoned by the House (except for imprisonment overnight in the custody of the Serjeant-at-Arms) was in 1880.[9] Only two outsiders – both newspaper editors – have been reprimanded since the beginning of the century.[10] In fact the only punishments of significance imposed by the House are on its own members and there have been occasions fairly recently on which members have been expelled.[11] In the great majority of cases, however, the House is prepared to accept the apology of the person concerned and then to regard the matter as closed. If it had not been for this, the House might have been forced by now to give up its powers.

In 1966 the Select Committee on Parliamentary Privilege was set up by the House to review the law and procedure relating to privilege and to consider whether any changes should be made. A number of criticisms were made against the present procedure. It was suggested by some that the penal power of the House should be transferred to the courts or some other body – it was felt that under the present procedure the House was a judge in its own cause – but this was rejected by the committee.[12] The committee did, however, make a number of recommendations for reform but so far most of them have not been adopted.[13]

It has already been pointed out that there is no code specifying what constitutes a contempt of Parliament; consequently the House is free to punish any activity which, in its view, impedes its work. Usually, however, the House follows its previous practice in deciding what is a contempt and it is therefore possible to give a general outline of the sort of conduct that is likely to incur the displeasure of the House.[14]

Fairly obvious examples of contempt would be if the proceedings of the House were disrupted (by a Member or by an outsider), if the rules and orders of the House were disobeyed or if a witness refused to give evidence before a committee of the House. A Member who deliberately misled the House[15] or who was guilty of serious misconduct in debate might also be punished.

An offer of money or other advantage to an M.P. to promote some matter in the House is a contempt under a Resolution of 2 May 1695.[16] If the Member accepts the offer he would also be guilty of contempt. There are, however, various roundabout ways of offering an inducement which pressure groups commonly use with apparent immunity. Donations to an M.P.'s constituency party, free trips to foreign countries (dressed up as 'fact-finding' visits), consultancy fees (paid, for example, by public relations firms), directorships of companies, and sponsorship[17] by trade unions are all quite common and regarded as legitimate so long as the pressure group makes no overt attempt to use the relationship as a lever to influence the M.P.[18]

An attempt to intimidate an M.P. with regard to his activities in the House could also be a contempt. Most examples of this, however, have been extremely trivial and suggest a rather petty mentality. For example, in 1935 the House held[19] that a letter sent to M.P.s by the League for the Prohibition of Cruel Sports was a contempt because, after asking the M.P.s for their views on blood sports, it concluded: 'If we do not hear from you, we shall feel justified in letting your constituents know that you have no objection to cruel sports'. In another case in 1946[20] a political group put up posters in London saying: 'Names of M.P.s voting for bread rationing in the Commons on Thursday will be published here as public enemies and dictators'. This was also held to be a contempt. No punishment was imposed in either case but nevertheless it seems incredible that a group of supposedly thick-skinned politicians could feel threatened by tactics of this sort.

Public statements that undermine the dignity and prestige of Parliament have also on occasion been treated as contempts. Most of the cases in this category are even more petty than those mentioned previously; for example, when petrol was rationed in 1956 (at the time of Suez) the *Sunday Express* published an article suggesting that M.P.s had failed, out of self-interest, to protest against the rather large supplementary allowances of petrol that they had been given. This was held to be a contempt and the editor was summoned before the bar of the House to express his apologies.[21] A cartoon on similar lines published in the *Evening News* at about the same time was also held to be a contempt.[22] These cases suggest that some M.P.s are excessively sensitive to criticism. The use of the penal powers of the House in situations of this kind is fairly rare; were this not so, contempt of Parliament could be a serious threat to the freedom of the press.[23]

THE RIGHTS AND IMMUNITIES OF INDIVIDUAL MEMBERS

The most important privilege enjoyed by individual Members is that of free speech in Parliament. This is protected by an immunity from legal liability on account of anything said or done in the course of parliamentary proceedings and is necessary if Parliament is to function effectively. Although the history of this privilege goes back at least as far as the reign of Richard II,[24] the starting point for any modern discussion must be Article 9 of the Bill of Rights 1689.[25] This reads:

That the freedom of speech and debates or proceedings in Parliament ought not to be impeached or questioned in any court or place out of Parliament.

Thus no Member can be sued for defamation on account of anything said in debates nor can such words form the basis of any criminal charge such as sedition or a breach of the Official Secrets Acts.[26] Evidence cannot even be brought in court proceedings of anything taking place in the House without the consent of the House[27] and it is also probable that executive action, such as internment in time of war, on account of words spoken in proceedings in the House would be a breach of privilege.[28]

Legal proceedings in breach of this immunity would be stopped by the courts as soon as the position was realized – normally the writ would be struck out as disclosing no cause of action – but on some occasions the House has not waited for this to happen and has threatened to use its penal powers against the person bringing the action.

Although Members are immune from actions in the courts, there is nothing to prevent the House itself from punishing a Member on account of words spoken in debate and if a Member abused his privilege of free speech by making an unjustified attack on anyone the House would punish him for contempt by suspending or even expelling him from the House.[29] Thus, though the citizen is prevented from going to court, he can look to the House for redress if he is defamed.

Since the scope of the privilege is limited to things done in the course of 'proceedings in Parliament', it is important to define what exactly is covered by this phrase. In general it includes 'everything said or done by a Member in the exercise of his functions as a Member in a committee of either House, as well as everything said or done in either House in the transaction of Parliamentary business'.[30] Asking a question in Parliament and giving notice of such a question would be covered[31] and, since the protection applies to actions as well as words, it also covers voting, giving notice of a motion and presenting a petition or a report of a committee. Moreover, the protection is not limited to Members: officers of the House carrying out the orders of the House and members of the public giving evidence before a committee would also be protected.[32]

Not everything, however, which takes place within the precincts of the House forms part of the proceedings. For example, a private conversation between two Members – even if it took place in the chamber during a debate – would not normally be privileged[33] and it has also been held that a letter posted within the precincts of the House by a member of the public to an M.P. is not privileged.[34]

Generally speaking, privilege does not apply to things which take place outside the House, but there may be exceptions to this. Thus it has been said:[35]

Cases may, however, easily be imagined of communications between one member and another, or between a member and a minister, so closely related to some matter pending in, or expected to be brought before, the House, that though they do not take place in the chamber or a committee room they form part of the business of the House, as, for example, where a member sends to a Minister the draft of a question he is thinking of putting down or shows it to another member with a view to obtaining advice as to the propriety of putting it down or as to the manner in which it should be framed.

Such matters may well be included within the concept of proceedings in Parliament.

In *ex parte Wason*[36] it was held that a charge against two peers and the Lord Chief Baron of conspiring to pervert the course of justice by making false statements in proceedings on a petition in the House of Lords was a charge which could not be maintained in a court of law. Thus, since the conspiracy could have taken place outside the House, it seems that an agreement outside the House to do something in the course of proceedings in the House cannot be the subject of criminal proceedings.

In the London Electricity Board Case[37] it was held by the House, rejecting the view of the Committee of Privileges, that a letter written by an M.P. to a Minister criticizing the activities of a nationalized industry was not a proceeding in Parliament. This decision could be criticized on the ground that a letter to a Minister is often used as a substitute for a parliamentary question and, since the latter is a proceeding in Parliament, it is anomalous that the former is not also protected.[38] It is, however, necessary to draw a line somewhere and even if the letter is not protected by absolute privilege it is probably protected by qualified privilege.[39]

Just because words spoken in parliamentary proceedings are privileged it does not follow that publication of debates outside the House is protected.[40] If the whole debate is published, qualified privilege attaches to it, not by privilege of Parliament, but by analogy with the rule protecting the publication of judicial proceedings[41] (in both cases it is in the public interest that publication should take place). Qualified privilege will also attach to selective reporting of parliamentary proceedings so long as it is fair and accurate.[42] It does not matter that the speaker in Parliament was malicious so long as the reporter was not. This rule is important because it is unlikely that many papers would report parliamentary proceedings unless they could be selective.[43]

Papers published by order of, or under the authority of, either House are protected under the provisions of the Parliamentary Papers Act 1840 (passed as a result of the decision in *Stockdale* v. *Hansard*).[44] This also gives protection to anyone who publishes a copy of such a paper. The publisher of an extract or abstract of a parliamentary paper is protected if he can prove that he acted *bona fide* and without malice.

Freedom of speech is indirectly protected by the power of the House to exclude the public from its proceedings and to prohibit the publication of debates. In the eighteenth century the House passed a number of resolutions prohibiting any publication of debates.[45] These resolutions have long been a dead letter and in 1971 the House formally declared that reporting the proceedings of the House and its committees is not a breach of privilege except where the proceedings are conducted with closed doors or where publication is expressly forbidden.[46] Publication in these circumstances could be punished as contempt of Parliament and the House's penal powers could also be used against anyone who published a deliberately misleading report.

Freedom of speech is not the only immunity enjoyed by members of Parliament. Freedom from civil arrest is also a parliamentary privilege though it has lost most of its importance since the abolition of imprisonment for debt. The justification for this privilege was that the House was entitled to the first claim on the services of its members and for this reason the privilege only applies when the House is in session and for forty days before and after each session, a period originally required for travel to and from Parliament.[47] The privilege does not apply to arrest on any criminal charge (though it is customary to inform the Speaker when this occurs) and it also does not apply to internment by the Government under emergency legislation[48] (though in some circumstances this might be the most vital immunity of all for Members of Parliament to possess).

In the case of arrest for contempt of court the immunity applies in the case of civil contempt but not in the case of criminal contempt.[49] In a recent case[50] the wife of a peer applied for a writ of attachment against her husband for contempt of court for failure to comply with a Registrar's Order under the Married Women's Property Act 1882 to give her certain items of property; this was held to be civil contempt and the husband's claim to privilege was upheld.

It seems hard to justify the continued existence of this privilege today. It is not necessary for the functioning of the House and it can hinder private citizens who are trying to enforce their rights against M.P.s. The Select Committee on Parliamentary Privilege recommended that legislation be brought in to abolish it[51] but so far nothing has been done to implement this.

PRIVILEGES OF THE HOUSE IN ITS CORPORATE CAPACITY

There are a number[52] of privileges enjoyed by the House in its corporate capacity; but the most important is the right of the House to have control over its own composition and proceedings. The courts recognize that the jurisdiction of the House in these matters is exclusive and they will refuse to consider any case in which such issues are raised. This immunity from the jurisdiction of the courts is important from the constitutional point of view and is one of the factors which preclude the courts in Britain from playing a very active role in constitutional questions.[53]

The right of the House to control its own composition is the basis of the House's power to expel its members. This power is used when someone is considered unfit to be a member and is normally restricted to the cases where a member has been convicted of a serious crime or has committed a gross contempt on the House; but if, for example, the Government were to use its majority in the House to put through a resolution expelling all the members of the Opposition, the courts would be powerless to intervene. The power of the House to decide disputed election returns has now been given to the courts[54] but the House still decides whether a member has become disqualified by virtue of circumstances which have arisen since his election.[55]

The case which illustrates most vividly the reluctance of the courts to interfere in the affairs of Parliament is *Bradlaugh* v. *Gossett*.[56] Bradlaugh was elected as Member of Parliament for Northampton in

1880 but was not allowed by the House to take the oath of allegiance because he was an atheist. Under the Parliamentary Oaths Act 1866, if a member sat or voted in the House without taking the oath[57] he was liable to a penalty and his seat was vacated as if he were dead. Bradlaugh lost his seat under this provision but was re-elected by his constituents. During the next four years he was twice expelled from the House and re-elected each time. Finally the House passed a resolution directing the Serjeant-at-Arms to exclude him from the House until he undertook not to disturb its proceedings. Bradlaugh then applied to court for a declaration that the resolution was invalid and for an injunction to prevent the Serjeant-at-Arms barring him from the chamber.

The court, however, was unable to grant him a remedy since the matter was outside their jurisdiction. 'If injustice has been done', said Lord Coleridge C. J.,[58] 'it is injustice for which the Courts of law afford no remedy.' This was true even though the case turned on the interpretation of a statute, the Parliamentary Oaths Act. The reason for this was given by Stephen J.:[59] 'the House of Commons has the exclusive power of interpreting the statute, so far as the regulation of its own proceedings within its own walls is concerned . . . even if that interpretation should be erroneous, this Court has no power to interfere with it directly or indirectly.'[60]

Besides having the power to control its own composition the House also has the power to regulate its own procedure. It lays down its own rules of procedure but it is not responsible to any external authority for following the rules it lays down. This is shown by the case of *Edinburgh and Dalkeith Railway* v. *Wauchope*[61] in which Wauchope argued that he was not bound by a private Act of Parliament because he had not been given proper notice of it as required by the Standing Orders of the House. This argument was rejected by the court. Lord Campbell said:[62]

All that a Court of Justice can do is look to the Parliamentary roll; if from that it should appear that a bill has passed both Houses and received the Royal assent, no Court of Justice can inquire into the mode in which it was introduced into Parliament, nor into what was done previous to its introduction, or what passed in Parliament during its progress in its various stages through both Houses.

Since, however, the exclusive jurisdiction of the House is limited to matters which form part of its proceedings, anything which is not part of those proceedings can be dealt with by the courts. This distinction is applicable in the case of crimes committed within the precincts of the House.[63] If the criminal act is part of the proceedings in the House, for example a speech in debate which is alleged to be seditious, the jurisdiction of the courts would be excluded; but if it is not part of the proceedings then the courts can try the case. Thus in 1970 when a member of the public threw a canister of CS gas into the chamber from the strangers' gallery, he was tried in the ordinary courts. Since, however, an act such as this would also be a contempt of Parliament (because it disrupts proceedings in the House), the House would probably have had concurrent jurisdiction.

PARLIAMENT AND THE COURTS

The question which must now be considered is this: which body has ultimate jurisdiction over matters of parliamentary privilege – the courts or the two Houses of Parliament? There is no doubt that parliamentary privilege depends on an objective and knowable body of law – the law of Parliament – and not on the arbitrary assertion of either House. It is also accepted that neither House can create new privileges by resolution: only an Act of Parliament can do this. But when it comes to interpreting and applying the law of Parliament in a particular case, who is to be the ultimate judge?

This problem could arise whenever a member or officer of the House raises a question of privilege outside the House. Normally in this situation the courts would decide whether the claim was justified and give judgment accordingly. But in some cases in which the law was unclear it is possible that the courts might give a different decision from that which the House would have given if the case had come before them. In these circumstances the House might expect the court to accept their interpretation of the law and might try to use their penal powers to impose their view. This is possible because the House has always regarded a denial of parliamentary privilege by any person as being a contempt; consequently if a litigant and his advisers insist on asking the courts for a ruling on a matter on which the House has itself pronounced, they run the risk of being punished for contempt of Parliament. In one very old case, in fact, the Commons went so far as to imprison two judges for contempt because they refused to accept the Commons' view on a matter of privilege.[64]

The best illustration of these problems is the series of events concerning Stockdale, Hansard and the Sheriff of Middlesex. Stockdale was the publisher of a book on anatomy which contained illustrations of human sex organs. Apparently it circulated among the prisoners at Newgate gaol and the Inspectors of Prisons in a Report published in 1836 described it as being 'of the most disgusting nature' and stated that the plates were 'obscene and indecent in the extreme'. The Report was published by Messrs Hansard, the printers of the House of Commons, by order of the House. Stockdale took exception to the description of his book and brought an action for libel against Hansard in 1836.[65] Hansard raised two defences: first, that the statements concerned were true; and secondly, that, as the Report was published by order of the House, it was protected by parliamentary privilege. The jury found for Hansard on the first point and the action consequently failed; but the judge, Lord Denman C. J., made comments indicating that he did not accept the validity of the second point.

As a result of these proceedings a parliamentary committee was set up to consider the legal position regarding papers published by order of the House and, after it had reported, the House expressed its view on the matter in the following resolutions, which were passed on 31 May 1837:[66]

That the power of publishing such of its Reports, Votes, and Proceedings as it shall deem necessary or conducive to the public interests, is an essential incident to the constitutional functions of Parliament . . .

That by the law and privilege of Parliament, this House has the sole and exclusive jurisdiction to determine upon the existence and extent of its privileges; and that the institution or prosecution of any action, suit or other proceedings, for the purpose of bringing them into discussion or decision before any court or tribunal elsewhere than in Parliament, is a high breach of such privilege, and renders all parties concerned therein amenable to its just displeasure, and to the punishment consequent thereon . . .

That for any court or tribunal to assume to decide upon matters of Privilege inconsistent with the determination of either House of Parliament thereon, is contrary to the law of Parliament, and is a breach and contempt of the Privileges of Parliament.

This assertion by the House of its claims was unequivocal and it was not long before the challenge was taken up.

Shortly after the publication of the first Report, Hansard published a second document which contained the reply of the Inspectors

to criticisms of their original Report and this repeated the statements about Stockdale's book. Stockdale therefore brought a second
action in 1837.[67] The House of Commons instructed Hansard to
defend the action solely on the ground of privilege and not to raise
the defence which had succeeded in the previous action. This time
Stockdale won the action. The court held that the House was not the
sole judge of its own privileges; that the court was not bound to
follow the House's view of the law; and that papers published by
order of Parliament were not privileged. Damages were assessed at
£100 and this sum was paid to Stockdale.

The matter did not end there, however, because Stockdale soon
began a third action against Hansard for further publication of the
alleged libel. This time the House instructed Hansard not to defend
the case and damages were assessed at £600 against him. The judgment was enforced by the Sheriff of Middlesex (an office which was
actually held by two men) who levied execution on Hansard's goods
to satisfy the judgment. However, the sheriffs, perhaps uneasy about
what the House might do, did not hand over the money to Stockdale.
Stockdale then applied to court for an order that the sheriffs pay
him the money; but before this application was heard the Commons
summoned the sheriffs and, when they refused to return the money,
resolved that they be committed for contempt. The Speaker then
signed a warrant that they be taken into the custody of the Serjeant-
at-Arms.

When the court heard Stockdale's application, the sheriffs were
already in custody. The sheriffs were in an impossible position: if
they wished to obtain their release from imprisonment by the
Commons they would have to return the money to Hansard; but if
they did not pay it over to Stockdale they would be imprisoned by
the court for contempt. In spite of this the court granted Stockdale's
application and ordered the sheriffs to pay over the money.[68]

Meanwhile attempts were made to secure the release of the sheriffs
and an application for a writ of habeas corpus was brought before the
court.[69] In his return to the writ, the Serjeant-at-Arms, who had the
custody of the sheriffs, stated that he held the men by virtue of a
warrant of the Speaker which stated that they were 'guilty of a contempt and breach of the privileges of this House'. Lord Denman
C. J., who had given judgment in all the previous cases, held that the
sheriffs were not entitled to be released. He stated that when
persons were committed to prison by order of the House, the court

could judge whether the committal was justified only if the grounds for the committal were expressly stated in the warrant. If, as was the case here, no specific ground was stated, the court had no power to go behind the warrant and had to accept the decision of the House.[70] This was indeed a remarkable judgment since the ground of committal was, as the court knew perfectly well, that the sheriffs had carried out the orders of the court.

The result of these proceedings was deadlock,[71] which was eventually broken by Parliament passing a statute, the Parliamentary Papers Act 1840, which conferred privilege on papers published by order of either House. Thus, although the specific point at issue – whether parliamentary papers are privileged – was finally settled in favour of Parliament, the vital question of jurisdiction was never resolved. To this day, therefore, there are two views on this question. The Commons have never withdrawn the resolutions of 31 May 1837 that the ultimate jurisdiction lies with them and the courts have maintained their view that if an issue of privilege is raised in proceedings before them, they have the power and the duty to decide the matter independently of Parliament. That this is still the view of the courts is illustrated by the following extract from the judgment of Scarman J. in 1963 in *Stourton* v. *Stourton*,[72] the case mentioned previously in which a peer claimed the privilege of immunity from civil arrest before the courts:

I do not think, however, that I, sitting in the High Court of Justice, must necessarily take the law that I have to apply from what would be the practice of the House. I think I have to look to the common law as deduced in judicial decisions in order to determine in the particular case whether the privilege arises and, if so, its scope and effect . . .

Thus, though both sides have in recent years taken care to avoid a clash, the basic difference remains and a new clash could, in theory at least, occur at any time.

The possibility of such a clash arose when the London Electricity Board case came before the Commons in 1957.[73] This case concerned an M.P. who had written a letter to a Minister criticizing certain actions taken by the London Electricity Board. The Minister had passed the letter on to the board and they wrote to the M.P. threatening to sue him for libel on account of statements contained in the letter. The M.P. considered that the letter was a proceeding in Parliament and was consequently protected by privilege but, instead of waiting until the action was brought and claiming privilege before the courts, he instead raised the matter in the House. His claim was considered by the Committee of Privileges which reported, first, that the letter was a proceeding in Parliament and, secondly, that the action of the board in threatening to sue the M.P. for libel was a breach of privilege. As it happened the Commons rejected the Committee's Report on the ground that the letter was not a proceeding in Parliament, and the board did not proceed with their action. The whole affair, therefore, ended quietly; but if the House had accepted the Report and if the board had continued with their action, the courts and the House could have been in conflict again.[74]

It is important, however, not to ignore the large area of agreement which does exist between the courts and the Commons. First, the courts recognize the exclusive jurisdiction of the House in matters concerning its composition and internal proceedings. The only difficulty here, however, is that the courts would probably claim the right to decide when a matter concerned the internal proceedings of the House and thus fell within that exclusive jurisdiction. Secondly, the courts recognize the power of the Commons to summon persons before them and, if necessary, imprison them for contempt. As we have seen, the courts will not inquire into the ground on which they were found guilty of contempt, provided it is not stated in the warrant. It is, however, possible that there might be a dispute about the extent of this power and in such a situation the courts would probably claim the right to decide the matter for themselves. The House, on the other hand, does not in theory concede any jurisdiction to the courts but in practice it is often prepared to accept their decision. For these reasons, therefore, it is extremely unlikely that a new trial of strength will take place between the courts and the Commons.

13
Politics and the Mass Media

Politics is impossible without communication – persuading, convincing and bargaining with people – and mass democratic politics is impossible without mass communication. Today the main media of mass communication are the written word and broadcasting, and of these the press and television are the most important. Older forms of political communication such as public meetings and mass rallies are today often more useful as a means of obtaining press and TV publicity than as a means of direct communication with those present.

There are, of course, significant differences between newspapers and television. The visual presentation of events has greater emotional impact and television is able to bring home to the public the realities of foreign wars and domestic disaster in a way that the press could never do. It also provides a very effective medium for politicians to put across their personalities to the public in order to win the loyalty and confidence of the electorate. Newspapers, on the other hand, can provide a more detailed coverage of events and, because they owe no duty to be politically impartial, they can use more controversial material. Corruption or inefficiency in public bodies, scandals involving prominent politicians, in-fighting among opposition leaders, or the failure of Government policies – all these can be exposed in the press with considerable effect. Sometimes a single newspaper can influence Government policy by discovering and publishing facts which embarrass or discredit the Government – for example the publicity given in *The Sunday Times* in 1971 to the maltreatment of internees in Northern Ireland. The mass media, therefore, have an important role to play in the political system and the laws and practices governing their operation are of direct interest to constitutional lawyers.

TELEVISION

Television in Britain is controlled by the British Broadcasting Corporation and the Independent Broadcasting Authority. The BBC is a public corporation established by Royal Charter in 1926[1] and headed by a Board of Governors who are appointed and dismissable by the Crown on the advice of the Prime Minister.[2] It is a non-profitmaking body financed by a grant from Parliament equal to the net revenue from licence fees and is not permitted to broadcast paid advertisements or sponsored programmes without the consent of the Minister of Posts and Telecommunications.[3] The BBC has a broadcasting licence[4] under the Wireless Telegraphy Act 1949 and this contains important limitations on what may be broadcast. The Corporation is legally obliged to observe these conditions and those in its Charter: failure to do so could result in the revocation of the Charter.[5]

The Independent Broadcasting Authority was established by statute in 1954,[6] and is now governed by the Independent Broadcasting Authority Act 1973. The members of the Authority are appointed and dismissable by the Minister for Posts and Telecommunications.[7] The Authority does not make the programmes itself: it provides the equipment and contracts out the right to produce programmes to the programme companies (Granada, Thames, etc.), which obtain their revenue from the sale of advertising time. The IBA also has a broadcasting licence from the Minister but, unlike the BBC's licence, it does not contain any restrictions on the programmes that may be broadcast. Such restrictions are, however, contained in the Act.

Under its licence agreement the BBC is required to broadcast an impartial account of proceedings each day in Parliament[8] and to broadcast Government announcements when asked to do so by a Minister.[9] The Licence agreement also gives the Minister of Posts and Telecommunications the power to order the Corporation not to broadcast any material or class of material specified by him in a written notice, but if this is done the Corporation has the right to announce that such a ban has been imposed.[10] This is, of course, a very wide power and could be used to ban programmes or topics which were harmful to the Government. In fact, it has not been used in this way and only a small number of fairly general directives have been made under it.[11]

In 1927 the Corporation was directed not to broadcast its own opinion on current affairs or matters of public policy and in 1955 another directive was made prohibiting it from transmitting party political broadcasts except those arranged by the Corporation in agreement with the leading political parties.[12] In 1955 a directive was made prohibiting the Corporation from making broadcasts about matters which were to be debated in Parliament within fourteen days of the broadcast, but this gave rise to strong criticism and was withdrawn after the BBC had undertaken not to do anything which would derogate from the primacy of Parliament as the forum for debating the affairs of the nation.[13] It should finally be mentioned that the licence agreement gives the Minister the power to take over the Corporation if in his opinion an emergency has arisen in which it is expedient in the public interest that this be done.[14] This power has never been used, though it has been said that during the Suez crisis in 1956 the Prime Minister, Sir Anthony Eden, contemplated such a takeover.[15]

The restrictions on the IBA are of a similar kind. The Authority must satisfy themselves that nothing is included in any programme which is likely to encourage crime, to lead to disorder or to be offensive to public feelings.[16] Sufficient time must be given to news and current affairs and all news must be given with accuracy and impartiality. Due impartiality must be preserved in programmes dealing with politics, industrial disputes or current public policy,[17] and the Authority must not give its own opinion on these matters. In applying the rule concerning impartiality, however, a series of programmes may be considered as a whole and a later programme can 'balance' an earlier one. Subliminal broadcasting is prohibited.[18] As in the case of the BBC, the IBA is required to broadcast Government announcements, and there is also provision for the Minister to prohibit the Authority from broadcasting anything specified in his notice.[19] Finally, advertisements cannot be broadcast if they relate to religion, politics or an industrial dispute.[20] As a result of this, the Authority have refused advertisements for the *Morning Star*, and in 1971 they rejected a series of advertisements in favour of the Common Market.[21]

Although the powers which the Government has over the two corporations are potentially very extensive, it is generally accepted

that they will not be used for party political advantage. The relationship between the Government and the corporations was described as
follows in a White Paper on broadcasting in 1966:[22]

Both the BBC and ITA [now the IBA] are public corporations, wholly
responsible for the content of their programmes, and for the day-to-day
conduct of their affairs. The principle that the public corporations should
be independent of the Government has been upheld by successive
Administrations since the beginning of broadcasting in the United Kingdom.

In spite of this tradition of independence, however, there is some
evidence that Government pressure has been brought from time to
time on the corporations to refrain from broadcasting certain items.[23]

The political broadcasting of the corporations falls into three
categories: party political broadcasts, Ministerial broadcasts, and
regular programmes on political topics. Party political broadcasts
are broadcasts produced by a political party and transmitted (free of
charge) by the BBC and IBA. They are, in effect, 'plugs' for the
party concerned and, since political advertising is forbidden on
television, they constitute the only means available to the parties of
putting across their policies on television in programmes under their
own control. The arrangements for these broadcasts – including the
amount of time allocated to each party – are made by a committee
consisting of representatives of the BBC and IBA on the one hand
and of the parties on the other. Only the Conservative, Labour and
Liberal parties are represented, however. Plaid Cymru and the
Scottish National party once applied for membership but were
refused.[24]

Party political broadcasts are, of course, much more numerous
during a general election campaign than otherwise and the basis for
apportioning the broadcasts between the parties is also different.
Between elections the proportion of votes gained at the previous
general election is taken as the basis for allocating broadcasts but
during an election the number of candidates nominated is used.
During the 1970 general election the Conservative and Labour
parties were each given five broadcasts lasting ten minutes and the
Liberals were given three. Plaid Cymru and the Scottish National
party were each given one five-minute broadcast which was transmitted only in Wales and Scotland respectively. There was also a
rule that any party nominating at least fifty candidates on a national
basis would be given one five-minute broadcast at a national level.

Only the Communist party qualified under this. The non-election broadcasts during 1970 were allocated as follows: the Conservatives and Labour each got two broadcasts of fifteen minutes and three of ten minutes; the Liberals had two ten-minute broadcasts and the SNP and Plaid Cymru were each given one five-minute broadcast transmitted locally.[25]

This system has been attacked by the smaller parties as being unfair to them. They accuse the big parties of carving up the time among themselves and it could be argued that the small parties do not have a fair chance of attracting greater support if they are given so little time on television. However, the present system used between elections – based on the proportion of *votes* gained at the previous election – is more advantageous to small parties than would be a system based on the proportion of *seats* they gained; and it is hard to see what other basis could be used for allocating election broadcasts. Whether it is desirable to have party political broadcasts at all is, of course, another question. Here the interests of the parties and the viewers may conflict: the parties are generally in favour of the present system but it is doubtful whether it produces very good television.

Ministerial broadcasts are made on the basis of an *aide-mémoire* agreed to by the BBC and the two big parties on 3 April 1969.[26] These broadcasts fall into two categories: first, there are broadcasts which Ministers wish to make in order to explain legislation or administrative policies approved by Parliament or to seek the co-operation of the public in matters where there is a general consensus of opinion. In these circumstances there is no right of reply for the Opposition. The second category concerns broadcasts in which the Prime Minister or a senior Minister comments on recent events of prime importance. The Opposition does have a right of reply to these broadcasts and there is normally a third programme in which a discussion takes place between spokesmen for the Government, the Opposition and the Liberals.

The most important kind of political broadcasting is, of course, the ordinary programmes broadcast by the BBC and IBA. These may consist of interviews with political figures, discussions, or reports on current affairs. They probably have much more impact on viewers than the broadcasts made by the parties, partly because there is a tendency to discount party political broadcasts as propaganda, and partly because many politicians come across much better when facing an independent interviewer than in the artificial atmosphere of a scripted production.

In order to make good political programmes the producers must have the freedom to be controversial, but the power of television is so immense that it would be intolerable if that freedom were not exercised in a responsible way. The various instances in which claims have been made that controversial programmes were suppressed or cut because they offended vested interests can be matched by cases in which individuals or institutions have felt that they were treated unfairly by television producers. The furore caused in 1971 by a BBC programme on the Labour leadership entitled 'Yesterday's Men', in which the participants were said to have been induced to take part by misleading statements on the nature of the programme, gave rise to demands for a broadcasting council to be set up to hear complaints against the BBC. It was felt to be wrong for the Governors to have the dual function of overseeing the management of the Corporation and investigating complaints. The Government declined to act but the BBC itself decided to set up an independent Programmes Complaints Commission under the chairmanship of Lord Parker, the former Lord Chief Justice. The function of the Commission is to consider cases where the complainant has already made use of the BBC's own complaints procedure but is dissatisfied with the result. The Commission considers complaints by individuals and organizations who feel that they have been treated unfairly. This covers unwarranted invasion of privacy and misrepresentation but not questions of taste or of general broadcasting policy. The Commission have no punitive powers and any action taken if they decide a complaint is justified depends on the BBC. Publicity is, however, given to their findings.[27]

Television is a new phenomenon of immense social importance and it is not easy to discover the most appropriate legal and political framework for its operation. The main alternatives to the British system are to hand television completely over to private enterprise (as in America) or to have it directly controlled by the State (as in France). Neither of these seems satisfactory: complete commercial control generally results in low quality programmes and direct State control can easily reduce the television service to an organ of Government propaganda. It therefore seems likely that British television will continue to be in the hands of public corporations but there may be changes in the powers and responsibili-

ties of the corporations. In particular, more effective machinery
for dealing with complaints may be set up.

THE PRESS

Two institutions of importance for political journalism are the Press
Gallery and the Lobby in the House of Commons.[28] The members of
the Press Gallery are the parliamentary reporters who report debates
in the House. In addition to the seats in the Press Gallery parliamentary reporters are also given the use of writing rooms and a
restaurant. In this way the House recognizes the importance of the
reporters' work in bringing the activities of the House to the attention of the public. The heyday of the parliamentary reporters was,
however, in the nineteenth century; today the focus of politics has
moved away from Parliament, and proceedings in the House no
longer attract such great interest.

The work of the Lobby correspondents is more important. They
also frequent the Palace of Westminster but they are concerned with
what happens behind the scenes rather than on the floor of the
House. They derive their name from the fact that they have the
privilege of going into the Members' Lobby just outside the Chamber (members of the public are only allowed to enter the Central
Lobby of the House) and this is a convenient place to meet Ministers
and other M.P.s as they enter and leave the Chamber. The select
group of journalists who are entitled to this privilege are those whose
names appear on the Lobby List, which is drawn up by the Serjeant-
at-Arms under the authority of the Speaker. This list is made up of
representatives from the national daily and Sunday papers, news
agencies, provincial dailies, BBC and ITN. It contains over a
hundred names. Journalists from overseas papers and from the
weeklies are excluded. Lobby members are given briefings twice a
day by members of the Prime Minister's press staff and they also
have access to briefings by the Leader of the House, the Leader of
the Opposition and Ministers. Another privilege is that they are
given copies of Government documents before publication, though
they are not allowed to refer to them until they are officially published.

The Lobby has an elected committee which organizes the Lobby
meetings and other activities of the Lobby. It also drafts the rules of
the Lobby. These are contained in a booklet entitled *Lobby Practice*,
which is given to each new Lobby man when he is admitted. These

rules were secret until recently but they have now been published.[29] The most important principles governing the Lobby are that information which is given by a Minister, M.P., civil servant or party organizer 'on Lobby terms' can be used by the Lobby men only if the source is not revealed. Thus when the story appears in a newspaper it will be attributed to 'usually well-informed circles', 'sources close to the Government' or some other circumlocution. Never will it be said that X, the Minister for so-and-so, said it. The second rule is that if information is said to be 'off the record' it may not be used directly at all. It is, however, valuable as background information which may indicate general trends.

The relationship between politicians and political journalists is beneficial to both sides: the journalist gets inside information and the politician gets the publicity he wants. A deliberate leak may be used by the Government to test public opinion or prepare the public for a new development, while individual politicians may use it as a weapon in internal party disputes. The relationship can only exist, however, as long as the journalist keeps to the rules: if he does not, he will find that no more information is given to him. One occasion when this happened was in 1965 when *The Sunday Times* appointed Mr Anthony Howard as their 'Whitehall correspondent'.[30] Howard's job was to reveal the inside workings of the civil service and in his first article he discussed policy clashes inside Whitehall, naming the civil servants involved and revealing the policies they were advocating. This conflicted with the convention of Ministerial responsibility – that the Minister in charge of the department takes the blame for failures and the credit for successes in his department – and would have threatened the anonymity and political impartiality of the civil service. Apparently, the matter was discussed in Cabinet and all members of the Government were instructed to refuse to give interviews to Howard. A Whitehall circular was also sent out instructing civil servants that he was not to be spoken to. The result was that *The Sunday Times* decided to drop the idea and Howard went to America to become the Washington correspondent of *The Observer*.[31]

The withholding of information is one weapon the Government has to discipline journalists who step out of line. On other occasions an informal approach may be made to the proprietor of the paper. In some circumstances the threat of an action for libel may be effective in silencing the press. This can be used if the press is about to publish a discreditable story about an individual Minister or civil servant. Juries often give extremely high damages against newspapers and a threat of action will deter the paper from publishing unless it is confident that it can prove its allegations in court. There are, however, two other constraints on the freedom of the press which are of more direct constitutional importance. These are the Official Secrets Acts and D Notices.

THE OFFICIAL SECRETS ACTS

Before 1889 there was no legislation against spying or leaking official information. The need for some sort of legislation to protect official secrets was made clear by a number of cases in the latter half of the last century in which information from highly confidential Government documents was published in the press to the great embarrassment of the Government. Thus in 1858 the *Daily News* published two dispatches from the High Commissioner of the Ionian Islands just after Gladstone had set out to investigate the state of affairs there. The leak was traced to a man called Guernsey, who was a frequent visitor to the Colonial Office Library where one of the librarians was a friend of his. He had apparently taken a copy of the dispatches from the library and passed it on to the *Daily News*. He was charged with stealing the document but was acquitted by the jury after his counsel had argued that an essential element of the crime of larceny – the intention to deprive the owner permanently of his property – was missing.[32]

Another case arose in 1878 when *The Globe* published details of a secret agreement between Britain and Russia just as the Congress of Berlin was getting under way. A copying clerk who held a temporary post in the treaties department of the Foreign Office at the pay of ten pence an hour was accused of being the source of the leak. He was a regular contributor to *The Globe* and had paid the sum of £42 into his bank account just after the articles had been published. Nevertheless, there was not sufficient evidence to convict him of larceny and the proceedings against him were dismissed.

The first legislation to prevent occurrences of this kind was the Official Secrets Act 1889. There were a number of convictions under it but it was felt to be too narrowly drawn to provide adequate protection against foreign agents spying in this country. In the period leading up to the First World War the Germans carried on fairly blatant espionage operations and further legislation was thought to be necessary to thwart their activities. A new Official Secrets Act was therefore passed in 1911. The Bill was introduced at a time of great international tension and after it was passed in the House of Lords it went through all its stages in the Commons in less than an hour. It repealed the 1889 Act and re-enacted its provisions with amendments which greatly extended its scope. If it had been introduced in less critical times it would undoubtedly have aroused substantial opposition. The 1911 Act is still the basis of the law but it was amended and further extended by the Official Secrets Act 1920. A small, but important, limitation was introduced by the Official Secrets Act of 1939.[33]

Section 1 of the 1911 Act makes it an offence to do any of the following 'for any purpose prejudicial to the safety or interests of the State': first, to go near a 'prohibited place' (defence installations, etc.); secondly, to make any sketch or note that might be useful to an enemy; or thirdly, to obtain or communicate to anyone any document that might be useful to an enemy. It is provided that in certain circumstances the onus is on the accused to prove that his purpose was innocent. The maximum penalty, originally seven years, was raised to fourteen by the 1920 Act.[34] There is a minimum penalty of three years. This section was intended to deal with spying (though it has in fact been used against nuclear disarmers)[35] and is unlikely to cause many problems for newspapers.

The important section from the point of view of the press is section 2 of the 1911 Act.[36] This applies to any person who has in his possession any document or information which either had been entrusted to him in confidence by a person holding office under Her Majesty,[37] or which he had obtained through his position as a person holding such office. Such a person is guilty of an offence if he does any of the following things: first, if he communicates the document or information to any unauthorized person;[38] secondly, if he retains it in his possession when he has no right to do so; thirdly, if he fails to comply with any directions issued by lawful authority concerning its disposal; and finally if he fails to take reasonable care of it. The section also provides that if anyone receives any document or information knowing (or having reasonable ground to believe) at the time when he receives it that it was communicated to him in contravention of the Act, he is guilty of an offence. His only defence is that it was communicated to him contrary to his desire. The maximum punishment under section 2 is two years' imprisonment.

These provisions are very far-reaching. For example, if a civil servant gives official information to a journalist without authority the civil servant and the journalist may be guilty of an offence under the Act. Moreover, if a newspaper publishes information given in confidence to a journalist by a civil servant, the journalist and his editor may be guilty of an offence if the publication was unauthorized. The fear of prosecution under the Act can inhibit the press from disclosing malpractices in Government departments or from pointing out that the policies actually being pursued by the Government are not in line with official statements made by Government spokesmen. One press representative has said that newspapers dare not admit that they have access to confidential official documents and may therefore be unable to justify criticisms of Government departments. The criticism may be well founded but without the supporting evidence to back it up it may be dismissed as inaccurate and the reputation of the paper would then suffer.[39]

The 1920 Act created additional offences as well as tightening up the wording of the previous Act and extending some of its provisions. For example it is laid down in section 1(2) that if anyone obtains possession of an official document 'by finding or otherwise' and fails to return it to the proper authority (or to a policeman) he is guilty of an offence punishable by two years' imprisonment. This could apply to a journalist who obtained an official document by chance or through a mistake by a Government official and refused to return it.

The provision which caused the greatest concern was section 6 of the Act. This gave the police the right to question anyone who had any information relating to an offence or suspected offence under either of the Acts. Failure to give the information to the police was an offence punishable by up to two years in prison. This provision could be used to make journalists reveal the sources of leaks from inside Government departments. Thus in 1930 when three London newspapers published the news of Gandhi's impending arrest in India the Attorney-General authorized the police to question the editors of the papers. This caused a great outcry because the Government had given an assurance when the Bill was being debated in the Commons that the section would be used only in the context of spying. Nevertheless a similar case occurred in 1937 when a journalist on a Manchester newspaper was fined £5 for refusing to disclose the source of information he had obtained concerning the contents of a police circular.

The matter finally came to a head in 1938 when an M.P., Mr Duncan Sandys, sent the Secretary of State for War a letter and draft parliamentary question in which he gave details of the inadequacies of the anti-aircraft defences around London. The Government wanted to find out where he had acquired this information and he was interviewed by the Attorney-General. Sandys was told that failure to reveal his sources could make him liable to imprisonment under section 6. The result of this was a parliamentary storm and the setting-up of a Select Committee. Finally the Government agreed to amend section 6 so as to restrict its operation to cases of spying. The Official Secrets Act 1939 was therefore passed and this limited the provisions of section 6 to those cases where an offence under section 1 of the 1911 Act was suspected.

The Official Secrets Acts, and especially section 2 of the 1911 Act, raise very important questions concerning the role of the press in a democracy. When should the press be prepared to publish information obtained as a result of a breach of confidence by a civil servant? In what circumstances has the Government a right to prevent publication? If, for example, a civil servant in the Department of Defence or the Foreign Office tells a journalist that the Government is secretly giving military assistance to one side in a foreign war when its official policy is one of strict neutrality, should the newspaper publish the story or keep quiet? On the one hand it could be argued that the public has a right to know the true facts concerning Government policy: democracy can function only if public opinion is well informed. On the other hand, however, it might be said that secret operations are a legitimate means of achieving foreign policy objectives and that deceit cannot always be avoided in affairs of state. (Who expects a Chancellor of the Exchequer to admit that a devaluation is about to take place?) The attitude that newspapers will take to situations such as the one given above will often depend on whether they support the policy in question. If they do, they may decide not to publish; if they do not, they will regard it as their 'duty' to the public to expose the duplicity of the Government.

Irrespective of the rights and wrongs of publication in this sort of situation, there is still the question whether the criminal law should be involved. It has sometimes been suggested that where there is no question of espionage there should be no legal penalty for the publication of official information. If this were the case the civil servant concerned would be disciplined (probably dismissed) but nothing would happen to the journalist. However, there are cases in which the disclosure of official information could do great harm to the national interest. The most obvious examples of this are in the fields of finance (e.g. a proposed devaluation), defence (e.g. details of a new weapon) and law enforcement (e.g. security precautions taken with regard to bullion shipments). There are also cases in which legitimate private interests could be compromised: members of the public who are obliged to give details of their private affairs to Government officials (e.g. in regard to taxation or social security benefits) have a right to demand that this information be treated in strict confidence.

The problem in drafting a statute of this kind is to devise a form of words that covers the cases which need to be covered but which does not interfere with the legitimate activities of the press. This is difficult to do. The solution adopted by the present Acts is to cover a much wider area than necessary and then to provide that no prosecutions may be brought without the consent of the Attorney-General.[40] It is the job of the Attorney-General to see that no prosecutions are brought unless the public interest so requires. In making a decision of this kind the Attorney-General is constitutionally obliged to put party considerations on one side and act solely in the public interest: if it were suspected that a prosecution was politically motivated it could be very damaging for the Government. Nevertheless, it is unsatisfactory that the rights of the press should depend on the judgment of a man who is after all a politician.

A different solution was proposed by a Committee set up by the Government in 1971 to consider the operation of section 2 (the Franks Committee).[41] They identified four categories of information which they regarded as of sufficient importance to justify the use of criminal sanctions. These were:

1. Information relating to defence and internal security, foreign relations, or the currency and reserves;
2. Information likely to assist criminal activities or impede law enforcement;
3. Cabinet documents;
4. Information entrusted to the Government by a private individual or concern.

They proposed that it should not be an offence to disclose official information unless it fell into one of these four categories. The only exception would be where the disclosure was made for the purpose of private gain. (In this latter case it would continue to be an offence for a Crown servant to disclose *any* official information.)

The Committee proposed an additional safeguard in the case of information in the first category (which is clearly the most important). This would be protected only if it had been classified by the Government as secret and this could be done only if, in the Government's view, its disclosure would cause serious injury to the national interest. Where the information was contained in a document, the document would have to be marked with the word *secret* or the words *defence – confidential*. If a prosecution were to be considered the classification of the information allegedly leaked would have to be reviewed by the Minister personally. He would have to decide whether the classification was justified at the time of the alleged disclosure: if he decided that it was, he would give a certificate to that effect and this would be conclusive in any court.

The Committee proposed that these recommendations should be put into effect by repealing section 2 of the Official Secrets Act and passing a new Act to be called the Official Information Act: it was felt undesirable that spying and leakages should be dealt with in the same Act.

These proposals have been criticized on the ground that they do not go far enough. Some critics feel that the court ought to make the ultimate decision whether information in the first category had been properly classified. However, when the Home Secretary announced in June 1973 that the Government accepted the essential recommendations of the Franks Committee, his statement suggested that on certain points the Government did not intend to go quite as far as the Committee proposed.[42]

D NOTICES

In addition to the legal restraints imposed by the Official Secrets Acts there is also a system of voluntary censorship generally known as the D Notice system. D Notices (*D* stands for *Defence*) are formal letters sent to the editors of newspapers, TV and radio news programmes, certain periodicals concerned with defence matters and, occasionally, book publishers. They contain a request that nothing should be published about certain specific items or general topics in order to safeguard national security. The subjects covered by D Notices are restricted to defence and security matters. The Notices are issued on the authority of a body called the Services, Press and Broadcasting Committee which consists of representatives of the Government and the communications industry. Its composition in 1967 was as follows.[43] On the Government side there were five civil servants – the Permanent Under-Secretary at the Ministry of Defence (who was chairman of the Committee), a representative from the Ministry of Technology (Aviation) and three other civil servants from the Ministry of Defence. Subsequently two of the latter were replaced by representatives from the Foreign Office and the Home Office. The other eleven members of the Committee represented the press (both national and provincial), technical periodicals, news agencies, the BBC and ITN. In 1968 a spokesman for book publishers was added.

The Services, Press and Broadcasting Committee is the only body which can issue D Notices and since officials are heavily outnumbered by press representatives a Notice cannot go out unless the latter are convinced that it is justified. The members of the Committee are given confidential information by the Government to enable them to form a judgment on the security grounds for censorship of particular topics. Once issued a D Notice remains in force until it is withdrawn and in 1967 there were sixteen Notices in operation. It is impossible to discover the contents of all these Notices since D Notices are themselves regarded as confidential by the Committee and by most editors. (The reason for this is that knowledge of the items British security is concerned about could be useful to foreign intelligence organizations.) However, in 1967 extracts from two Notices were published.[44] One of them read (in part) as follows:

Dear Sir, 27.4.56

Will you please in the national interest make no reference to the following:

(i) Secret intelligence or counter-intelligence methods and activities in or outside the United Kingdom.

(ii) Identities of persons engaged in intelligence or counter-intelligence duties, whether actively engaged in such duties or in a clerical or administrative capacity, and of whatsoever status or rank.

(iii) Any information from which the number, duties or type of staff or other details of the organization of M.I.5 could be ascertained.

(iv) Any information from which could be deduced the addresses where our Intelligence Services operate.

(v) Special methods of training the Intelligence staff.

In conclusion may I ask you to bear in mind that the task of the Intelligence Services in a democratic country is far from easy and earnestly request you, when in doubt, to act on the principle that as little publicity as possible should be given to their activities?

Yours faithfully,

GEORGE P. THOMSON (*signed*)
Secretary to the Committee

The system first came into operation in 1912, the year after the Official Secrets Act 1911 was passed. The Committee was then called the Admiralty, War Office and Press Committee. It ceased to operate in 1939 when war broke out and its functions were taken over by the Press Censorship Department of the Ministry of Information. This department issued D Notices (agreed to by representatives of the press) and Private and Confidential Letters, which were issued by the Chief Censor on his own authority. At the end of the war the Committee was reconstituted in its present form.

The procedure starts with a proposal from a Government department that a D Notice should be issued on a certain topic. A draft is discussed with the Secretary of the Committee who will give his opinion whether the press representatives are likely to accept it. Some proposals do not pass beyond this stage. If the Secretary thinks the proposal is reasonable he will advise on detailed points of presentation and then circulate the draft among the members of the Committee for their comments. If it is approved the Notice is issued by the Secretary in the name of the Committee. In cases of special urgency the Secretary is authorized to adopt an emergency procedure: the Notice is sent out on his own responsibility provided it is first approved by at least three of the press representatives, who meet together for this purpose.

It is important to emphasize that there is no statutory authority for the Committee or for the Notices it issues. There is, therefore, no legal sanction for the breach of a D Notice as such. Publication of the information concerned may constitute a breach of the Official Secrets Acts, but D Notices are not limited to matters which infringe the law and in some cases it would not be possible for a prosecution to be brought. It may, therefore, be said that a D notice is both a warning and a request: a warning that publication may be contrary to the Official Secrets Acts and a request that the paper should observe restraint even when the Acts do not apply. In the latter case a newspaper which ignored a D Notice might be exposed to public criticism by the Government for compromising British security and it might find itself cut off from the flow of confidential information that reaches the press from official sources. In the last analysis, however, the system depends on the consent and voluntary co-operation of the press and this is why the Committee is largely made up of its representatives.

The system is supported by both the Government and the press because it benefits both sides: it gives editors guidance concerning what they can safely print and it provides a means for the Government to prevent disclosure of secret information. For these reasons the system normally works smoothly and D Notices are almost always obeyed. There have, however, been occasions when they have not. Usually these have been the result of inadvertence on the part of editors but a number of cases have occurred in which deliberate breaches have taken place. Thus in 1967 the *Daily Express* and the *Guardian* published the names of the heads of the two main branches of British Military Intelligence (after they had been revealed in an American periodical) and *The Sunday Times* announced that in publishing their account of the Philby story they were breaking a D Notice. In neither case was there a prosecution.

It will be seen from the specimen D Notice reproduced above that the prohibitions are sometimes fairly broad and general. It follows from this that editors may at times be unsure whether a particular news story is covered by a D Notice or not. When this occurs the story can be taken to the Secretary of the Committee who will give his opinion on the interpretation of the relevant D Notice. This 'advisory service' is one of the most important parts of the Secretary's job and he is apparently available at virtually all times of the day and night so that the story will not be held up if it is cleared. The Secretary has no authority to give 'rulings' on the interpretation of D Notices but his opinion is treated with respect by journalists and is rejected, if at all, only after careful consideration by the editor.

The Secretary is obviously the key person in the system and if he were not prepared to give on-the-spot interpretations of D Notices the system would probably break down. The first Secretary after the last war was Admiral G. T. Thomson. He was succeeded by Colonel L. G. Lohan, who held the post until he resigned in June 1967 as a result of the cable vetting affair. The next Secretary was Vice-Admiral Sir Norman Denning, a brother of Lord Denning M. R., who served until 1972, when he was replaced by Rear-Admiral

Kenneth Farnhill. The Secretary's job, which is full-time, needs both tact and careful judgment and in the past was made more difficult by the fact that he was not only required to interpret D Notices but in addition was given the job of persuading papers to refrain from printing stories that were not covered by a Notice, when this was desirable in the national interest. This dual role was the cause of the misunderstanding that arose over the cable vetting story.

This affair started in February 1967 when the defence correspondent of the *Daily Express*, Mr Chapman Pincher, was told by a former employee of two cable offices that copies of in-coming and out-going cables and overseas telegrams were taken away for vetting by the security services as a routine measure.[45] Pincher telephoned the Press Relations Branch of the Ministry of Defence to ask them if there was any truth in the story. They denied it. He also contacted the Public Relations Branch of the Post Office who told him that there was some substance in the story but not all cables were collected. Pincher's next step was to contact Colonel Lohan, the Secretary of the Services, Press and Broadcasting Committee. Colonel Lohan told him that there was no D Notice applicable to the story.

At this point, however, the Foreign Office and the Security Services heard that the story was about to be published. A conference was held at the Foreign Office to discuss what should be done. It was decided that the story was covered by two D Notices (one of them being the one set out above) and it was agreed that Colonel Lohan should be asked to get the *Express* to agree not to publish. Colonel Lohan then arranged to have lunch with Chapman Pincher at a London restaurant to try to persuade him to drop the story. Unfortunately there was a misunderstanding between the two men at the meeting: Pincher thought that Lohan was appealing to him on general grounds and was not arguing that the matter came within a D Notice. This was not what Colonel Lohan intended.

Pincher then put the whole matter before his editor. He assured him that Colonel Lohan did not consider that a D Notice was involved but had asked for the suppression of the story on general security grounds. The editor took the decision to publish and this is what eventually happened in spite of a number of late-night telephone calls that took place as the presses began to turn out copies of the next day's paper. These included a phone call from Mr George Brown, the Foreign Secretary, to Sir Max Aitken, the proprietor of the *Daily Express*, who was dining at the Garrick Club. This also resulted in a misunderstanding: George Brown thought that Sir Max had promised to suppress the story unconditionally; Sir Max maintained that his promise applied only if publication would involve the breach of a D Notice.

The publication of the story had wide repercussions. The Prime Minister claimed that the story was sensationalized and inaccurate and accused the *Daily Express* of breaking two D Notices. This was resented by the press and a political row followed. A committee of Privy Councillors under Lord Radcliffe was set up to investigate the matter[46] and they reached the conclusion that the *Express* story was 'not inaccurate in any sense that could expose it to hostile criticism on that score'. They also concluded that publication of the story was not a breach of any D Notice. They considered that at first reading the interception of cables would appear to come within the first item in the Notice of 27 April 1956 (above), which referred to 'secret intelligence or counter-intelligence methods and activities in or outside the United Kingdom', but a narrower interpretation of this D Notice had prevailed in practice and it was not therefore right to say that the publication of the story was a breach of the Notice.

The Government then took the unusual step of publishing a White Paper in which they rejected the findings of the Committee on these points: they maintained that the story *was* untrue and that it *did* break a D Notice.[47] In the Commons debate that followed Mr Harold Wilson made what was regarded by many observers as a rather unfair attack on Colonel Lohan, who resigned as a result of the affair. Relations between the press and the Labour Government were severely strained and Wilson referred to the whole matter in his book as 'one of my costliest mistakes'.[48]

In the White Paper the Government outlined a number of changes they intended to put into effect to improve the system. All of them except one were recommended by the Committee of Privy Councillors. First, it was decided that the two D Notices which were in issue should be rewritten to make their meaning clearer. Secondly, the Government stated its intention of discussing with the press the possibility of setting up a 'court of appeal' or other arbitration machinery acceptable to both sides so that disputes regarding the interpretation of Notices could be resolved (though this idea had been rejected by the Committee of Privy Councillors). Thirdly, it was accepted that in future the Secretary would act only within the framework of the D Notice system: if a case came to him which lay 'at or beyond the borderline' of the system he would report it to the Chairman of the Committee. Appeals to the press on wider grounds would not in future be made by the Secretary. A deputy to the Secretary would be appointed so that the Secretary would not be 'on call' at all times of the day and night. Finally, the Secretary would go through the positive vetting procedure[49] so that he could be informed of the full reasons why it was desired to suppress any particular story: it was thought that journalists would have more confidence in his judgment if they knew that he was aware of all the facts.

CONCLUSIONS

As has been shown, the Government has a number of formal powers which can be used to prevent publication of material by the media: a D Notice can be issued, a prosecution threatened under the Official Secrets Acts, or, in the case of broadcasting, a directive can be issued by the Minister of Posts and Telecommunications. It is unlikely, however, that these powers would ever be used for party political purposes – the publicity that would result from such an action would be very damaging. In practice the Government is more likely to use informal means such as a quiet phone call to the proprietor of a newspaper or an unofficial approach to the Governors of the BBC.[50]

Protecting the media from unjustified Government pressure is only one problem, however. The other problem is the protection of the public from the media. The libel laws, the Press Council, and the BBC's Programmes Complaints Commission are the most important institutional means of doing this. Opinions differ sharply whether these means are sufficient.

14
Special Tribunals and Local Inquiries

SPECIAL TRIBUNALS

In the course of the administration of Acts of Parliament, disputes may arise. Frequently, and especially in the social services, the Acts provide that disputes shall be settled by special tribunals created for the resolution of those disputes. Each Act will establish such tribunals for the disputes which arise under it, and so a large number of tribunals exist, each concerned with a special type of dispute.

The most recent general study of these tribunals is contained in the report[1] of the Committee on Administrative Tribunals and Enquiries which was chaired by Lord Franks. As a result of the recommendations of that Committee, the Tribunals and Inquiries Act was passed in 1958 and amended in 1966. These two Acts were replaced by an Act of the same name in 1971. The Act of 1958 established the Council on Tribunals to keep under review the constitution and working of tribunals listed in the Act; and to consider and report on particular matters referred to the Council by Ministers with respect to any tribunals, whether or not listed in the Act.

To understand what kind of functions are performed by tribunals, we must look at some of the most important.

Under the Immigration Appeals Act 1969[2] a Chief Adjudicator, nineteen full-time and twelve part-time adjudicators were appointed. Their function is to hear appeals from persons who are refused admission into the United Kingdom or who are admitted under conditions or who have been ordered to be deported, and in some other circumstances. From the decisions of adjudicators there is a right of appeal to the Immigration Appeal Tribunal. In 1971, there were 1944 cases heard by adjudicators and 118 heard by the Tribunal.[3]

The Industrial Training Act 1964 established industrial training boards for the training of persons over school age for employment in industrial and commercial activities. To raise money towards meeting its expenses, an industrial training board was empowered to impose, in accordance with orders made by the Minister, a levy on employers. The Act required the Minister to establish tribunals to hear appeals from any employer who claimed that he ought not to have been assessed to a levy or ought to have been assessed in a smaller amount.[4] Tribunals sat in different centres and in 1971 heard 223 cases. These industrial tribunals were later used to hear cases arising under other Acts, particularly for appeals and applications (which totalled 8,651 in 1971) relating to payments required to be made by employers to employees who became redundant.[5]

A third example is different again. The Lands Tribunal was constituted under the Lands Tribunal Act 1949. It is a highly expert and professional body the main function of which is to decide a variety of questions affecting the value of land, particularly for the determination of compensation payable when land is compulsorily acquired; and hearing appeals from local valuation courts on the fixing of rateable values. The Tribunal disposed of 1,108 cases in 1971. Local valuation courts are also administrative tribunals and heard 24,515 cases in 1971.

Yet another type of function is exercised by the fifteen Mental Health Review Tribunals which were set up under the Mental Health Act 1959 and which heard 1,021 cases in 1971. In a large number of situations where action is taken or is proposed to be taken in relation to a person who is said to be suffering from mental disorder, that person or another may appeal to a Review Tribunal consisting of legal members, medical members and other members.

One of the most important groups of tribunals is set up under the National Insurance Act 1965 and the National Insurance (Industrial Injuries) Act 1965. Under the first of these Acts,[6] any person who applies for national insurance benefit (such as unemployment, sickness, maternity or widow's benefit) or for any other payments under the Act, and who is refused, may appeal to a local appeal tribunal and thence to a National Insurance Commissioner. A similar structure of tribunals exists for industrial injuries with the addition of medical appeal tribunals. In 1971, local tribunals heard 29,334 cases, medical appeal tribunals 17,614 cases and the Commissioners 2,261 cases.

Of similar importance are the appeal tribunals constituted under the Ministry of Social Security Act 1966. The great majority of the 29,648 cases heard in 1971 concerned supplementary benefits, being appeals from the refusal of the Supplementary Benefit Commission to make payments to persons whose resources were insufficient to meet their requirements. The purpose of these payments is to help those who are not employed and whose income from all sources falls below the standards laid down.

Rent tribunals were set up under section 69 of the Rent Act 1968. These are empowered to consider the rents of certain furnished accommodation and to approve the rent or to reduce it to such amount as they think reasonable. In 1971 they considered 15,793 cases.

Under the Road Traffic Act 1960, licences must be obtained by those who wish to run certain public service vehicles, carrying passengers for hire or reward. The licensing authorities are traffic commissioners and in 1971 they dealt with 17,212 applications.

Finally the Industrial Relations Act 1971 established the National Industrial Relations Court and greatly increased the function of Industrial Tribunals first created in 1964. A great number of issues may be taken either to the Tribunals with appeal to the Court, or directly to the Court, including many 'unfair industrial practices'.

As we have said, these are examples only of tribunals. Amongst those not mentioned are agricultural land tribunals, the Air Transport Licencing Board, an appeal tribunal for betting levy, national health services tribunals, the comptroller-general and other officers for patents and designs, and general and special commissioners for tax purposes.

All this adds up to a very considerable body of special tribunals and with such diversity, description of their characteristics can easily be misleading. We may venture a few generalizations. The members of tribunals are normally appointed by the appropriate Minister for it will be seen that all tribunals concern some part or other of government functions. Frequently they hold office 'according to the terms of their appointment' and do not enjoy the permanency that attaches to judges. A member of the Lands Tribunal may be removed from office during the term for which he is appointed only if the Lord Chancellor (who appoints him) considers he is unfit to continue in office or incapable of performing his duties. Although this leaves the decision to the Lord Chancellor, it does effectively limit his powers to dismiss.[7] No power of a Minister other than the Lord Chancellor to terminate a person's membership of listed tribunals (which includes most of the important tribunals) is exercisable except with the consent of the Lord Chancellor, the Lord President of the Court of Session (for Scotland) or the Lord Chief Justice of Northern Ireland, depending on the areas within which the tribunals sit.[8]

The Tribunals and Inquiries Act 1971 provides that the chairmen of certain tribunals shall be selected from a panel of persons appointed by the Lord Chancellor. This applies to local tribunals for national insurance and medical appeal tribunals for industrial injuries; some national service tribunals, supplementary benefit appeal tribunals and (normally) rent tribunals.[9] Some other tribunals also are required to be composed partly or wholly of lawyers or other professionals;[10] but laymen commonly fill many of the positions especially where the number of tribunals is considerable. Most of the members of the 167 local tribunals for national insurance in England and Wales are laymen, appointed from panels representing employers and employed persons.

It must not, however, be assumed, because Ministers appoint and because security of tenure is not ensured, that these tribunals are mere extensions of Government departments. To a very large extent they act independently and would both resent and resist interference from the departments. Nor have departments any great interest in seeking to exert such influence. Through legislation, Ministers make and can remake the context in which tribunals work and the laws which it is their duty to apply. The application of those laws to individual cases is not a matter of concern to the department unless, in unlikely and extreme circumstances, the interpretation given by tribunals so departs from what the departments assumed to be the law that the policy of the legislation is threatened. If this did happen, then the Minister would make new regulations or introduce a bill.

Before the report of the Franks Committee and the passing of the Tribunals and Inquiries Act 1958, concern was justifiably expressed about the rules of procedure of some of the tribunals. The defects were never considerable but there was an absence of supervision. As a result of the provisions of that Act, as we have seen, the Council on Tribunals exercises general supervision. But more importantly, the Council must be consulted by Ministers before they make procedural rules. This enables the Council to ensure that at least minimum standards are provided and Ministers would rarely choose to make political trouble for themselves by refusing to accept the advice of the Council on such matters.

The Tribunals and Inquiries Act 1971 provides that where any listed tribunal gives any decision it shall furnish a statement of the reason for the decision if requested to do so.[11] Either under this Act or under Acts setting up tribunals, the decisions of tribunals may be appealed from on a point of law to the High Court.[12]

Constitutional objections used to be raised to the institution of these tribunals on the ground that they exercised functions which 'properly' belonged to the ordinary courts. A similar objection was made against delegated legislation on the ground that this was a usurpation by the executive of the functions of the legislature. But the fact is that the ordinary courts are not well suited to deal with the great mass of cases brought before tribunals – and this for a variety of reasons. The ordinary courts are extremely expensive, slow in operation and highly formal in their procedures. Moreover, judges are not expert in the understanding and interpretation of much of the legislation which comes before tribunals. This is not to say that judges could not become so but this would mean that they would have to be specialists, and it is easier to appoint specialist tribunals with men and women, being lawyers or not as the need arises, who have the necessary expertise. In this way, greater coherence, greater consistency and greater certainty can be developed.

The formal procedures in the ordinary courts and the rules of evidence which they apply are largely designed to ensure fairness and equality of treatment between parties. The more informal procedures of tribunals carry dangers and it is to these that attention has been recently directed. While the criticism of the procedures of tribunals was exaggerated in the past, it stimulated the setting up of the Franks Committee, the passing of the Tribunals and Inquiries Acts and the creation of the Council on Tribunals. Today the most serious defect in the operation of tribunals results from the non-availability of legal aid. Often no hardship may follow, partly because the expense involved may be slight and partly because organized interests (especially trade unions for industrial injuries) may ensure that a party is adequately advised by an experienced representative who may speak on the party's behalf before the tribunal. But a party may not realize that he needs expert assistance or may be wholly unable (especially before supplementary benefit tribunals) to pay even a small fee to obtain it. Free advice and representation are provided by a number of voluntary organizations. But the gap remains.

LOCAL INQUIRIES

Special tribunals in making decisions in individual cases are seldom empowered to take into account questions of policy. To a large extent they operate under statutes and regulations which explicitly or implicitly lay down the policies to be followed. Their function is to interpret the meaning of those statutes and regulations and to apply principles to individual cases. If they take into account public policy or the needs of the community it is within a narrow range. Often they are dealing with rights claimed by parties and their duty is to decide whether or not those rights are made out, not to consider what is desirable or wise. Indeed, as we have seen, the reason why Ministers are content to allow tribunals to make decisions without Governmental interference is precisely because they operate within policies determined by Ministers and expressed in those statutes and regulations.

Inquiries are, however, instruments of government. They are part of the process of decision-making, not only for individual cases but for policy formation. Again, examples must be given to explain these generalities.

Typically, inquiries are into a dispute which has arisen between public, generally local, authorities and particular persons affected by decisions made.

Public inquiries may be held into a very great variety of disputes[13] but by far the largest number of inquiries are concerned with compulsory purchase of land for housing and for town and country planning purposes, with slum clearance orders, and with planning applications. In the period 1966–8, the average annual number of inquiries was: for slum clearance orders, 220; for slum clearance compulsory purchase orders, 700; for compulsory purchase for housing, 120; for compulsory purchase for housing under planning provisions, 54; for the approval and amendment of development plans, 75; for calling-in of planning applications by the Minister, 97; for appeals against refusal of planning permission, 4,247.[14]

When a local authority has decided that it wishes to clear slum housing in a particular area, it must choose one of two methods of proceeding. The first is to acquire the land (generally compulsorily) and then to demolish buildings; the second is to require the owners to clear the land of buildings. Under the first method the ownership of the land passes to the local authority; under the second it remains with the owners. Both compulsory purchase orders and clearance orders, though made by local authorities, must be confirmed by the Secretary of State for the Environment before they can become operative. Frequently owners, and others with interests in the land, object to the making of the order and write to the Minister accordingly. If this happens, then the Minister will appoint one of his inspectors to hold a local inquiry. Local authorities also have powers to acquire land compulsorily for a large number of their functions and, most importantly, for building houses. Again, if there are objections there will be a local inquiry.

The other main occasion for local inquiries arises under three sets of provisions concerned with town and country planning.[15] First, under the statutory provisions which operated from 1947 until 1968, each local planning authority was required to prepare a development plan showing how, in fairly broad terms, it was intended to control the use of land. Areas were zoned in the plan as, for example, residential or industrial or for open space or for highways or for agriculture or for new housing. This could have considerable consequences for the owners of land and they were enabled to object to any of the provisions of the plan. The plan was subject to confirmation by the Minister and before he confirmed, with or without modifying the plan, he caused a local inquiry to be held. Under the Town and Country Planning Act 1968, old-style development plans are replaced by structure plans and local plans. Both are prepared by local planning authorities but, in the ordinary case, only structure plans require Ministerial approval. Both are open to objections and local inquiries are provided for.[16]

The second set of provisions concerned the control of development. The principle of the planning Acts is that no one may 'develop' land (most commonly by building on it) or change its use without first obtaining the permission of the local planning authority. If that permission is withheld, or unacceptable conditions are imposed, the applicant may appeal to the Minister who appoints an inspector[17] to hold a local inquiry before coming to a decision. The grounds on which permission may be withheld must of course be planning grounds but this is a very wide category. The grounds may relate to the design of the proposed building, including such small matters as

the colour of bricks or of tiles; to important questions like the extent
to which building is to be permitted in rural areas or how far 'green
belts' of unbuilt-on land should be preserved around towns and cities;
whether petrol stations should be permitted in residential areas;
whether a private house should be used as a nursing home; whether
high buildings are appropriate in particular areas; what density
building should be in different kinds of areas; how much access
should be allowed from new estates on to main roads and where the
access should be; whether caravan sites or motels should be allowed;
whether sand or gravel should be extracted from land; what advertisements of what size should be permitted; and so on.[18]

The third set of provisions arises from the power given to the
Secretary of State to direct a local planning authority to refer an
application for planning permission to him instead of being dealt
with by the local planning authority, (this is the 'call-in' power).[19] A
major difference between the provisions relating to compulsory
purchase orders, clearance orders and development plans on the one
hand, and applications for planning permission on the other, is that
none of the former can come into operation (whether or not there are
objections) until the Minister has confirmed them; whereas, if a local
planning authority grants planning permission, the Minister is in the
ordinary case not involved at all.[20] The grant of permission does not
require Ministerial confirmation; and no one can appeal against
the grant of permission. The power to call-in an application therefore gives the Minister the opportunity to consider the application before the local planning authority has decided. If either the
applicant or the local planning authority so desire, the Minister
appoints an inspector to hold a local inquiry before he makes his
decision.

The principal parties at a local inquiry are the local housing or
planning authority and the objector or the applicant. Members of
the general public may attend the inquiry and may, at the discretion
of the inspector, give evidence. The principal parties are often represented either, for the local authorities, by a member of the legal
department, or, for others, by a solicitor or barrister. Sometimes,
members of the public (especially where they are members of
organized groups like amenity societies) are represented also by
lawyers. Wraith and Lamb[21] record in round figures for 1961-7,
with no significant variations from year to year, that in planning
appeal hearings 25 per cent of appellants were represented by

barristers, 40 per cent by solicitors, 20 per cent by members of other professions and 2 per cent by 'friends'. This leaves 13 per cent who represented themselves.

The principal parties will probably call witnesses, including expert witnesses, to give evidence to support their case; and those witnesses may be cross-examined by the other side and questioned by the inspector. The inspector, either alone or with representatives of both sides, will inspect the land which is the subject matter of the inquiry.

Before planning inquiries are opened, the local planning authority publishes a written statement of its case; if the Minister has called in the application he publishes a written statement of any points which seem to him to be likely to be relevant. The applicant, if so required by the Minister, publishes a similar statement. If any other Government department makes submissions, the applicant may apply for that department to be represented at the inquiry.

The applicant opens the case at the inquiry and has the right of final reply.

Until 1958, the report made by the inspector to the Minister was confidential. The decision was taken in the department in the name of the Minister, after consideration of the report and the recommendation of the inspector. Since 1958, the inspector's report is published along with the Minister's decision. The Minister is not, of course, bound by the inspector's recommendation but if he departs from it this will now be known and the Minister will be obliged in his decision letter to explain why it is that he has not accepted that recommendation. The Minister is unlikely to differ from the inspector's findings of fact. He may differ on the conclusions which are to be drawn from those facts or on the policy decision which should flow from them. But if the Minister does depart from his inspector's recommendation, this is most likely because the Minister takes into account wide policy considerations. For example, it may have been the policy of the department not to permit large-scale development in a particular area in or near the London Green Belt. In line with this policy, the local planning authority may have rejected an application and the inspector may have recommended that the appeal be not allowed. But evidence may have been accumulating of the great and increasing demand for more housing in the south-east and the Minister may feel obliged to release more land for housing and so to overrule his inspector and allow the appeal. It seems likely that, since 1958, civil servants in the department have been more reluctant to differ from the inspector because of the political trouble which the Minister may be landed into if he departs from his inspector's recommendation.

Since 1968, in less important[22] but numerous planning cases, inspectors have been authorized to make decisions themselves without reference to the department or to the Minister.

In compulsory purchase inquiries, the procedure is substantially similar. The Minister is required to notify the local 'acquiring' authority of the substance of each objection received; and the acquiring authority must publish a written statement of their reasons for making the compulsory purchase order. The acquiring authority opens and has the right of final reply. There is no provision enabling the inspector in any case to decide the question. He reports to the Minister who decides.

The Franks Committee[23] was required to consider and make recommendations on the working of such administrative procedures as included the holding of an inquiry or hearing by or on behalf of a Minister. Much of the argument that took place during its deliberations in 1956 and 1957 has now passed into history either because many of its recommendations have been adopted or because those which were not adopted have ceased to agitate opinion. Some of the witnesses wanted inspectors to be more independent of the department concerned; and the case for and against the publication of inspectors' reports was hotly argued. When the Council on Tribunals was established under the Tribunals and Inquiries Act 1958 its terms of reference were extended to include the duty, in the words of the Act of 1971, to consider and report on such matters as might be referred to the council by Ministers, or as the council might determine to be of special importance, with respect to administrative procedures involving or which might involve the holding by or on behalf of a Minister of a statutory inquiry.[24] The Act empowers the Lord Chancellor to make rules regulating the procedure to be followed in connection with statutory inquiries and he is required before doing so to consult with the council.[25] The Act also provides that where any Minister notifies any decision taken by him after the holding of an inquiry, it is the duty of the Minister to state his reasons for that decision.[26]

Any general assessment of the value of local inquiries and of their effectiveness has to begin by asking what is their purpose. The answer must be that they have no single purpose and are seen differently by the different parties. In the department's view – and therefore in the inspector's view – the primary purpose is to inform the mind of the Minister. He is by statute put in a position in which he is required to make a decision – whether to confirm an order or plan, whether to allow or reject an appeal, whether (in either case) to modify what is put before him. Although he may seem to be adjudicating between two parties – the local authority on the one hand and the appellant or the objector on the other – he is in fact doing much more than this. He is applying policy to a concrete situation. More, he may often be making policy in arriving at the decision in the particular dispute.

Departmental policy on planning and housing questions varies, according to the subject matter, from the hard and defined (where little variation is likely) to the soft and vague or even nonexistent. Or though it has been well defined hitherto, the time may have come to change the policy. For example, Governments are inclined to favour housebuilding, sometimes to relieve the general shortage, at other times to promote slum clearance. Or a policy may be adopted to extend green belts or to relax the provisions preventing development within them. Attitudes to gipsies vary from year to year; so do policies about traffic, or about office accommodation. Governments make decisions not in conditions of removed and abstracted objectivity but in the midst of pressures, of conflict, of political strife. And many decisions, particularly on matters concerned with town and country planning, are embedded in controversy. So local inquiries are a part, generally a large part, of the procedure whereby Ministers acquire information. But when all the information is in and all the factors, political and other, are taken into account, the decision has to be made.

From the viewpoint of the local authority, the local inquiry is the place where they resist the attack on the decision they have made. It forces them to marshal their arguments – perhaps more importantly, the possibility of a local inquiry forces them to make sure that their decision is well founded when it is made. Local authorities must make their case by showing how the public interest is properly served by their decision and to do this they must show, in the case of compulsory purchase for housing for example, what are the needs of the area and why this method is the best or the only method for meeting those needs. Or, if their decision was to refuse planning permission, they must show why they did so and must meet the arguments put forward by the would-be developers.

For the individual applicant or the individual objector, the local inquiry is the best opportunity he will have to seek to persuade the decision-makers that he has right or justice or common sense or the public interest on his side. It is his day in court, when he is confronted by his adversaries and can seek to overthrow them.

Finally the general public or that part of it which, for whatever reasons, has a particular interest in the matter, is presented with an opportunity to express its view either in support of the local authority or against the local authority. Sometimes, especially when organized groups are involved (like the Council for the Preservation of Rural England, or amenity societies under the Civic Trust, or conservationists of many kinds), the contributions from the public are of the greatest importance. But not only when there are organized groups. One individual man or his family may be particularly affected by the way the decision goes and although he may not be an official 'party' at the inquiry, his position may be crucial.

Given all these different viewpoints the procedure by local inquiry is probably the best that could be devised, despite its disadvantages. It may be a lengthy process, it can be expensive, but alternatives seem less effective. Some criticize the procedure on the ground that the information needed by the department could be more efficiently obtained by an investigation rather than by an adversary public hearing. But this, while it might best serve the needs of the department, would be least likely to satisfy the individuals affected. They would be unable to hear the arguments advanced by the other side and so be unable to answer them. Also the general public would be excluded. Public hearings publicly conducted remove much suspicion from the minds of those who would otherwise be doubtful about the purity of the motives of both local authorities and property developers. No procedure by itself can prevent corruption or inefficiency but it can introduce some safeguards. Secrecy is the first enemy of good administration.

15
Governmental Liability

This chapter is concerned with the liability of the central Government and other public authorities to be sued in courts of law. The liability of the Crown (central Government) will be the main issue considered because most of the rules of law which put public authorities in a different position from private individuals are limited to the Crown; but where these rules do apply to other public authorities they will be considered as well.

Before the Crown Proceedings Act 1947 was passed the Crown was in strict law immune from all proceedings. Historically, the King had always been subject to the law in theory, but in practice there was no means of enforcing it against him: the courts were the King's courts and the King could not be sued in his own courts. Moreover, since writs were issued in the King's name they could not be issued against him.[1]

This position was mitigated in practice by various devices, the most important of which was the petition of right. This was a petition to the Crown by the subject for his just rights which was voluntarily referred by the Crown to the courts for decision. The suppliant had first to obtain the consent of the Crown and this was signified by endorsing the petition with the words '*fiat justicia*' (let justice be done). Then the case could be tried by the courts in the ordinary way except that the judgment took the form of a declaration of the rights of the suppliant. This could not be enforced legally but in fact it was always respected by the Crown. If the Crown refused to grant its *fiat* the subject had no remedy (there was no appeal against such refusal) but in practice it was always granted whenever the subject had a possible claim.

The petition of right procedure was available for the recovery of land and other property from the Crown, for damages for breach of contract and in certain other cases. It was not, however, available for claims in tort.[2] But though the Crown had immunity from such claims, no such protection was granted to a servant of the Crown. Thus if a civil servant, a soldier or some other servant of the Crown committed a tort against the subject, he could be sued in the ordinary way in the courts. The fact that he acted on the orders of the Crown was no defence.[3] Moreover in time the Crown adopted the practice of accepting moral responsibility for the torts of its servants and paying any damages out of public funds. The action became in reality one against the Crown, though in form it was against an individual. In fact, if the plaintiff was uncertain as to which official should be sued, the department concerned would help by giving him the name of an appropriate defendant.

It might seem, therefore, that the subject was in substance given a satisfactory means of obtaining a remedy, but there were two difficulties. First, although in a particular case it might be clear that some Crown servant had committed a tort, it might be impossible to discover *which* Crown servant was responsible. In these circumstances the Crown would nominate someone to be the defendant and would not make anything of the fact that there was no evidence that he was personally liable. Where this was done, however, the idea that the action was against the servant was a pure fiction and in 1946 the House of Lords condemned this practice.[4] Another defect was that in certain torts liability could rest *only* on the Crown: for example, if a Crown employee was injured in a Crown factory and he claimed that his employer had failed in his duty to provide a safe system of work, the only possible defendant was the Crown; and in 1947 a worker in a Ministry of Supply ordnance factory failed to obtain a remedy for this reason.[5] Clearly the time had come for the law to be reformed.

The outcome was the Crown Proceedings Act 1947, which revolutionized the law by making the Crown liable to be sued in the courts in much the same way as anyone else. Section 1 of the Act provided that wherever a claim against the Crown could previously have been enforced by petition of right, it could now be enforced as of right without any need for the Crown's *fiat* while section 2 made the Crown liable in tort in a large range of situations. In spite of this, however, there still remain a number of special rules affecting Crown liability and there are some important instances in which the Crown (and sometimes other public authorities) is in a different position from private citizens.

FETTERING THE POWERS OF PUBLIC AUTHORITIES

During the First World War the British Government instituted a 'ship for ship' policy in an attempt to thwart the German blockade of British ports. This meant that neutral ships in British ports were allowed to leave only if they were replaced by other ships of the same tonnage. The owners of a Swedish ship called the *Amphitrite* wanted to send her to England in 1918 and in order to prevent her being detained they wrote to the British Legation in Stockholm to ask whether a guarantee could be given that if she sailed to England she would be allowed to leave freely. The answer was that the *Amphitrite* would earn her release if she came to England with a full cargo consisting of at least 60 per cent approved goods. On the strength of this undertaking she sailed to England with an approved cargo and was duly released and returned to Sweden. Her owners then wanted to send her on another voyage to England and obtained a similar assurance from the British Legation before she set out. She again carried an approved cargo but this time she was detained in a British port and eventually her owners sold her in order to avoid further loss.

After the war her owners brought a petition of right in the English courts claiming damages against the Crown for breach of contract.[6] It was not disputed that the undertaking to release the ship was made with the full authority of the Government but the court held that there was not an enforceable contract. In the opinion of the court the undertaking was merely an expression of intention to act in a particular way in a certain event. Rowlatt J. said:[7]

My main reason for so thinking is that it is not competent for the Government to fetter its future executive action, which must necessarily be determined by the needs of the community when the question arises. It cannot by contract hamper its freedom of action in matters which concern the welfare of the State.

Judgment was therefore given for the Crown.[8]

The rule laid down in this case, therefore, is that the Crown lacks the capacity, at least in certain circumstances, to enter into a contract that will 'fetter its future executive action'. This decision might have seemed very unfair to the suppliants: they were not obliged to

send their ship to England and they did so in reliance on the undertaking given by the British Government. Moreover, the Government
wanted the ship to come to England because it would bring much-
needed goods (the proviso concerning 60 per cent approved cargo
ensured this).

However, the basic powers of government cannot be subject to
bargain and it could be argued that the shipowners should have
known that the Government did not intend to enter into a legally
binding contract. There was no evidence that the Government was
not acting in good faith at the time when the undertaking was given
and if it was regarded as no more than an expression of intention no
complaint could be made if subsequent events necessitated a change
of policy.

The principle on which this case was decided has been applied in
a long line of cases concerned with public authorities other than the
Crown.[9] It was formulated in the following words by Lord Birken-
head in a case decided by the House of Lords in 1926:[10]

. . . if a person or public body is entrusted by the Legislature with certain
powers and duties expressly or impliedly for public purposes, those persons
or bodies cannot divest themselves of these powers and duties. They cannot
enter into any contract or take any action incompatible with the due
exercise of their powers or the discharge of their duties.

The question which must be asked, therefore, is whether the contract
is *compatible* with the functions of the body. The test is not whether in
any conceivable circumstances the contract might possibly interfere
with the functions of the body, but whether there is any *likelihood*
that it will.[11]

When applied to statutory bodies this principle could be regarded
as based either on public policy or on the doctrine of *ultra vires*, but in
regard to the Crown it must be regarded as resting on public policy.
Since the Crown derives its powers not only from statute but also
from the prerogative, the principle cannot in the case of the Crown
be limited to statutory powers. The precise limits of the principle are
not easy to formulate but it is clear that it is of restricted application:
the mere fact that a power possessed by a public body is in some way
limited does not invalidate the contract. Otherwise it would be very
hard for public bodies to contract at all since almost every contract
limits the exercise of their powers in some way.

A good illustration of this is *Blake* v. *Hendon Corporation*.[12] In this case the Corporation had a statutory power to dedicate land as a public park; it also had a statutory power to let land. It was argued that it could not dedicate a piece of land because this would deprive it of the power to let the land. It could, of course, be equally well argued that it could not let the land because this would prevent it from dedicating it.[13] The result would be that the authority would be unable to exercise either of its powers. This would be absurd and the court had no difficulty in rejecting the argument that the principle applied in this situation.

Another case of a similar kind was *Dowty Boulton Paul Ltd* v. *Wolverhampton Corporation*.[14] In 1936 the corporation had conveyed land to the company and had agreed that the company could use an adjoining airfield, which was owned by the corporation, for a period of ninety-nine years. The company manufactured and repaired aircraft and presumably would not have bought the land if they had been unable to use the airfield. In 1970, however, the corporation decided to close the airfield and use the land for a housing estate. They claimed that the agreement was not binding because it fettered their powers to use the land for any purpose other than that of an airfield. This contention was not accepted by the court, but the company's application for an injunction was refused; they had to be content with the remedy of damages. This was a good decision: it would have been wrong if the court had forced the corporation to keep the airfield open just for the benefit of the company (which had used it very little in recent years) but they were entitled to damages to compensate them for the breach of the agreement.[15]

In neither of the two preceding cases could it be said that the agreement was incompatible with the functions of the local authority. A good example of an agreement which was incompatible is *William Cory & Son Ltd* v. *London Corporation*.[16] The corporation was the health authority for the Port of London and in this capacity they had passed by-laws requiring boats carrying refuse on the river to have coverings of a certain standard so as to prevent the pollution of the river. The corporation was also the sanitary authority for the City and in this capacity they entered into a contract with the company in 1936 for the removal of refuse from the City by barge. Clause 1 of this contract contained provisions concerning the use of coverings which were more stringent than the by-laws then in force. In 1948, however, the corporation decided to pass new by-laws which were stricter than both the old by-laws and the terms of the contract. The company argued that the contract contained an implied term that the corporation would not make such by-laws and the question was whether such a term would be valid.[17] The court held that it would not. Lord Asquith put the matter like this:[18]

If the suggested term were express, it would have to take some such form as this: 'True we are charged by Parliament with the duty of making such by-laws with reference to refuse as may be called for from time to time by considerations of public health. But even if these considerations call, and call peremptorily, for a provision not less stringent than that made by the 1948 by-laws, even if a second plague of London is likely to occur, unless such provision is made, we undertake in such an event to neglect or violate our statutory duty so far as the requirements of such a by-law may exceed the requirements imposed by cl. 1 of our contract with the claimants.' Such a contractual provision would seem to be plainly invalid.

These cases have been considered in some detail to show how the principle works in practice. Not all the cases are easy to reconcile[19] and it is often difficult to predict how the courts will apply the principle in different situations. Some of the earlier cases seem to have given too wide a scope to the principle but in recent years it has been applied more narrowly.[20] It has indeed been argued that the principle should be abolished altogether. The Crown cannot be forced to refrain from any action it wants to take because the remedies of specific performance and injunction are not available against it[21] and if it wants to break its contract it can do so provided it pays compensation.[22] This argument cannot, however, be applied to other public authorities and it could be said that contractors should know that no public authority can make an agreement that disables it from carrying out its functions. Provided it is applied moderately and flexibly the doctrine does not seem to work injustice and it is unlikely that the courts today would apply it unless to do so was required by the public interest.[23]

APPROPRIATION OF FUNDS

At one time it was thought that the provision of funds by Parliament was a condition precedent to the validity of a Government contract. The main authority for this view was a dictum by one of the judges who decided the case of *Churchward* v. *The Queen* in 1865.[24] However, in this case the contract contained an express provision that payment was to be made out of 'monies provided by Parliament' and it was expressly provided in the Appropriation Acts passed during the years preceding the case that none of the monies provided by Parliament was to be used for this purpose. The dictum is, therefore, in no way binding and in 1934 the High Court of Australia expressly decided that appropriation of funds by Parliament was not a condition of the validity of a Government contract.[25]

Appropriations by Parliament relate to money to be spent, not to commitments for future expenditure which will not have to be met within the coming year. It would, therefore, be impossible for Parliament to appropriate funds for a contract which was due to run for more than a year – as many Government contracts do – and if prior appropriation were necessary the Government would be unable to enter into long-term contracts. The building of a motorway or the development of a missile would then become impossible since such contracts must obviously run for a number of years.

It seems fairly clear, therefore, that there is no such rule though, of course, payment cannot be made to a contractor without parliamentary approval. This does not mean that there must be a specific appropriation for each contract entered into by the Government; all that is necessary is that the contract should relate to a service for which money has been provided. Even if no money were appropriated, or if Parliament were specifically to provide that no money was to be used for the contract, this would not mean that the contract would be invalid. The contractor would be able to sue the Crown and obtain judgment. Satisfaction of the judgment would, however, depend on a grant of money by Parliament but in practice Parliament would, of course, provide the necessary funds.

ESTOPPEL

Estoppel is a doctrine of law that applies generally in legal relations between private persons. It arises if one person represents to another that certain facts exist and the other person acts on the basis of that representation and suffers loss as a result. Then the first person is estopped (prevented) from denying in subsequent legal proceedings that the representation was true. The effect of this doctrine, which is sometimes regarded as a rule of evidence and sometimes as a rule of substantive law, is that the person who was misled by the representation can, if he wishes, insist that the legal proceedings be conducted on the basis that the representation was true.

Despite some earlier doubts, it is now accepted that estoppel can apply to the Crown.[26] There are, however, two important limitations on the scope of estoppel in the case of both the Crown and other public authorities. The first is the doctrine of *ultra vires*.[27] If a public authority has no power to do a certain act, it cannot obtain that power by means of an estoppel.[28] If this were not so it would mean that a public authority could enlarge its powers through misrepresentation. In the words of Lord Greene M. R.:[29]

The power given to an authority under a statute is limited to the four corners of the power given. It would entirely destroy the whole doctrine of *ultra vires* if it was possible for the donee of a statutory power to extend his power by creating an estoppel.

The second limitation arises if a statutory duty is imposed on a public authority. Estoppel cannot prevent the authority from performing its duty. This is well illustrated by the case of *Maritime Electric Co.* v. *General Dairies Ltd.*[30] The appellant was a private company which sold electric power in the city of Fredericton in New Brunswick (Canada). It was a 'public utility' company within the meaning of the Public Utilities Act of New Brunswick[31] and section sixteen of this Act provided:

No public utility shall charge, demand, collect or receive a greater or less compensation for any service, than is prescribed in such schedules as are at the time established . . .

The respondent, a dairy in Fredericton, bought electricity from the power company but, due to an error by the latter in calculating the amount of electricity used, they were charged only one-tenth of the correct sum. More than two years later the power company realized its mistake and demanded the balance of the money. The dairy (which had calculated their payments to the farmers who supplied them with cream on the basis of the charges made for electric power) claimed that the power company was estopped from denying the correctness of its charges. The Privy Council held, however, that since the company had no legal power to charge less than the scheduled rates, it could not be estopped from claiming the correct sum.[32]

It is clear that if the Maritime Electric Company had entered into a contract to sell power at less than the statutory charge the contract would have been void. This raises the question of the relationship between this doctrine and the doctrine concerning the fettering of public powers: would the doctrine of estoppel be excluded whenever its operation would fetter the powers of a public body in a way that could not be done by contract? There is no direct authority but it seems logical that this should be so.

The rules applied in the cases discussed so far are reasonably clear but they can produce injustice where members of the public are misled by public authorities. For example, in the *Maritime Electric Company* case the dairy had relied on the statements received from the power company when they decided how much to pay the farmers. When they were then obliged to pay more for their electricity they ended up out of pocket. In order to remedy this, judges in some recent cases have applied estoppel more widely.

The first of these cases is *Robertson* v. *Minister of Pensions*.[33] This case concerned the right of an army officer to receive a disability pension and this depended on whether the disability was attributable to military service. The officer wrote to the War Office in 1941 and was told in reply, '. . . . your case has been duly considered and your disability has been accepted as attributable to military service.' When he received this letter he naturally thought that the matter was settled and consequently refrained from getting an independent medical opinion. Unfortunately, however, the administration of disablement claims had been transferred from the War Office to the Ministry of Pensions and the War Office was not, therefore, the proper department to deal with the matter. Some time later (after the X-ray plates had been lost) the Minister of Pensions decided that the disability was not attributable to military service. The officer appealed to the court.[34]

The argument he put forward was that the Minister of Pensions was estopped by the War Office letter from denying that the disability was attributable to military service. There were, however, a number of objections which could be made to this. First, the authority responsible for granting the pension was the Minister of Pensions. How could the Minister of Pensions be estopped by a letter, not from his own Ministry, but from the War Office? This objection was met by arguing that both departments were agents of the Crown: the War Office letter bound the Crown and consequently bound the Minister of Pensions, who was a Crown servant acting on behalf of the Crown. This was accepted by the court.[35]

The second problem was that it could be argued that the officer should have known that the War Office had no power to deal with the matter and he should not, therefore, have relied on their letter. However, the letter did not say that the War Office had made the decision: it merely said that a decision had been made and the officer was entitled to assume that the matter had been put before the competent authority (a medical officer or board appointed or recognized by the Minister of Pensions) [36] and they had made the decision. The representation, therefore, was simply one of fact: that a competent authority had made the decision. The officer had relied on this by failing to obtain an independent medical opinion. All the elements of estoppel seemed to be present.

Denning J. (as he then was) accepted this argument and decided in favour of the officer. [37] In the course of his judgment he laid down the principle which he considered to be applicable: [38]

... if a government department in its dealings with a subject takes it upon itself to assume authority upon a matter with which he is concerned, he is entitled to rely upon it having the authority which it assumes.

This principle was much wider than was necessary for the decision and was subject to strong criticism a few years later.

This occurred in the case of *Howell* v. *Falmouth Boat Construction Co. Ltd* [39] where it was argued by the owner of a ship that he was not obliged to pay for repairs which had been carried out on it because the repairers had not obtained a licence to do the work. This had happened during the last war and there was a regulation in force which made it an offence to carry out repairs on any ship without a licence from the Admiralty. A licensing official had given oral permission for the repairs to be done but no written licence had been issued until after the work had been started. In the Court of Appeal Denning L. J. (as he had then become) said that the repairers could not be regarded as having acted illegally since they had been given permission by the official. He then repeated the principle put forward in *Robertson*'s case. The House of Lords held on other grounds that no offence had been committed but they were not prepared to accept this principle. Lord Simonds referred to Lord Denning's principle and continued: [40]

My Lords, I know of no such principle in our law nor was any authority for it cited. The illegality of an act is the same whether or not the actor has been misled by an assumption of authority on the part of a government officer however high or low in the hierarchy. I do not doubt that in criminal proceedings it would be a material factor that the actor had been thus misled if knowledge was a necessary element of the offence, and in any case it would have a bearing on the sentence to be imposed. But that is not the question. The question is whether the character of an act done in face of a statutory prohibition is affected by the fact that it has been induced by a misleading assumption of authority. In my opinion the answer is clearly No. Such an answer may make more difficult the task of the citizen who is anxious to walk in the narrow way, but that does not justify a different answer being given.

Lord Normand also said:[41]

... neither a minister nor any subordinate officer of the Crown can by any conduct or representation bar the Crown from enforcing a statutory prohibition or entitle the subject to maintain that there has been no breach of it ...

It is clear, therefore, that at least where a criminal offence is involved estoppel cannot operate.

The next case was *Southend-on-sea Corporation* v. *Hodgson (Wickford) Ltd.*[42] In this case the respondent company had wanted to establish a builders' yard in Southend and had found a piece of land that seemed suitable. Before buying it, however, they wanted to make sure that they would be able to use it as a builders' yard and they wrote to the borough engineer to find out. He replied: 'The land ... has an existing user right as a builders' yard and no planning permission is therefore necessary.' The company then bought the land and started to use it. Unfortunately, however, the corporation subsequently received a large number of complaints about the user of the land and evidence was produced that it had no existing use as a builders' yard. The corporation therefore served an enforcement notice on the company requiring them to cease using the land for this purpose. The question before the court was the validity of this notice.

The argument of the company was that the corporation was estopped by the Borough Engineer's letter from denying that the land had an existing use as a builders' yard. This was a representation of fact[43] which had been acted on by the company when they bought the land. The court, however, held that the case was covered by the rule that estoppel cannot prevent the carrying out of a statutory duty. It was true that the corporation was not under a duty to serve an enforcement notice when the necessary planning permission had not been obtained – they merely had a discretion to do so – but the court considered that there was no difference between a statutory duty and a statutory discretion, since the corporation was under a duty 'to exercise a free and unhindered discretion'[44] – i.e. to exercise their discretion in the way which they believed best promoted the public interest. They would be prevented from doing this if they were estopped from considering the real user of the land. Therefore estoppel did not operate.

In 1970 another case came before the courts which raised issues very similar to those in the *Southend* case. This was the case of *Lever (Finance) Ltd* v. *Westminster Corporation*.[45] The company in this case wanted to develop a piece of land and they obtained planning permission from the corporation to build fourteen houses on the basis of a detailed plan. Later they wanted to move the site of one of the houses 17 feet nearer to the boundary of the land. The developers' architect spoke over the telephone to the corporation's planning officer and asked him whether the change would require further planning permission. The officer, who had unfortunately lost the relevant file, told him that the variation was not material and no further planning permission was necessary. In fact the variation was material and planning permission should have been obtained. When the house in question was being built the neighbours complained to the corporation. The architect subsequently applied for further planning permission but this was refused and the planning committee decided to issue an enforcement notice. The developers then went to court and asked for a declaration that they were entitled to complete the house on the site where it was. This was granted. In the Court of Appeal, where the judgment of the lower court was upheld, the main judgment was given by Lord Denning (who was now Master of the Rolls). He decided that the corporation were bound by the statement of their officer. This decision plainly conflicted with that in the *Southend* case. Lord Denning dealt with that case in the following way:[46]

I know that there are authorities which say that a public authority cannot be estopped by any representations made by its officers. It cannot be estopped from doing its public duty: see, for instance, the recent decision of the Divisional Court in *Southend-on-sea Corporation* v. *Hodgson (Wickford) Ltd*. But those statements must now be taken with considerable reserve.

He then went on to state the principle he considered applicable:[47]

If an officer, acting within the scope of his ostensible authority, makes a representation on which another acts, then a public authority may be bound by it, just as much as a private concern would be.

This is a slightly less sweeping version of the principle first put forward in *Robertson*'s case – the word 'may' suggests that the rule will not apply in all circumstances – but it seems clear that Lord Denning's views remain basically unaltered.[48]

These are the leading cases on the problem and it is plain that they are to some extent inconsistent. The reason for this is that there are two conflicting policy considerations pulling in different directions: on the one hand it is unfair that a member of the public should suffer as a result of relying on official advice; on the other hand it is undesirable that public authorities should be prevented from doing their duty because one of their officers has made a mistake. This dilemma appears most clearly in a case like *Southend-on-sea Corporation* v. *Hodgson (Wickford) Ltd.*[49] The company in this case quite understandably felt that they had been badly treated by the corporation. But if the court had applied estoppel it would have meant that the people living in the vicinity of the land would have had to put up with a builders' yard in what was presumably a residential area. Why should they suffer because of a mistake by a council official?

It is true that in many of the cases the person misled might also be thought in some measure to blame: thus if the officer in *Robertson* v. *Ministry of Pensions*[50] had written to the Ministry of Pensions instead of the War Office the misunderstanding over his pension would never have arisen. Likewise in the town planning cases the person concerned could have obtained an official decision on the question by applying in proper form to the planning authority instead of asking a council official[51]. The common feature of all these cases, however, is that the official concerned did assume authority in the matter. It was this assumption of authority by a person in an official position that was really the cause of the trouble and for this reason there should be some remedy where his information turns out to be unreliable.

Besides this policy conflict there is also a conceptual problem. If the rules concerning *ultra vires* and statutory duties are strictly applied there is very little room for estoppel. For example, the effect of the decision in *Lever (Finance) Ltd* v. *Westminster Corporation*[52] was that the planning officer was able to give a binding decision on a question which should have been decided by the council.[53] He had no power to do this and according to the *ultra vires* doctrine his decision should have been invalid.[54] Secondly, there is the argument put forward in the *Southend* case that a planning authority is under a statutory duty to consider all planning questions on their merits. This is undoubtedly true and it would follow from this that the application of estoppel in such a case would infringe the rule concerning statutory duties.

There may be some cases in which the application of estoppel is justifiable[55] but in many cases a better solution would be to hold that the authority is not bound by estoppel but that the person misled has an action for damages in tort against the officer and the authority in those cases where the statement is made negligently.[56] This solution would have the merit of compensating the person misled without preventing the authority from fulfilling its statutory duty.

AGENCY

What happens if an official concludes a contract on behalf of a public authority and it is subsequently discovered that he had no authority to do so? This is a question of some importance because members of the public do not always have any means of knowing who is authorized to contract on behalf of a public authority. Government contracts, for example, are usually concluded by civil servants who receive their authority from internal departmental rules which are not made public. In private law the contractor might find a remedy in the doctrine of ostensible or apparent authority. Under this doctrine, which is closely related to estoppel, a principal is bound by a contract concluded by his agent, even if the agent acted outside his authority, if the principal represented by words or by conduct to the contractor that the agent had authority to act. If the principal made no representation the contractor can sue the agent for breach of an implied warranty of authority – i.e. for leading the contractor to believe that he was authorized.

In public law, however, the contractor is in a weaker position. It has been held by the courts that the doctrine of implied warranty of authority does not apply to Crown servants.[57] The servants of other public authorities are probably liable under this doctrine but there is no justification for an exception in favour of Crown servants.

There is also a decision of the Privy Council which suggests that it may be difficult to establish a representation by the Crown that one of its servants had authority to act on its behalf. This is the case of *A.-G. for Ceylon* v. *Silva*.[58] Under the Ceylon Customs Ordinance the Principal Collector of Customs was empowered to sell goods that remained unclaimed for more than three months in the customs

warehouse. Acting under this power he advertised some steel plates
for sale and these were bought by Silva. The plates had in fact
belonged to the Crown and, since the Crown was not bound by the
Ordinance, the Principal Collector had no authority to sell them. He
therefore refused to deliver the plates and Silva sued the Crown for
damages for breach of contract. He claimed that even if the Principal Collector had no actual authority to sell the goods, the Crown
was nevertheless bound by the contract because the Principal Collector was acting within his apparent authority.

The Privy Council rejected this argument. They pointed out that
for the doctrine to apply the representation must be made by the
principal (the Crown) and not by the agent:[59]

No representation by the agent as to the extent of his authority can amount
to a 'holding out' by the principal. No public officer, unless he possesses
some special power, can hold out on behalf of the Crown that he or some
other public officer has the right to enter into a contract in respect of the
property of the Crown when in fact no such right exists.

It might have been thought that by appointing the Principal Collector to his post the Crown was representing that he had authority
to sell the goods. But his authority came from the Ordinance and, as
the Ordinance did not apply to Crown goods, the Privy Council considered that he could not be regarded as having such authority.

This judgment might have been legally correct but it was rather
hard on the buyer (as was recognized by the Privy Council). At first
sight it seems to leave little scope for the operation of the doctrine of
apparent authority where the Crown is concerned but this decision
may not be as restrictive as it appears at first sight. First of all,
the case was rather unusual in that the Principal Collector's authority was derived from legislation so that in theory the limits of that
authority could have been discovered by a contractor. Secondly,
the Privy Council specifically left open the question whether the
appropriate Minister could hold out an officer as having authority
to bind the Crown.[60] Finally, the phrase 'unless he possesses some
special power' in the passage quoted above implies that there are
some situations in which an officer does have the power to represent
that another officer is entitled to contract on behalf of the Crown.
One case in which it has been suggested[61] that this would be so is
where the officer making the representation is himself authorized to
conclude the contract. If he represented to a contractor that another

officer had the necessary authority the Crown would be bound. If this is correct the scope of the doctrine with regard to the Crown may not be as narrow as has been supposed.

CROWN LIABILITY IN TORT

It is provided in the Crown Proceedings Act 1947 that the Crown is subject to the same liability in tort as a private person in respect of torts committed by its servants and agents.[62] This is subject to the proviso that the Crown is not liable unless the servant or agent is himself liable.[63] There are a few rather rare situations in which a master is liable in private law for the torts of his servant even though the servant is not himself liable.[64] The Crown would not be liable in these circumstances, though there is no good reason why it should be protected in this way.[65]

The term 'agent' is defined in the Act to include an independent contractor; so the Crown is liable for the torts of independent contractors employed by it to the same extent as it would be if it were a private person.[66] The Act does not, however, define the term 'servant' and it is not always easy to decide which persons are servants of the Crown. There is no doubt that Ministers (expressly included by section 38(2) under the definition of 'officer'), civil servants and members of the armed forces are Crown servants. There is less certainty about the holders of certain public offices and it seems that the matter depends on the degree of control which the Crown through its Ministers can exercise over them in the course of their duties.[67] If they have a substantial degree of independence they may not be Crown servants.[68]

It is also provided in the Act[69] that where functions are imposed on an *officer* of the Crown by common law or by statute, the Crown is liable for torts committed by the officer in the course of performing his functions to the same extent as it would if those functions had been imposed by instructions lawfully given by the Crown. The Act defines 'officer' as including a servant of the Crown[70] but it is not clear what categories of persons other than servants are officers of the Crown. On the basis of the test of governmental control, it would seem that policemen and judges are not Crown servants.[71] They may, however, be officers of the Crown, but the Crown would still not be liable on their account because of two provisions in the Act. The first is section 2(6) which provides that the Crown is not liable for the torts of its officers unless the officer was directly or indirectly appointed by the Crown and was paid wholly out of the Consolidated Fund or certain other funds. Since all policemen are paid partly out of the local rates this excludes liability on their account. Secondly, section 2(5) provides that the Crown is not liable for anything done by anyone discharging responsibilities of a judicial nature or any responsibility concerned with the execution of judicial process. This excludes liability for judges.[72]

Apart from liability for torts committed by its servants and agents, the Crown Proceedings Act also imposes liability in three other important situations.[73] First, it is provided that the Crown is subject to the same liability as a private person in respect of the duties owed by a person at common law to his servants and agents by reason of being their employer. This includes, for example, the duty of an employer to provide a safe system of work. Secondly, the Crown is liable in respect of the breach of the duties attaching at common law to the ownership, occupation, possession or control of property. This, for example, would extend to the Crown liability under the rule in *Rylands* v. *Fletcher*.[74] Finally, the Crown is liable for breach of statutory duty if the duty is binding on the Crown, provided it is also binding on persons other than the Crown and its officers. However, as will be seen below,[75] many statutes are not binding on the Crown.

THE ROYAL PREROGATIVE AND ACTS OF STATE

Under the prerogative[76] the Crown has the power to take possession of, or to destroy, the property of private persons in time of war or national emergency.[77] This is known as the defence prerogative and its purpose is the defence of the realm. At common law there is a right to compensation, although this was established only in 1964. This was in the case of *Burmah Oil Co. Ltd* v. *Lord Advocate*[78] which arose out of events which took place in Burma (then a Crown colony) during the last war. When the Japanese army was advancing into Burma and it became clear that they would soon occupy the whole country, the General Officer Commanding, on the basis of directions from the British Government, ordered the destruction of oil wells and other installations in Burma belonging to the plaintiffs. This was done in order to deny these facilities to the enemy. The question before the House of Lords was whether the plaintiffs were legally entitled to compensation. The case was dealt with on the assumption that no statutory powers to destroy the property existed and the majority of the court considered that the destruction was carried out under the prerogative. It was held by the majority that the acts of the Crown were lawful but that compensation was payable. The only case in which there is no right to compensation is battle damage, i.e. damage deliberately or accidentally inflicted in the course of actually fighting the enemy. The destruction in this case was not battle damage and compensation was therefore payable.

The victory of the plaintiffs was, however, short-lived. Soon after the decision was announced a statute was passed to change the law. This was the War Damage Act 1965, which provided as follows:[79]

No person shall be entitled at common law to receive from the Crown compensation in respect of damage to, or destruction of, property caused (whether before or after the passing of this Act, within or outside the United Kingdom) by acts lawfully done by, or on the authority of, the Crown during, or in contemplation of the outbreak of, a war in which the Sovereign was, or is, engaged.

Since this provision was retroactive it meant that the Burmah Oil Company was deprived of its compensation. The Act does not, however, entirely nullify the general principle laid down in the case: for example the Act would not apply to the requisitioning, as distinct from the destruction, of property.

It is, of course, unlikely that this prerogative power will be used very often, because legislation is normally passed at the outbreak of war to give the Crown power to requisition and destroy property. Such legislation always provides for compensation and there is a rule that when a statute grants the Crown a power which covers the same ground as a prerogative power, but which imposes conditions or limitations, the Crown must act in accordance with the statutory provisions and cannot claim that it is acting under the prerogative.[80] This rule was laid down in the case of *A.-G.* v. *De Keyser's Royal Hotel*[81] which concerned the requisitioning of a hotel during the First World War. A statute granted the power to do this and provided for compensation but the Crown claimed that it was not obliged to pay compensation because it had a prerogative power to requisition the hotel. (At this time it had not been established that compensation was also payable under the prerogative.) The House of Lords, however, held that the Crown could not make use of the prerogative in these circumstances.

Certain acts performed by the Crown in the course of its relations with foreign countries – for example, the declaration of war, the signing of a treaty or the annexation of territory – are usually referred to as acts of State. The importance of the doctrine of act of State lies in the fact that in certain circumstances the plea of act of State can prevent the courts from considering whether any legal liability results from the commission of such an act. This does not mean that the act is lawful, but merely that it is outside the jurisdiction of the British courts to consider whether it is lawful or not: the only means by which redress can then be obtained is through diplomatic channels or before an international tribunal. However, it is not certain that this legal immunity results from every act of State: or perhaps it would be more accurate to say that the term 'act of State' has two meanings and it is only when the narrower meaning applies that the jurisdiction of the courts is ousted.[82] To avoid confusion the term 'act of State' will, therefore, be used hereafter only in the sense of an act of such a character that the courts have no jurisdiction to determine its lawfulness.

The exact relationship between act of State and the prerogative is not clear but it seems that all acts of State are performed under the prerogative. It does not, however, follow that all prerogative acts are acts of State. Thus, for example, the taking or destroying of property under the defence prerogative is not an act of State; the courts have full jurisdiction to determine the legality of such acts and, as has already been mentioned, there is at common law a right to compensation.

It is an important principle that the defence of act of State cannot apply to any act done within the U.K. The foremost authority for this is the case of *Johnstone* v. *Pedlar*[83] which concerned an American citizen who had been arrested in Dublin in 1918 (when the whole of Ireland was part of the U.K.). The police found some money in his possession, which they took from him and refused to return. He brought an action for the detention of the money and the defence of act of State was raised. The House of Lords held, however, that the defence could not apply to acts committed within the U.K. even if the plaintiff was an alien.[84]

The doctrine can operate where the act takes place outside the realm. It will protect not only the Crown itself but also anyone who acted on Crown orders or whose act was subsequently ratified by the Crown. This is illustrated by the old case of *Buron* v. *Denman*.[85] The plaintiff in this case was a Spaniard who was engaged in the slave trade in West Africa. The defendant was a British naval officer who had been instructed to suppress the slave trade. He had landed on the coast of West Africa and destroyed the plaintiff's barracoon (a fort used for holding slaves) and released his slaves. In doing this he had exceeded his instructions but his actions were subsequently ratified and adopted by the Crown and this was held to constitute a defence to the action in trespass which was brought against him.

It does not follow from this, however, that legal proceedings can be thwarted simply because the defence of act of State is raised. The courts always have the power to decide whether the act, even if it was done on the orders of the Crown, had the quality of an act of State. This was illustrated in the most recent case on the subject, *A.-G.* v. *Nissan*,[86] which arose out of the activities of the British peace-keeping force in Cyprus. In 1963 serious disturbances broke out between the Greek and Turkish communities on the island and an agreement was made between the British and Cypriot Governments that British troops would assist the Cypriot Government to restore peace. The British force then commenced operations in pursuance of this agreement and a contingent of this force took over a luxury hotel near Nicosia for use as their headquarters. The hotel belonged to the plaintiff, who was a United Kingdom citizen, and he subsequently brought legal proceedings against the Crown in England in order to obtain compensation.

His claim was put forward under three heads: first, that the actions of the Crown were lawful acts under the prerogative which gave him a right to compensation (as had been decided in the *Burmah Oil* case); secondly, on the basis of a contract which he claimed the British High Commissioner had made with him; and thirdly, he claimed damages for trespass to his chattels. One of the defences raised by the Crown was that the taking of the hotel was an act of State. This was, however, rejected by the House of Lords when the case came before them on a preliminary issue. It was held by the majority of the court that the quality of the act was not that of an act of State. The judgments were, however, rather vague on exactly what the essential qualities of an act of State are. Thus Lord Pearce said, after pointing out that the treaty did not expressly provide for the occupation of the hotel:[87]

No doubt it was a sensible place for them to be stationed. But, had it not existed, they would have been stationed elsewhere. There is nothing in the facts pleaded to suggest that the occupation of the hotel was a sine qua non of the performance of the treaty. It was quite a subsidiary matter. In my opinion it did not have the character of an act of State.

Lord Pearson said:[88]

As to the alleged act of state, it is necessary to consider what is meant by the expression 'act of state', even if it is not expedient to attempt a definition. It is an exercise of sovereign power. Obvious examples are making war and peace, making treaties with foreign sovereigns, and annexations and cessions of territory. Apart from these obvious examples, an act of state must be something exceptional. Any ordinary governmental act is cognizable by an ordinary court of law (municipal not international): if a subject alleges that the governmental act was wrongful and claims damages or other relief in respect of it, his claim will be entertained and heard and determined by the court. An act of state is something not recognizable by the court: if a claim is made in respect of it, the court will have to ascertain the facts but if it then appears that the act complained of was an act of State the court must refuse to adjudicate upon the claim. In such a case the court does not come to any decision as to the legality or illegality, or the rightness or wrongness, of the act complained of: the decision is that because it was an act of state the court has no jurisdiction to entertain a claim in respect of it. This is a very unusual situation and strong evidence is required to prove that it exists in a particular case.

Sending troops into a foreign country would normally be an act of State and the same would apply to military operations which were necessary to achieve their object (such as blowing up a bridge or shelling enemy positions) but actions not militarily necessary for attaining the objectives of the operation might not be included.

Until recently it was thought by many writers that the defence of act of state could never apply if the plaintiff was a British subject (or at least a U.K. citizen), but doubt was thrown on this rule in *Nissan's* case where only one judge (Lord Reid) based his decision on it. The main argument in favour of such a rule is that if a foreigner is injured by British action he can complain to his own Government which might take steps through diplomatic channels to obtain redress; a citizen of the United Kingdom cannot do this. (On this basis, of course, the defence should be available against the citizens of independent Commonwealth countries since their Governments can take diplomatic action just as effectively as foreign governments.) However, it might be thought that if a U.K. citizen chooses to live in a foreign country he cannot expect to be in a better position than the local citizens if his property is destroyed in the course of military operations against that country.

The arguments seem, therefore, to be fairly evenly balanced. If, however, the nationality of the person concerned were taken into account, the defence of act of State should be excluded only in the case of U.K. citizens; the citizens of independent Commonwealth countries should be in the same position as aliens.

The act of State doctrine relates to events that lie at the frontier of law and power politics. All States have to take high-handed action at times in order to safeguard what they regard as their vital interests and Britain would be unduly hampered in her foreign policy if the courts tried to impose legal restraints on such actions. The lawfulness of these acts should be decided by international law and disputes should be settled diplomatically or before international tribunals. However, if the Government was allowed to raise the plea of act of State with regard to its domestic actions the foundations of civil liberties and the rule of law in this country would be completely undermined; and this applies just as much where the persons affected are aliens as where they are citizens. It is, therefore, right that the defence should not operate within the U.K. and colonies. Some writers, however, suggest that it should be excluded when the act takes place anywhere within the Queen's Dominions; but this would mean that the defence could not apply to acts committed within those independent Commonwealth countries which recognize the Queen as their Head of State (though not the republics, such as Cyprus, and those Commonwealth countries with indigenous monarchs) and this seems inappropriate since these countries are just as independent politically as any foreign country.

CROWN IMMUNITY FROM STATUTES

There is a well-established rule that statutes do not bind the Crown unless it is expressly provided in the statute or is a necessary implication from the words of the statute that the Crown is intended to be bound.[89] It is not always clear exactly when the Crown is bound 'by necessary implication' and it seems that in earlier times a more liberal approach was adopted than is the case today.[90] Thus, until the middle of the nineteenth century the courts tended to approach the matter by looking at the policy of the statute in order to decide whether Parliament intended the Crown to be bound. In the second half of the nineteenth century, however, the courts adopted a stricter approach in line with the general tendency to interpret statutes more literally. Thus, in a case decided in 1887, but not reported until 1903, it was stated that a necessary implication would not arise unless the legislation would otherwise be meaningless.[91]

The present-day position is best illustrated by the decision of the Privy Council in *Province of Bombay* v. *Municipal Corporation of Bombay*[92] in which it was held that a statute giving the municipality power to carry water-mains through any land 'whatsoever in the city' did not apply to land owned by the Crown. The Board stated:[93]

If . . . it is manifest from the very terms of the statute, that it was the intention of the legislature that the Crown should be bound, then the result is the same as if the Crown had been expressly named.

Their Lordships went on to say:[94]

If it can be affirmed that, at the time when the statute was passed and received the royal sanction, it was apparent from its terms that its beneficent purpose must be wholly frustrated unless the Crown were bound, then it may be inferred that the Crown has agreed to be bound.

However, the Board disapproved the principle, put forward in the court below, that a necessary implication would arise if the legislation could not operate with reasonable efficiency unless the Crown were bound.[95]

The results of this restrictive approach can be rather strange. Thus in *Cooper* v. *Hawkins*[96] a War Office employee who was driving a street locomotive through Aldershot in 1903 in order to deliver a load of coal to a balloon factory was charged with breaking the speed limit (of two miles an hour) imposed by the Locomotives Act of 1865. It was held, however, that the statute did not bind the Crown and since he was a Crown servant and had been driving the locomotive in the course of his duty he could not be convicted. It has also been held that the Rent Restriction Acts 1920–3 did not bind the Crown so that Crown tenants and even sub-tenants could not benefit from them.[97] Today, however, a great many statutes contain clauses specifically providing for the Crown to be bound.[98]

Even though the immunity of the Crown from onerous statutes is quite considerable, it has been suggested by various writers that the Crown can take advantage of a statute that confers a benefit even though there is no express or implied provision that the statute applies to the Crown.[99] This could even mean that the Crown might be able to claim the benefit of a statute when its operation favoured the Crown but claim immunity when it did not. This point was considered, but not decided, by Scrutton L. J. in *Cayzer, Irvine & Co.* v. *Board of Trade*:[100]

The only remaining question, which is one of great historical interest and importance, is whether the Crown can successfully say: 'We are not bound by the statute but we are at liberty to take advantage of it.' At first sight such a statement appears somewhat strange. There is undoubtedly a long series of statements in textbooks repeating each other for some centuries; but there is something to be said for the view argued by Sir John Simon that they start with a passage in an unsuccessful argument of a law officer which was not even relevant to the case before the Court, but which has been taken out by a text-writer and repeated for centuries until it was believed that it must have some foundation.

The rule is, therefore, rather doubtful. It seems fairly clear that if the Crown claims the benefit of a right given by statute it must accept any restrictions or conditions attaching to the right in the statute (or in an amending statute): it cannot claim that the part of the statute that imposes the restriction does not apply to it.[101]

The common law position has, however, been altered by the Crown Proceedings Act. Section 31(1) provides:

This Act shall not prejudice the right of the Crown to take advantage of the provisions of an Act of Parliament although not named therein; and it is hereby declared that in any civil proceedings against the Crown the provisions of any Act of Parliament which could, if the proceedings were between subjects, be relied upon by the defendant as a defence to the proceedings, whether in whole or in part, or otherwise, may, subject to any express provision to the contrary, be so relied upon by the Crown.

The first part of this merely preserves the common law rights of the Crown but the second part establishes that the Crown can always rely on a *defence* in a statute unless there is an express provision to the contrary.

When the Crown is not bound by a statute the immunity also applies to Crown servants provided they are acting in the course of their duties. Thus, as was seen above, a War Office employee who broke a speed limit while acting in the course of his duty was acquitted once it was established that the statute imposing the limit did not bind the Crown.[102] Likewise a Crown servant enjoys immunity from taxation in respect of money received by him on behalf of the Crown[103] (though not, of course, in respect of his personal income).

It is also said that agents of the Crown are entitled to immunity when they are acting on behalf of the Crown and there are some cases which have held that immunity from having to pay rates extends to certain persons who are not even servants or agents of the Crown but are regarded as being '*in consimili casu*' with servants and agents (i.e. in the same position as them). It is not clear exactly who falls into this category but assize court buildings and judges' and policemen's lodgings are exempt from rates for this reason.[104] It has been stated by Lord Asquith that:[105]

Persons will tend to be placed in this category if the public functions which they discharge are closely connected with the exercise of the Royal prerogative; e.g. *inter alia*, the administration of justice, the preservation of public order, the making of war and the conclusion of peace.

The courts seem anxious, however, to limit this category as much as possible. It is not clear whether such persons would be entitled to immunity from statutes other than those imposing rates or taxes.

Although there are some circumstances in which the Crown obviously should be exempt from a statute – there is no reason, for example, why the Crown should pay income tax to itself – the immunity given by the present law is far too wide. It would be better if the rule were turned the other way round so that all statutes would apply to the Crown unless the Crown was expressly or impliedly exempt. This would limit the Crown's immunity to those cases where it is really necessary and would be more in keeping with the idea of the rule of law.

PROCEDURE AND REMEDIES

The Treasury publishes a list of Government departments which can sue or be sued in their own name. Where none of these departments is appropriate the action is brought by or against the Attorney-General.[106] In most respects the action proceeds in the same way as it would if private parties were involved but there are restrictions on the remedies that may be obtained against the Crown. Thus it is provided by section 21(1) of the Crown Proceedings Act that no injunction or order for specific performance, for the recovery of land or for the delivery of property can be made against the Crown. Section 21(2) provides:

The court shall not in any civil proceedings grant any injunction or make any order against an officer of the Crown if the effect of granting the injunction or making the order would be to give any relief against the Crown which could not have been obtained in proceedings against the Crown.

The effect of this seems to be that Ministers and other servants of the Crown[107] cannot be restrained by injunction when acting in their official capacities. Thus in *Merricks* v. *Heathcoat-Amory*[108] an attempt was made to obtain an injunction against the Minister of Agriculture to prevent him from seeking parliamentary approval for a scheme for marketing potatoes. It was held, however, that in laying the scheme before Parliament the Minister was acting in his capacity as an officer of the Crown and accordingly no injunction could be made.

The Act does, however, provide[109] that a declaration can be given in lieu of an injunction or the other orders mentioned and, since the Crown will always respect such a declaration, this will normally be just as good. It is, however, quite common in legal proceedings for one of the parties to obtain an interim injunction to maintain the *status quo* until the main action is decided. Unfortunately it has been held[110] that the courts cannot grant such a thing as an interim declaration; so there is no equivalent remedy to an interim injunction when the Crown is involved.

If a judgment is given against the Crown no order for execution can issue. Instead the court issues a certificate stating the amount of money payable and this is paid by the appropriate Government department.[111] The idea behind this provision and the provisions concerning injunctions and orders for specific performance is probably that it would be unseemly if Government property were seized in execution or if a Minister were to be imprisoned for contempt of court. It is also possible that it was envisaged that on certain occasions the Government might deliberately break the law where the safety of the country demanded this. Such action can always be legitimated *ex post facto* by a retrospective Act of Parliament; but if it were possible to obtain an injunction against the Crown or the relevant Minister the Government could be involved in a clash with the courts. It is unfortunate, however, that no solution to the problem of the interim injunction has been found.

CROWN PRIVILEGE IN THE LAW OF EVIDENCE

A few months before the outbreak of the Second World War the British submarine *Thetis* sank during a trial dive. Relatives of the men who had lost their lives decided to sue the builders of the ship for negligence. In order to prove their case they wanted the shipbuilders to produce various documents including the contract between the shipbuilders and the Admiralty, plans, specifications, letters and a foreman's notebook. On instructions from the Admiralty, the shipbuilders objected to the production of these documents and an affidavit sworn by the First Lord of the Admiralty was presented to the court in which he stated that he believed it would be injurious to the public interest for any of the documents to be disclosed to any person.

As Britain was by this time at war, and as the documents must have contained many technical details which would have been of great use to the enemy, it was not surprising that the court refused to order their production. However, when the case came before the House of Lords, the Lord Chancellor, Lord Simon, took the opportunity to lay down the law in general terms as to when the Crown could claim that documents should not be produced in the course of civil proceedings on the ground that this would be contrary to the public interest.

Lord Simon stated that there were two circumstances in which a claim of privilege might be upheld: first, if the contents of the particular document were such that its production would not be in the public interest (for example, where disclosure would be injurious to national defence or to relations with foreign countries); and secondly, if the document belonged to a class which should be withheld, as a class, irrespective of the contents of the particular document in question. This second ground would normally only apply to communications with, or within, Government departments and the reason why it was thought desirable for all documents falling into such a class to be withheld was that it was felt that 'the candour and completeness of such communications might be prejudiced'[112] if the possibility existed that their disclosure might be ordered at some future time.

Duncan v. *Cammell, Laird & Co.*[113] – this was the name of the case – was not, of course, the first time a court had refused to order the production of a document on the ground that this was contrary to the public interest. But what was so important about the case was that the House of Lords laid it down as a general rule applying in all civil proceedings that if the appropriate Minister took objection in due form to the production of a document, the court had to treat this as conclusive and could not examine the document itself so as to reach an independent decision. It was this rule, which made the Government the final arbiter as to which documents should be withheld, that aroused criticism of the strongest kind and which was eventually overruled a quarter of a century later.

The way in which this came about was very interesting from the point of view of the doctrine of precedent. The rule had been undermined by criticism for some time; then the House of Lords held in a Scottish case that it was not part of the law of Scotland.[114] Commonwealth courts refused to follow it[115] and the Court of Appeal rebelled.[116] Finally in 1967 the House of Lords repudiated the rule in the case of *Conway* v. *Rimmer*.[117] This was an action for malicious prosecution by a former probationary police constable (Conway) against his former superintendent (Rimmer). The documents in question were four reports written by Rimmer about Conway when the latter was on probation and a report sent by Rimmer to his chief constable with the intention that it be given to the Director of Public Prosecutions in connection with the prosecution of Conway on a criminal charge. It was this prosecution, which failed, that was the foundation of the action for malicious prosecution.

Clearly the documents could have been very important in establishing the plaintiff's case and both parties in fact desired their production, but the Home Secretary objected on the ground that they fell within a class which should be protected from disclosure. In other words this was a 'class' case, not a 'contents' case as was *Duncan* v. *Cammell, Laird*. The reason why protection was wanted for this class of documents appeared to be the 'candour' argument: that future reports would be less candidly written if these reports were made public.

The House of Lords recognized that two important policy considerations could conflict in cases such as this. On the one hand, the efficient running of the public service, and sometimes even the safety of the country, could require that certain documents be kept secret; on the other hand, it might be impossible to do justice in a particular case unless such documents were produced. In the court's view the solution to this dilemma is that these conflicting considerations should be weighed up in each case in order to decide what the right solution is. The interests of the State must be balanced against the rights of the individual. The court held, moreover, that it is the judge who must make this decision. It was recognized that in some cases the public interest will be of such a nature that no private interest could prevail against it. In others the reasons given by the Minister will be of such a character that a judge would be unable to appreciate their weight. But these would be exceptional cases: normally the judge would first consider the reasons given by the Minister in his affidavit and then, if he was not convinced, he could examine the documents privately himself in order to decide whether they should be put in as evidence. (In *Conway* v. *Rimmer* itself the House of Lords examined the documents and decided that they should be produced.)

Where privilege is claimed on the basis of the content of the particular document it would be only in rare cases that the courts would not uphold the Minister's claim. Even where privilege is claimed on a 'class' basis the courts will pay a great deal of respect to what the Minister says. Certain classes of documents – for example Cabinet papers, Foreign Office dispatches or high-level departmental minutes – would probably never be disclosed. But in the case of more routine documents, especially where the 'candour' argument is put forward, the courts are likely to prove much harder to convince. Some of the judgments were in fact rather scathing about the 'candour' argument,[118] but it is a fact of human nature that most people are likely to tone down unpleasant comments about someone else if they know that what they said might become publicly known. There is also the problem of libel: it is true that public officers writing reports will normally be protected by qualified privilege but if judges and M.P.s feel that absolute privilege is necessary to protect them in their duties, why should civil servants and police officers not have similar protection?

This problem is well illustrated by *Rogers* v. *Secretary of State for the Home Department*.[119] This case concerned the Gaming Board, which was set up by Act of Parliament 'to keep under review the extent and character of gaming in Great Britain'[120] and had the duty of deciding whether to grant a certificate of consent to anyone wishing to open a gambling establishment. In this case a company had applied for certificates in respect of a number of bingo clubs it wished to open and the Board wrote to the Sussex police asking them to give any information they had about the director of the company. A reply was received from the assistant chief constable and the certificates were subsequently refused. The director of the company claimed to have been sent a copy of the assistant chief constable's letter by an anonymous person and he instituted proceedings against the assistant chief constable for criminal libel on the basis of what was allegedly written in the letter. Clearly it was essential to his case that the original letter be produced in court but the Home Secretary issued a certificate[121] claiming privilege on the ground that if such communications were disclosed the Board might find it difficult in future to obtain the full and frank information it needs.

This was a strong argument. The reason why Parliament set up the Gaming Board was to ensure that gambling in Britain would not be taken over by criminal elements; consequently it was very important for the Board to vet all applicants for licences very carefully. Under the Act they were obliged to take into consideration 'the character, reputation and financial standing'[122] of applicants. To do this they would have to collect a good deal of information about an applicant and this would normally be supplied by the police and various other people. If such information is liable to be disclosed, however, it is less likely to be given. Even though the police would still co-operate with the Board it is unlikely that police informers (often members of the underworld themselves) would be prepared to give information if they knew that it might be made public. The court recognized this and held that the documents should not be disclosed.

Finally, a few remaining points about Crown privilege should be mentioned. (The House of Lords in *Rogers*' case said that the term 'Crown privilege' was misleading since it is not really a privilege of the Crown but a rule of evidence based on the public interest; nevertheless it is a convenient term to use.) First: although most cases are concerned with documents, the rule can apply to oral evidence as well.[123] Secondly: although the matter is normally raised by the appropriate Minister, it can if necessary be raised by a party, a witness or even by the court itself.[124] Thirdly: the rule is not restricted to documents emanating from, or in the possession of, a Government department;[125] nor need the Crown be a party to the proceedings. Finally, almost all the cases where the question has arisen have been civil proceedings; in criminal proceedings evidence is much less likely to be excluded on this ground but police informers would normally be protected.

16
Judicial Review

INTRODUCTION

This chapter is concerned with the role of the judiciary in the administrative process. Courts do not, of course, have any direct concern with administration. They are concerned with law and they can, therefore, intervene only if a breach of the law has occurred. If, however, a public authority has acted illegally, the courts have the power and the duty to take action if the matter is brought before them. The starting point of judicial review is *ultra vires*. If a statute gives a public authority power to do something, that power is always limited. There will be limits on what may be done; the purposes for which the power may be used will often be specified; and the procedure that must be followed may be laid down. If the authority steps outside these limits it will be acting beyond its powers (*ultra vires*): its action will be unlawful and the courts will intervene.[1]

At its simplest, therefore, judicial review is the means of ensuring that the will of Parliament is obeyed. It is an essential corollary of parliamentary supremacy. If it were only this, however, judicial review would be little more than a branch of statutory interpretation. But the courts have gone further. They have not concerned themselves merely with what the legislation actually says, or what the legislative body clearly intended; they have also read into the legislation requirements which are supposedly implied by the words used but which are actually the creation of the courts. They have thus built up a body of judge-made law which is deemed to apply to all public authorities unless it is clearly and expressly excluded by the relevant legislation. The pretext for the courts' intervention is still usually *ultra vires* but in some circumstances this is wearing rather thin and it may be better in some cases to regard the common law, rather than the supposed meaning of the relevant legislation, as the basis of their intervention.

It might be useful at the outset to say something about remedies since a discussion of the circumstances in which the courts take action will not make proper sense unless the remedies available are kept in mind. There are two ways in which a remedy may be obtained: by a direct challenge or by a challenge in collateral proceedings. In the former case the object of the proceedings is simply to impugn some act of the administration (or, in the case of failure to act, to require action to be taken); in collateral proceedings the immediate purpose of the proceedings is something quite different and the validity of the administrative act arises incidentally. An example will make this distinction clear. Assume that a local authority makes a by-law that is thought to be invalid. A person affected by it has two choices: he can either go to court and ask to have it declared invalid (direct challenge); or he can ignore it and wait for the local authority to take enforcement proceedings. If he is charged with a breach of the by-law, he can claim that it is invalid and the court will then have to determine its validity before it can decide whether he has committed an offence. This is a challenge in collateral proceedings. In many circumstances, however, an opportunity to challenge an administrative act in collateral proceedings will not arise and then a direct challenge will be the only possibility.

Where a direct challenge is made the remedies used are rather specialized. These are the prerogative[2] orders of certiorari, prohibition and mandamus; the equitable remedy of injunction; and the declaration, which has equitable characteristics but is in some ways *sui generis*. Certiorari and prohibition are similar in many ways and their functions are to some extent complementary: certiorari is used to quash a decision that has already been made, prohibition is awarded to prevent an authority considering a matter which it has no right to decide. Thus the choice between these two remedies is normally a matter of time: if legal action is taken before the decision is made prohibition is appropriate; otherwise application will be made for certiorari. Mandamus is used where a public official or body has failed to act; it is an order to compel the performance of a public duty and failure to obey it can be punished as contempt o court.

The procedure is similar for all three prerogative remedies. First, an application is made to a Divisional Court of the Queen's Bench division for leave to apply for the order. This application is made *ex parte* and must be supported by verifying affidavits. If leave is granted, the application is made by originating motion to the Divisional Court. The notice of motion must be served on all persons directly affected and they can oppose the application. Evidence is normally by affidavit but in exceptional cases the deponents of affidavits may be cross-examined orally.

An injunction is basically a private law remedy but it is also used in public law cases to prohibit a public authority from doing something illegal. In private law an injunction is sometimes given to order someone to do a positive act (mandatory injunction) but this is hardly ever done in public law cases since the appropriate remedy would be mandamus. Likewise an injunction is not normally given to prevent the institution of proceedings before a tribunal: prohibition is the proper remedy here.

A declaration was also originally a private law remedy but today it is important in public law since it has greater flexibility than the remedies mentioned so far. A declaration is simply a statement by the court of the legal position with regard to a certain question and it can be used to determine the powers and duties of a public authority. There is no order addressed to the authority and no direct sanction, but this does not matter since public authorities can always be relied upon to obey the law once their legal position is clarified.

In some cases remedies are provided by statute against decisions or acts of public authorities. The nature of these remedies depends, of course, on the statute in question: sometimes it may provide for an application to be made to court to quash an order that is beyond the powers of the authority; in other cases it may provide for an appeal from the decision of the authority, usually only on a point of law. An important difference between review and appeal is that in the latter case the court can normally substitute its decision for that of the administrative body; in the case of review the court simply quashes the decision and the administrative body can then reconsider the matter if it wishes.

It is not easy to say how successful the courts are in their attempts to control public administration. There is no sure test whether they have succeeded in improving the quality of administration – or whether they have, in fact, succeeded only in placing additional obstacles in the way of the administrators. One advantage, however, which judicial control has over executive control is that the judges are not usually concerned with the political influence of the complainant: whether he belongs to an important and vociferous group; whether he can influence votes; or whether his case has caught the public attention. The courts are concerned with principles, more flexible and imprecise in this area than in others – but principles which nevertheless can give as much comfort to the small man, the individual who stands on his own, as to a politically important organization.

This is the strength of judicial control. Its weaknesses are several. Courts lack expert knowledge of the problems of administration; they cannot intervene unless someone is prepared to start legal proceedings; when they do intervene they can only deal with the case before them: they cannot lay down rules for related situations; they cannot easily oversee the way in which their orders are carried out; finally, there is the unfortunate fact that judicial proceedings are often rather slow and almost always expensive. The cost of legal proceedings in the high court usually deters all save the poor (who can obtain legal aid), the rich, and those who are backed by some group or organization. This fact detracts from the role of the courts as the protector of the individual and is one of the greatest weaknesses of judicial review as a method of control over administration.

One of the problems of writing about judicial review is the lack of hard-and-fast rules. The task of reconciling the principles laid down in the cases on this topic is almost impossible; and even if it could be done the code that might emerge would be of limited use for the prediction of future decisions. The fact is that in this area the courts are guided more by policy than by precedent, more by what they think is fair and reasonable than by rigid rules. There has also been a marked change in the attitudes of the courts in the last ten to fifteen years and they seem to be pursuing a more interventionist policy than in the past. For this reason there is little point in a detailed study of many of the older cases except in order to illustrate the swings of judicial policy.

NATURAL JUSTICE

The procedural requirements that the courts have sought to impose on administrative authorities are usually summed up in the phrase 'natural justice'. This is basically a question of fairness. Natural justice does not require the procedural technicalities normally applicable in court proceedings but is based on two simple principles: the right to a hearing before a decision is taken affecting one's interests (*audi alteram partem*); and the absence of bias on the part of the decision-maker (*nemo judex in sua causa*).

The Scope of Natural Justice

The principles of natural justice do not have to be followed in every administrative decision and the first question to consider is, therefore: in what circumstances does natural justice apply? Before attempting to answer this question, however, two preliminary points should be made. First, although the courts usually pose the question in the form given above, it does not necessarily follow that the same considerations apply to each of the basic principles of natural justice: it is possible that the scope of the rule against bias may not be the same as that of the rule that a hearing must be given – though there is no very obvious reason why it should not be. Secondly, the actual content of natural justice may vary in different circumstances; for example, the exact content of the 'hearing' and the procedural rights that go with it will not be the same in all cases. Natural justice is not an 'all or nothing' requirement; in some cases the courts will require no more than elementary fair play, while in others more detailed safeguards will apply.

The duty to observe natural justice will, of course, arise if there is an express or implied requirement to this effect in legislation; but the courts may impose a duty to follow natural justice even if the relevant legislation is quite silent on the point. This is illustrated by one of the best known of the older cases, *Cooper* v. *Wandsworth Board of Works*,[3] which was decided in 1863. This case concerned a man's right to his property and this naturally struck a chord in the Victorian judges. The facts were that a statute had been passed providing that no one could put up a building in London without first giving notice to the district Board of Works. Cooper disobeyed this statute. He started to build a house in Wandsworth without informing the Wandsworth Board of Works. The statute provided that if notice was not given the Board of Works had the power to demolish the house. The Wandsworth Board of Works consequently pulled down Cooper's half-finished house. He then brought an action for damages against them in trespass. Their defence was that they had committed no trespass because their actions were authorized by the statute. But the court held that the Board should have given Cooper the chance to explain his failure to inform them before taking the drastic action provided for in the statute. By not doing this they had rendered their subsequent action unlawful and Cooper was therefore entitled to damages.[4]

It should be emphasized that there was nothing in the statute requiring a hearing to be given before a building was demolished. The court therefore grafted a provision on to the statute that made the power of the Board to demolish a building contingent on their first giving a hearing. Byles J. said in his judgment: '. . . a long line of decisions . . . establish that, although there are no positive words in the statute requiring that the party shall be heard, yet the justice of the common law will supply the omission of the legislature'.[5]

When will the courts imply a duty to obey natural justice? This is not a question that can be answered in a few words but there are two theories that seek to lay down a general principle as to when the duty will arise. Neither theory has any generally recognized name but they may be referred to as the 'analytical' theory and the 'interest' theory. The analytical theory was influential in the past but the interest theory is more important today. The former will be considered first.

The analytical theory is based on the classification of functions and according to it the duty to follow natural justice depends on the nature of the decision to be made by the public authority: if the decision is essentially of a judicial nature natural justice will apply; otherwise it will not. The nature of the decision does not depend, however, on the nature of the body making it: the fact that the authority is not a court or tribunal does not mean that its decision is not of a judicial nature; conversely, a court or judge may perform functions that are not judicial.

This theory raises the question whether decisions can be classified according to their nature and whether it is possible to formulate a set of criteria to distinguish a judicial decision from, say, an administrative one. The decisions taken by public authorities are in practice so varied that it is not very easy to do this but it is usually said that a decision is of a judicial nature if it authoritatively declares the legal rights of the parties and was arrived at by ascertaining the facts, interpreting the law and applying the law to the facts. It is contrasted with an administrative decision, which is normally based on discretion. Many decisions are of course based on a mixture of law and discretion and in this case the characterization of the decision as judicial or administrative depends on the relative importance of these two elements.

At first sight this theory might seem both logical and reasonable. Unfortunately, however, it has two very serious drawbacks. First of all, in practice it is almost impossible to decide in many cases whether the decision in question is judicial or not. Secondly, it is far too restrictive. There are in fact many kinds of decision of an apparently administrative nature to which natural justice ought to apply. The *Wandsworth Board of Works* case is a good example. The Board had no authority to declare Cooper's legal rights but they had a power to pull down his house if notice was not given before its construction. Their decision to exercise this power was based on discretion and was clearly an administrative one. Yet this was a case in which it was desirable that there should be a duty to grant a hearing. The analytical theory was in fact discussed in the case and, though it does not appear to have been accepted by the court, the majority of judges made a point of saying that the Board's decision *was* judicial. This was very unfortunate because it set the pattern for later cases; for many years the courts paid lip service to the theory but got round it in practice by classifying as judicial, decisions which appeared to be clearly administrative. This terminological imprecision caused a great deal of confusion; it also meant that the theory itself was of little value because the courts often made no serious attempt to classify decisions according to any objective criteria.

Later cases tried to lessen the absurdity of applying the tag 'judicial' to an administrative decision by inventing a new term, 'quasi-judicial'. This term recognized that the decision was not purely judicial but implied that it had a judicial element. However no satisfactory definition of it has ever been given and it is often said that a decision is quasi-judicial if there is a duty on the decision-maker to observe natural justice.[6] This definition, of course, is useless if the object of classifying the decision is to discover whether natural justice is applicable.

The confusion created by the analytical theory has been abated to a large extent as a result of the recognition by the courts that natural justice can apply to a purely administrative decision. *Ridge* v. *Baldwin*[7] marked an important turning point when the House of Lords held that natural justice applied to a decision by a Watch Committee to dismiss a chief constable. The chief constable had been acquitted on a criminal charge of conspiracy but the judge had commented adversely on his leadership of the force. The Watch Committee thereupon dismissed him; but the court held that his dismissal was void because he had not been given a hearing.

A later case where the point was dealt with more explicitly was *Re H.K. (An Infant.)*[8] In this case Lord Parker C. J. held that natural justice applied to a decision by an immigration officer as to whether an immigrant was entitled to admission to Britain under section 2(2) of the Commonwealth Immigrants Act 1962.[9] Lord Parker said in his judgment that he doubted whether the immigration officer was acting in a judicial or quasi-judicial capacity. But he thought that even if he were not acting in such a capacity he was required to act 'fairly'. He continued:[10]

> Good administration and an honest or bona fide decision must, as it seems to me, require not merely impartiality, nor merely bringing one's mind to bear on the problem, but acting fairly; and to the limited extent that the circumstances of any particular case allow, and within the legislative framework under which the administrator is working, only to that limited extent do the so-called rules of natural justice apply, which in a case such as this is merely a duty to act fairly. I appreciate that in saying that it may be said that one is going further than is permitted on the decided cases because heretofore at any rate the decisions of the courts do seem to have drawn a strict line in these matters according to whether there is or is not a duty to act judicially or quasi-judicially. It has sometimes been said that if there is no duty to act judicially or quasi-judicially there is no power in the court whatever to interfere.

Since this case it has become fully accepted that natural justice can apply to a decision of an administrative nature.

The fact that natural justice can apply to a purely administrative decision does not, however, completely destroy the usefulness of the analytical theory. It is still of value for at least three reasons. First, if the decision is of a judicial nature, natural justice will normally apply. Secondly, if the decision is of a purely ministerial character natural justice will not apply. A decision is ministerial when there is no element of discretion or independent judgment: it is neither judicial nor administrative in the sense in which these terms have been used. There would be no point in requiring natural justice to be followed in these circumstances because it could not affect the content of the decision in any way. Thirdly, natural justice will not normally apply to a legislative function.[11] This is not very easy to define but it is concerned with laying down rules of general application. If the number of people who might be affected is very large it would not be possible to grant them all a hearing.

It is, of course, true that most of the cases coming before the courts are concerned with administrative decisions and in this situation the analytical theory is of little use because it does not tell us *which* administrative decisions must be made according to the rules of natural justice. This is where the second theory is of use. This is the 'interest' theory. According to this theory the applicability of natural justice depends on the impact of the decision on the interests of the individual affected. The more seriously his interests are affected the more likely it is that natural justice will apply. The questions to be considered are: first, does the decision directly affect an individual person's interests; secondly, is the interest affected one which the courts are prepared to protect; and thirdly, how seriously is the interest affected? The interests of the individual, however, are not the only interests to be considered. There is also the public interest. This requires, for example, that the administrative process should not be unduly hampered by unreasonable procedural requirements. The interests of the individual concerned must be balanced against the public interest and the extent to which natural justice will apply (if it applies at all) will depend on the way the balance is struck.

One of the best examples of the 'interest' approach is *Durayappah* v. *Fernando*,[12] a case decided by the Privy Council on appeal from Ceylon. The relevant legislative provision was as follows:

If . . . it appears to the Minister that a municipal council is not competent to perform, or persistently makes default in the performance of, any duty or duties imposed upon it, or persistently refuses or neglects to comply with any provision of law, the Minister may, by Order . . . direct that the council shall be dissolved . . .

Acting under this power the Minister made an order dissolving the Jaffna Municipal Council on the ground that it was not competent to perform its duties. The question before the Privy Council was whether the Minister was obliged to grant a hearing before making the order.

The Board started off by saying that it would be wrong to attempt to give an exhaustive classification of the cases where the principles of natural justice apply. However, the following statement was made as regards the general approach to be adopted:[13]

In their Lordships' opinion there are three matters which must always be borne in mind when considering whether the principle [of natural justice] should be applied or not. These three matters are: first, what is the nature of the property, the office held, status enjoyed or services to be performed by the complainant of injustice. Secondly, in what circumstances or upon what occasions is the person claiming to be entitled to exercise the measure of control entitled to intervene. Thirdly, when a right to intervene is proved, what sanctions in fact is the latter entitled to impose upon the other. It is only upon a consideration of all these matters that the question of the application of the principle can properly be determined.

Each of these matters was then considered in turn. First, it was pointed out that the council was a public corporation entrusted with the administration of a large area and the discharge of important duties. It also owned a lot of property. Secondly, the grounds on which the Minister was entitled to act were specified in the legislation. At least two of these grounds (persistent default in the performance of its duties and persistent refusal or neglect to comply with the law) involved very serious charges against the council. Even if this argument did not apply to the ground actually applicable in the case (incompetence) it would be unreasonable to hold that the necessity for granting a hearing depended on the ground on which the decision was eventually made. Finally, the sanction that could be imposed – the dissolution of the council – was as complete as could be imagined. The council would lose all its property. The case therefore fell within the principle of *Cooper* v. *Wandsworth Board of Works*[14] 'where it was held that no man is to be deprived of his property without having an opportunity of being heard'.[15] The Board considered that this principle applied as much to a corporation as to an individual. Consequently it was decided that the Minister was under a duty to grant a hearing.

It is not easy to list the interests that will be protected because the courts have not always followed a consistent line. In particular there was a period from the end of the First World War to the late fifties when the courts seemed to stage a retreat and limit the scope of natural justice to a considerable extent. The turn of the tide came in the early sixties with the decision of the House of Lords in *Ridge* v. *Baldwin*[16] and since then case after case has applied natural justice to new situations. This trend is still continuing and a point has now been reached where it has been said that the principles of natural justice will apply to all decisions affecting individual rights unless the circumstances are such as to indicate the contrary.[17]

It is impossible to foresee how much further this policy will be carried but at present one can say that in the absence of counter-vailing policy considerations, natural justice will usually apply to decisions affecting individuals when the following interests are at stake: liberty and freedom of movement, property, reputation or good character, the right to earn one's living, and the possession of an office or status. The case of *Re H.K. (An Infant)*[18] showed that natural justice applies to at least some immigration decisions (free-dom of movement). It was held in earlier cases, however, that it does not apply to a decision to deport an alien[19] or to a refusal to extend his period of stay in this country.[20] This question is no longer of great practical importance, however, since the right of appeal to a tribunal has now been granted by statute against most immigration deci-sions.[21]

Natural justice will normally apply to a decision to confiscate or destroy private property[22] or in proceedings in which a person is accused of discreditable conduct.[23] It will apply to a decision by a trade union to expel one of its members[24] (which could result in the loss of his job) or a decision by a professional body which affects a person's right to practise his profession. It will also usually apply to a decision to revoke a licence to engage in a business or occupation.[25] It was held in *R. v. Metropolitan Police Commissioner, ex p. Parker*[26] that the Metropolitan Commissioner of Police could revoke a taxi driver's licence without a hearing and in *Nakkuda Ali v. Jayaratne*[27] the Privy Council held that natural justice did not apply to a decision to revoke a textile dealer's licence. These cases were, however, both decided during the period when the courts adopted a restrictive atti-tude and it is doubtful whether similar decisions would be made today.[28]

Natural justice applies to a decision to dismiss someone from a public office, provided he can be dismissed only for cause.[29] Failure to follow natural justice will normally mean that the dismissal is invalid and the person concerned will be entitled to a declaration by the court that he still holds the office. Public servants who are dis-missable at pleasure do not normally have the benefit of natural justice.[30] At common law a private employer can dismiss an employee without complying with the provisions of natural justice. If the dismissal is in breach of contract the employer may have to pay damages but the employee will not be entitled to reinstatement.[31]

It will be clear from what has already been said that natural justice does not apply only to decisions made by public authorities. It can also apply to 'semi-public' bodies like trade unions, sporting associations (such as the Football Association),[32] voluntary associations[33] and political parties.[34] Universities are bound by natural justice when conducting disciplinary proceedings against a student (at least if the penalty is serious, such as expulsion or suspension)[35] and it has been held that, if non-academic considerations (such as personal and family problems) are taken into account, a hearing must be granted before deciding whether a student who has failed his examinations will be required to leave the university.[36] It has, on the other hand, been held by the Privy Council that a professor has no right to a hearing before dismissal,[37] but this case was decided some time ago and it is doubtful whether it would be followed today.[38]

Even if the interest affected is one which would normally be protected, natural justice may nevertheless be excluded if the public interest so requires. Circumstances where this might be the case are: where a wide range of persons are affected so that it would not be practicable to grant them all a hearing; where the full application of natural justice might lead to the disclosure of confidential information; where action has to be taken with great urgency; or where prior notice to the individual concerned might defeat the whole object of the action – for example, in the case of the arrest of a suspect who is likely to flee if warned in advance. The presence of one of these factors does not, however, necessarily mean that natural justice will be totally excluded. It may be possible to reconcile the conflicting interests at stake by granting a limited form of hearing.

Finally, it should be pointed out that natural justice can be excluded by the legislation granting the power in question. If an Act of Parliament expressly or by clear implication provides that natural justice will not apply in a certain case this will, of course, be accepted by the courts. The same is true where natural justice is excluded by delegated legislation except that the courts may be less willing to interpret it as implicitly excluding natural justice and in certain cases it is possible that the courts might consider an express provision to be *ultra vires* – but this would depend on the parent Act.[39]

It is not clear whether a voluntary association can exclude natural justice by its rules. There is some authority for saying that a rule would be contrary to public policy and consequently void if it purported to exclude natural justice in a situation where it would normally apply and this is probably the case with regard to trade unions and other bodies which control the right to work in certain kinds of employment.[40] If, on the other hand, the rules of a voluntary association provided for natural justice to be observed to a greater extent than that required by the common law, this would probably be enforced by the courts. Moreover, an undertaking by a public or semi-public body to grant a hearing in a particular case will normally oblige the body to follow the rules of natural justice in deciding that case even if they would not otherwise have been obliged to do so. Furthermore, if the body gives an undertaking as to the way in which it will exercise a power, it will not normally be able to act contrary to that undertaking (even if the undertaking is not binding on it) without first granting a hearing to the person to whom the undertaking was made.[41]

The Right to a Hearing

Exactly what the right to a hearing entails depends on the circumstances. Where there are two parties in contention and the decision-maker has to decide between them, the procedural rights of the parties are likely to be more extensive than in a one-party situation (where there is only one person concerned in addition to the decision-maker). Whether there are one or two parties may, of course, depend on the procedure adopted. Thus, for example, in the case of disciplinary proceedings in a trade union or university the rules might provide for someone to play the part of 'prosecutor', in which case there would be two parties, or they might provide that the disciplinary authority itself would initiate the proceedings and gather evidence, in which case there would only be one party. There appears to be no authority as to whether natural justice would require one of these procedures to be adopted in preference to the other in any given situation but in the case of a serious disciplinary charge the former might be more appropriate.

In all cases the person concerned must be given the opportunity to put his case to the decision-maker before the decision is made. He should normally be entitled to do this orally but in some cases the opportunity to present written submissions would be sufficient. In some situations it might be permissible for the hearing to take place before some person other than the decision-maker but in this case the person conducting the hearing should prepare a report setting out the evidence and the contentions of the parties and this should be considered by the decision-maker before making the decision.[42]

The person concerned should be given sufficient notice of the proceedings to enable him to prepare his case. He should also be given sufficient information to enable him to know what sort of case he has to meet. If some kind of charge is made against him, he should know what he is accused of doing. If he has to prove certain facts in order to obtain a favourable decision – for example, the granting of a licence – he must be told what those facts are. If the authority is prepared to accept that certain facts exist but is doubtful about some other matter, the person concerned should be told what that matter is, so that he can attempt to satisfy the authority.

If there are two parties to the proceedings it would be improper for the decision-maker to hear one party behind the back of the other. Each party should know the submissions of the other party and should normally be allowed to hear the evidence put forward by his opponent. If witnesses are called by one party, the other party should be able to cross-examine them.

Does the right to a hearing entail the right to be legally represented at the hearing (assuming it is oral)? The argument in favour of granting a right to legal representation is that a layman cannot always adequately present his case. He may be nervous or inarticulate. He may not know what facts should be brought to the notice of the decision-maker in order to establish his case and he may not know how to establish those facts. He may be unable to cross-examine witnesses or to bring out the weaknesses of his opponent's case. All these things could be done by a good lawyer (either a barrister or solicitor) and the presence of a lawyer would mean that the party's case was adequately presented.

There are, however, disadvantages in allowing legal representation. If one party has a lawyer, the other will feel that he must have one too. Since the services of a lawyer are expensive this means that the hearing could cost the parties a lot of money. The introduction of lawyers is also likely to make the proceedings more complicated and technical. The result of this is that there will be greater delay. Finally, if the decision-maker is not legally qualified he might feel inadequate; consequently it might be felt desirable either to provide him with legal advice or to appoint lawyers as decision-makers. Delay, expense and inflexibility are the price of legal representation.

How are these conflicting considerations to be resolved? No definite answer has been provided by the courts but it seems likely that they will hold that legal representation should be allowed in some cases but not all.[43] The complexity of the issues and the importance of the decision are likely to be the main factors. If a man's whole career is at stake in a disciplinary hearing before a professional body it would be reasonable to allow him to be represented by counsel; but if the maximum penalty were a £5 fine, it might be more satisfactory if lawyers were kept out.[44]

A good example of the way the courts balance conflicting interests in natural justice cases is *R. v. Gaming Board for Great Britain, ex parte Benaim*.[45] This case concerned an application for a certificate of consent under the Gaming Act 1968. Under this Act gambling can take place only in premises licensed for the purpose. The licence is granted by the licensing justices but before a person can apply for a licence he must obtain a certificate of consent from the Gaming Board. The function of the Board is to decide whether the applicant is a fit person to run a gaming club and it is required to take into account his character, reputation and financial standing.[46] The reason why these provisions were enacted was that gambling in Britain (as elsewhere) had become closely connected with organized crime and it was thought that the only way to eliminate the criminal element in gambling was to set up a licensing system under which only those who were above suspicion would be allowed to operate gaming clubs.

In this case the application was made by two men, Benaim and Khaida, on behalf of one of the most famous and fashionable gaming clubs in Britain – Crockford's. The applicants had a long meeting with the Board at which they were asked numerous questions. The Board clearly indicated to the applicants what matters were troubling them and they gave them the opportunity to put their case. Some time later the Board informed the applicants that a certificate of consent had been refused. The applicants then brought proceedings for an order of certiorari to quash the decision on the ground that the Board had not observed natural justice. They also asked for an order of mandamus to require the Board to give them more information.

The Court of Appeal refused to grant either order. It held that the Board was obliged to follow the rules of natural justice to the extent of acting fairly. But the court considered it had done this.

There were two main points at issue. First, the applicants claimed that the Board should have given them reasons for refusing the licence. The court held that there was no obligation on the Board to do this. Secondly, the applicants wanted to know the source of the information the Board had concerning them. The court ruled that the Board was not obliged to tell them this: in view of the fact that many gaming clubs had criminal associations, potential informants might be afraid to give information to the Board if there was a possibility that their names might be made known to the club concerned.[47] The Court also considered that the Board did not have to give details of the information it had if this might give away the informant's identity. All that was necessary was that the applicants be told clearly what was alleged against them so that they could rebut it. This the Board had done.[48]

Bias

If it is wished to challenge a decision on the ground of bias, it is not necessary to prove that the decision-maker was actually biased in the sense that his decision was influenced by improper considerations:[49] it is enough if facts can be shown to exist which cast reasonable doubt on his impartiality. This will normally be the case if the adjudicator has an interest in the outcome of the case; if he is associated with someone who has such an interest; or if he has in some way already committed himself on the point in issue.

The most serious case is where the decision-maker has a financial interest in the outcome of the case. One of the best-known examples of this is *Dimes* v. *Grand Junction Canal Company*, decided in 1852.[50] In this case the rule was applied to a judge – no less a person than the Lord Chancellor in fact – who had affirmed a decree in favour of a company in which he was a shareholder. On appeal to the House of Lords the decree was set aside. Lord Campbell said:

No one can suppose that [the Lord Chancellor] could be, in the remotest degree, influenced by the interest that he had in this concern; but, my Lords, it is of the last importance that the maxim that no man is to be a judge in his own cause should be held sacred. And that is not to be confined to a cause in which he is a party, but applies to a cause in which he has an interest.

Another case was *R*. v. *Hendon R.D.C.*, *ex p. Chorley*.[51] This case concerned an application to the Hendon Rural District Council for permission to develop a certain piece of land. The owner of the land had entered into a provisional contract to sell it but the contract was conditional on the Council's permission being granted. The estate agent acting for the owner was a councillor and he was present when the application was considered (and granted). The court held that his interest in the matter – his fee if the sale went through – was sufficient to invalidate the decision even though he took no part in the proceedings before the Council.

The courts are very strict where a pecuniary interest is involved but, of course, a line must be drawn somewhere and if the interest is remote and depends on an unlikely contingency it may be ignored. To give some idea of where the line is drawn one might contrast *Re Hopkins*,[52] where it was held that magistrates who were shareholders in a railway company were disqualified from hearing a charge against a passenger accused of travelling on the company's train without the right ticket, with *R*. v. *Burton*, *ex p. Young*[53] in which it was held that a magistrate who was a member of the Incorporated Law Society could hear a charge brought by the society against a person accused of falsely pretending to be a solicitor. The only way in which the magistrate in the latter case might have been affected financially by his decision would have been if the prosecution had failed, costs had been awarded against the society, and the society had been dissolved – thus entitling its members to a share in its assets.

A financial interest is not the only thing that will disqualify a decision-maker. He will also be disqualified if he is in any sense a party to the proceedings – for example, if someone who has acted as prosecutor in disciplinary proceedings also takes part in reaching the decision.[54] The same will apply if a decision-maker has acted as advocate for one of the parties.

There is a rule that if the adjudicator has already given a ruling on the point at issue he will be disqualified from adjudicating in subsequent proceedings.[55] The rationale for this is that his mind will not be open. If there is an appeal to another body, or a re-hearing or confirmation of the decision by such a body, anyone who is a member of the body which gave the original decision is disqualified from taking part in the proceedings before the second body.[56] Here there are probably two underlying ideas: first that the adjudicator will not have an open mind; and secondly that he might in some sense be regarded as the respondent in the appeal, or at least as having an interest in its outcome. The first idea would probably apply only if the adjudicator in question had actually taken part in the original decision but the second could be applicable even if he had not. This is illustrated by the decision of the Court of Appeal in *Hannam* v. *Bradford Corporation*.[57] This case concerned the dismissal of a schoolteacher by the governors of the school. The local education authority had the power to veto the dismissal and after it had taken place the staff sub-committee of the Corporation held a meeting to consider the matter and decided not to exercise the power. Three members of the sub-committee were also governors of the school but they had not attended the meeting of the governors at which it was decided to dismiss the teacher. Nevertheless, the court considered that their presence at the meeting of the sub-committee was contrary to natural justice.[58]

Another situation in which a decision-maker may be disqualified is where there is some personal connection between himself and a party to the proceedings. He may be disqualified by reason of kinship with a party, friendship (or, on the other hand, personal animosity) or a professional, business or employer – employee relationship. For example, a solicitor or barrister might be disqualified from adjudicating in a case if a client of his was a party, at least if the relationship with the client was continuing or very recent.

A good example of disqualification on these grounds is *Metropolitan Properties Co.* v. *Lannon*.[59] This case concerned proceedings before a rent assessment committee to determine fair rents for a number of flats owned by the Metropolitan Properties Company. The chairman of the rent assessment committee was a solicitor who lived with his father, who was a tenant of a flat owned by another property company in the same group as the Metropolitan Properties Company. He had advised his father in his dealings with his landlords about the fair rent for his flat and had also advised other tenants in the same block of flats as his father. In other words, he was both professionally and personally involved in proceedings against the same landlords (in essence) with regard to the same issue (fair rents). The Court of Appeal therefore quashed the decision of the rent assessment committee (which had been very unfavourable to the landlords) and remitted the case to another assessment committee.

A personal relationship with a party will not, of course, always result in disqualification and the courts are much less strict in this situation than in the case where there is a financial interest. The exact test that should be applied is the subject of some controversy but the best formulation is probably that given by Lord Denning M. R. in *Metropolitan Properties Co.* v. *Lannon*. He said:[60]

The court looks at the impression which would be given to other people. Even if he was as impartial as could be, nevertheless if right-minded persons would think that, in the circumstances, there was a real likelihood of bias on his part, then he should not sit.

This is, therefore, a 'reasonable man' test. However, it may happen that in some cases the appearance to a casual on-looker might be rather bad but if the full facts were known there would be no cause for suspecting bias. In these circumstances the test must be applied not only on the basis of the facts known to the party complaining but also on the basis of 'such further facts as he might readily have ascertained and easily verified in the course of his inquiries'.[61]

The various situations already discussed are not necessarily the only ones in which a likelihood of bias could arise and the test laid down by Lord Denning could be applied to any set of facts (except where there is a financial interest, in which case a stricter test is applied). However, an adjudicator will rarely, if ever, be disqualified merely because he holds strong views on the point in question so long as he has not associated himself with one side in the dispute. Thus, for example, a licensing justice is not disqualified because he is a teetotaller nor would a Roman Catholic be disqualified from hearing a case concerning abortion or divorce. 'Ideological bias', therefore, is not normally taken into account. The only exception to this might be if the adjudicator had made a statement indicating that he would not consider the point at issue with an open mind.

There are two special cases in which an adjudicator who would normally be disqualified will nevertheless be permitted to make the decision. The first is where he is expressly or impliedly exempted from disqualification by legislation. For example, if it is provided by Act of Parliament that any dispute between a local authority and its employees as regards the pensions of the latter is to be decided by the local authority itself – as was provided by the Local Government Superannuation Act 1937[62] – a decision by the local authority would not be invalid on account of bias even though it would plainly be a judge in its own cause.[63] Secondly, in certain rare cases an adjudicator may be exempt from disqualification by necessity. This would be the case either if the person concerned were the only person allowed by law to make the decision or if all possible adjudicators were biased.[64]

Even if an adjudicator is disqualified his decision will normally stand if the complainant waived his right to object. He will be taken to do this if he does not object as soon as is reasonably possible after he becomes aware of the relevant facts. Thus if a party learns before the decision is made of facts that would normally disqualify the adjudicator and decides to keep quiet until he knows which way the decision has gone, he will find that he will be deemed to have waived the right to object and will be unable to challenge the decision.[65]

One final point: it will be apparent from the cases that have been discussed that a decision made by a group of people may be invalidated if a single one of them is biased, even though there would have been a majority in favour of the decision if the biased adjudicator had been excluded. The reason for this is that the public cannot normally know how much he has influenced the other decision-makers and the whole proceedings will therefore be suspect.[66]

DECISIONS OF FACT AND LAW

Jurisdiction

In discussing decisions of fact and law it is essential to grasp the distinction between the case where a person is entitled to make a decision on a question of fact or law which is not binding on anybody and the case where a person is empowered to make a binding decision on such a question. Anyone, whether he is a public official or private citizen, is entitled to make a non-binding decision on a question of fact or law. Thus, a motorist looking for a parking place in a crowded city may have to decide whether he is allowed to park in a particular street. This might be a question of law (e.g. the meaning of a traffic sign) or a question of fact (the time of day it is). But such a decision is in no way binding and if he mistakenly thinks that parking is permitted, his belief will not prevent his being convicted of a parking offence.

On the other hand courts and tribunals are empowered to make binding decisions on questions of fact or law. Such decisions determine the legal rights of the persons concerned and the doctrine of *res judicata* applies to them. Subject to what will be said below, they cannot be challenged unless there is provision for an appeal. Thus if the motorist mentioned above is charged with a parking offence and the magistrate who hears the case mistakenly decides that he was entitled to park in the street in question, he will not be convicted. The difference between the magistrate's decision and the motorist's is that the former is legally binding while the latter is not.

It quite often happens that public officials are required by law to make decisions of fact or law in order to know whether they are permitted to take a particular action. However, the fact that the official is required to make the decision does not of itself mean that it is binding. For example, assume a statute provides: if X is so, the Minister may do Y. Let us assume that X is a question of fact. Here the Minister's power to do Y is conditional on X being so and before he acts he must decide whether X is so. If he does Y when X is not so, he is acting *ultra vires* and the courts will intervene; moreover, the fact that he makes a mistaken decision that X is so will not make his action any the less illegal.[67]

The statute might, however, say: if the Minister is satisfied that X is so, he may do Y. Here the condition of his being able to do Y is not that X is in fact so, but that the Minister is satisfied that it is so. For this reason it is known as a 'subjective' condition. The matter depends on the state of the Minister's mind: if he honestly believes that X is so his action will be valid;[68] it is only where he is not satisfied that it is so that the courts will intervene – if his state of mind can be proved.

Similar principles can be applied to decisions by inferior tribunals (tribunals and inferior courts such as magistrates' courts and county courts). Such bodies have power to give binding decisions on questions of fact and law but their jurisdiction (power to give binding decisions) is limited. Thus, for example, a magistrates' court does not have jurisdiction to try a murder case. If it does try such a case its decision will be invalid and the High Court will set it aside in the same way that an *ultra vires* decision of an administrative authority is set aside.

The jurisdiction of an inferior tribunal may, however, depend on a preliminary question of fact or law. Thus a statute may say: if X is so the tribunal may decide question Y. For example, a rent tribunal may have jurisdiction to decide the rent of a dwelling provided it is unfurnished. In this case the condition on which the jurisdiction depends is that the dwelling is unfurnished. This involves questions of fact and the question of law of what 'unfurnished' actually means in this context. Where the jurisdiction of a tribunal depends on a preliminary question such as this, does the tribunal have jurisdiction to decide the preliminary question as well as the main question? If it does, any decision on the preliminary question will be binding and consequently it will not be possible to set aside a decision on the main question on the ground that the tribunal was acting outside its jurisdiction. The result will be the same as in the case of a 'subjective' condition for the exercise of an administrative power. If, on the other hand, the tribunal does not have jurisdiction to decide the preliminary question, the courts will be able to set aside its decision whenever it makes a mistake on a preliminary issue.

According to one theory inferior tribunals always have jurisdiction to decide such preliminary questions. This is known as the 'pure theory of jurisdiction'[69] and it states that a judicial body has power to make a binding decision on any question which it is legally obliged to consider. According to this theory the jurisdiction of a body is determinable at the commencement and not at the conclusion of the proceedings. Once it has embarked on the consideration of a question which it has power to consider it does not lose its jurisdiction by coming to a wrong conclusion on a question of fact or law. Since it must always consider the preliminary question in order to know whether it has jurisdiction to decide the main question, any decision on the preliminary question must be within its jurisdiction.

This theory has had some support from the courts in the past[70] but it is not generally accepted today. A good illustration is *R*. v. *Fulham, Hammersmith and Kensington Rent Tribunal, ex p. Zerek*.[71] Under the Rent Restriction Acts the tribunal had jurisdiction to determine what rent was reasonable for a dwelling-house provided it was unfurnished. In this case the landlord had originally agreed to let the premises unfurnished but when the tenant arrived with his furniture to take possession, the landlord refused to admit him unless he agreed that the landlord should hire his furniture from him and he would then take the rooms with the furniture in them. He had also to sign a receipt for £12 (for the hire of the furniture) although this sum had not in fact been paid to him.

On these facts the rent tribunal held that the letting was really unfurnished and they reduced the rent. The landlord claimed that the tribunal was acting beyond its jurisdiction and applied for an order of certiorari to quash its decision. The court held that the tribunal's decision that the premises were unfurnished was correct and therefore no problem of jurisdiction arose. However the court made it quite clear that it did not accept the pure theory of jurisdiction. Thus Devlin J. said:[72]

> When, at the inception of an inquiry by a tribunal of limited jurisdiction, a challenge is made to their jurisdiction, the tribunal have to make up their minds whether they will act or not, and for that purpose to arrive at some decision on whether they have jurisdiction or not. If their jurisdiction depends upon the existence of a state of facts, they must inform themselves about them, and if the facts are in dispute reach some conclusion on the merits of the dispute. If they reach a wrong conclusion, the rights of the parties against each other are not affected. For, if the tribunal wrongly assume jurisdiction, the party who apparently obtains an order from it in reality takes nothing. The whole proceeding is, in the phrase used in the old reports, *coram non judice*.

In other words, a tribunal cannot give itself jurisdiction by a wrong decision on a preliminary question.[73] If it wrongfully takes jurisdiction its decision will be a nullity. If a rent tribunal exceeds its jurisdiction the landlord could have the decision quashed by the High Court or he could simply ignore it and sue the tenant for the original rent. The tenant might raise the decision as a defence but once the court was satisfied that it was invalid it would no longer be of any effect.[74]

Since a decision of an inferior tribunal on a preliminary question can be challenged in the courts, it is very important to distinguish clearly between such a question and a question within the jurisdiction of the tribunal. Various expressions are used by courts and writers to indicate this distinction. Thus a preliminary question may also be referred to as an 'incidental question', a 'collateral question', a 'question going to jurisdiction', or a 'jurisdictional question'. All these expressions mean the same thing. However, in spite of the plethora of words to describe such a question it is often extremely difficult to distinguish between a jurisdictional question and a question within the jurisdiction of the tribunal. The end result is very confusing and the courts sometimes decide first on policy grounds whether they wish to review the decision in question and, if they do, they then characterize it as jurisdictional. This enables the courts to intervene when they feel that there has been an injustice but it often makes it impossible to say in advance whether a decision is reviewable or not.[75]

Does a decision on a question of fact otherwise *within* a tribunal's jurisdiction become a jurisdictional question if the tribunal had no evidence for its decision? This question was answered in the negative by the Privy Council in *R*. v. *Nat Bell Liquors Ltd*:[76]

It has been said that . . . a justice who convicts without evidence is acting without jurisdiction to do so. Accordingly, want of essential evidence, if ascertained somehow, is on the same footing as want of qualification in the magistrate, and goes to the question of his right to enter on the case at all. Want of evidence on which to convict is the same as want of jurisdiction to take evidence at all. This, clearly, is erroneous. A justice who convicts without evidence is doing something that he ought not to do, but he is doing it as a judge, and if his jurisdiction to entertain the charge is not open to impeachment, his subsequent error, however grave, is a wrong exercise of a jurisdiction which he has, and not a usurpation of a jurisdiction which he has not.

Thus if a tribunal has jurisdiction to decide a question of fact it does not lose its jurisdiction because there is no evidence for its finding. Two qualifications should, however, be made to this: first, the courts have not been entirely consistent on this point and there have been cases which point to the opposite conclusion.[77] Secondly, a finding of fact for which there is no evidence can be regarded as an error of *law*; if this appears 'on the face of the record' the courts are entitled to quash the decision. The reason for this will now be considered.

Error of Law on the Face of the Record
All the principles discussed so far have been derived from the basic principle of *ultra vires*. Where a question of law is involved there is, however, another principle that has nothing to do with *ultra vires*. This is the principle that the court may, on an application for certiorari, quash the decision of an inferior tribunal if the tribunal has made an error of law (whether jurisdictional or non-jurisdictional) provided that the error appears 'on the face of the record' of the tribunal. There is no logical explanation for this principle, only an historical one.

The writ (now order) of certiorari was originally a means by which the King, through the Court of King's Bench, could control the activities of inferior courts. It was an order in the King's name to the judges of the inferior court to deliver up to the Court of King's

Bench the record of their proceedings with regard to a specified matter. The Court of King's Bench could then examine the matter and quash the proceedings if an error was revealed.

From the seventeenth century onwards certiorari was used to quash decisions of inferior courts if an error of law appeared on the record as well as where there was an excess of jurisdiction. In criminal matters justices were obliged to set out the proceedings in detail and convictions were quashed for the smallest irregularity. Parliament reacted to this excessive supervision by passing the Summary Jurisdiction Act in 1848 which provided for a standard form of conviction omitting all mention of the evidence or the reasons for the decision. The effect of this was that errors of law were rarely revealed on the record. In civil matters justices were never required to prepare such a detailed record though they sometimes voluntarily set out their reasons so that the Court of King's Bench could give its opinion. However, section 10 of the Summary Jurisdiction Act 1857 provided for justices to state a case for the opinion of the court without the need for certiorari. For these reasons the use of certiorari to quash for error of law on the face of the record became rare by the end of the nineteenth century and almost forgotten by the middle of the twentieth. It was, however, revived in 1951 in *R. v. Northumberland Compensation Appeal Tribunal, ex p. Shaw*[78] and is now a valuable means of controlling administrative tribunals when there is no provision for an appeal.

Since a non-jurisdictional error of law can be quashed only if it is apparent from the record of the tribunal it is very important to decide exactly what constitutes the record. The briefer the record, the less likely it is that an error of law will be revealed. According to Lord Denning in the *Northumberland* case the record consists of the document which initiates the proceedings, the pleadings (if any) and the adjudication.[79] In some cases a document delivered by a tribunal at the same time as its decision, or a document referred to in the decision, may also form part of the record.[80] Tribunals are not obliged at common law to give reasons for their decisions but if they choose to do so, and incorporate them in the adjudication, they will form part of the record.

Under section 12 of the Tribunals and Inquiries Act 1971 various tribunals (listed in Schedule 1) are obliged to furnish a statement, either written or oral, of the reasons for their decision if they are requested to do so on or before the giving or notification of the decision.[81] Any such statement of reasons, even if oral, is deemed to be part of the record.[82] If a tribunal to which these provisions apply fails to give reasons, or gives reasons which are inadequate or unintelligible, the court can order it to give sufficient reasons.[83]

If no reasons are given by a tribunal it is unlikely that any error of law will appear on the record. However, such an error may appear if the tribunal gives its findings of fact and these are not sufficient to lead to the conclusion reached by the tribunal. Moreover, if the evidence is incorporated in the record (which tribunals are not obliged to do), a finding of fact for which there was no evidence could constitute an error of law on the face of the record. A mere error of fact, of course, is not a ground for quashing the decision unless it goes to jurisdiction.

Finally, it should be mentioned that in the case of many tribunals there is statutory provision for an appeal on a point of law to the High Court.[84] Where this is the case an application for certiorari for any error of law on the face of the record will not be necessary.

DISCRETIONARY POWERS

A discretionary power is a power which is exercisable according to the discretion of the person to whom it is granted. He, therefore, has a choice whether to exercise it or not. In the eyes of the law there is normally no single right way in which such power should be exercised, and in this it differs from a power to decide questions of fact or law, where in theory there is always one right decision. In spite of this, however, there are a number of grounds on which the courts can intervene.[85] Broadly speaking, one might regard these as falling into two categories: failure to exercise a discretion and abuse of discretion.

Failure to Exercise a Discretion

Failure to exercise a discretion is quite different from failure to exercise a discretionary power. The person to whom a discretionary power is given is not obliged to exercise the power but he is obliged in appropriate circumstances to make a considered decision whether to exercise the power or not. If he refuses even to consider the matter the courts will intervene.

There are various ways in which someone might refuse to exercise a discretion besides the obvious one of a direct refusal to consider the matter. Where a discretionary power has been granted to an authority or named individual, that power cannot normally be delegated to someone else unless this is expressly or implicitly permitted by the relevant legislation.[86] If the person empowered to exercise the discretion unlawfully delegates it to another person, a decision by the latter will be invalid and the person granted the discretion will be ordered by the courts to exercise the discretion himself. The same will apply if the person granted the power acts under the dictation of someone else or if he grants the latter a veto over the use of the power.[87]

An example of this sort of situation is *Lavender* v. *Minister of Housing and Local Government*.[88] Under section 23 of the Town and Country Planning Act 1962 an appeal lay to the Minister of Housing from a refusal of planning permission by a local planning authority. At the time of this case he had adopted a policy of refusing planning permission for gravel-working in reservation areas of high quality agricultural land unless the Minister of Agriculture was informed and did not object. In effect this gave the Minister of Agriculture a veto in all appeals of this kind. In the case in question the Minister of Agriculture was opposed to permission being granted and the appeal was rejected. It was held by the court, however, that there had been an improper delegation and the Minister of Housing had failed to exercise his discretion. The decision was quashed.

This does not mean that an authority entrusted with a discretionary power may not consult with other authorities and take their views into account when making the decision.[89] There are many situations in which the views of other authorities would be relevant to the decision and where this is so it is quite proper – indeed desirable – that they should be taken into account. However, the final decision must be made by the person to whom the discretion is given and in making it he must weigh up all relevant considerations. An agreement not to exercise the power if another authority objects prevents the person granted the discretion from considering whether in a particular case the views of the other authority might not be outweighed by other considerations.

To what extent may an authority entrusted with a discretionary power adopt rules or policies for the exercise of the power? It is obvious that an authority with a large number of cases to decide – for example, applications for a licence – would want to lay down such rules. The advantages of doing so are that individual decisions would be easier to make and there would be a greater degree of consistency. The disadvantage is that the authority might fail to take all the circumstances of a particular case into account.

The solution to this problem adopted by the courts is to allow public authorities to make rules to guide them in the exercise of their discretion provided they are prepared to depart from the rules where this is desirable.[90] The rules themselves, of course, must not be designed to achieve improper objectives and they must not be based on irrelevant considerations. If the rules themselves are bad the authority will be guilty of an abuse of discretion if it follows them.[91] Normally the authority should tell anyone concerned with a particular case what the relevant rules are and listen to any arguments he might put forward as to why an exception should be made in his case or the rule itself changed. If all this is done and the authority sees no reason to modify or depart from the rules, it is in order for the authority to decide the case according to the rules.

Abuse of Discretion

An abuse of discretion takes place if the person concerned exercises the power for an improper purpose, if he takes irrelevant considerations into account, if he fails to take relevant considerations into account or, in some cases, if he acts unreasonably. These different grounds overlap to a considerable extent, but it is convenient to consider each separately.

If the legislation granting the power specifies the purpose for which it is to be used, its exercise for some other purpose will be invalid. A good example of this is *R. v. Leigh (Lord)*.[92] This case concerned a former chief constable who had been granted a pension by the police authority on the ground that he was incapacitated from performing his duties. Under the legislation in force at the time a police authority had the power to call a police pensioner for a medical examination in order to ascertain whether the incapacity for which the pension had been granted still existed.

The ex-chief constable was living abroad and he was required to attend an examination in England even though only three months had elapsed since his last examination. The real reason for doing this was that the police authority wanted to enable a warrant of arrest to be issued against him in connection with bankruptcy proceedings. When he failed to attend the examination the police authority cancelled his pension; but the court held that the decision to require him to attend the examination was invalid as it was made for an improper purpose and the authority therefore had no power to cancel the pension.

What happens where the person entrusted with the power has two purposes in mind, one legitimate and the other illegitimate? Two cases which illustrate this problem may be considered, although neither provides a satisfactory solution. The first is *Westminster Corporation* v. *London and North Western Railway Company*.[93] It was provided by statute: 'Every sanitary authority may provide and maintain public lavatories . . . in situations where they deem the same to be required.' Acting under this power, the corporation built public lavatories underneath the middle of a street and provided access by means of a subway from either side. The effect of this was that the subway could be used as a means of crossing the street by persons who had no desire to use the lavatories. It was argued that the corporation had abused its powers by doing this. Lord Mac-Naghten dealt with this point as follows:[94]

It is not enough to shew that the Corporation contemplated that the public might use the subway as a means of crossing the street . . . it must be shown that the Corporation constructed this subway as a means of crossing the street under colour and pretence of providing public conveniences which were not really wanted at that particular place.

This does not really face the problem of a dual purpose but it seems to suggest that as long as the corporation believed that lavatories were required in that place, it did not matter that they also took into account the desirability of providing a means of crossing the street. But what would the court have decided if it had been shown that the corporation believed that lavatories were required at two separate sites and had chosen the site in question in preference to the other because of the need for providing a safe means of crossing the street at that point?

A case in which the problem arose in a starker form (but was answered in an even less satisfactory way) was *R.* v. *Governor of Brixton Prison, ex p. Soblen*.[95] This case concerned the validity of a deportation order against a man called Soblen who had been convicted in the United States of conspiracy to deliver defence information to the Soviet Union. He jumped bail and fled after his trial and eventually arrived in England. The Home Secretary issued a deportation order against him with the intention of putting him on board an aircraft bound non-stop for America. Soblen wanted to go to Czechoslovakia instead and he challenged the validity of the deportation order on the ground that its effect would be to extradite him to the U.S.A. (which was unlawful because his offence was not extraditable). In the Court of Appeal Lord Denning M. R. said that the whole issue turned on the Home Secretary's *purpose* in making the order. If his purpose was legitimate (to remove Soblen from the United Kingdom because the Home Secretary considered that his presence here was not conducive to the public good)[96] the order was valid; if it was illegitimate (to return him to the United States so that he could serve his sentence) it would be invalid.

This analysis is excellent as far as it goes, but it does not deal with the possibility that the Home Secretary might have had two purposes. Since Soblen appeared to be a Soviet agent there were good grounds for believing that his presence in Britain would not be conducive to the public good. But there was also evidence that the U.S. Government had asked the British Government for his return and no doubt the Home Secretary was anxious to oblige. The fact that the Home Secretary seemed determined that he should go to America and not to Czechoslovakia suggests strongly that this was one purpose he had in mind. Lord Denning in fact ignored the possibility that there might be a dual purpose and once he had decided that the Home Secretary had reasonable grounds for deporting Soblen, he held the order to be valid.

These cases raise the question whether it makes any difference if the purpose for which the power was granted was in fact fulfilled, even though the person concerned was trying to achieve something different. If a public lavatory was in fact needed in the street in question, would it matter if the provision of a subway was the real motive of the corporation? If there were in fact legitimate grounds for deporting Soblen, did it matter if the Home Secretary's prime concern was to get him back to America? This way of looking at the problem is, of course, a shift from a subjective point of view to an objective one and this runs counter to the basic principle involved, i.e. the purpose for which the power was actually exercised. Nevertheless, it is a factor which may influence the courts: why upset a decision which in its end result is quite proper?[97]

If the exercise of a discretionary power is influenced by irrelevant considerations, or if relevant considerations are not taken into account, the courts may hold that there has been an abuse of discretion. This ground of invalidity overlaps to a great extent with the previous one since a person with an improper purpose in mind will usually be influenced by irrelevant considerations or fail to take relevant considerations into account: considerations that are relevant for one purpose may be irrelevant for another.

If an irrelevant consideration influenced the decision it seems not to matter that the decision was also influenced by relevant considerations. So long as the influence of the irrelevant consideration was substantial the decision will be invalidated.[98] In view of this, it might be advantageous to rely on this ground rather than improper purpose in those cases where the person concerned had two purposes. If one purpose was illegitimate it is probable that irrelevant considerations were taken into account, and if the challenge is made on this basis it might be possible to avoid the problems that arise where an authorized purpose is combined with an unauthorized one. One cannot be entirely certain, however, that this tactic will always be successful in inducing the courts to side-step the problem.

It has been assumed up to now that the relevant legislation has specified the purposes for which the power is to be exercised and the considerations that are to be taken into account. Even if this is not the case, however, the courts will often decide for themselves what the intended purpose is and what considerations are relevant. This is done by looking at the legislation as a whole in order to discover the policy behind it. This technique can produce very desirable results at times; but it also permits the courts to read their own values and preconceptions into legislation and to discover purposes that were never intended by Parliament.

A case which might be regarded as an example of this is *Roberts* v. *Hopwood*.[99] Under an Act of Parliament the Poplar Borough Council had the power to pay its employees 'such . . . wages as [it] may think fit'. In the exercise of this power it decided that the minimum wage for its employees was to be £4 per week for the year 1921–2. This was the same as in the previous year even though there had been an enormous fall in the cost of living since then; it was also considerably more than the going wage for this kind of work at the time. In fixing this wage the Council, which was strongly left-wing, admitted that it was not concerned only with economic considerations but also with social considerations: it thought that £4 was the minimum that should be paid irrespective of the cost of living and prevailing wage rates. The House of Lords held that this was an invalid exercise of its discretion. Their Lordships obviously thought that the Council should pay the minimum wages consistent with an efficient work-force; if they allowed themselves to be influenced by wider considerations they were acting illegally.

A similar decision in more recent times was *Prescott* v. *Birmingham Corporation*.[100] The Corporation had the power by statute to charge such fares as they thought fit on the municipal bus service subject to any prescribed statutory maxima for the time being in force. They decided to introduce a scheme to allow old people to travel free at certain times. The court, however, held that this was illegal:[101]

We think it is clearly implicit in the legislation, that while it was left to the defendants to decide what fares should be charged within any prescribed statutory maxima for the time being in force, the undertaking was to be run as a business venture, or, in other words, that fares fixed by the defendants at their discretion, in accordance with ordinary business principles, were to be charged.

The Corporation could not, therefore, 'go out of their way to make losses by giving away rights of free travel'. However, Parliament seems to have regarded the matter differently since, shortly after this decision, it passed the Public Service Vehicles (Travel Concessions) Act 1955 which authorized schemes such as this.

Unreasonableness is generally said to be another ground on which a discretionary decision can be upset. This, again, largely overlaps with the previous grounds since the reason why the decision is unreasonable will often be because, for example, relevant considerations have not been taken into account. One example often given of an unreasonable decision is the dismissal of a school-teacher because she has red hair. But this is obviously also a case of taking irrelevant considerations into account.[102] However, there may be some cases in which a decision is unreasonable without any other ground of invalidity being present. This may occur if all the right considerations are taken into account but such undue weight is given to one of them that the result is unreasonable.[103]

If the relevant legislation expressly requires the power to be exercised reasonably the courts will normally have no difficulty in giving effect to this. Even if no express mention of reasonableness is made the courts may still intervene, but in this case the test applied is very strict:[104]

It is true the discretion must be exercised reasonably. Now what does that mean? ... if a decision on a competent matter is so unreasonable that no

reasonable authority could ever have come to it, then the courts can interfere. . . . It is not what the court considers reasonable, a different thing
altogether.

It is not often that this test is satisfied.

A recent example of the application of an express requirement of
reasonableness was *Backhouse* v. *Lambeth London Borough Council*.[105]
Under section 62(1) of the Housing Finance Act 1972 local authorities were required to make increases in the rents of council houses.
There was, however, an exception to this. Section 63(1) provided
that 'If the authority made a general rent increase in the first half of
1972–3 which produces £26 or more per dwelling in 1972–3 they
shall not make an increase towards fair rents in that year.' The
council hit upon the plan of increasing the rent of just one house by a
sum so large that this alone would produce an increase of £26 per
dwelling in the total rent for all their houses. It was hoped that this
would bring the council within the provisions of section 63(1) and
they would not have to increase the rents of any other houses. The
ability of the council to do this depended on another statute, the
Housing Act 1957. Section 111(1) of this gave the council the
power to make 'such reasonable charges for the tenancy or occupation of the houses as they may determine'. This section expressly
required the council to set reasonable rents and the court had no
difficulty in deciding that £18,000 per week was not a reasonable
sum of a house of which the rent had previously been just over £30
per month. However, since the council was confessedly motivated by
the desire to get round the Housing Finance Act the case could have
been decided on the ground of improper purpose.

An abuse of discretion can normally be established without any
evidence that the person granted the discretion knew that he was
acting improperly. In those cases where the courts determine the
purpose for which the power may be exercised (or the considerations
that are relevant) through a consideration of the general policy of
the statute, it is quite possible that the person granted the power
might honestly have thought that he was acting legitimately. This,
however, will not prevent the courts from invalidating the action. If
it can be established that the person concerned knew that he was
acting wrongly (which is rare), he may be regarded as having acted
in bad faith. This would certainly be the case if he was motivated by
personal favouritism or animosity. It is not, however, usually necessary to go so far as to establish bad faith except in a few special

situations (e.g. where it is sought to establish personal liability on the part of the person exercising the power).

DELEGATED LEGISLATION

If Parliament passes a statute the courts have no power to declare it invalid and this is so even if the correct parliamentary procedure was not followed.[106] But where legislative power is delegated by Parliament[107] the courts are fully entitled to consider the validity of the subordinate legislation made under the power and they can take appropriate action if it is invalid. The ground on which this is done is the familiar doctrine of *ultra vires*.

The doctrine of *ultra vires* applies to only a limited extent in the case of a procedural irregularity. Failure to comply with a procedural requirement when making delegated legislation does not necessarily invalidate the legislation: this will occur only where the requirement is mandatory, not where it is directory. It is, however, difficult to tell (in the absence of specific statutory provision) whether any particular requirement is mandatory or directory though the former classification is normally adopted in the case of a particularly important requirement.

A duty to consult specified bodies before making the legislation might be regarded by the courts as mandatory; a duty to lay the instrument containing the legislation before Parliament ought on general principles to be mandatory but it is not at all clear that this is so.[108] The provisions of the Statutory Instruments Act 1946 regarding the printing and issue of statutory instruments are merely directory,[109] but it is provided by section 3(2) of the Act that if criminal proceedings are brought for the contravention of a statutory instrument, it is a defence to prove that the instrument had not been issued by Her Majesty's Stationery Office at the time of the alleged contravention. This defence will not, however, apply if the prosecution proves that reasonable steps were taken to bring the purport of the instrument to the attention of the public in general, persons likely to be affected by it, or the person charged.

These problems do not arise in the case of substantive *ultra vires*. If power is given to legislate only on certain topics, or for certain purposes, or in certain circumstances, the limits of the power must not be over-stepped. As in other areas, however, the courts have gone further than merely enforcing the expressed limitations on the power and they have construed even the widest grants of power as being subject to implied limitations derived from general constitutional principles. What the courts have done in fact is to create a number of presumptions that prevent subordinate legislative authorities from doing certain things without express authority in the relevant statute.

One of the most important of these presumptions is directed against subordinate legislation that attempts to oust the jurisdiction of the courts. There have been a number of cases in which the courts have struck down provisions of this nature. One of them is *R. & W. Paul Ltd* v. *The Wheat Commission*.[110] Under section 5 of the Wheat Act 1932 the Wheat Commission had power to make by-laws to provide 'for the final determination by arbitration of disputes' with regard to certain matters. Acting under this power the Commission made a by-law providing that all disputes on a certain question should be referred to arbitration. The by-law also purported to exclude the operation of the Arbitration Act 1889 (which gave the right to obtain a ruling from the courts on a disputed point of law arising in the course of an arbitration). By excluding the application of the Arbitration Act the Commission was depriving parties to the dispute of the right to go to court and this, the Court held, they had no power to do without express authorization in the empowering Act.

Another presumption is that subordinate legislative authorities do not have the power to impose a tax without an express provision in the empowering Act. One of the leading cases on this point is *Attorney-General* v. *Wilts United Dairies Ltd*.[111] The facts of this case were as follows. During the First World War the office of Food Controller was established to regulate the supply and consumption of food. Under Regulation 2F of the Defence Regulations (made under the Defence of the Realm Consolidation Act 1914) he had power to make orders regulating 'the production, manufacture, treatment, use, consumption, transport, storage, distribution, supply, sale or purchase of, or other dealings in, or measures to be taken in relation to any article (including orders providing for the fixing of maximum and minimum prices) where it appears to him necessary or expedient to make any such order for the purpose of encouraging or maintaining the food supply of the country.' This was actually a sub-delegated power but it was nevertheless couched in very wide terms. In 1919 he made an Order to fix the maximum price of milk and since the south-west of England was more productive than elsewhere, he decided to set a lower maximum price there than in the rest of the country. He also provided that whenever milk was taken from the lower-price area to the higher-price area, the sum of two-pence per gallon should be paid to him (this being the difference in the price of milk in the two areas). The courts, however, held that the Food Controller had no power to do this as it was a form of taxation. The following quotation[112] explains their reasons:

. . . if an officer of the executive seeks to justify a charge upon the subject made for the use of the Crown (which includes all the purposes of the public revenue), he must show, in clear terms, that Parliament has authorized the particular charge. The intention of the Legislature is to be inferred from the language used, and the grant of powers may, though not expressed, have to be implied as necessarily arising from the words of a statute; but in view of the historic struggle of the Legislature to secure for itself the sole power to levy money upon the subject, its complete success in that struggle, the elaborate means adopted by the Representative House to control the amount, the conditions and the purposes of the levy, the circumstances would be remarkable indeed which would induce the Court to believe that the Legislature had sacrificed all the well-known checks and precautions, and, not in express words, but merely by implication, had entrusted a Minister of the Crown with undefined and unlimited powers of imposing charges upon the subject for purposes connected with his department.

Two other cases concerning regulations under the Defence of the Realm Consolidation Act 1914 make an interesting contrast. Section 1 of the Act gave power to the Crown in Council to make regulations 'for securing the public safety and the defence of the realm'. One regulation made under this power (Regulation 2B) gave the Government the power to take possession of stores of various kinds and provided that the compensation, which would be deter-mined by a tribunal, did not have to be based on the market value. In *Newcastle Breweries Ltd* v. *The King*[113] a large quantity of rum had been requisitioned for the Navy and the compensation offered had been about one third of the market value. There already was statu-tory provision for requisitioning property subject to the payment of full compensation (i.e. based on the market value) and in the event of a dispute this was to be determined by a county court judge. The effect of Regulation 2B was, therefore, to take away the right to full compensation and to substitute the tribunal for a county court judge. The Court considered that these provisions could not reasonably be regarded as necessary for securing the public safety and the defence of the realm and were consequently outside the power conferred by the Defence of the Realm Consolidation Act. Salter J. said:[114]

> It is an established rule that a statute will not be read as authorizing the taking of a subject's goods without payment unless an intention to do so be clearly expressed. . . . This rule must apply no less to partial than to total confiscation, and it must apply a fortiori to the construction of a statute delegating legislative powers.

The breweries were, therefore, entitled to be paid the 'fair market value' for the rum.

Another regulation made under the same general power was Regulation 14B which gave the Home Secretary the power to intern persons of 'hostile origin or associations' irrespective of whether or not they were British subjects. In *R. v. Halliday, ex p. Zadig*[115] the House of Lords held that this regulation was valid even though there was no express provision for internment in the enabling Act. It is true that internment might well have been necessary for 'securing the public safety and the defence of the realm' and the case was decided in the middle of the war, but nevertheless it is almost incredible that so drastic a step as imprisonment without trial could be introduced without express statutory authorization.

Another ground on which delegated legislation may be struck down by the courts is that it is unreasonable. This ground of invalidity has been applied in several cases to local authority by-laws but it is generally thought not to be applicable to statutory instruments made by Ministers or the Crown in Council. Of course, implied *ultra vires* could cover the same ground as unreasonableness and the courts are quite willing to invalidate statutory instruments on the basis of implied limitations in the enabling Act. Moreover, it is far from clear whether unreasonableness is not itself a special category of implied *ultra vires*: one could say that Parliament intended the power granted to be used only in a reasonable way.

The test of unreasonableness seems to be generally the same as in the case of discretionary powers of an executive nature, i.e. it is not a question of whether the judge thinks the by-law is desirable or necessary but whether any reasonable man could think this to be so. The leading case on the subject is *Kruse* v. *Johnson*[116] and the following quotation gives some idea of what the courts regard as unreasonable (and also gives some support to the idea that unreasonableness is a category of implied *ultra vires*):[117]

... I do not mean to say that there may not be cases in which it would be the duty of the court to condemn by-laws ... as invalid because unreasonable. But unreasonable in what sense? If, for instance, they were found to be partial and unequal in their operation as between different classes; if they were manifestly unjust; if they disclosed bad faith; if they involved such oppressive or gratuitous interference with the rights of those subject to them as could find no justification in the minds of reasonable men, the court might well say, 'Parliament never intended to give authority to make such rules; they are unreasonable and *ultra vires*'. But it is in this sense, and in this sense only, as I conceive, that the question of unreasonableness can properly be regarded. A by-law is not unreasonable merely because particular judges may think that it goes further than is prudent or necessary or convenient, or because it is not accompanied by a qualification or an exception which some judges may think ought to be there.

Uncertainty also appears to be a ground of invalidity, at least in the case of by-laws, and, since the power to make subordinate legislation is a discretionary power, it would seem that in principle the rules concerning abuse of discretion (considered in the previous section) would apply to the making of delegated legislation.

What happens if delegated legislation conflicts with a statute? It sometimes happens that Parliament gives subordinate legislative authorities the power to amend either the enabling Act or another Act and where this is done the subordinate legislation will, of course, prevail provided the statute amended was passed prior to the enabling Act. Since subordinate legislation can have no greater validity than it would have if it were contained in the parent Act, it would seem to be constitutionally impossible for subordinate legislation to amend a statute passed after the enabling Act: a later statute will always prevail over an earlier one.[118] If there is no express authorization to amend Acts of Parliament the courts will probably take the view that the subordinate legislative authority was not intended by Parliament to have this power. In this case any conflict will be resolved in favour of the statute irrespective of when it was passed.

REMEDIES
Something has already been said about remedies at the beginning of this chapter. Unfortunately, however, the law in this area is not as

straightforward as it might be and some of the problems that arise require consideration. In most branches of the law, if a person has a legal right there is usually also a remedy to enforce it. This is not always the case in administrative law; or perhaps it would be more accurate to say that the mere fact that a public authority has acted contrary to the law does not necessarily mean that the citizen can obtain a remedy against it. It is not enough, therefore, to study the various grounds on which the act or decision of a public authority may be open to challenge; even if this has been established the would-be litigant must still discover whether there is an available remedy.

Choice of Remedies

Although there might seem to be a satisfactory range of remedies available in administrative law, there are a number of technical problems that make it difficult to choose the appropriate way of proceeding. It is not intended to discuss these technical defects in detail, but some brief points may be made.

The prerogative orders suffer from a number of defects. The most important of these are as follows:

1. Since the prerogative orders are exclusively public law remedies, they cannot apply to domestic bodies such as trade unions or professional associations.[119]

2. As a result of the special procedure for these orders, there is no provision for discovery of documents. This can make it difficult to obtain the necessary evidence.

3. It is sometimes said that certiorari and prohibition (but not mandamus) apply only to a body that is under a duty to act judicially.[120] This limitation has, however, been ignored in some cases and it is unclear how far it applies today;[121] but there does seem to be a rule that these remedies cannot be used to control delegated legislation.

4. In the case of certiorari there is a strict time limit. If the application is brought more than six months after the date of the order that is challenged, leave to apply will not be granted without a satisfactory explanation of the delay.

These defects do not apply to injunctions or declarations. There is, however, one kind of proceeding in which these latter remedies cannot be used: if the ground of invalidity is error of law on the face of the record, certiorari must be used to quash the decision. Another disadvantage of these remedies is that the rules for *locus standi* are stricter than in the case of the prerogative remedies, especially certiorari and prohibition. This problem is discussed below.

Additional problems arise where it is wished to challenge action taken by, or on behalf of, the Crown. Certiorari and prohibition cannot issue against the Crown although they can issue against Ministers or other persons acting on behalf of the Crown. The position is similar with regard to mandamus, except that this order will not issue against a Crown servant if the duty in question is owed only to the Crown and not towards any other person.[122] Injunctions are prohibited against the Crown. They are also prohibited against officers of the Crown if the effect of granting the injunction would be to give a remedy against the Crown that could not have been obtained in proceedings against it.[123] A declaration, on the other hand, is available against the Crown and against Crown servants in the same way as against anyone else.

One answer to the problem of choosing the right remedy might be to apply for a combination of remedies in the hope that at least one would prove appropriate. Unfortunately, however, it is not possible to apply for one of the prerogative orders in conjunction with a non-prerogative remedy. This is also due to the special procedure applicable in the case of the prerogative remedies. It is possible to apply for two or more prerogative orders – for example, certiorari to quash an invalid decision and mandamus to require the authority to consider the matter afresh according to law – but the combination which is most likely to be desired, a declaration in conjunction with one of the prerogative orders, is impossible. The applicant must first try to obtain, for example, certiorari and if that fails on a technicality, he can apply for a declaration in new proceedings.

There is no justification for the excessive technicality of administrative law remedies and there is no reason why there should not be one all-purpose remedy that would combine the advantages of the old remedies without their technical drawbacks. This question is being considered by the Law Commission and it is to be hoped that reform will not be too long delayed.

Ouster Clauses

Sometimes when Parliament gives power to a public authority there is a provision in the empowering statute limiting or excluding the jurisdiction of the courts to review the acts and decisions of the authority. Such a provision is often known as an 'ouster clause' (because it ousts the jurisdiction of the courts). However, just as the courts have adopted a policy of opposition to provisions in subordinate legislation that oust their jurisdiction, so have they also attempted wherever possible to restrict the effect of ouster clauses in statutes.

This tradition of opposition to ouster clauses dates back to the seventeenth century and is still very strong today. Various techniques are used to evade the effect of such clauses: in some cases the courts have been prepared to ignore them in a rather blatant manner; in others subtle linguistic arguments have been put into service in an attempt to show that they do not really mean what they say.

One form of ouster clause that was once fairly common is known as a finality clause. It reads: 'Any decision of . . . shall be final.' This clause has long been treated by the courts as not preventing judicial review; it merely takes away a right of appeal (which, however, can exist only if a statute has made provision for it.) Thus in *R. v. Medical Appeal Tribunal, ex parte Gilmore*[124] Lord Denning said:

> . . . on looking again into the old books I find it very well settled that the remedy by certiorari is never to be taken away by any statute except by the most clear and explicit words. The word 'final' is not enough. That only means 'without appeal'. It does not mean 'without recourse to certiorari'. It makes the decision final on the facts, but not final on the law. Notwithstanding that the decision is by a statute made 'final', certiorari can still issue for excess of jurisdiction or for error of law on the face of the record.

Two points should be noted with regard to this: first, although Lord Denning said that a finality clause makes the decision final on the facts, this refers only to facts within the jurisdiction of the body concerned; secondly, the case in question was an application for certiorari (since the ground of invalidity was error of law on the face of the record) but where other remedies, such as a declaration, are available a finality clause will be equally ineffective.

At one time in the past statutes sometimes contained 'no certiorari' clauses. These expressly took away the right to certiorari by providing that the decision 'shall not be removed by certiorari'. The courts, however, were prepared to grant certiorari even in the face of these clauses.[125]

Attempts were sometimes made to protect delegated legislation from review by providing that the regulations in question 'shall have effect as if enacted in this Act'. The courts have not been consistent in their interpretation of this kind of clause and there are conflicting dicta in decisions in the House of Lords.[126] However, there is authority for saying that such a clause is designed only to protect regulations that are within the empowering Act; since *ultra vires* regulations would not be within the Act, they would not be protected.[127]

These problems are now of much less importance in view of the Tribunals and Inquiries Act 1971. Section 14(1) provides as follows:[128]

As respects England and Wales or Northern Ireland, any provision in an Act passed before 1st August 1958 that any order or determination shall not be called into question in any court, or any provision in such an Act which by similar words excludes any of the powers of the High Court, shall not have effect so as to prevent the removal of the proceedings into the High Court by order of certiorari or to prejudice the powers of the High Court to make orders of mandamus.

As regards statutes passed after 1 August 1958 and remedies other than certiorari and mandamus the law remains as before.

There is an important qualification to the above provision, which is found in section 14(3). This reads:

Nothing in this section shall affect section 26 of the British Nationality Act 1948 or apply to any order or determination of a court of law or where an Act makes special provision for application to the High Court or the Court of Session within a time limited by the Act.

This proviso is important because it is quite common for a statute to give the right to challenge an order or decision within a limited period and to prevent review thereafter. One statute where this occurred was the Acquisition of Land (Authorization Procedure) Act 1946. Paragraph 15 of the First Schedule of this Act provided that compulsory purchase orders could be challenged on certain grounds within six weeks. The following paragraph provided:

Subject to the provisions of the last foregoing paragraph, a compulsory purchase order . . . shall not . . . be questioned in any legal proceedings whatsoever.

In 1956 in *Smith* v. *East Elloe Rural District Council*[129] the House of Lords held (by a majority of three to two) that this clause was effective to oust the jurisdiction of the courts after the six-week period even when the order was challenged on the ground of fraud (bad faith). This case was decided before the Tribunals and Inquiries Act but it would not have been affected by the Act.

A different approach was taken in a case concerning the Foreign Compensation Commission. This is a body which has been given the task of distributing money received by the Government as compensation for British assets confiscated in foreign countries. Under section 4(4) of the Foreign Compensation Act 1950 it was provided as follows:

The determination by the commission of any application made to them under this Act shall not be called in question in any court of law.

This was very similar to the clause in the *East Elloe* case, but in spite of that the House of Lords held in 1968 in *Anisminic* v. *Foreign Compensation Commission*[130] that a decision of the Commission based on an error of law going to jurisdiction could be quashed.[131] The reasoning of the court was that a decision of the Commission that was beyond its jurisdiction was a nullity and was not, therefore, a 'determination'. In other words they interpreted the word 'determination' in the provision quoted above to mean a valid determination, not a purported determination that was in reality a nullity. On this reasoning a clause of this kind would never prevent judicial review except, perhaps, in the case of a decision which was not void but merely voidable.[132]

Parliament responded to this decision by passing the Foreign Compensation Act 1969. This provided for an appeal to the Court of Appeal by way of case stated on questions of law.[133] Subject to this,[134] there was an ouster clause in similar terms to the previous one, but it was also provided in the same section:[135]

In this section 'determination' includes . . . anything which purports to be a determination.

It is hard to see how the courts could get round this.[136]

It is not entirely clear what the authority of the *East Elloe* case now is. It was not formally overruled in the *Anisminic* case, neither was it satisfactorily distinguished. There were, however, a number of critical remarks about it and it is clear that a majority of the court would have been prepared to overrule it if this had been necessary. One difference between the two cases was that the ouster clause in the *East Elloe* case operated only after a six-week period; in the *Anisminic* case there was a total ban on review. This could be a ground for distinguishing the two cases but the logic of the *Anisminic* decision would apply equally well where there was a limited period for review. In practical terms, however, this distinction is not without merit: in many situations it might be administratively desirable for any challenge to be made as quickly as possible. This is obviously the case where land is compulsorily purchased since building on the land cannot start if the validity of the order is in doubt. In view of this, the courts may well look with more favour on ouster clauses which come into operation after a limited period.

Discretion

All the main administrative remedies – certiorari, prohibition, mandamus, injunction and declaration – are discretionary remedies, that is to say that the court is not obliged to grant them even if the applicant proves that the administrative authority acted unlawfully. Failure to grant a remedy does not necessarily mean that the action of the authority is validated – it may still be open to collateral attack – but in practice it often has this effect.

There are various grounds on which this discretion may be exercised. If the applicant's case is unmeritorious (though technically justified) a remedy may be refused and this may also occur if the applicant is guilty of unreasonable delay (even if he is inside the time limit for the remedy in question).[137] In some circumstances a remedy may not be granted if the applicant is regarded as having waived his rights: for example, if a decision is challenged on the ground that there was a real likelihood of bias on the part of the decision-maker, a remedy may be refused if the applicant knew the facts at the time of the hearing and did not raise the matter until the decision had gone against him.[138]

In some natural justice cases a remedy has been refused on the ground that the end result was fair. For example, in *Glynn* v. *Keele University*[139] a student was fined £10 and excluded from the university residence (but not from the university itself) for appearing naked on the university campus (apparently as part of a protest). The student challenged this decision by applying for an injunction. The court held that he ought to have been given a hearing but decided to exercise its discretion against granting the remedy. The student did not dispute that he had done what he had been accused of doing and, since the court considered that the punishment was quite proper, it was felt that he had suffered no injustice.[140]

The fact that there is a statutory remedy open to the applicant, such as an appeal to a higher administrative authority or even to the courts, does not normally preclude the granting of one of the ordinary administrative remedies. The court may, however, in its discretion refuse to grant such a remedy if the alternative is as convenient, beneficial and effective as the remedy requested. In some cases, of course, there may be an ouster clause precluding the granting of any save the statutory remedy; it is also possible that the courts may construe the relevant legislation as implicitly excluding all other remedies.[141] As has been explained above, the courts are normally hostile to such provisions but if the statutory remedy is fair and effective the court may be more willing to refrain from exercising jurisdiction.

Locus Standi

The fact that a public body has acted unlawfully does not necessarily mean that proceedings can be brought by someone who is not personally affected. If a busybody (or public-spirited citizen, according to taste) applies to court for a remedy, he may be told that the affair is none of his business and that he has no *locus standi* to bring the proceedings. *Locus standi* (standing) means the right to bring proceedings, the right to challenge an act or decision of a public body.

In what circumstances will a person be regarded as having *locus standi*? No consistent answer has been given to this question by the courts.[142] In some cases almost anybody who is in fact affected by the order or decision is allowed to apply to court; in others it has been held that the applicant must have a special interest in the matter above that of members of the general public, or have suffered special damage peculiar to himself. Moreover, a person who might in fact have been seriously affected may be held to have no interest recognized by law.

The requirements for *locus standi* are not the same for all remedies. The attitude of the courts is more liberal in the case of the prerogative remedies, which are of a public nature, than in the case of the private law remedies of injunction and declaration. It is said that a court may in its discretion grant certiorari to anyone; someone who is personally affected *must* normally be granted the remedy (unless there are special reasons why the court should exercise its discretion against him).[143]

Two recent cases illustrate the approach of the courts with regard to mandamus. *R. v. Commissioners of Customs and Excise, ex p. Cooke and Stevenson*[144] concerned a tax on bookmakers imposed by the Finance Act 1969. Under the Act the tax was payable either annually or in two half-yearly payments. There was a great deal of protest from bookmakers against the tax and finally it was announced in the press that bookmakers could pay the tax by monthly intalments. There was no legal authority for this concession and two bookmakers who had paid the tax as provided by the Act applied to the court for mandamus against the Commissioners of Customs and Excise (who were responsible for collecting the tax) to require them to insist that the tax be paid under the terms of the Act. The court accepted that the Government were acting quite illegally in what they were doing but refused to grant mandamus because the applicants had no *locus standi*. The argument of the applicants was that if the tax was enforced as provided by law, rival bookmakers would be put out of business and they would therefore face less competition. The court rejected this argument on the ground that the purpose of the Finance Act was to collect a tax and not to regulate betting by limiting the number of bookmakers. Their interest was not, therefore, a legitimate one and did not give them *locus standi*. In a much earlier case, however, it was held that a brewer had *locus standi* to apply for certiorari to challenge a liquor licence granted to his trade rivals.[145]

In *R. v. Hereford Corporation, ex p. Harrower*[146] the standing orders of the corporation provided that before the corporation entered into contracts of certain kinds, public notice should be given and a reasonable number of persons on the corporation's list of contractors should be invited to tender.[147] In the case in question the corporation was about to enter into a contract with the Midland Electricity Board to provide heating for some flats and they had neither given notice nor invited tenders. The applicants were electrical contractors on the corporation's list of approved contractors. The corporation had not complied with the standing orders because they had no heating design engineer on their staff and it was therefore impossible for them to send out specifications for tender. The court held that the applicants did not have sufficient interest to apply for mandamus in their capacity as potential contractors but they did have *locus standi* in their capacity as ratepayers.[148] This suggests that the object of the provisions concerning tenders was to protect the interests of ratepayers (by making sure that the corporation obtained value for money) rather than to protect the rights of potential contractors.

As was stated previously, the rules of *locus standi* are stricter in the case of injunction and declaration. However, the difficulties of *locus standi* in the case of these two remedies can be overcome by means of a relator action. A relator action is an action brought by the Attorney-General at the relation (request) of the applicant. The Attorney-General has *locus standi* to bring proceedings on a wide range of matters affecting the public and in a relator action a private person can take advantage of his superior standing. The Attorney-General has a discretion whether to allow proceedings to be brought in his name (although he is usually fairly liberal in the exercise of this discretion) and he has the power to control the proceedings; normally, however, the relator (as the applicant is called) is given a free hand in the conduct of the case.

When can proceedings for an injunction be brought by a private person without the intervention of the Attorney-General? In *Boyce* v. *Paddington Borough Council*[149] Buckley J. said that this could be done in two cases:

first, where the interference with the public right is such as that some private right of his is at the same time interfered with . . .; and, secondly, where no private right is interfered with, but the plaintiff, in respect of his public right, suffers special damage peculiar to himself from the interference with the public right.

Where these conditions are not met a relator action must be brought. The only exception is that a private citizen may be allowed to sue in his own name if the Attorney-General improperly refuses permission for a relator action or if the matter is so urgent that his permission cannot be obtained.[150]

The rules of *locus standi* in the case of a declaration are similar to those for an injunction. A case which illustrates the strict view sometimes taken by the courts is *Gregory* v. *London Borough of Camden*.[151] In this case it was held that, where planning permission to build a school was wrongly given, the neighbours did not have standing to obtain a declaration. The court held that the Town and Country Planning Acts (which made it necessary to obtain planning permission) were not passed for the benefit of any particular class of the public – such as neighbours – but for the benefit of the public in general. This decision (which has been subject to criticism) may be contrasted with a much earlier case in which certiorari was granted to an adjacent landowner in similar circumstances.[152] This is perhaps an illustration of the difference between certiorari and declaration. (The applicants in the *Camden* case could not obtain certiorari because they discovered the facts too late to come within the six-month time limit applicable to this remedy.)

The abolition of the doctrine of *locus standi* would not be desirable. There is no reason why a person with no interest in the matter should be allowed to bring proceedings if those most closely affected see no reason to do so. Difficulties might arise where there is a duty owed to the public in general but in this case relator proceedings could normally be brought.

Void or Voidable?

A great deal of confusion and difficulty has been caused by the question whether invalid decisions in administrative law are void or voidable. The first problem is the exact meaning of these terms. The word 'voidable' means something different in the law of contract, for example, from what it means in the law of marriage: a voidable contract is one which is valid unless and until it is set aside by the party at whose option it is voidable; a voidable marriage, on the other hand, is one which is valid unless it is set aside by the *court* at the suit of a party. Until recently the law was that when a voidable marriage was annulled the decree operated retrospectively (for most purposes) so that the marriage was deemed never to have existed.[153] This was never the case in the law of contract.

In view of this terminological inconsistency in other branches of the law it is not surprising that there is some confusion in administrative law. However, what is generally meant by the distinction is that a void act or decision is of no effect at all and may, in theory, be simply ignored by those concerned. A voidable act or decision, on the other hand, is valid and effective unless set aside or quashed by the court in proceedings properly instituted for the purpose.

This distinction is not quite so fundamental as it sounds because the uncertainties of administrative law are such that in most cases one cannot be sure whether a decision is valid or not without a court ruling and it is consequently desirable to go to court whether the decision is thought to be void or voidable. There are, however, a number of situations in which the distinction has practical consequences. The most obvious is where the validity of the decision arises in collateral proceedings. Here a voidable decision should be treated as valid (unless it has previously been set aside in separate proceedings) while a void one can be treated as of no effect. Another case is where the remedy asked for is a declaration. Since this is merely a statement of the pre-existing legal situation it is not a suitable procedure for challenging a voidable decision; an application for certiorari to quash would be the proper procedure.

In what circumstances is a decision void and when is it merely voidable? It is impossible to give a confident answer to this question since the relevant cases are confused and contradictory. It is generally thought that error of law on the face of the record makes a decision voidable and this is supported by the fact that declaration cannot be used as a remedy in this case.[154] Most other grounds of invalidity are thought to make the decision void but the position where there has been a breach of natural justice is very controversial. In 1852 it was decided in *Dimes* v. *Grand Junction Canal Company*[155] that a breach of the rule against bias made a decision voidable and it was stated that such a decision could not be challenged in collateral proceedings. However, in 1893 it was held in *Cooper* v. *Wandsworth Board of Works*[156] that a decision given without a hearing could be challenged in collateral proceedings. There seems to be no good reason why the position should be different depending on whether the ground of invalidity is bias or failure to give a hearing. *Dimes'* case might, however, be distinguished on the ground that it concerned a decision of a court while in *Cooper's* case the decision was that of an administrative authority. The main argument for saying that a decision is merely voidable is that this protects those carrying out the decision from liability in tort if the decision turns out to be invalid; but it is not obvious why those carrying out the order of a court should be in need of greater protection than those carrying out the decision of an administrative authority.

Two recent cases in which the problem has been considered are *Ridge* v. *Baldwin*,[157] decided by the House of Lords, and *Durayappah* v. *Fernando*,[158] decided a few years later by the Privy Council. Both these cases concerned a decision that was vitiated through failure to give a hearing and at first sight they appear to be directly contradictory. In *Ridge* v. *Baldwin* there was a majority of three judges against two in favour of the proposition that the decision was void, while in *Durayappah* v. *Fernando* the Privy Council held that such a decision was voidable. The conflict between these cases, however, seems to be the result of confusion over the meaning of the term 'voidable' and the point that the Privy Council was concerned with establishing in *Durayappah* v. *Fernando* was that it is up to the person refused the hearing to take steps to set it aside. If he does not challenge it, no one else can.[159] This was what the Privy Council meant by voidable and there is no doubt that most, if not all, of the judges in *Ridge* v. *Baldwin* would have agreed with this.[160] It seems fairly clear, for example, that if the decision is in favour of the party denied a hearing, the other party cannot attack it. There is little doubt that the same rule applies in the case of bias. Moreover, the person denied natural justice must himself take action with reasonable promptitude, otherwise he will lose the right to complain.[161] This, however, does not necessarily mean that a decision contrary to natural justice is voidable in the sense in which the term is normally used in administrative law: one could simply say that if no objection is made within a reasonable time by the person denied natural justice, the decision is validated;[162] if, however, he does not waive his rights in this way, the decision is void *ab initio*.[163]

The fact that the decision can be attacked only by the person who was denied natural justice does not mean that a declaration cannot be granted if he does challenge it: several cases establish that this remedy can be used in natural justice cases.[164] The position with regard to collateral proceedings is unclear. The answer which *should* be given to this question is, it is suggested, to allow collateral proceedings provided the plaintiff acts as soon as possible. Assume for example that an order is made to demolish a private house and the order is invalid for lack of a hearing (as in *Cooper* v. *Wandsworth Board of Works,* above). If the owner knows what is happening and does nothing until the demolition is completed, it would be wrong for him to be able to sue for damages; he should have taken action before the demolition was started. On the other hand, if he knew nothing about the matter until the damage was done, it would be only right to allow him to obtain compensation. This solution can be supported by saying that his failure to act in the first case took effect as a waiver of his rights. If the order was invalid for bias the same reasoning should apply: if he did not know of the facts that constituted bias until the house was demolished he should be allowed to sue for damages; otherwise the waiver doctrine should apply.

Finally, a word should be said about ouster clauses. It is sometimes stated that an ouster clause is more effective where the decision is voidable than where it is void. It is clear, however, that at least certain kinds of ouster clause do not prevent review of voidable decisions. Thus a 'finality' clause does not bar review for error of law on the face of the record (which is generally regarded as making the decision voidable.[165] On the other hand, the reasoning in *Anisminic v. Foreign Compensation Commission*[166] is hardly applicable to a voidable decision. It will be remembered that in this case a provision stating that a 'determination by the commission . . . shall not be called in question in any court of law' was circumvented by holding that an invalid decision was not a 'determination'. This presupposes that the decision was a nullity before it was considered by the court and would not apply to a decision that was merely voidable. It remains to be seen, however, whether the courts will follow the logic of this argument.

17
The European Community

Since the last war Britain and Europe seem to have danced a curious minuet: when one side advanced the other retreated. In September 1946 Winston Churchill made a speech at the University of Zürich in which he called for 'a sort of United States of Europe'. His audience might have thought that Britain would lead the way towards this goal; but this was not to be the case. In 1950 Robert Schuman, Foreign Minister of France, launched a plan to pool Franco-German coal and steel production under a supra-national High Authority. This organization was open to other countries. Belgium, the Netherlands, Luxemburg and Italy expressed the desire to join in; Britain did not. The Six went ahead without Britain and in 1952 the European Coal and Steel Community, the first of the Communities, came into existence. In 1955 a conference was held in Messina, Sicily, to plan a wider merger. Britain was invited to take part, but the comparatively junior official who was sent on behalf of the U.K. was soon withdrawn, and Britain again stood back. In 1957 the Six signed in Rome the treaties creating the European Economic Community and the European Atomic Energy Community. These treaties came into force on 1 January 1958. There were then three Communities – ECSC, EEC and Euratom – and Britain was outside all of them.

Britain saw herself excluded from the most important economic grouping in Europe and therefore proposed a free trade area for the whole of Western Europe. The difference between a free trade area and a customs union, which was what the EEC was intended to become, is that in a free trade area customs duties are abolished between the participating countries but there is no common external tariff on imports from outside. A customs union, on the other hand, has both these features. Britain did not wish to enter into a customs union because she wanted to be free to retain her system of preferences for imports from the Commonwealth. Moreover, the British were also opposed to the supra-national elements which were a cardinal feature of the three European Communities. The British proposal for a West European free trade area was viewed with suspicion by many in the Six who regarded it as an attempt to dilute their own concept of European unity. Negotiations consequently broke down and Britain then formed her own trade group with the rump of the European countries: Norway, Sweden, Denmark, Austria, Switzerland and Portugal. In 1959 these countries signed a convention in Stockholm to set up the European Free Trade Association (EFTA).[1] But EFTA, with little more than half the population of the EEC, was really only a stop-gap.

At the beginning of the sixties British attitudes towards Europe began to change and the first hesitant steps were taken towards a new partnership. In 1961 the Conservative Government decided to open negotiations with the Six. But now the European attitude had changed as well. The first French veto took place in 1963 and Britain was rebuffed. In 1967 Britain tried again when the Labour Government applied for membership; but this was rejected when de Gaulle applied his veto a second time. Britain's application was not, however, formally withdrawn and when de Gaulle disappeared from the scene in 1969 the way was open for a third attempt to join. Negotiations finally began in June 1970, just after the Conservatives returned to power, and this time they were successful. The terms were accepted by the House of Commons by a majority of 112 in October 1971, and the Treaty of Accession was signed in January 1972.[2] The European Communities Act was passed in 1972 and Britain became a member on 1 January 1973.

Britain's initial aloofness and subsequent change of attitude were based on a number of factors. The history of the last War, in which Britain remained unconquered; Britain's economic, political and cultural links with the Commonwealth and the United States – links strengthened by common political and legal traditions as well as by a common language; and perhaps also a certain sense of superiority often felt towards Continental Europe – these all made it difficult for British leaders to accept that Britain should throw in her lot with her European neighbours. But developments in the decades following the end of the War brought changes. The decline of the Commonwealth both as a political force and as a market for British goods, as well as the end of the special relationship with America, meant that there was no alternative grouping for Britain to join; while the rapid rise in living standards and economic development within the Six in contrast to Britain's own sluggish rate of growth meant that, in the economic sphere at least, it was no longer possible to look down on the Continentals.

Whatever the merits and demerits of joining the Community there is no doubt that the effects of membership on the British constitution are very important. If Britain's membership is not terminated by a future Government and if the Community continues to evolve towards 'a sort of United States of Europe' the effects of joining will be profound. Even if one restricts oneself to the rather fragile supranational structure that exists at the present time, it is clear that British constitutional law has entered a new era. In certain important matters legislative power has been transferred from Westminster to Brussels and in relation to these matters the House of Lords is no longer at the apex of the judicial system. Precedents laid down in Luxemburg will have to be followed in England. English lawyers will have to familiarize themselves with laws drafted in a foreign legal idiom which cannot always be easily understood unless one realizes that they were originally written in French and were based on Continental legal concepts. These are the immediate effects of joining the Community.

WHAT THE COMMUNITY DOES

The European Coal and Steel Community is limited to coal and steel and Euratom is limited to the field of nuclear energy; but the EEC is not restricted to any section of the economy and the three Communities together, therefore, cover all aspects of economic activity. The basic objective of the Communities is economic expansion and the raising of living standards. The most important policies that are pursued to attain this objective are those contained in the EEC Treaty.[3] First, there is the establishment of a customs union between the Member States. This involves the abolition of customs duties, quantitative restrictions and similar measures which hinder the free movement of goods within the Community; it also requires the establishment of a common external tariff on goods imported from outside the Community.[4]

The customs union came fully into effect between the Six in 1968 and the new members will be integrated into the system in stages according to a time-table laid down in the Treaty of Accession. This transitional period should be complete in 1977.

The establishment of a common trade policy towards the rest of the world is a Community objective and this is closely related to the establishment of a customs union.[5] It requires that trade agreements between Member States and third countries should be replaced by Community agreements, that international trade negotiations (especially in GATT) be undertaken by the Community, and that uniform policies be worked out on matters such as anti-dumping regulations and export credits. Much has been achieved in this area – the Community, for example, has concluded numerous trade and association agreements with third countries – but a common policy has not yet been fully implemented in all respects.

Another objective of the Community is the abolition of all obstacles to the free movement of persons, services and capital within the Community.[6] A great deal has been done to implement this. Workers from all countries in the Community have the right to seek employment in any Member State and discrimination is forbidden against workers from another Member State as regards employment, pay and conditions of work.[7] Progress has been slower, however, as regards the abolition of restrictions on the right of professional people, businessmen and companies to establish themselves in other countries of the Community.

One of the major areas of Community activity is agriculture, where a common policy has been implemented to protect the interests of the farmers.[8] The Common Agricultural Policy as it works at present is very complicated and not very satisfactory, resulting in high prices and large surpluses which have to be bought up by the Community authorities. It is, however, of great political importance since the farming community in most Member States is larger and more powerful politically than in Britain.

Transport is another area in which a common policy is to be established,[9] but only limited progress has been made so far. The Treaty also contains important anti-trust provisions[10] and the Community authorities have the power to impose heavy fines on firms which infringe the rules. The Community is trying to promote the harmonization of laws in the member states in so far as these affect trade within the Community.[11] The harmonization of indirect taxation is another Community objective[12] and agreement has been reached on the adoption of a uniform system of value-added tax (VAT).

These are just some of the areas where the Community has adopted common policies. Co-ordination of policies and co-operation already extends into many fields, such as economic and monetary policy,[13] (especially as regards balance of payments problems) cultural and social matters,[14] and even political questions. It is clear from this that the EEC is much more than just a common market.

INSTITUTIONS

The principal Community institutions are the Commission, the Council, the Assembly (European Parliament) and the Court of Justice. Of the three political institutions, the Commission and the Council are the most important: the European Parliament is not directly elected and its functions are mainly advisory. The Council is composed of representatives of the Member States and it is the forum where the Governments attempt to resolve conflicts of national interest. The Commission is independent of the national Governments and it is supposed to advocate the Community interest. Thus the views of the Council are likely to be no more than the lowest common denominator among the conflicting interests of nine national Governments; the Commission is expected to provide the supra-national element.

The relationship between the Commission and the Council was intended to be a carefully balanced compromise between supranationalism on the one hand and inter-governmental negotiation, the basis of most international organizations, on the other. The exact powers and functions of these two bodies are laid down in the Treaties and vary, depending on the subject-matter, but in general it is the function of the Commission to make proposals (based on the provisions of the Treaties and the objectives of the Communities) and it is the function of the Council to accept or reject them. The Council, therefore, has the final say but the Commission has an important power of initiative. It is provided in the Treaty[15] that the Council cannot *amend* a proposal from the Commission unless all the members of the Council agree; but if a proposal is rejected by the Council the Commission would normally make the necessary amendments itself. The usual procedure, in fact, is for the Commission to hold consultations before submitting a proposal in order to meet possible objections in advance. In addition to the power of initiative, the Commission also has certain independent decision-making powers.

Strictly speaking, there are still three Communities – the European Coal and Steel Community, the European Economic Community and the European Atomic Energy Community. Today, however, the main institutions are common to all three. This was always so in the case of the Assembly and the Court; but originally there were separate Councils and Commissions[16] for each Community. In 1967 these bodies were merged[17] but the step has not been taken of merging the Communities themselves. The three Communities are still governed by three separate Treaties (as amended by later agreements) and the powers of the Community organs differ under the different Treaties. Thus, for example, the Commission has somewhat greater powers when it is acting with regard to the European Coal and Steel Community (under the ECSC Treaty) than when it is acting with regard to the EEC. The discussion that follows, however, will be limited to the EEC as this is the most important of the three Communities.

The Commission

The Commission consists of thirteen members appointed by the Governments of the Member States who must all agree to each appointment. Only nationals of Member States may be Commissioners and not more than two Commissioners may be nationals of the same State.[18] There are in fact two Commissioners from each of the larger countries (Britain, France, Germany and Italy) and one from each of the others. The members of the Commission are appointed for a four-year term which is renewable.[19] Once appointed, a member of the Commission cannot be removed by the Council or the Governments of the Member States. The Court of Justice, however, has the power compulsorily to retire Commissioners for incapacity or misconduct[20] and the Commission can be removed as a whole by a vote of censure passed by a two-thirds majority in the European Parliament.[21]

It is provided by the Treaty that when a Commissioner's term of office expires he remains in office until someone has been appointed to replace him.[22] This is important because it might not be possible to obtain the unanimous consent necessary to appoint a new member.

A President and two Vice-Presidents of the Commission are appointed from among its members for a renewable two-year term by the Governments of the Member States acting unanimously.[23]

The headquarters of the Commission are in Brussels where it has a large, modern building which functions in much the same way as the headquarters of a British Government department. It has a staff of over 5,500 (including all grades). There are various departments, each headed by a director-general who is responsible to the member of the Commission in charge of the department. Each Commissioner has departmental responsibilities which are allocated among the Commissioners when a new Commission takes office. All the languages of the Community have official status (English, French, German, Italian, Dutch, Danish and Irish) but French is normally used as the working language. Documents are, however, translated into all the official languages and this is a task which occupies the time of a large number of officials.

Before making proposals the Commission consults fully, not only with representatives of the national Governments, but also with interest groups and other non-governmental organizations. Many such groups are now organized at Community level. There are also a number of official bodies set up either by the Treaties or by the Community authorities to advise the Commission and the other Community institutions on different aspects of Community policy. These bodies are too numerous to mention in detail but one of the most important is the Economic and Social Committee. Its members are chosen by the national Governments and one-third represent trade unions in the Community, one-third represent employers' organizations and one-third represent other groups such as consumers, professional associations and farmers.[24] There are also a large number of specialist bodies composed of experts in fields such as agriculture, monetary problems, transport and science.

It is not easy to find an exact parallel to the Commission in British Government. The Commissioners are more than civil servants. The Treaty lays down that they shall be completely independent in the performance of their duties and that they shall neither seek nor take instructions from any Government or from any other body.[25] They take their decisions by a majority vote[26] and they have important independent powers of initiative and decision.

It would be equally wrong to regard them as the equivalent of the Cabinet. First of all, they lack the power of a British Cabinet. In most matters of importance they cannot take decisions themselves: their proposals have to be accepted by the Council before action can be taken. They are also in quite a different political position from a British Cabinet. A cardinal feature of a British Cabinet is that it is politically responsible to a democratically elected Parliament and through it to the electorate. It is true that the European Parliament can dismiss the Commission by means of a vote of censure (if a two-thirds majority is obtained); but it is the Council and the Governments of the Member States that exercise most influence over the Commission.

The status of the Commission is the product of the ambiguous nature of the Community itself – part international organization, part government – and it is a serious weakness that the Commission is not responsible to, and does not derive its authority from, a directly elected European Parliament; but this would have been too great a step towards federalism for the national Governments to have accepted when the Communities were created. It is, however, a step that must be taken some time in the future if the Community is to progress further.

The Council of Ministers

The Council consists of one representative from each Member State. The office of President is held for a term of six months and rotates among the members.[27] The delegates chosen by the Governments are normally Ministers and the person sent to Brussels depends on the topic before the Council. Foreign Ministers are usually sent to represent their Governments when major political questions are to be discussed, but Ministers of Agriculture, Labour or Finance are sent when these matters are under consideration. Members of the Commission also attend meetings of the Council but they do not, of course, have the right to vote.

When the Communities were created it was intended that they should be more than inter-governmental organizations. Thus two supra-national elements were built into the structure of the Communities: an independent Commission and majority voting in the Council. Majority voting was not, however, something that most countries found easy to accept. Therefore, although the Treaty states that the Council will act by a majority of its members 'save as otherwise provided',[28] it is in fact provided that all important decisions are to be taken either unanimously or by a 'qualified majority'.

Where the Council is required to act by a qualified majority the votes of its members are weighted.[29] The four big countries, the U.K., France, Germany and Italy, are given ten votes each; Belgium and the Netherlands each get five votes; Ireland and Denmark get three votes each; and Luxemburg is given two votes. The total number of votes is therefore fifty-eight and a qualified majority is forty-one votes. Thus the big four cannot override the wishes of the others, and any grouping that can command a total of eighteen votes can block a proposal that requires a qualified majority. It is also provided in the Treaty that if the Council is not acting on a recommendation of the Commission, a qualified majority in addition requires that at least six Member States cast their votes in favour of the proposal.

The position under the Treaty, therefore, is that it is only in the case of comparatively unimportant matters that a simple majority is sufficient. Normally a qualified majority is required; and for very important questions – for example, the admission of new Members[30] – the Council must be unanimous.

The Treaty provisions are not, however, the whole story. A convention has grown up – much insisted upon by the French – that no Member State will be overruled on any question which it regards as vital to its interests.[31] The rule of unanimity therefore prevails in practice and the principle of majority voting only applies to questions of comparatively minor significance. Decisions on important questions are usually reached on the basis of 'package deals' in which each country gives way on certain points in order to secure agreement on what it considers most important. It is common Community practice to set a deadline for reaching agreement and to hold marathon bargaining sessions often lasting all night in which it seems that the stubbornness of the delegates is finally overcome by fatigue and agreement is announced to the press round about dawn. So far this system has usually worked. But one day something better will have to be found.

The Assembly

The European Assembly (Parliament) is meant to represent the peoples of the Member States.[32] Its members are not, however, directly elected but are chosen by the parliaments of each Member State from among their own members.[33] The number of delegates from each country depends on the size of the country concerned. The

U.K., France, Germany and Italy each have thirty-six delegates; Belgium and the Netherlands have fourteen each; Denmark and Ireland have ten delegates each, and Luxemburg has six.[34] The total membership is 198. The method by which the delegates are selected varies in each country. In most countries the delegates are chosen from both houses of the legislature; but in Germany all the delegates are from the lower house.

Provision is made in the Treaty[35] for the Assembly to draw up proposals for the direct election of its members according to a uniform procedure in all Member States. These proposals are to be put before the Council, which has the power, provided it acts unanimously, to recommend appropriate provisions to Member States for adoption in accordance with their respective constitutional requirements. The European Parliament made such proposals as long ago as 1960 but the Council has never acted on them in spite of the fact that they have been strongly supported by the Commission. One problem is that direct elections would make sense politically only if the Assembly were given real power, but the Governments of some Member States are not prepared to accept this.

The most important power that the Assembly has is that of dismissing the Commission on a vote of no confidence if a two-thirds majority is obtained.[36] This power is not likely to be used. It would precipitate a crisis and would not achieve a great deal since the Assembly would have no say in the appointment of the new Commissioners. Moreover, the old Commissioners would remain in office until the Council had agreed on their successors.[37] In 1970 it was agreed by the Council that the European Parliament would be given certain powers over the Community's budget. The Assembly has no power to legislate and its other powers are purely advisory. It has to be consulted before major decisions are taken and its members have the right to address questions to both the Commission and the Council.[38]

The Assembly normally meets about eight times a year and sits for about a week at a time. Its members do not sit according to their country but according to the political group to which they belong, and voting is normally on political rather than national lines. The main groups represented are the Communists, Socialists, Christian Democrats, Gaullists, Conservatives and Liberals. At the time of writing the British Labour Party is boycotting the Assembly.

One problem that all members have to face is that of finding the time to attend the sessions of the European Parliament – and its various specialist committees – in addition to their national Parliaments. Even if there were no other considerations, this fact alone would seem to make it inevitable that some new method of choosing the members of the Assembly will have to be devised.

The Court of Justice

The Court of Justice has its seat in Luxemburg. There are nine Judges, who are appointed for terms of six years by the Governments of the Member States acting unanimously.[39] They must possess the qualifications required for appointment to the highest judicial office in their own countries or be jurisconsults (legal experts) of recognized competence.[40] There is no provision in the Treaty for Judges to represent the various Member States but normally there is one Judge from each country. The President of the Court is elected by his fellow Judges for a term of three years and he is eligible for re-election when his term of office expires.[41]

There are also four Advocates-General whose function is to assist the Court by presenting impartial arguments based on the public interest as distinct from the interests of the parties to the case.[42] They play a very important part in the work of the Court. Their arguments are published in the reports of cases before the Court and are often more illuminating than the judgments of the Court. There is no analogous office in England[43] but officers of this kind are found in a number of Continental countries. Thus the *Commissaire du Gouvernement* in the French *Conseil d'État* has a similar role. The provisions relating to the appointment of Judges apply equally to the Advocates-General.[44] A Judge or Advocate-General cannot be dismissed during his term of office unless, in the unanimous opinion of the other Judges and Advocates-General, 'he no longer fulfils the requisite conditions or meets the obligations arising from his office' – in other words, he is no longer qualified for office or is guilty of misbehaviour.[45]

The court sits either in chambers or in plenary session. In the former case there are either three or five judges on the bench and in a plenary session there must be at least seven. Certain categories of cases must be heard in plenary session.[46] The procedure is modelled more on the Continental, than the English, system. The Court exercises much more initiative in discovering the facts as well as researching into the law. Written briefs and argument play a more important part than in English courts. The plaintiff normally has the right to choose the language of the proceedings (provided it is one of the official languages). If, however, the Commission is the plaintiff and the defendant is a Member State, the language of the proceedings is that of the defendant. All documents are translated into all the official languages and there is simultaneous translation for oral proceedings. The court delivers a single judgment in each case: no dissenting or concurring judgments are permitted.

COMMUNITY LAW

Community law is a unique system. It has affinities with international law since its foundation is a set of treaties. But the Community Treaties are much more than ordinary international treaties: they establish legislative, executive and judicial institutions and they create rights that can be invoked by private individuals in the national courts of the Member States.

If Community law is distinct from international law, it is also separate from the national law of the Member States. It is an autonomous legal system and, though it is applied by national courts, it receives its most authoritative interpretation from the European Court of Justice. National legislatures cannot alter Community law and the European Court has laid down that in the event of a conflict between Community law and national law the latter must give way.

The most important sources of Community law are the Treaties establishing the Communities. These are the ECSS Treaty (1951), the E.E.C. Treaty (1957) and the Euratom Treaty (1957). They are supplemented by Protocols and Annexes and they have been amended by later Treaties. The most important of these are the Rome Convention of 1957 on certain institutions common to the Communities, the Brussels Treaty of Merger (1965), which unified the institutions of the three Communities, the Luxemburg Treaty on Budgetary Matters (1970) and the Treaty of Accession (1972).

There are also three other kinds of international agreement that can create Community law. There are provisions in the Treaties that envisage conventions between the Member States on certain subjects related to the Treaty.[47] These conventions are usually regarded as a source of Community law. Secondly, Article 228 of the EEC Treaty provides for agreements between the Community and third states.

Such agreements are negotiated by the Commission and concluded by the Council after consultation with the Assembly. They can only be entered into if they are compatible with the Treaty and a ruling on this point from the European Court can be obtained by Member States, the Commission or the Council before the agreement is concluded. These agreements are also regarded as a source of Community law. Finally, there are decisions of the Governments of Member States meeting in the Council. These decisions are usually considered to be international agreements in a simplified form and are a source of Community law. There is no provision for them in the Treaties and they appear to be outside the control of the European Court. For this reason they might be regarded as an unfortunate development but they have played an important part in the Community; for example they were the means used to accelerate the setting up of the customs union between the Six.

All the sources of Community law considered so far are international agreements of one kind or another. They are based on international law and are sometimes called primary sources. The Community itself, however, also has legislative power and the acts of Community organs are a source of Community law. They are referred to as secondary sources and derive their validity from Community law itself and not from international law.

Executive and Legislative Powers of the Community

The executive and legislative powers of the Community are exercised by the two principal organs of the Community, the Council and the Commission. They obtain their powers from the Treaties and cannot act in excess of the powers granted to them. Article 189 of the EEC Treaty classifies the official acts of the Council and Commission as falling into five categories – regulations, decisions, directives, recommendations and opinions.

Regulations are the main form of Community legislation (although the term 'legislation' is not used in the Treaties, possibly because it was feared that this would upset the parliaments of the Member States). They are binding on everyone and are directly applicable. This means that the authorities of the Member States do not have to do anything to implement them: they are automatically binding throughout the Community. There are a number of provisions empowering the Council or the Commission to make regulations for specified purposes:[48] the most common formulation is to provide that the Council will make the regulation on a proposal from the Commission after consulting the Assembly. This gives each organ a say in the making of the regulation.

Directives are addressed to a Member State and are binding on that State. They specify the result that must be achieved but allow the national Government to decide how to bring it about. They are often used when uniformity throughout the Community is not essential and they are normally implemented by executive or legislative action at a national level. Directives can only be addressed to a State, but (as will be seen below) this does not prevent individuals from obtaining rights under them. There are provisions in the Treaties granting both the Council and the Commission the power to issue directives.

A decision is binding on the person to whom it is addressed. Decisions can be made by both the Council and the Commission and can be addressed to individuals, companies or Member States. Decisions are usually concerned with individual cases. They implement Community law and are usually regarded as executive rather than legislative. For example, they might grant exemptions or authorizations; or they may impose fines for breach of Community law.

Recommendations and opinions are not legally binding.

Regulations, directives and decisions must be reasoned.[49] This means first, that the instrument must state the Treaty provision under which it was made; secondly, it must contain a reference to any proposal or opinion which formed part of the procedure for making it (e.g. if a regulation is made by the Council on a proposal from the Commission after an opinion has been obtained from the Assembly); and thirdly, the body making the instrument must give its reasons for making it. This last requirement is met by something like the preamble of a British statute although the phraseology is based on Continental forms.

Regulations are published in the Official Journal of the Community and they enter into force on the date specified in them or, if no date is given, on the twentieth day after publication.[50] The Official Journal is published in all the official languages of the Community and all texts of the regulation are equally authentic. Directives and decisions have to be notified to the addressees and take effect upon notification. They do not have to be published in the Official Journal but in practice they often are.

Direct Effect

When can Community law be invoked by a private citizen in the ordinary courts of a Member State? This depends on whether the provision in question is directly effective.[51] This is a question within the jurisdiction of the European Court and it has held that it depends not on the form of the provision (whether it is in a Treaty, regulation, etc.) but on its nature. It will be directly effective if it is clear and unconditional and does not require implementation by a Community organ. A simple prohibition can have this effect. Thus Article 12 of the EEC Treaty provides:

Member States shall refrain from introducing between themselves any new customs duties on imports or exports or any charges having equivalent effect, and from increasing those which they already apply in their trade with each other.

In the well-known case of *N.V. Algemene Transport – en Expeditie Onderneming van Gend en Loos* v. *The Netherlands Fiscal Administration*[52] (usually called the '*van Gend & Loos*' case) the European Court held that Article 12 was directly effective. It follows from this that a national law that introduced a new customs duty contrary to this Article would be invalid and a private person who was required to pay such a duty could invoke its invalidity in the national court.

At one time it was thought that a provision of Community law that imposes a positive duty on a Member State could not be directly effective. It now seems, however, that such a provision can be directly effective if it fulfils the requirements mentioned above and does not leave any significant margin of choice to the Member State as to the way in which it will carry out the duty.[53]

It has also been established that Treaty provisions and regulations are not the only forms of Community law that can produce direct effects. Decisions addressed to Member States[54] and directives[55] can also have direct effect. Since decisions and directives are binding only on the person to whom they are addressed, they cannot impose obligations on anyone else. They can, however, confer rights on private citizens which can be enforced in the national courts against the State concerned. The same test for direct effectiveness is applied as in the case of other forms of Community law. It will, however, be fairly rare in practice for decisions and directives to satisfy this test.

Enforcement of Community Law

Community law is enforced against Member States and Community organs by means of proceedings in the European Court. The Commission has power in certain cases to impose fines on individuals and companies for an infringement of Community law and these are enforced by the national authorities in the Member States.[56] Directly effective provisions of Community law are enforced by national courts.

THE JUDICIAL POWER OF THE COMMUNITY

The judicial power of the Community is vested in the European Court. The function of the Court is to maintain the rule of law in the Community and to interpret and apply Community law.[57] It has jurisdiction in a number of situations.

Proceedings against Member States

Proceedings against a Member State for a breach of Community law may be brought either by the Commission or by another Member State. If the Commission decides that a Member State has failed to fulfil an obligation under the Treaty (which includes a breach of secondary Community law, i.e. regulations, directives and decisions)[58] it must notify the State concerned and give it an opportunity to submit observations. Then it must deliver a reasoned opinion on the matter. If the State does not comply with the opinion within the period laid down by the Commission, the latter may bring the matter before the Court.[59] It should be noted that the Commission is obliged to deliver the reasoned opinion once it concludes that the Member State has failed to obey the Treaty, but it has a discretion whether or not to refer the matter to the Court.

If a Member State wishes to bring proceedings against another Member State it must first bring the matter before the Commission.[60] The Commission must give each of the States concerned an opportunity to submit its case and to comment on the submissions of the other State. Then the Commission must deliver a reasoned opinion. After this has been done,[61] the plaintiff State can go before the Court. Although there have been a number of cases in which the Commission has brought proceedings against a Member State, there have been no cases so far brought by another Member State. The reasons for this are probably partly political (court actions might be detrimental to good relations between the countries concerned) and partly because the Commission will normally bring the necessary proceedings.

Article 171 of the EEC Treaty states that if the Court finds that a Member State has failed to fulfil an obligation under the Treaty, the State in question 'shall be required to take the necessary measures to comply with the judgment of the Court of Justice'. There is no direct method of enforcing such a judgment but if a Member State failed to respect it, serious political consequences would follow.

Under Article 182 of the EEC Treaty the Court has jurisdiction to adjudicate in a dispute between Member States which 'relates to the subject matter' of the Treaty if the dispute is submitted to it under a special agreement between the States concerned. This 'voluntary urisdiction' has not so far been used.

Judicial Review of Community Action

It is important not only that Member States should obey Community law but also that the Community organs should do so. To ensure this the European Court has been given power to review the legality of the acts of the Council and Commission. This power of judicial review is similar to that exercised by British courts in relation to the acts of British public authorities.[62] There are two cases to consider: unlawful action by Community authorities and unlawful failure to act. Unlawful action will be considered first.

Article 73 of the EEC Treaty gives the Court jurisdiction to review the legality of acts of the Council or Commission other than recommendations or opinions (which are omitted because they are not legally binding). This means that the acts that will normally be reviewed are regulations, directives and decisions. Proceedings can be brought by a Member State or by another Community organ. Private individuals (or companies) can also bring proceedings if they are directly affected.

It is a general principle of both English and Community law that proceedings for judicial review can be brought only by someone who is directly affected. This is the doctrine of *locus standi*.[63] Member States and Community organs always have *locus standi* in proceedings of this kind (just as the Attorney-General always has *locus standi* in England where the public interest is affected). An individual, however, has *locus standi* only with regard to a decision addressed to him or 'a decision which, although in the form of a regulation or a decision addressed to another person, is of direct and individual concern' to him.[64] This means that if an act, such as a regulation, affects everyone in general, no private individual will have *locus standi* to challenge it. It should, however, be stressed that it is not the form, but the substance, of the act that determines this.

There are four grounds on which Community acts can be set aside. They are derived from French administrative law but are not very different from the grounds applied by English courts. The first is lack of competence (jurisdiction). This is equivalent to substantive *ultra vires* in English law.[65] Community organs can act only when they are empowered to do so by Community law; if they perform an unauthorized act, or step outside their powers, they are acting *ultra vires* and their actions will be declared invalid by the court.

The second ground is the infringement of an essential procedural requirement. This is the equivalent of procedural *ultra vires* in English law. As in English law, not every procedural irregularity will result in invalidity: this will occur only if the procedural requirement is important. For example, if the Treaty provided that the Assembly must be consulted before a decision was taken by the Council, failure to do this would result in invalidity.

The third ground is infringement of the Treaty 'or any rule of law relating to its application'.[66] This is a wide ground that overlaps with the previous grounds and also covers any violation of Community law.

The last ground is 'misuse of powers'.[67] This is a translation of the French term '*détournement de pouvoir*' and its equivalent in English administrative law is improper purpose.[68] This means that if a power to act is exercised for a purpose other than that for which it was given, the act in question will be invalid. In order to establish that a misuse of power has occurred the purpose for which the power was given must be ascertained. If it can then be shown that the Community organ in question used it for a different purpose, the Court will declare the act invalid.

Proceedings for review must be brought within two months from the date on which the measure in question was published or was notified to the plaintiff.[69] Regulations have to be published in the Official Journal and directives and decisions must be notified to the addressee. In the absence of notification time runs from the date on which the addressee became aware of the measure. The reason for this very short time limit is to avoid uncertainty as to the validity of official acts of the Community but it means that anyone wishing to challenge Community action must take proceedings quickly.

Similar principles apply where the Council or Commission is guilty of failure to act. Another Community organ or a Member State again has *locus standi* in all cases, but individuals can bring proceedings only if the Community organ in question has failed to address an act to them.[70] Before legal proceedings can be taken the Community organ must be called upon to act and given a period of two months to take action or justify its failure to do so; when this period has elapsed, proceedings can be brought within the next two months. If an infringement of Community law is established, the organ concerned must take the necessary steps to comply with the Court's judgment.[71]

Challenge to Community Acts in Collateral Proceedings

The provisions just considered apply only in proceedings directly aimed at establishing the invalidity of Community acts. It is, however, quite possible that the validity of such an act might arise incidentally (collaterally) in other proceedings before the European Court; for example if a company was fined for breach of a regulation it might bring proceedings in the Court to have the decision imposing the fine set aside on the ground that the regulation was invalid.[72] This situation is covered by Article 184 of the EEC Treaty which provides that where a regulation of the Council or Commission is in issue in proceedings before the Court, a party may challenge its validity (on the basis of the four grounds considered previously) even though the time limit for direct proceedings has expired. In such a case the Court could not annul the regulation; it could only declare that it did not apply to the case before it. But the effect of this would be to make it impossible to enforce the regulation against anyone else.

The right to challenge the validity of regulations in collateral proceedings is of great importance in view of the fact that the rules of *locus standi* usually make a direct challenge impossible for a private citizen.

Preliminary Rulings

It is not only in the Community Court that questions of Community law can arise. Directly effective provisions of Community law can be invoked in national courts. When this occurs it is, however, desirable that national courts should not have the final say on questions of Community law since this could produce conflicting interpretations in different countries. Article 177 of the EEC Treaty therefore lays down a procedure for a reference to the European Court for a preliminary ruling.

Under Article 177 the following matters can be referred to the European Court:

1. The interpretation of the Treaty;
2. The validity and interpretation of acts of the institutions of the Community;
3. The interpretation of the statutes of bodies established by an act of the Council, where those statutes so provide.

It is important to note that not only the interpretation but also the validity of the acts of Community organs can be considered by the Court. Thus if one party in a case before a national court relies on a directly effective regulation and the other party claims that it is invalid, the national court can refer the question to the European Court. This is another example of a collateral challenge to the validity of a regulation and what was said above on this would apply here as well.

A national court[73] may request the European Court to give a ruling on one of these questions if the national court considers that it cannot give judgment on the case before it without first deciding the question of Community law. Any national court *may* request such a ruling; it is not, however, obliged to do so unless it is a court 'against whose decisions there is no judicial remedy under national law'.[74] The exact interpretation of this provision could cause problems. For example, appeal from the Court of Appeal to the House of Lords is not as of right but only with leave: is the Court of Appeal therefore obliged to refer questions of Community law to the European Court? The answer to this is not clear but in practice it is likely that it will do so. There is, however, a fairly widely accepted doctrine (known as the *acte clair* doctrine) that a reference need not be made if there is no real doubt as to the meaning of the Community provision in question: if the Community law is clear the national court can apply it without referring it to the European Court.

When a reference is made the proceedings before the national court are suspended while the case goes to the European Court. The Registrar of the European Court notifies the parties to the case, the

Member States and the Commission that the reference has been made. The Council is also notified if the proceedings concern an act of the Council. All persons or bodies notified are entitled to put their contentions before the Court.[75]

The function of the European Court is, of course, to decide only the point of law referred to it. It cannot decide any question of fact, nor can it apply the law to the facts. These are all matters for the national court, which also has exclusive jurisdiction to interpret national law. The European Court can say that a particular provision of Community law has a certain meaning and is directly effective; it can also lay down the general principle that Community law prevails over national law; but it cannot decide whether a particular provision of national law is in conflict with Community law, and it certainly cannot declare the national provision to be invalid. These matters fall within the jurisdiction of the national court.

Once the Community Court has given its ruling the case returns to the national court for the final decision.

Other Cases

The European Court has jurisdiction to give judgment pursuant to any 'arbitration clause' contained in a Community contract[76] and it is common for Community contracts to provide that the Court will have exclusive jurisdiction to determine any dispute arising out of the contract. The applicable law will usually be specified by the contract itself. Article 215 of the EEC Treaty provides that the Community must pay compensation for damage caused by its institutions or by its servants when acting in the course of their duty. Actions for compensation are heard by the European Court[77] which gives judgment according to the 'general principles common to the laws of the Member States'.[78] Two other matters coming within the Court's jurisdiction are disputes between the Community and its employees[79] and questions relating to penalties imposed under a regulation made by the Council if the regulation in question so provides.[80]

COMMUNITY LAW IN THE UNITED KINGDOM

It is a general principle of British law that a treaty entered into by the U.K. does not in itself affect British law. In British eyes international law and internal British law are two quite separate legal orders: a treaty is binding in international law but will only have internal effect if appropriate legislation is passed by Parliament. In view of this, Britain's accession to the Community Treaties had to be implemented by legislation and this was done by the European Communities Act 1972, which provides the legal foundation for Britain's membership of the Communities.

The Act starts off by defining the Community Treaties.[81] The eight major treaties are listed by name.[82] In addition to these the following are regarded as Community Treaties: first, treaties entered into between one of the Communities (with or without any of the Member States) and a third country; and secondly, treaties ancillary to any Community Treaty which are acceded to,[83] or entered into, by the U.K. Both these categories apply to future as well as past treaties. However, no treaty entered into by the U.K. after the date on which the Treaty of Accession was signed (22 January 1972) is to be regarded as a Community Treaty unless it is specified as such in an Order in Council of which a draft has been approved by resolution of each House of Parliament.[84] The only exceptions are pre-accession treaties to which the U.K. accedes on terms settled before the date of the Treaty of Accession.[85]

Section 2 is the most important section of the Act. Sub-section (1) provides that directly effective Community law is binding in the U.K. This covers all 'rights, powers, liabilities, obligations and restrictions from time to time created or arising by or under the Treaties . . . as in accordance with the Treaties are without further enactment to be given legal effect . . . . in the United Kingdom.' Three points should be noted concerning this provision: first, it includes secondary Community law ('created . . . under the Treaties'); secondly, it includes future Community law ('from time to time created . . .'); thirdly, it makes clear that the question whether a particular provision is directly effective is decided by Community law.

The same sub-section also provides that Community remedies and procedures will be available and effective in the U.K. An example of such a procedure is the reference for interpretation under Article 177 of the EEC Treaty.

Sub-section (2) is concerned with Community obligations which are not directly effective. These are obligations which have to be implemented by each Member State, and the purpose of the sub-section is to enable the Government to do this by means of subordinate legislation. This may be contained either in an Order in Council or in a regulation made by a Minister or department designated for the purpose by Order in Council. In both cases the subordinate legislation must be in the form of a statutory instrument and must be approved by Parliament.[86]

The breadth of this power is very great. Subject to two limitations, subordinate legislation made under it may include 'any such provision (of any such extent) as might be made by Act of Parliament'.[87] The limitations are, first, that the subordinate legislation must be made for one of the purposes specified in the Act. These are:

1. To implement Community obligations (or to enable them to be implemented);
2. To enable the U.K. to exercise rights enjoyed by it under Community law (both present and future);
3. To deal with matters arising out of, or related to, the above obligations and rights;
4. To deal with the coming into force or operation of section 2(1).

Secondly, there are four things that such subordinate legislation cannot do.[88] It cannot impose or increase taxation; it cannot operate retroactively (i.e. take effect as from a date before it was made); it cannot itself grant the power to make subordinate legislation (except the power to make rules of procedure for a court or tribunal); and it cannot create a new criminal offence punishable by imprisonment of more than two years[89] or a fine of more than £400 (or £5 a day, if the fine is calculated on a daily basis).

Section 3(1) deals with the application of Community law in U.K. courts. It provides that any question as to the meaning or effect of the Treaties or the meaning, effect or validity of secondary Community law is to be regarded in the U.K. as a question of law (unlike questions of foreign law, which are regarded as questions of fact) and, if not referred to the European Court under Article 177 of the EEC Treaty, decided by the U.K. court according to the principles laid down in any relevant decision of the European Court. In other words, when questions of European law are in issue, British courts must follow precedents laid down by the European Court.

The enforcement in the U.K. of judgments of the European Court (and of decisions of the Council or Commission imposing fines or penalties)[90] is provided for in an Order in Council made under the power given by section 2(2).[91] Such judgments or decisions are registered by the High Court (after the Secretary of State has appended an enforcement order) and are then enforced in the same way as ordinary High Court judgments.

These provisions provide for the operation of Community law in Britain. Community law is not to be regarded as a foreign legal system but it is clearly distinct from national British law. The apex of the judicial system, as far as Community law is concerned, is not the House of Lords but the European Court in Luxemburg. What is the relative status of Community law and British law? It has already been pointed out that in the eyes of the European Court Community law must prevail over national law in the event of a conflict between the two. This is so even if the provision of national law was enacted later than the provision of Community law. Whether this will be accepted by the courts of the U.K. is, however, a difficult question.

It seems clear that the draftsmen of the European Communities Act intended that Community law should prevail. This is provided for in Section 2(4) of the Act:

[A]ny enactment passed or to be passed, other than one contained in this Part of this Act, shall be construed and have effect subject to the foregoing provisions of this section . . .

Since the 'foregoing provisions' of the section include sub-section (1), which provides for the binding effect of directly effective Community law in the U.K. (including future Community law), and sub-section (2), which gives the Government the power to make subordinate legislation to implement Community obligations, it seems clear that the intention of the provision quoted above was to secure the primacy of Community law. This is buttressed by section 3(1) which provides that any question as to the 'effect' of the Treaties or a Community instrument is to be decided 'in accordance with the principles of any relevant decision of the European Court'. One such principle is the primacy of Community law.

There is little doubt that these provisions are effective where a British statute passed prior to the European Communities Act is in issue. A provision in such a statute would have to give way to a directly effective provision of Community law, irrespective of whether the latter was contained in a Treaty or in secondary legislation. (It would also be irrelevant whether the secondary Community legislation was enacted before or after the European Communities Act or the conflicting British statute.) The same would apply where a statute passed prior to the European Communities Act conflicted with subordinate legislation made under section 2(2).

What is the position where there is a conflict between an Act of

Parliament passed *after* the European Communities Act and a provision of directly effective Community law? If one applies the traditional principles of British constitutional law it seems that the Act of Parliament must prevail (unless it contains an express or implied provision that it is to take effect subject to Community law).[92]

This follows from the doctrine of the sovereignty of Parliament: any Act passed by Parliament must be obeyed by the courts even though an earlier Act may have purported to prohibit the passing of such an Act. The provisions of the European Communities Act are ineffective in so far as they seek to limit the power of Parliament to legislate in the future. A future Act of Parliament must be obeyed by the courts no matter what the European Communities Act or the European Court may say.

Under the traditional theory the European Treaties would be regarded as incorporated by reference in the European Communities Act and the same would apply to secondary Community law enacted before the European Communities Act was passed. Future secondary Community law would be regarded as delegated legislation. The rule regarding delegated legislation is that it has the same force and effect as if it were contained in the empowering Act, i.e. the European Communities Act. The same, of course, applies to provisions incorporated by reference. Since a later Act of Parliament always prevails over an earlier one, any Act passed after the European Communities Act would prevail over any provision of Community law.[93]

The same would apply if there were a conflict between an Act of Parliament passed after the European Communities Act and subordinate legislation made under section 2(2) of the European Communities Act.

If this theory is followed by the courts it means that the U.K. can never fully carry out her obligations of membership of the Community. Parliament can never give primacy to Community law because the doctrine of parliamentary sovereignty forbids it.

This, however, is not the whole story. The doctrine of parliamentary sovereignty is not something which has existed from the beginning of time, nor is it self-evident in logic. It was developed by writers and courts to meet the needs of the times. It is not immutable: it can be changed by the courts if they decide to follow another doctrine. As Lord Denning said in a recent case concerning the Common Market, 'Legal theory must give way to practical politics'.[94] Britain's entry into the Community is a political fact. It is conceivable that a future Government may in a few years' time take Britain out of the Community. The political and economic consequences of such a move would be serious. Moreover, they will become more serious as time goes on and the Member States become linked together more and more tightly. Eventually withdrawal will cease to be a practical possibility and by that time – if not before – the courts will recognize that new political realities demand a new fundamental principle. The doctrine of parliamentary supremacy will cease to be the bedrock of the Constitution and the primacy of Community law will be accepted. This has already been recognized by the courts of some of the other Member States[95] and it may be that British courts will follow their example.

Notes

CHAPTER 1

1 *Prohibitions del Roy* (1607) 12 Co. Rep. 63.
2 See Chapter 17.

CHAPTER 2

1 *British Political Parties* (2nd rev. edn 1963), pp. 635 et seq.
2 See *The Party Organization* (1971) published by the Conservative Central Office.
3 The Scottish Conservative and Unionist Association and the Ulster Unionist Council are formally separate bodies.
4 The 1922 Committee consists of all backbench Conservative Members of Parliament.
5 See pp. 53–4.
6 *The Party Organization*, p. 33.
7 See *Party Organization* (1972) published by the Labour Party; and see Sara Barker, *How The Labour Party Works* (1971). To some extent these rules will be affected by local government reorganization.
8 Trades Councils are now rarely affiliated.
9 Commonly referred to as the General Management Committee or G.M.C.
10 He must also, if eligible, be a member of a trade union.
11 Which must also accept the programme, principles and policy of the party (Party Constitution Clause III (1)(a)).
12 Op. cit., p. 532.
13 Sara Barker, op. cit., p. 9.
14 There may also be additional women delegates and Young Socialist delegates.
15 Where a borough contains more than one constituency, the constituency parties come together to form a central party.

16 Such federations may exist for Labour parties generally within County Council areas.

17 The Secretary of the party also attends and speaks but customarily does not vote.

18 Op. cit., p. 187 and note 1.

19 Ibid., p. 484 and note 1.

20 McKenzie's book is subtitled 'The Distribution of Power within the Conservative and Labour Parties' and considers at length the answer to this question.

21 Austin Ranney, *Pathways to Parliament* (1964), p. 3.

22 For one of the few examples to the contrary (Nigel Nicolson and Bournemouth East and Christchurch Conservative Association in 1956–9) see Ranney, op. cit., pp. 64–5; and Nigel Nicolson, *People and Parliament*.

23 In 1972, Mr Dick Taverne (Labour M.P. for Lincoln since 1962) was disowned by his constituency party after he had voted with the Government in favour of the United Kingdom's entry into the EEC. The National Executive Committee of the Labour party dismissed his appeal and he resigned his seat. In the resulting by-election on 1 March 1973, Mr Taverne stood as a Democratic Labour candidate against an official Labour candidate, an official Conservative and others. He won the seat, polling 58·2% of the vote (compared with the 51% he polled at the general election in 1970) and obtaining a majority of 13,191 over the official Labour candidate (his majority over the Conservative candidate in 1970 had been 4,750). At the general election of 1974 Mr Taverne held his seat with a majority of 1,293. Also in 1974 Mr E. J. Milne who had been Labour M.P. since 1960 was not adopted as candidate by his constituency party at Blyth. He stood as Independent Labour at the general election and was returned with a majority of 6,140 over the official Labour candidate.

24 See above p. 16.

25 Ranney, op. cit., citing D. E. Butler and R. Rose, *The British General Election of 1959*, p. 122.

26 Ranney, op. cit., pp. 60–1.

27 Ranney, op. cit., pp. 133–7.

28 In both parties placement is often more important at a by-election, which may have been occasioned by a resignation to make way for an eminent but seatless member of the party.

29 The N.E.C. may in certain circumstances nominate, but this power is very seldom exercised.

30 *The Selection of Parliamentary Candidates*, p. 276.

31 Ibid.

32 *The Party Organization*, p. 29.

33 Op. cit., p. 193.

34 McKenzie says this can mean only the work of the party outside Parliament. Op. cit., p. 485.

35 See below, p. 198.

CHAPTER 3

1 For a study of the more recent history of the electoral system, see D. E. Butler, *The Electoral System in Britain Since 1918* (2nd edn 1963).

2 Multi-member constituencies were common in the nineteenth century and were finally abolished only in 1948.

3 For a detailed evaluation of the British system and the alternatives to it (such as proportional representation), see Enid Lakeman, *How Democracies Vote* (3rd edn 1970) and W. J. M. Mackenzie, *Free Elections* (1958).

4 For examples of seats won since the War on less than 34 per cent of the vote, see Peter Pulzer, *Political Representation and Elections in Britain* (1967), p. 55.

5 The table is based, for 1945–66, on Craig, *British Parliamentary Election Statistics 1918–1968*, and for 1970 on *The Times' House of Commons*, 1970.

6 S. 2 (1).

7 S. 2(3) of the 1949 Act.

8 Sch. I, Pt I of the 1949 Act.

9 S. 1 (1) (a) of the 1958 Act. For Scotland and Northern Ireland, see ibid., s. 1 (1) (b) and (d).

10 He took over the functions of the Minister of Housing and Local Government in 1970. The Minister of Housing and Local Government had previously taken over from the Minister of Health. For Scotland, Wales and Northern Ireland, see Sch. I, Pt I of the 1949 Act.

11 S. 2(1) (f) and Sch. I, Pt III.

12 S. 1 (2) of the 1958 Act. For Scotland and Northern Ireland, see ibid.

13 1949 Act, Sch. II.

14 See the Second Periodical Reports of the Commissions: Cmnd. 4084 (England); Cmnd. 4085 (Scotland); Cmnd. 4086 (Wales); and Cmnd. 4087 (Northern Ireland). All were published in 1969.

15 See the Second Schedule to the 1949 Act, as amended by the 1958 Act.

16 1958 Act, s. 2(2).

17 Ibid.

18 For a discussion of the factors which influenced the English Commission in deciding to begin a general review in 1965, see paragraphs 4–10 of their Second Periodical Report (*supra*).

19 The procedure which must be followed is set out in Sch. I, Pt III of the 1949 Act as amended by the 1958 Act.

20 Local inquiries may be held whenever the Commission thinks fit, but the 1958 Act (s. 4(2)) provides that they must be held whenever objections are made by a local authority or by a hundred or more electors in the constituency affected. When preparing their last report the English Commission considered about 1,200 written representations and held 70 local inquiries. In 40 cases revised or modified recommendations were made as a result of a local inquiry.

21 The Report of the Scottish Commission is presented to the Secretary of State for Scotland.

22 1949 Act, s. 2(5)

23 Ibid., ss. 2(5) and 3(3).

24 Ibid., s. 3(4) and (6).

25 S. 3(7) of the 1949 Act. This is a very strong ouster clause. It reads: 'The validity of any Order in Council purporting to be made under this Act and reciting that a draft thereof has been approved by resolution of each House of Parliament shall not be called in question in any legal proceedings whatsoever.' For a discussion of provisions of this kind, see below, pp. 356–60.

26 *The Times*, 15 December 1954.

27 *The Times*, 18 December 1954 (Roxburgh J); reversed [1955] 1 Ch. 238 (C.A.).

28 See note 25 above.

29 *Per* Evershed M. R. (giving the judgment of the court) at p. 251.

30 Apart from the political problems that would arise there are also considerable technical difficulties. An injunction will not lie against the Home Secretary in these circumstances: *Merricks* v.

Heathcoat-Amory and the Minister of Agriculture, Fisheries and Food
[1955] Ch. 567 and ss. 21(2) and 38(2) of the Crown Proceedings Act, 1947. This point was considered, but not finally
decided, in *Harper's* case. An interim declaration cannot be
obtained instead: *Underhill* v. *Ministry of Food* [1950] 1 All E.R.
591; *International General Electric Co. of New York* v. *Customs and
Excise Commissioners* [1962] Ch. 784. For further discussion of the
cases in the text, see de Smith, (1955) 18 M.L.R. 281; Butler,
'The Redistribution of Seats' [1955] *Public Administration* 125 at
140 et seq.; and Craig, 'Parliament and Boundary Commissions' [1959] *Public Law* 23 at 34 et seq.

31 Before the draft orders were introduced an attempt was made
by an elector to obtain an order of mandamus to compel the
Home Secretary to carry out the provisions of the Act: *R.* v.
*Secretary of State for the Home Department, ex parte McWhirter, The
Times*, 21 October 1969. When the application came before the
Court, however, the Home Secretary had already undertaken
to lay the draft orders before Parliament and in view of this the
application was withdrawn. The Home Secretary made an
ex gratia contribution to the applicant's costs.

32 The largest constituency, Billericay (124,215) was over six times
the size of the smallest, Birmingham, Ladywood (18,884).
Labour won 58 of the 77 constituencies with under 45,000 voters
and the Conservatives won 70 of the 90 constituencies with over
80,000 voters. Labour won 120 out of the 168 seats in which the
electorate had declined since 1954. These figures are taken from
Peter Bromhead, 'The British Constitution in 1970' (1971)
XXIV *Parliamentary Affairs* 104 at 109. They suggest that
Labour did stand to lose from a redistribution of seats.

33 The principal statutory provision is the Representation of the
People Act (R.P.A.) 1949, s. 1.

34 The Electoral Registers Act 1949, s. 1(3) as substituted by the
Electoral Registers Act 1953, ss. 1(1) and (4).

35 R.P.A. 1949, s. 6(2). For Scotland and Northern Ireland, see
ibid., ss. 6(3) and (4).

36 R.P.A. 1949, s. 9(1); for Northern Ireland, see s. 9(2).

37 Ibid., s. 45(1).

38 Ibid., s. 45(2); for Scotland, see sub-ss. (8)–(10); for Northern
Ireland, see sub-s. (11).

39 R.P.A. 1949, ss. 1 and 4. To vote in Northern Ireland a person

must be resident in Northern Ireland during the whole of the three-month period ending on the qualifying date: ibid., s. 1(2).

40 R.P.A. 1949, s. 10; R.P.A. 1969, ss. 2 and 3.

41 For voting by proxy and by post see R.P.A. 1949, ss. 12-15; and R.P.A. 1969, ss. 5 and 6.

42 [1970] 3 All E.R. 7.

43 It is expressly provided in R.P.A. 1949, s. 1(1) that a person cannot vote in more than one constituency.

44 The Peerage Act 1963, s. 6. The holders of Irish peerages are no longer disqualified from voting: ibid., s. 5(b).

45 R.P.A. 1969, s. 4.

46 The incapacity applies if it is stated in the report of an election court that the person concerned is personally guilty or if he is convicted of such a practice; however, in certain cases a court may mitigate or remit the incapacity. A person guilty of a corrupt practice cannot vote in any constituency; in the case of a person guilty of an illegal practice the incapacity applies only to voting in the constituency where the offence occurred. See R.P.A. 1949, ss. 140, 151 and 152.

47 R.P.A. 1949, s. 1.

48 R.P.A. 1969, s. 1.

49 Act of Settlement 1700, s. 3; Status of Aliens Act 1914, s. 3; British Nationality Act 1948, s. 31 and Sch. 4.

50 Family Law Reform Act 1969, s. 1(4) and Sch. 2, para. 2.

51 Erskine May, *Parliamentary Practice* (18th edn 1971), p. 35.

52 Sitting members have one month to make their decision. See below, p. 224.

53 Bankruptcy Act 1883, ss. 32(1)(b), 32(2) and 33(1); Bankruptcy Act 1890, s. 9.

54 S. 2.

55 Criminal Law Act 1967, ss. 1 and 10(2) and Sch. 3, Pt III.

56 Parliamentary privilege does not confer any immunity on M.P.s from arrest or imprisonment on a criminal charge: see below, p. 247.

57 Representation of the People Act 1949, ss. 139, 140, 151 and 152. The law is actually more complicated than indicated by the text.

58 By the Welsh Church Act 1914, s. 2(4). But the disestablishment of the Church of Ireland did not relieve its clergy of their disqualification.

59 Report from the Select Committee on Clergy Disqualification (H.C. 200 of 1952–3). See also the Report of the Select Committee on the House of Commons Disqualification Bill (H.C. 349 of 1955–6).

60 S. 3.

61 S. 1(4).

62 S. 1(1) and Sch. 1.

63 Listed in Sch. 1, Pt I.

64 Listed in Sch. 1, Pts II and III.

65 S. 2(1) as amended by the Ministers of the Crown Act 1964, ss. 3(2) and 5(1) and Sch.2.

66 The disqualifying effect of these offices was preserved by the House of Commons Disqualification Act 1957, s. 4.

67 See below, pp. 49–50.

68 May, *Parliamentary Practice* (18th edn 1971), pp. 108–9. The House used to decide all disputes relating to disqualification but this power was taken away by statute in the case of disputed elections. See the Representation of the People Act 1949, s. 107 (1).

69 See s. 7 of the Act. The applicant must, however, give security for up to £200 for costs. This procedure can be used if the disqualification existed at the time of the election provided that the question has not been, and is not about to be, decided by an election court.

70 See s. 2 of the Act and May, op. cit., pp. 48–9. This procedure can be used whether or not the disqualification existed at the time of the election.

71 *Re Parliamentary Election for Bristol South East* [1964] 2 Q.B. 257.

72 But Parliament is automatically dissolved after five years: the Septennial Act, 1715, as amended by the Parliament Act, 1911, s. 7.

73 R.P.A. 1949, s. 17.

74 See the timetable, R.P.A. 1949, Sch. II. Pt I, as amended by R.P.A. 1969, Sch. I.

75 Each candidate must appoint an agent but he may appoint himself: R.P.A. 1949, s. 55. The agent's job is to see to the organizational side of the campaign and to keep accounts of all money spent.

76 The deposit is returned if the candidate obtains more than one-eighth of the votes cast. The purpose of this is to discourage

frivolous candidates. For details, see R.P.A. 1949, Sch. II, Rules 10 and 54. Candidates are now permitted to have their political affiliations stated on the nomination and ballot papers: R.P.A. 1969, s. 12(1). Previously this was not allowed.

77 The main treatises on election law are Schofield, *Parliamentary Elections* (3rd edn 1959) and Parker's *Conduct of Parliamentary Elections* (1970).

78 Prosecution may take place before an election court or before the ordinary courts. Corrupt practices may be tried on indictment or summarily; illegal practices may only be tried summarily. See R.P.A. 1949, ss. 146–9. The maximum penalty for personation (voting as someone else, a corrupt practice) is two years' imprisonment. R.P.A. 1949, s. 47.

79 R.P.A. 1949, s. 99.

80 Ibid., s. 100.

81 Ibid., s. 101.

82 Ibid., ss. 96 and 153(2).

83 Ibid. s. 94.

84 R.P.A. 1949, s. 64(2) as amended by R.P.A. 1969. The limit is £750 plus, in a county constituency, 5p for every six registered voters and, in a borough constituency, 5p for every eight registered voters.

85 [1952] 1 All E.R. 697 (Central Criminal Court).

86 *The Kinross and West Perthshire Election Petition, The Times,* 24 December 1964 (reprinted in Geoffrey Wilson, *Cases and Materials on Constitutional and Administration Law* (1966), p. 152). See now the Representation of the People Act 1969, s. 9(4) amending s. 63(1) of the Act of 1949.

87 Political advertising on television is prohibited by the Television Act 1964, s. 7(3) and Sch. 2, para. 8.

88 S. 19.

89 For a more detailed discussion of the problem, see Rose, 'Money and Election Law' (1961) 9 *Political Studies* 1.

90 R.P.A. 1969, s. 9(5) amending R.P.A. 1949, s. 80(1).

91 R.P.A. 1969, s. 9(1) and (2).

92 Ibid.

93 R.P.A. 1949, Sch. II, Rules 51–3.

94 Ibid., s. 107.

95 Ibid., ss. 108 and 110.

96 Ibid., s. 123.

97 Ibid., s. 124. For appeals, see ss. 126 and 137.

98 Ibid., s. 139(1).

99 Parker's *Conduct of Parliamentary Elections* (1970), pp. 332–40.

100 R.P.A. 1949, s. 142.

101 Relief from these penalties may be obtained in certain circumstances: ibid., ss. 138(3), 145 and 152.

102 Above, p. 44.

103 *In re Parliamentary Election for Bristol South East* [1961] 3 W.L.R. 577 (discussed above pp. 44–5).

104 See David Butler and Richard Rose, *The British General Election of 1959* (1960), Appendix v. (quoted in Geoffrey Wilson, *Cases and Materials on Constitutional and Administrative Law* (1966), p. 159).

105 The petitioner must give security for costs in the sum of £1,000 when he presents the petition (R.P.A. 1949, s. 119), but the costs may be greater than this.

CHAPTER 4

1 E.g. the sovereign is never a minor; and cannot be sued in a personal capacity.

2 Above, p. 3.

3 Apart from avery limited prerogative power to legislate.

4 Given by Civil List Acts.

5 All general propositions have exceptions. Several of those closely associated with Mr Chamberlain when he was Prime Minister in the late 1930s overcame that disadvantage and one of them (Sir Alec Douglas-Home) became Prime Minister.

6 Or, as with Mr Winston Churchill, have much to do with himself.

7 The 1922 Committee consists of all backbench Conservative M.P.s.

8 There have never been more than three candidates, but presumably only one candidate can be eliminated on each ballot, so a third ballot (or more) might be necessary if there were four or more candidates.

9 But if he wishes to establish new departments he will need to do so by legislation unless the office is that of a Secretary of State.

10 The Prime Minister is traditionally First Lord of the Treasury but the Treasury is headed by the Chancellor of the Exchequer.

11 The other principal department was Posts and Telecommunications headed by a Minister not in the Cabinet.

12 See note 11.

13 For one account see J. P. Mackintosh, *The British Cabinet* (2nd edn, 1968), pp. 510–18.

14 See below, pp. 205–6.

15 See below, pp. 114–15.

16 See Cmnd. 4506.

17 Ibid., para. 23.

18 What follows is broadly true of all departments but there are minor differences in many departments.

19 Cmnd. 5178, p. 8.

20 See ibid., p. 75, para 3.

21 Ibid., page 9, para 7.

22 For general accounts of the work of departments see the *New Whitehall Series* of the Royal Institute of Public Administration.

23 *National Income and Expenditure 1972* (Central Statistical Office), tables 1, 4 and 5.

24 See below, pp. 215–16.

CHAPTER 5

1 This definition was first put forward by the Royal Commission on the Civil Service, 1929–31 (Tomlin Commission), Cmd. 3909 (1931), para. 9.

2 The figures in this paragraph are taken from the Report of the Civil Service Department, 1969, p. 7. The Government has a policy of dispersal, i.e. sending as many civil servants as possible out of London, mainly to the Development Areas.

3 *The Civil Service*, Cmnd. 3638 (1968).

4 *Civil Service Manpower*, 1969 (Statistics Division, Civil Service Department), p. iv.

5 Minister for the Civil Service Order 1968 (S.I. 1968 No. 1656), made under s.1 of the Ministers of the Crown (Transfer of Functions) Act 1946.

6 This was another of the recommendations of the Fulton Report. The suggestion that the committee should include eminent people from outside the service was not, however, accepted.

7 For a detailed study of this method of recruitment see *The Method II System of Selection* (Davies Committee) Cmnd. 4156 (1969).

8 These figures are taken from *Staff Relations in the Civil Service* (H.M. Treasury 1965), p. 5 and relate to 1965.

9 See s. 162 of the Act.

10 See *Staff Relations in the Civil Service* op. cit., Appendix III.

11 Ibid., Appendix VI.

12 For a detailed study see S. J. Frankel, 'Arbitration in the British Civil Service' [1960] *Public Administration* 197.

13 See below, pp. 85–7.

14 See below, pp. 86–7 and especially the quotation from *Kodeeswaran* v. *Attorney-General for Ceylon*.

15 See paras. 55–7 of the Report of the Board of Inquiry appointed by the Prime Minister to investigate certain Statements affecting civil servants, Cmd. 3037 (1928), where these principles were first set out.

16 These rules apply mainly to employment with firms having special connections with the Government – e.g. firms which have government contracts or receive government subsidies – and they are intended to prevent the civil servants dealing with such firms being influenced by the prospect of a job with them in the future.

17 See the *Report of the Committee on the Political Activities of Civil Servants,* Cmd. 7718 (1949).

18 See vol. 4 of the Fulton Report, p. 401.

19 House of Commons Disqualification Act 1957. See above, p. 43.

20 See in general on this topic: David Williams, *Not in the Public Interest* (1965), Chaps. 3, 7, 8 and 9; David Jackson, 'Individual Rights and National Security' (1957) 20 M.L.R. 364; Mark Joelson, 'The Dismissal of Civil Servants in the Interests of National Security' [1963] *Public Law* 51.

21 The purge procedure also covers Fascists but it is unlikely that they present a serious threat. They were probably included for the sake of ideological balance.

22 See the statement by the Prime Minister, Clement Attlee, on 15 March 1948 (448 H.C. Deb., col. 448).

23 See the statement by Enoch Powell (who was then Financial Secretary to the Treasury) on 29 January 1957, 563 H.C. Deb., col. 152.

24 In these terms of reference the term 'Communist' includes 'Fascist'.

25 See 563 H.C. Deb., col. 155 (29 January 1957).

26 If this happens, he may lose his pension. It is unlikely that this

procedure is affected by the Industrial Relations Act 1971: under s. 162(7) a Minister can issue a certificate exempting any class of employment from the Act for the purpose of safeguarding national security.

27 See below, pp. 320–36.

28 Joelson, 'The Dismissal of Civil Servants in the Interests of National Security' [1963] *Public Law* 51.

29 For a general discussion see J. D. B. Mitchell, *The Contracts of Public Authorities* (1954), pp. 32–52; Leo Blair, 'The Civil Servant – Political Reality and Legal Myth' [1958] *Public Law* 32; Leo Blair, 'The Civil Servant – A Status Relationship?' (1958) 21 *M.L.R.* 265; H. H. Marshall, 'The Legal Relationship between the State and its Servants in the Commonwealth' (1966) 15 *I.C.L.Q.* 150.

30 [1896] 1 Q.B. 116.

31 *Dunn* v. *McDonald* [1897] 1 Q.B. 555 (C.A.).

32 *Denning* v. *Secretary of State for India* (1920) 37 T.L.R. 138; *Terrell* v. *Secretary of State for the Colonies* [1953] 2 Q.B. 482.

33 *Riordan* v. *War Office* [1959] 3 All E.R. 552.

34 *Rodwell* v. *Thomas* [1944] 1 K.B. 596.

35 [1934] A.C. 176.

36 At p. 179.

37 [1896] A.C. 575 (P.C.).

38 Besides *Kodeeswaran* v. *Att.-Gen. of Ceylon* (below), see *Lucas* v. *Lucas* [1943] P. 68 at 74 and 75; *Rodwell* v. *Thomas* [1944] 1 K.B. 596 at 602; *Terrell* v. *Secretary of State for the Colonies* [1953] 2 Q.B. 482 at 497–8; and *Riordan* v. *War Office* [1959] 3 All E.R. 552 at 557. The only opinion to the contrary is an *obiter dictum* of Denning J. (as he then was) in *Robertson* v. *Minister of Pensions* [1949] 1 K.B. 227 at 231.

39 *Kodeeswaran* v. *Att.-Gen. of Ceylon* [1970] A.C. 1111 at 1118. The fact that the Board referred to *Reilly's* case immediately after making this statement shows that they were not unaware of what had been said in that case.

40 See, for example, *Terrell* v. *Secretary of State for the Colonies* [1953] 2 Q.B. 482.

41 See below, pp. 300–2.

42 See D. W. Logan, 'A Civil Servant and his Pay' (1945) 61 *L.Q.R.* 240 at pp. 249 et seq; and Mitchell, op. cit., pp. 32 et seq. Prior to the last century, however, a public office was regarded as a kind

of property which could often be bought and sold; so it is doubtful whether much reliance can be placed on the old law.

43 This has now been replaced by the Supreme Court of Judicature (Consolidation) Act 1925, s. 12(1) and the Appellate Jurisdiction Act 1876, s. 6.

44 Compare *Terrell* v. *Secretary of State for the Colonies* [1953] 2 Q.B. 482 at 499–500 (Lord Goddard) with *Riordan* v. *War Office* [1953] 3 All E.R. 552 at 557 (Lord Diplock).

45 [1953] 2 Q.B. 482.

46 See s. 162.

47 Under s. 162(7) a Minister can exempt certain classes of civil servant from the provisions of the Act for the purpose of safeguarding national security. See also ss. 27 and 28, under which certain part-time or temporary civil servants may be excluded. Under s. 31 the parties to a procedure agreement may agree to substitute rights under an internal arbitration agreement for those given by the Act. It is not known at the time of writing whether the Crown and the staff associations will conclude such an agreement.

48 The fullest discussion is to be found in Logan, 'A Civil Servant and his Pay' (1945) 61 *L.Q.R.* 240.

49 *Mitchell* v. *The Queen* [1896] 1 Q.B. 121 n; *Leaman* v. *The King* [1920] 3 K.B. 663.

50 In addition to the cases cited below, see *Gibson* v. *East India Company* (1839) 5 Bing. N.C. 262 at 274; and *High Commissioner for India* v. *Lall* 1948 L.R. 75 I.A. 225.

51 1926 S.C. 842 at 860.

52 [1943] P. 68.

53 R.S.C. O. XLV, r. 1. The case could (and should) have been decided on the ground that Order XLV does not bind the Crown: see Logan, 'A Civil Servant and his Pay' (1945) 61 L.Q.R. 240 at 266. See now the Crown Proceedings Act 1947, ss. 27(1) (a) and 38(2) which provide that an order of attachment cannot be made against the Crown in respect of a civil servant's salary.

54 In addition to the cases cited below, see *The Queen* v. *Doutre* (1884) 9 App. Cas. 745 (P.C.); *Picton* v. *Cullen* [1900] 2 I.R. 612; *Owners of S.S. Raphael* v. *Brandy* [1911] A.C. 413; and *Cameron* v. *Lord Advocate* 1952 S.C. 165.

55 (1923) 39 *T.L.R.* 294.

56 At this time Post Office employees were civil servants.

57 [1970] A.C. 1111.

58 Ibid., at p. 1123.

59 See the Superannuation Act 1965, ss. 79 and 80; see also the Superannuation Acts of 1859 (s. 2) and 1834 (s. 30). See further *Nixon* v. *A.-G.* [1931] A.C. 184.

60 Superannuation Act 1972, s. 2 (6) and (7).

61 Leo Blair, 'The Civil Servant – A Status Relationship?' (1958) 21 *M.L.R.* 265.

62 *Inland Revenue Commissioners* v. *Hambrook* [1956] 2 Q.B. 641 at 654.

63 Above, p. 86. See Blair, 'The Civil Servant – Political Reality and Legal Myth' [1958] *Public Law* 32, at 43–6.

64 See, for example, the passage from the judgement in *Kodeeswaran* v. *Att.-Gen. for Ceylon* quoted above, pp. 86–7.

65 *Reilly* v. *The King* [1934] A.C. 176 at 179.

66 The Privy Council went on to point out that 'a power to determine a contract at will is not inconsistent with the existence of a contract until so determined'. In other words, the Crown's power to dismiss at pleasure does not prevent the relationship from being contractual.

67 There does not seem to be any justification for Lord Goddard's opinion that the trend of the judgment in *Reilly's* case was that the relationship is not normally contractual.

68 [1959] 3 All E.R. 552 at 557.

69 The Privy Council suggested that one such case may be where the appointment is made directly by the Crown by Letters Patent: *Kodeeswaran* v. *Attorney-General for Ceylon* [1970] A.C. 1111 at 1118.

70 The Fulton Report states that in 1967 (which seems to have been a fairly typical year) dismissals and compulsory retirements of permanent staff in the grades of Executive Officer (and equivalents) and above on the grounds of misconduct or inefficiency numbered 22. This is 0·015 per cent of the permanent staff in these groups (Cmnd. 3638, vol. 1, p. 43).

71 See Blair, 'The Civil Servant – A Status Relationship?' (1958) 21 *M.L.R.* 265 at 275; see also Blair, 'The Civil Servant – Political Reality and Legal Myth' [1958] *Public Law* 32.

72 Under s. 27(1) (f) an employee who works less than 21 hours per week is excluded; under s. 28(a) an employee who is dismissed before he has been in employment for two years is also excluded.

73 A case which illustrates the need for such a right is *Cameron* v.

Lord Advocate 1952 S.C. 165. In this case a Scotsman made a contract in Scotland through the Crown Agents with the Custodian of Enemy Property in the Cameroons to work as a Field Assistant in the Cameroons for at least 18 months. When he arrived in West Africa, however, he was told that the Custodian had no power to make the contract. In this situation there would be no remedy under the Industrial Relations Act: see ss. 27(2) and 28(a). (The Scottish courts were apparently prepared to give a remedy in this case but it is not clear whether this was justifiable under the traditional rule.)

74 There are some exceptions to this: for example immigration officers have the power to exclude non-patrials from the U.K. See the Immigration Act 1971, s. 4(1).

75 There are some decisions of great importance, however, which must be taken by the Minister personally, e.g. the refusal to make evidence available in legal proceedings on the grounds of Crown privilege. See below, pp. 113–16.

76 [1943] 2 All E.R. 560.

77 Regulation 51 (1) of the Defence (General) Regulations, 1939.

78 At p. 563.

CHAPTER 6

1 Evidence suggests that this is the minimum population needed to support a local authority responsible for major functions. Smaller authorities are likely to be too poor and their work is likely to be too limited in amount to justify the appointment of a full range of specialist officers.

2 This means the old City of London – the square mile in the heart of Greater London.

3 Cmnd. 4040.

4 See pp. 95–9.

5 Cmnd. 4040, paras. 85–108.

6 The counties and the metropolitan districts in England and Wales, and the non-metropolitan districts in Wales, are named in the schedules to the Act. For non-metropolitan districts in England, see Cmnd. 5148.

7 The 36 metropolitan districts are included in the 369 as they also perform the less important functions. As they are also in the 89, they are counted twice. For the full total of local authorities in

England and Wales, the Greater London Council, the City of London, the 32 London boroughs, the parishes and the communities must be added.

8 Department of the Environment Circular 121/72, Annex A. The letter (*a*) means that these are concurrent functions exercisable by county and district councils; (*b*) means that the function is exercised in consultation with district councils; (*c*) means that these functions are exercisable in some non-metropolitan districts under local Acts. The water and sewage functions and some of the personal social services (relating to health) are at present subject to reorganization. The police and fire functions are exercisable by amalgamated authorities.

9 See ss. 2–7, 21–6.

10 See ss. 9–17, 27–36.

11 See s. 137; this is a general provision applying to all local authorities.

12 See ss. 79–81.

13 See ss. 101–3.

14 General Rate Act 1967 s. 19. Appeal lies from the fixing of a rateable value to a local valuation court and thence to the Lands Tribunal: see ss. 76–7.

15 *Report of Committee of Inquiry into the Impact of Rates on Households* (Cmnd. 2582) para. 200. For more recent figures somewhat differently based, see *Economic Trends* No. 220 February 1972 p. xxv.

16 I.e. household income less income tax, surtax, and national insurance contributions.

17 See General Rate Act 1967, s. 49.

18 See Local Government Act 1972, ss. 147–150.

19 See Local Government Act 1966, ss. 1–5.

20 These two are the new associations set up in 1974. There is also an Association of District Councils.

21 The relevant expenditure at first totalled £5226m. but the Government subtracted £10m. as 'saving from economy and increased efficiency'; see H.C. 27 of 1972–3 and S.I. 1972 No. 2034.

22 See Local Government Act 1972, ss. 154–67.

23 None of these allowances applies to members of parish or community councils acting within their own areas. See Local Government Act 1972, ss. 173–8.

24 Cmnd. 4741.

25 At present agricultural land is not rated.

26 Cmnd, 4040 (1969).

27 See below, pp. 280–1.

28 See below, pp. 281–2.

29 Ss. 95–8.

30 S. 4; see also Housing Finance Act 1972, s. 99.

31 Local Government Act 1972, s. 112.

32 Education Act 1944, s. 88.

33 Local Authority Social Services Act 1970, s. 6.

34 Written in mid-1973.

35 This will depend on the extent to which the new associations of local authorities work together.

36 See F. W. Maitland, *The Constitutional History of England* (1908), p. 54.

37 See also pp. 255–61.

38 I.e. the Minister within whose general responsibility the function of the corporation falls.

39 As when Lord Hall was dismissed from the chairmanship of the Post Office in November 1970 on the ground that he did not have the necessary qualities of leadership. (See 807 H.C. Deb. col. 977–1040.)

40 Area Health Authorities include some members appointed by Regional Health Authorities and by local authorities – an exception to the normal ministerial appointment.

41 See H.C. 50 of 1972–3.

42 See Cmnd. 5178, p. 43. The totals differ from those on page 66 above because this table is at 1972 Survey prices.

43 Ibid., p. 44 para. 4.

44 Ibid., p. 45 para. 9.

45 Ibid., para. 10.

46 Ibid., para. 13.

47 The figures relate to slightly different dates at or about the beginning of 1972.

CHAPTER 7

1 Hence 'bobby'.

2 Royal Commission on the Police, 1962. Final Report, Cmd.

1728. For a minority view, see the Memorandum of Dissent by Dr A. L. Goodhart: ibid., p. 157.

3 Schedule 3 to the Act.

4 These figures are taken from the Report of Her Majesty's Inspectors of Constabulary for 1961 (H.C. 220 of 1961/2), pp. 34–5 and the Report of Her Majesty's Chief Inspector of Constabulary for 1970 (H.C. 417 of 1970/1), pp. 88–9 .

5 The Police Act 1964, s. 13.

6 Ibid., s. 14.

7 Ibid., ss. 41–3.

8 In 1970 the total authorized establishment of all the forces in England and Wales was 104,115 but the actual strength was only 89,251. This works out at an average of one policeman for every 471 people in the general population. In 1961 the equivalent figures were: total establishment, 78,215; actual strength, 72,699; population per policeman, 590. For the source of these figures, see note 4, above. By 1973 the total number of policemen in England and Wales reached 100,000.

9 The Metropolitan Police Force was established under the Metropolitan Police Act 1829. The City of London Police is governed by private Acts, the first being the City of London Police Act 1839.

10 The Police (Scotland) Act 1966.

11 The original legislation was the Constabulary (Ireland) Act 1836.

12 The Police Act 1964, s. 4(2).

13 Ibid., s. 6(1) and (3).

14 Ibid., s. 6(4).

15 Ibid., s. 5(1).

16 Ibid., s. 7(2).

17 Ibid., s. 33(3) (b).

18 Ibid., s. 1(1) as amended by the Local Government Act 1972, s. 272 and Sch. 30.

19 Ibid., s. 2(1) as amended by the Local Government Act 1972, s. 272 and Sch. 30.

20 Ibid., s. 3.

21 Ibid., ss. 2 and 3 as amended by the Local Government Act 1972, s. 217 and Sch. 27, Pt II, para. 18.

22 Ibid., s. 4 (1).

23 Ibid., s. 4(3) and (4).

24 Ibid., ss. 4(2) and 6(4).

25 Ibid., s. 4(2).

26 Ibid., s. 33(3) (a).

27 Ibid., s. 12.

28 Ibid., s. 5(4), (5) and (6).

29 Ibid., s. 29.

30 Ibid., s. 8.

31 Ibid., s. 8(4). There are some exceptions to this.

32 Ibid., s. 31.

33 Ibid., s. 33.

34 Ibid., ss. 60(1) and 33(6).

35 Ibid., s. 30.

36 Ibid., s. 38. This does not apply to the Metropolitan Police but the annual report of the Commissioner is presented to Parliament by the Home Secretary.

37 This paragraph is based on D. E. Regan, 'The Police Service: An Extreme Example of Central Control over Local Authority Staff' [1966] *P.L.* 13, pp. 15–21.

38 See the article cited in the previous note.

39 Administration of Justice Act 1973, s. 1(9); Metropolitan Police Act 1839, s. 4; Metropolitan Police Act 1856, ss. 1 and 2; and Metropolitan Police Act 1933, s. 1.

40 The Police Act 1964, s. 47.

41 Ibid., s. 44 and the Police Federation Regulations 1969 (s. 1. 1969/1787) reg. 4(2).

42 See the Regulations cited in the previous note.

43 The Police Act 1964, s. 44(2), as amended by the Police Act 1972.

44 The Police Act 1969, s. 4. The matters to be considered by the Council are specified in the section.

45 As the Council covers the whole U.K. there are representatives from Scotland and Northern Ireland as well as from England and Wales.

46 See Regan, op. cit., note 37 above, pp. 28–32.

47 The Police Act 1964, s. 46.

48 See T. A. Critchley, *A History of the Police in England and Wales* (1967), pp. 184–9.

49 [1930] 2 K.B. 364. See also *A.-G. for New South Wales* v. *Perpetual Trustee Co. (Ltd).* [1955] A.C. 457 at 489–90; and *Lewis* v. *Cattle* [1938] 2 K.B. 454 where it was held that a policeman is a

'person who holds office under His Majesty' within the terms of s. 2 of the Official Secrets Act 1911.

50 But not, it seems, a servant of the Crown: see the *dicta* in *Conway* v. *Rimmer* [1968] A.C. 910 at 953 and 974–5 (H.L.). The Crown is not liable for the torts of a policeman: see note 71, below.

51 See the Report of the Royal Commission on the Police, 1962, Cmnd. 1728, pp. 30–33.

52 The Police Act 1964, s. 4.

53 The Police Act 1964, s. 5(1).

54 685 H.C. Deb., 5s., c. 84.

55 By Lord Chesham, speaking on behalf of the Government: 213 H.L. Deb., 5s., c. 47.

56 Cmd. 7831 (1944).

57 Metropolitan Police Act 1829, s. 4.

58 See 330 H.C. Deb., 3s., cols. 1161–4, 1171–6 (1888); 220 H.C. Deb., 5s., c. 839 (1928); 314 H.C. Deb., 5s., cols. 1553–4 (1936); 571 H.C. Deb., 5s., col. 574 (1959).

59 Italics added.

60 Metropolitan Police Act 1839, s. 4.

61 Metropolitan Police Act 1856, s. 1.

62 The preamble to the Act does, however, read, '. . . And Whereas it is expedient . . . to constitute an Office of Police, which, acting under the immediate Authority of One of His Majesty's Principal Secretaries of State, shall direct and controul the Whole of such new System of Police within those Limits . . .'

63 [1968] 2 Q.B. 118.

64 The law was in rather an uncertain state at the time.

65 At p. 136.

66 [1930] 2 K.B. 364.

67 [1955] A.C. 457.

68 Section 1 of the Act was referred to in argument by counsel for the Commissioner (at p. 125) but it was not argued by either side that it empowered the Home Secretary to give directions to the Commissioner.

69 *The Report of the Royal Commission on the Police 1962*, Cmnd. 1728, pp. 30–3.

70 This argument is put forward by Geoffrey Marshall in his book *Police and Government* (1965).

71 It is not possible to sue the police authority (*Fisher* v. *Oldham*

Corporation [1930] 2 K.B. 364); nor can the Crown be sued: see the Crown Proceedings Act 1947, s. 2(6), which provides that the Crown is not liable for the acts of an officer of the Crown unless he was appointed by the Crown and is paid wholly out of central Government funds.

72 The Police (Discipline) (Amendment) Regulations 1967 (S.I. 1967 No. 185), Sch. 1.

73 For the procedure, see S.I. 1965 No. 543 as amended by S.I. 1967 No. 185.

74 The Police Act 1964, s. 49(1).

75 Ibid.

76 Ibid., s. 49(3).

77 Ibid., s. 33(3).

78 For the procedure, see S.I. 1965 No. 544 as amended by S.I. 1967 No. 186.

79 The accused is also given a copy.

80 The Police Act 1964, s. 37 and Schedule 5. The procedure is set out in the Police (Appeals) Rules 1965 (S.I. 1965/618).

81 There were also over 18,900 letters of appreciation.

82 The figures for preceding years were: 1970 – 8·2; 1969 – 8·0; 1968 – 8·6; 1967 – 10·4; 1966 – 9·7; 1965 – 11·0; 1964 – 16·0.

83 These figures are taken from the Report of Her Majesty's Chief Inspector of Constabulary for 1971 (H.C. Paper 290 of 1971/2), pp. 71–5. For similar figures for the Metropolitan Police Force, see the Report of the Commissioner of Police of the Metropolis for 1971 (Cmnd. 4986) (1972), pp. 33–4.

84 See the proposal for the appointment of a Commissioner of Rights by three members of the Royal Commission on the Police, 1962 (Cmnd. 1728) pp. 193–4, and Marshall, op. cit., pp. 110–12.

85 At present the Parliamentary Commissioner for Administration has no power to intervene.

86 The Police Act 1964, s. 50.

87 Ibid., s. 32.

88 827 H.C. Deb., 5s., cols 652–7 (2 December 1971).

89 851 H.C. Deb., 5s., cols 993–1003 (23 February 1973).

CHAPTER 8

1 In certain cases private citizens can also make an arrest.

2 Criminal Law Act 1967, s. 3(1).

3 [1967] 2 W.L.R. 129.

4 The boys' activity was in fact quite innocent.

5 Contrary to s. 51(1) of the Police Act 1964.

6 Winn L. J. was rather doubtful whether the policemen had the power to arrest the boys in the circumstances but he reached his conclusion on the ground that the policemen did not *intend* to arrest the boys when they caught hold of their arms: they only wanted to ask them some questions.

7 This is the position in France: see Glanville Williams, 'Requisites of a Valid Arrest' [1954] *Crim. L.R.* 6 at 8–10.

8 Ibid., pp. 12–14.

9 For an example of the problems that can arise, see *Alderson* v. *Booth* [1969] 2 W.L.R. 1252.

10 *Per* Parke B. in *Timothy* v. *Simpson* (1835) 1 C.M. & R. 757 at 763 (cited in Glanville Williams, 'Arrest for Breach of the Peace' [1954] *Crim. L.R.* 578).

11 See Glanville Williams, 'Arrest for Breach of the Peace' [1954] *Crim. L.R.* 578 at 579.

12 Ibid., pp. 583–4.

13 A more general provision is found in s. 11 of the Prevention of Offences Act 1851. It empowered anyone to arrest a person found committing an indictable offence at night.

14 It is provided by s. 24 (1) of the Criminal Justice Act 1967 that a warrant is not to be issued under s. 1 of the Magistrates' Courts Act unless either the offence is indictable or is punishable by imprisonment or the defendant's address is not sufficiently established for a summons to be served.

15 See especially s. 1.

16 The Magistrates' Courts Rules, S.I. 1968 No. 1920, rule 79 (2).

17 *Christie* v. *Leachinsky* [1947] A.C. 573.

18 [1961] 1 W.L.R. 153.

19 Contrary to s. 3 of the Prevention of Crimes Amendment Act 1885; see now s. 51(1) of the Police Act 1964.

20 See Glanville Williams, [1954] *Crim. L.R.* 6 at 17.

21 [1966] 2 Q.B. 414.

22 S. 40.

23 This is shown by *Gelberg* v. *Miller* [1961] 1 W.L.R. 153 (discussed above) in which the suspect happened to have committed another offence which justified his arrest.

24 Provisions of this kind have already been enacted with regard to specific offences: see, for example, the Firearms Act 1968, ss. 48 and 50. For a detailed consideration of the reform of the law of arrest, see D. A. Thomas, 'Police Powers' [1966] *Crim. L.R.* 639.

25 See D. A. Thomas, 'The Execution of Warrants of Arrest' [1962] *Crim. L.R.* 597 at 601–4.

26 Ibid.

27 *Dillon* v. *O'Brien and Davis* (1887) 16 Cox C.C. 245 (Ireland). See also *Ghani* v. *Jones* [1970] 1 Q.B. 693 (C.A.) at p. 706 (*per* Lord Denning M.R.).

28 It is unclear whether the suspect's home could be searched if the arrest took place elsewhere but this seems to be common police practice.

29 [1934] 2 K.B. 164.

30 It ought not to matter whether the articles are in fact used as evidence in criminal proceedings so long as the policeman had reasonable grounds for believing that they might be so used: see *Chic Fashions (West Wales) Ltd* v. *Jones* [1968] 2 Q.B. 299 at 312 (*per* Lord Denning M.R.) (C.A.).

31 See E. C. S. Wade, 'Police Search' (1934) 50 *L.Q.R.* 354.

32 [1970] 1 Q.B. 693 (C.A.).

33 At p. 709. In his third proposition Lord Denning says that the person *in possession* of the article must have committed the crime for which the article is evidence or his refusal to give it up must be 'quite unreasonable'. Since these propositions apply even if there is no arrest, it is hard to see why he objected to *Elias v. Pasmore*.

34 [1968] 2 Q.B. 299 (C.A.).

35 At p. 313.

36 *The Times*, 4 September 1971.

37 At p. 321.

38 See D. A. Thomas, 'The Law of Search and Seizure' [1967] *Crim L.R.* 3 at pp. 9–11.

39 For a discussion of stop and search powers, see Thomas op. cit. at pp. 11–18.

40 There is reason to believe, however, that in practice the police are able to exercise somewhat wider powers since members of the public do not normally object when the police wish to conduct a search.

41 [1970] 1 Q.B. 693 (C.A.).

42 Ibid., at pp. 708–9. The facts of the case were that the police were investigating the disappearance of a Pakistani woman whom they believed to have been murdered. They interviewed her relatives and took a number of documents, including their passports, from them. Subsequently the relatives took proceedings to obtain a court order for their return. The court ordered the return of the documents since it had not been established that they were evidence of any crime. The importance of the case lies in the general principles laid down by the Court of Appeal.

43 Above, p. 140.

44 *Kuruma* v. *R.* [1955] A.C. 197 (P.C.); *King* v. *R.* [1969] 1 A.C. 304 (P.C.).

45 *Mapp* v. *Ohio* 367 U.S. 643 (1961).

46 In 1956 material obtained from tapping the telephone of a criminal was found to implicate a barrister. It was passed to the Bar Council who made use of it in disciplinary proceedings. This action was criticized by a committee of Privy Councillors set up to investigate the matter and they recommended that in future information obtained by interception should not be disclosed to private bodies or domestic tribunals. The Government accepted this recommendation. (See the Report of the Committee of Privy Councillors appointed to inquire into the interception of communications, Cmnd. 283 (1957), paragraphs 91–101.

47 Figures for the number of warrants issued from 1937 to 1956 are to be found in Appendix 1 to the Report of the Committee of Privy Councillors appointed to inquire into the interception of communications (Cmnd. 283 (1957)). Since then the Government has refused to publish figures but it has been officially stated that the principles continue to be applied in the same way as before: see the statement in the Commons by the Minister of State, Home Office (Mr Carlisle) on 1 February 1973 (849 H.C. Deb., 5s., cols 1777–1784).

48 Ibid., para. 31.

49 It is possible that in some circumstances a breach of copyright might occur but if the letter was evidence of a crime the rule in *Ghani* v. *Jones* [1970] 1 Q.B. 593 (discussed above) would probably apply.

50 The Telegraph Act 1863, s. 45; the Telegraph Act 1868, s. 20; and the Post Office (Protection) Act 1884, s. 11.

51 S. 77 and Sch. 5.

52 The only exception is where a registered inland packet is lost or damaged; but even in this case the amount recoverable may not exceed the market value of the packet, excluding the value of the message: the Post Office Act 1969, s. 30.

53 *Triefus* v. *Post Office* [1957] 2 Q.B. 352.

54 Cmnd. 283 (1957), para. 123.

55 Ibid., paras. 85–6.

56 The only exception is that at election time candidates have a right to have access to halls owned by a local authority for the purpose of electioneering meetings: Representation of the People Act 1949, ss. 82, 83 and Sch. 7.

57 S.I. 1952 No. 776 made under the Trafalgar Square Act 1844 and the Parks Regulation Acts 1872 and 1926 (see especially s. 2 of the Act of 1926). The penalty for breach of the regulations is a fine of £5 (ibid.).

58 See The Hyde Park Regulations 1955 (S.I. 1955 No. 1750), paras. 3(11) and(13).

59 [1950] 2 K.B. 498.

60 At p. 502.

61 See ibid., s. 54. The maximum penalty is a fine of £20 (Criminal Justice Act 1967, 9 2(1) and Sch. 3, Pt I). For a case on this section see *Papworth* v. *Coventry* [1967] 2 All E.R. 41.

62 Stephen's *Digest* (9th edn), art. 235 (quoted in Ian Brownlie, *The Law Relating to Public Order* (1968), p. 77.

63 The original penalty of £2 was increased to £50 by the Criminal Justice Act 1967, s. 92(1), Sch. 3, Pt I.

64 See *Nagy* v. *Weston* [1965] I. W.L.R. 280 where a man who sold hot dogs from a van parked at the side of a wide road was convicted under the Highways Act.

65 *R.* v. *Clark* [1964] 2 Q.B. 315.

66 *Nagy* v. *Weston* (above).

67 [1963] 2 Q.B. 561.

68 The Public Order Act 1963, s. 1(1).

69 *Cooper* v. *Shield* [1971] 2 All E.R. 917, which held that a railway station was not a public place (because it was part of a building), would not apply under the new definition. 69a S. 9 (1) of the Act of 1936.

70 [1972] 2 All E.R. 1297.

71 [1972] 2 All E.R. 1 (Sub. nom. *Cozens* v. *Brutus*).

72 [1963] 2 Q.B. 744.

73 Appeal courts will rarely interfere with a decision on this point: see *Brutus* v. *Cozens* [1972] 2 All E.R. 1297 (H.L.).

74 Referred to in Brownlie, op. cit., p. 14.

75 It should be mentioned that there are also some local statutes and by-laws similar to section 5 of the Public Order Act. See, for example, section 54 of the Metropolitan Police Act 1839.

76 Race Relations Act 1965, s. 6.

77 Incitement to Mutiny Act 1797; Incitement to Disaffection Act 1934.

78 Police Act 1964, s. 53.

79 This is a common law offence and its exact scope is not very clear; but if a speaker stirred up his audience to commit acts of violence he would probably be guilty of sedition. Prosecutions no longer seem to be brought for this offence, however.

80 Under The Prevention of Crime Act 1953 it is an offence to be in possession of an offensive weapon in a public place without lawful authority or reasonable excuse. 'Public place' has the same wide definition as now applies to the Public Order Act. An offensive weapon can be anything (e.g. a stick for holding a banner) intended by the person who has it for use as weapon. There is also an offence of similar scope under the Public Order Act 1936, s. 4.

81 Criminal Damage Act 1971.

82 Police Act 1964, s. 51.

83 *R.* v. *Caird* (1970) 54 Cr. App. R 499 (C.A.).

84 On the question of police discretion in prosecution and the role of the Director of Public Prosecutions, see below, pp. 189–90.

85 Most of the offences that have been discussed do not qualify as arrestable offences under s. 2(1) of the Criminal Law Act 1967.

86 Public Order Act 1936, s. 7(3).

87 S. 54.

88 The Prevention of Crime Act 1953, s. 1(3); see also the Public Order Act 1936, ss. 4 and 7(3).

89 Highways Act 1959, s. 121(2).

90 *Per* Hayes J in *Humphries* v. *Connor* (1864) 17 Ir. C.L.R. 1,

reproduced in Geoffrey Wilson, *Cases and Materials on Constitutional and Administrative Law* (1966), p. 387.

91 *Thomas* v. *Sawkins* [1935] 2 K.B. 249 (Div. Ct.).

92 See s. 51(3) of the Police Act 1964. A similar offence was provided for in earlier legislation.

93 [1936] 1 K.B. 218 (Div. Ct.). See also *Piddington* v. *Bates* [1960] 3 All E.R. 660 (discussed below).

94 It is an offence under The Public Meeting Act 1908 to act in a disorderly manner for the purpose of preventing the transaction of business at a lawful public meeting. The Public Order Act 1936, s. 6 gave a power of arrest for this offence. There are of course many provisions under which the attackers could be arrested and charged.

95 (1864) 17 Ir. C.L.R. 1.

96 (1883) 15 Cox 435.

97 At p. 445.

98 (1882) 15 Cox 138.

99 [1902] 1 K.B. 167.

100 See also the Magistrates' Courts Act 1952, s. 91.

101 A superior court can imprison him for a longer period.

102 See David Williams, *Keeping the Peace* (1967), pp. 88–93.

103 This principle only applies in the absence of a statutory provision to the contrary (e.g. s. 5 of the Public Order Act).

104 There was a similar offence at the time under s. 8 of the County Police Act 1839 (now repealed). See the article by Daintith cited below.

105 See T. C. Daintith, 'Disobeying a Policeman: A Fresh Look at *Duncan* v. *Jones*' [1966] *Public Law* 248.

106 As amended by the Trade Disputes Act 1906, s. 2(2).

107 See *Ward, Lock & Co.* v. *Operative Printers' Assistants' Society* (1906) 22 T.L.R. 327 and *Fowler* v. *Kibble* [1922] 1 Ch. 487; contrast *J. Lyons & Sons* v. *Wilkins* [1899] 1 Ch. 255.

108 [1974] 1 All E.R. 314 (H.L.).

109 [1967] 1 Q.B. 91.

110 At pp. 158–9. They were no doubt also guilty of an offence under s. 121 of the Highways Act 1959.

111 [1960] 3 All E.R. 660.

112 At p. 663.

113 Of 1381, 1391, 1429 and 1623.

114 *R.* v. *Mountford* [1971] 2 All E.R. 81 (C.A.).

115 *Kamara* v. *D.P.P.* [1973] 2 All E.R. 1242 (H.L.). This case is of great importance since it establishes that a 'sit-in' can result in a very serious criminal charge.

116 See R. J. Coleman, 'Sit-Ins and the Conspiracy and Protection of Property Act 1875' [1970] *Crim. L.R.* 608.

CHAPTER 9

1 For example, this occurred when the decision of the House of Lords in *Burmah Oil Co.* v. *Lord Advocate* [1965] A.C. 75 was reversed by the War Damage Act 1965. See also the Northern Ireland Act 1972.

2 See Chap. 14.

3 See below, pp. 318–19.

4 This includes ex-Lord Chancellors: see the Appellate Jurisdiction Act 1876, ss. 5 and 24.

5 See below, p. 223.

6 [1973] 2 All E.R. 1242.

7 See S. A. de Smith, *The New Commonwealth and its Constitutions* (1964), pp. 137–43.

8 This is the current figure in mid-1973. See The Judges' Remuneration Order 1972 (S.I. 1972 No. 1104). See further the provisions cited in the following note.

9 Administration of Justice Act 1973, s. 9; Courts Act 1971, s. 18.

10 Louis Blom-Cooper and Gavin Drewry, *Final Appeal* (1972), p. 168 quoting R. F. V. Heuston, *Lives of the Lord Chancellors* (1964), p. 420.

11 The Appellate Jurisdiction Act 1876, s. 6; the Supreme Court of Judicature (Consolidation) Act 1925, s. 12(1).

12 The Courts Act 1971, ss. 17 and 21(6).

13 Administration of Justice Act 1973, ss. 1 and 2.

14 Louis Blom-Cooper and Gavin Drewry, *Final Appeal* (1972), pp. 166 et seq.

15 There is of course no evidence that the judgments of individual judges are influenced by their social backgrounds.

16 See Chapter 12.

17 This and the following paragraphs are based largely on A. Rubinstein, 'Liability in Tort of Judicial Officers' (1964) 15 *U. of Toronto L.J.* 317.

18 The position may be different where a judge is guilty of an unlawful failure to act. Under the Habeas Corpus Act 1679 a

judge who wrongfully refuses to issue a writ of habeas corpus is liable to a penalty of £500, recoverable by the prisoner. See also Rubinstein op. cit., pp. 324–6.

19 For example, issuing a warrant of arrest: see the cases cited in Rubinstein, op. cit., p. 330, n. 74.

20 This exception applies only when the officer is sued for damages; for the position where proceedings are taken to have the decision set aside, e.g. by certiorari, see pp. 336–40 below.

21 This does not prevent witnesses being prosecuted for perjury.

22 *O'Connor* v. *Waldron* [1935] A.C. 76 at 81.

23 *Law* v. *Llewellyn* [1906] 1 K.B. 487.

24 *Attwood* v. *Chapman* [1914] 3 K.B. 275; *Royal Aquarium* v. *Parkinson* [1892] 1 Q.B. 431.

25 E.g. military service tribunals during the First World War: *Co-Partnership Farms* v. *Harvey-Smith* [1918] 2 K.B. 405.

26 E.g. a court of referees under the Unemployment Insurance Acts: *Collins* v. *Whiteway (Henry) & Co. Ltd.* [1927] 2 K.B. 378.

27 The position as regards reporting judicial proceedings is as follows. Under the Law of Libel Amendment Act 1888, s. 3, as amended by the Defamation Act 1952, ss. 8 and 9, a fair and accurate report in a newspaper or broadcast of judicial proceedings in open court is absolutely privileged so long as it is published contemporaneously. In addition to this there is a qualified privilege at common law that protects fair and accurate reports of such proceedings provided they are not published maliciously. The privilege at common law applies to all reports, whether in newspapers or not, and the report does not have to be published contemporaneously with the proceedings. There are, however, various statutory provisions limiting the reporting of court proceedings, for example in committal proceedings and proceedings concerning children and matrimonial proceedings. There is also a common law power whereby the court may delay reporting until the end of the trial where this is necessary in the interests of justice. On all these restrictions see G. J. Borrie and and N. V. Lowe, *The Law of Contempt* (1973), pp. 62–9, 114–22.

28 It should also be mentioned that the Crown is not liable for anything done by anyone discharging functions of a judicial nature: the Crown Proceedings Act 1947, s. 2(5).

29 For the origin of this power, see Harry Street, *Freedom, the Law*

and the Individual (3rd ed 1972), p. 154. There is no limit on the length of the imprisonment or the amount of the fine.

30 A coroner may, however, have limited contempt powers.

31 County Courts Act 1959, s. 157.

32 Administration of Justice Act 1960, s. 11.

33 [1973] 3 All E.R. 54.

34 (1928) 44 T.L.R. 301.

35 He was, however, ordered to pay the whole costs of the proceedings between solicitor and client.

36 *Ambard* v. *Attorney-General for Trinidad and Tobago* [1936] A.C. 322 at 355.

36a See further, *R.* v. *Commissioner of Police for the Metropolis, ex p. Blackburn (No. 2)* [1968] 2 Q.B. 150.

37 *R.* v. *Commissioner of Police for the Metropolis, ex p. Blackburn* [1968] 2 Q.B. 118.

38 See the Prosecution of Offences Regulations 1946 (S.R. & O. 1946 No. 1467/L. 17) paragraph 6, for a list of these offences.

39 Under the Prosecution of Offences Act 1908, s. 2(3).

40 See the Report by JUSTICE, *The Prosecution Process in England and Wales* (1970) reprinted in [1970] *Crim. L.R.* 668.

41 There are three types of pardon: a free pardon, which wipes out both the conviction and the sentence; a conditional pardon, or commutation, which substitutes a lesser kind of punishment (e.g. life imprisonment instead of execution); and a remission, which merely reduces the sentence. A reprieve is not a pardon: it simply postpones the carrying out of the sentence. See E. C. S. Wade and Godfrey Phillips, *Constitutional Law* (8th edn 1970 by E. C. S. Wade and A. W. Bradley), p. 322.

CHAPTER 10

1 *Parliamentary Practice* (18th edn, 1971) Chap. XV. These figures relate to business on the floor of the House and exclude time spent in committees of all kinds meeting 'upstairs'.

2 See p. 219.

3 For the names of those involved, see *Who Does What in Parliament 1973* (Mitchell & Birt).

4 See below, pp. 53-4.

5 If there is a tie for the last place there is a further ballot to decide which of them shall fill that place.

6 This means that the trade union will pay a high proportion of the

election expenses and a limited annual contribution to the constituency party.

7 Op. cit., p. 223.

8 See p. 219.

9 But see p. 116.

10 Adjusted annual rate based on 9 months' operation.

11 For the Commissioner's report for 1972 see H.C. 72 of 1972–3.

12 See op. cit., esp. Chs XV–XVII.

13 See below, pp. 205–6.

14 He interprets strictly this question of propriety and often refuses to allow the motion.

15 See S.O. Nos. 1–5.

16 See p. 205.

17 See pp. 206 et seq.

18 In relation to nationalized industries, see pp. 114–15.

19 See Chap. 17.

20 Some Provisional Order Confirmation bills are also introduced and passed, as are similar bills under the Private Legislation Procedure (Scotland) Act 1936. They are local in application and are referred to as Order Confirmation bills.

21 Excluding Order Confirmation Bills.

22 Also the Merchant Shipping Bill which, because of the shortage of Government time and the intention of the Government to introduce other legislation, received a first but not a second reading. This cannot be accounted a 'defeat'.

23 See above, p. 203

24 The four days (until 7 p.m.) other than Fridays are for motions.

25 Time spent in committee off the floor of the House is additional.

26 See P. G. Richards, *Parliament and Conscience* (1970).

27 See May op. cit. Pt III. Akin to private bills are the bills for confirming provisional orders, and provisional orders under the Private Legislation Procedure (Scotland) Act 1936; and orders made under the Statutory Orders (Special Procedure) Acts 1945 and 1965.

28 See p. 215.

29 Common for Government bills; unusual for private Members' bills, see above, p. 210.

30 Standing Order No. 40. Exceptionally, Consolidated Fund and Appropriation bills go automatically to a committee of the whole House.

31 Each session the Speaker appoints a panel of chairmen from amongst the Members of the House. They act as neutral, impartial chairmen.

32 There is a Scottish Standing Committee for Scottish bills which is specially composed.

33 See above, p. 205.

34 Standing Order No. 73 enables bills to be sent to a standing Committee or the Scottish Grand Committee for consideration on report but since this was introduced in November 1967 only one bill has been so treated.

35 If they do not agree to procedure under the Parliament Acts may be invoked (see below, pp. 226–30).

36 See May op. cit., Chaps. XXXIV–XXXVIII.

37 He has general supervising duties in relation to private bills, on behalf of the House.

38 P. 900.

39 The modern practice is that all private bills, except those relating to individual persons, are introduced into the House of Commons: see May op. cit., p. 961.

40 Not every piece of subordinate or delegated legislation is designated a statutory instrument. Local authorities have statutory powers to make bye-laws and these are not statutory instruments.

41 Statutory Instruments Act 1946, section 2(1).

42 Ibid., section 3(2).

43 See for example Town and Country Planning Act 1971, section 287(2), (5), (6), (7).

44 For judicial safeguards, see pp. 350–4.

45 Section 4 provides that an instrument which is required to be laid before Parliament must normally be laid before it comes into operation; if this is not done, the Lord Chancellor and the Speaker must be notified.

46 See H.C. 5 of 1972–3.

47 As Ministers and other officeholders are not members of select committees, the number of available Members is about 535.

48 I.e. with the House of Lords.

49 See Chap. 12.

50 See pp. 200–2.

51 See pp. 111 et seq.

52 See pp. 217–18.

53 E.g. the Public Accounts, Expenditure, and Public Petitions Committees.

54 E.g. the Select Committees on Statutory Instruments and on Nationalized Industries.

55 E.g. in 1971–2, the committees on the civil list, on delegated legislation, and on parliamentary questions.

CHAPTER 11

1 Above, p. 40.

2 Before the dissolution of the monasteries in the reign of Henry VIII abbots and priors were also members of the Lords and the Lords Spiritual were often as numerous as the Lords Temporal.

3 This first occurred when the bishopric of Manchester was created in 1847: the Ecclesiastical Commissioners Act, 1847, s. 2. See further the enactments listed in May's *Parliamentary Practice* (18th edn 1971), p. 5, n. (h).

4 When the union with Ireland took place it was provided in the Union with Ireland Act 1800, Article 4, s. 2, that one archbishop and three bishops of the Irish Church were entitled to sit in the House of Lords, but they lost their seats when the Church of Ireland was disestablished in 1871: the Irish Church Act 1869, s. 13. Bishops of the Church in Wales lost their right to sit when the Church in Wales was disestablished by the Welsh Church Act 1914, s. 2(2).

5 S. 4.

6 It was held in the *Earl of Antrim's Petition* [1967] 1 A.C. 691 that the right to elect Irish representative peers ceased to exist when the Irish Free State (Agreement) Act 1922 was passed.

7 S. 5.

8 *Viscountess Rhondda's Claim* [1922] 2 A.C. 339.

9 S. 6.

10 The Law Lords are the Lord Chancellor, serving and retired Lords of Appeal in Ordinary, former Lord Chancellors and other peers who hold or have held high judicial office. Appeals are heard by the Appellate Committee which reports back to the House.

11 See Gavin Drewry and Jenny Morgan, 'Law Lords as Legislators' (1969) XXII *Parliamentary Affairs* 226.

12 *Wensleydale Peerage Case* (1856) 5 H.L.C. 958.

13 Sometimes the Prime Minister will consult with the Leader of the Opposition before advising the Queen on the creation of new peers. Thus, for example, when a new government comes to power after a general election members of the previous government who wish to retire from the Commons are often given peerages by the new Prime Minister. No new hereditary peerages have been created by either Mr Wilson or Mr Heath and new peers are now given life peerages.

14 For a more detailed discussion, see P. A. Bromhead, *The House of Lords and Contemporary Politics* (1958), Chaps 2, 3 and 4, and J. R. Vincent 'The House of Lords' (1966) XIX *Parliamentary Affairs*, 475.

15 Above, pp. 44–5.

16 Ss. 1–3.

17 Quintin Hogg was subsequently given a life peerage: see note (19), below.

18 See ss. 1 and 2 of the Act for further details.

19 Ibid. s. 3(2). When Quintin Hogg (who had previously disclaimed his peerage) became Lord Chancellor in 1970 he was made a life peer and thus became known again as Lord Hailsham.

20 Act of Settlement 1700, s. 3; Status of Aliens Act 1914, s. 3; British Nationality Act 1948, s. 31 and Sch. 4.

21 Standing Order No. 2 made on 22 May 1685.

22 Bankruptcy Act, 1883, s. 32. See further, May's *Parliamentary Practice* (18th ed. 1971), pp. 33–4.

23 See p. 41, above. May (op. cit., p. 34) also gives another disqualification: when the House in its judicial capacity has sentenced a member to expulsion a permanent disability may be created.

24 S.O. s Nos. 69–70; May, op. cit., p. 652.

25 S.O. No. 22; May, op. cit., p. 215.

26 Cmnd. 3799 (1968), p. 5.

27 Taken from the White Paper 'House of Lords Reform' Cmnd. 3799 (1968), p. 3.

28 Ibid., p. 4. All the figures in this paragraph are from this source and relate to the period 31 October 1967 to 1 August 1968. For further details, see the table, note 29 below.

29 The following table shows the political composition of the House on 1 August 1968. The figures for attendance are for the

ATTENDANCE AT THE HOUSE OF LORDS
By those who were members on 1 August 1968
for the period 31 October 1967 to 1 August 1968

Party	Peers who attended more than 33⅓% ('working House')			Peers who attended more than 5% but less than 33⅓%			Peers who attended up to 5%			Peers who did not attend*			Totals		
	C	S	Total	C	S	Total	C	S	Total	C	S	Total	C	S	Total
Labour	81	14	95	8	5	13	4	1	5	2	1	3	95	21	116
Conservative	38	87	125	24	86	110	9	70	79	6	31	37	77	274	351
Liberal	8	11	19	2	6	8	2	8	10	1	3	4	13	28	41
Peers not in receipt of a party whip	26	26	52	61	24	85	22	56	78	32	307	339	141	413	554
TOTAL	153	138	291	95	121	216	37	135	172	41	342	383	326	736	1,062

C = Created peers.
S = Peers by succession.
Attendance at committees of the House (other than the Appellate Committee) has been taken into account.
* Including 192 peers with leave of absence;
  81 peers without writs of summons.

period 31 October 1967 to 1 August 1968. (Source: Cmnd. 3799, p. 4).

30 See May, *Parliamentary Practice* (18th edn 1971) Chap. XXXI.

31 S. 1(1).

32 S. 1(2).

33 The words in square brackets were added by the 1949 Act.

34 It is generally assumed that sub-section (3) means that the bill is deemed to be rejected if it is not passed *by the end of the session in which it is sent up to the Lords*. In the circumstances in which this sub-section is applicable it appears that the bill could not receive the Royal Assent until the *next* session because the bill would not be deemed to be rejected until the session was over and it would then be too late for the Royal Assent to be given since this can only be done when Parliament is sitting. See James William Lowther (Viscount Ullswater), *A Speaker's Commentaries* (1925), vol. ii, pp. 112–15.

35 S. 1(3).

36 S. 2(2).

37 S. 3.

38 The Septennial Act, 1715.

39 In 1712 Queen Anne created twelve new peers to secure the approval of the Treaty of Utrecht in the House of Lords and in 1832 the threat of swamping the Lords with new peers was sufficient to ensure the passage of the Reform Act.

40 A majority of peers do not actually take the Conservative whip but they can be relied upon to support the Conservatives.

41 The Welsh Church Act 1914, the Government of Ireland Act 1914, and the Parliament Act 1949.

42 See Bromhead, *The House of Lords and Contemporary Politics* (1958), Chap. IX.

43 In this case the delay provided for in the Parliament Acts might have caused difficulties for the Government since the Home Secretary was required under s. 2(5) of the House of Commons (Redistribution of Seats) Act 1949 to lay the Reports of the Commissions together with draft Orders in Council to give effect to them before Parliament 'as soon as may be' after the Reports were received. Proceedings were in fact begun for mandamus to compel the performance of this duty. For further details, see above, p. 38.

44 Below, pp. 237–9.

45 These figures are taken from Ivor Burton and Gavin Drewry 'Public Legislation: A Survey of the Session 1968/69' (1970) XXIII *Parliamentary Affairs* 154 at 164.

The following table gives more detailed information concerning amendments in the House of Lords to Government bills sent up from the Commons:

Session	Number of Bills Sent up	Number of Bills Amended	Number of Amendments	Number of Amendments Rejected by Commons*
1946–7	43	17	996	53 (5)
1948–9	76	29	533	41 (10)
1964–5	45	18	203	11 (0)
1965–6	70	30	736	48 (10)

* Figures in brackets represent amendments in lieu of those disagreed to.

Source: P. G. Henderson, 'Legislation in the House of Lords' (1968) XXI *Parliamentary Affairs* 176 at 177.

46 *Anisminic Ltd* v. *Foreign Compensation Commission* [1969] 2 A.C. 147. See below, pp. 359–60.

47 Foreign Compensation Act 1969, s. 3.

48 Consolidation bills are bills designed to simplify the statute law by collecting all the provisions dealing with a particular topic found in various statutes and consolidating them into one statute.

49 The figures are taken from Ivor Burton and Gavin Drewry, 'Public Legislation: A Survey of the Session 1969/70' (1970) XXIII *Parliamentary Affairs* 308 at 312 and 321. (See also pp. 335–43.)

50 Ibid., at p. 312.

51 Bromhead, op. cit., Chap. XVI.

52 Ibid., pp. 148 and 175.

53 See p. 215.

54 See pp. 215–18.

55 Agreed Statement on the conclusion of the Conference of Party Leaders, Cmnd. 7380 (1948).

56 Above, p. 231.

57 *House of Lords Reform*, Cmnd. 3799 (1968).

58 The Parliament (No. 2) Bill.

59 777 H. C. Debs., 5s., col. 55. (3 February 1969).

60 Appendix II.

61 Crick, *The Reform of Parliament* (revised 2nd edn 1970), pp. 149–60.

CHAPTER 12

1 See the *Report from the Select Committee on Parliamentary Privileges*, H.C. 34 (1967–8), paras. 36–8 and Minutes of Evidence, p. 4.
2 Ibid., paras. 150–4 and Minutes of Evidence, p. 3.
3 Ibid., paragraph 180.
4 The London Electricity Board Case in 1957.
5 *Report from the Select Committee on Parliamentary Privileges* (above), paras. 193–7. See also May, *Parliamentary Practice* (18th edn, 1971), Chapter IX.
6 The House of Lords does have this power: May, op. cit., p. 123.
7 May, op. cit., p. 125.
8 Cf the case of John Wilkes: May, op. cit., p. 130.
9 *Report from the Select Committee on Parliamentarys Privileges* (above). paragraph 18.
10 Ibid.
11 E.g. Garry Allighan in 1947.
12 *Report from the Select Committee on Parliamentary Privileges* (above), paragraphs 138–46.
13 For an assessment of these proposals, see Colin Seymoure-Ur 'Proposed Reforms of Parliamentary Privilege: An Assessment in the Light of Recent Cases' (1970) XXIII *Parliamentary Affairs*, 211.
14 For a detailed account see May, *Parliamentary Practice* (18th edn, 1971), pp. 132–57.
15 E.g. Profumo's case, C.J. (1962–3) 246.
16 C.J. (1693–7) 331.
17 Sponsorship involves paying part of an M.P.'s election expenses and often paying him an allowance while he is in Parliament. There are quite a number of Labour M.P.s who are sponsored by trade unions. For further details see above, p. 119; see also Appendix III of the *Report from the Select Committee on Members' Interests (Declaration)*, H.C. 57 (1969–70).
18 For further information on the attempts by pressure groups to influence M.P.s see the Report cited in the previous note and J. D. Stewart, *British Pressure Groups* (1958), pp. 184–204. Two cases in which problems of this kind came before the House were Robinson's case, *Report from the Committee of Privileges*, H.C. 85

(1943-44) and Brown's case, *Report from the Committee of Privileges*, H.C. 118 (1946-7).

19   301 H.C. Deb., 5s., cols 1545-47 (14 May 1935).

20   *Report from the Committee of Privileges*, H.C. 181 (1945-6).

21   *Second Report from the Committee of Privileges*, H.C. 38 (1956-7); 563 H.C. Deb., 5s., col. 403 (24 January 1957).

22   H.C. 39 (1956-7). No action was taken in this case in view of the immediate apology by the editor.

23   The Select Committee on Parliamentary Privilege accepted that some M.P.s are over-sensitive to criticism and suggested rules that might be followed by the House in order to avoid a misuse of its powers in future: see the *Report from the Select Committee on Parliamentary Privilege*, H.C. 34 (1967-8), paras. 7, 8 and 48.

24   Haxey's case in 1397.

25   Since Article 9 was declaratory of the existing law it is possible that the scope of the privilege is actually wider than that of the Article. See further, S. A. de Smith, 'Parliamentary Privilege and the Bill of Rights' (1958) 21 *M.L.R.* 465.

26   See Duncan Sandys' case, *Report from the Select Committee on the Official Secrets Acts*, H.C. 101 (1938-39).

27   May, op. cit., pp. 85-86. See also *Church of Scientology of California* v. *Johnson-Smith* [1972] 1 Q.B. 522.

28   See Captain Ramsay's case, *Report from the Committee of Privileges*, paragraph 14, H.C. 164 (1939-40).

29   *Report from the Select Committee of Parliamentary Privilege*, paras. 60-7, H.C. 34 (1967-8). The Bill of Rights merely prevents words spoken in the course of parliamentary proceedings being questioned *outside* Parliament.

30   *Report from the Select Committee on the Official Secrets Acts*, para. 3. H.C. 101 (1938-9).

31   Ibid.

32   May, op. cit., pp. 81, 151 and 154. In *Goffin* v. *Donnelly* (1881) 6. Q.B.D. 307, 50 L.J.Q.B. 303, it was held that an action for slander could not be brought on account of statements made by a witness before a parliamentary committee.

33   *Report from the Select Committee on the Official Secrets Acts*, paragraph 10, H.C. 101 (1938-39); May, op. cit., p. 86. Compare the American decision of *Coffin* v. *Coffin* (1808) 4 Mass. 1.

34   *Rivlin* v. *Bilainkin* [1953] 1 Q.B. 485. In certain cases, however, a communication between a constituent and his M.P. may enjoy

qualified privilege: *R.* v. *Rule* [1937] 2 K.B. 375; *Beach* v. *Freeson* [1971] 2 All E.R. 854.

35 *Report from the Select Committee on the Official Secrets Act,* para. 4, H.C. 101 (1938–9).

36 (1869) L.R. 4 Q.B. 573.

37 *Fifth Report from the Committee of Privileges,* H.C. 305 (1956–7); 591 H.C. Deb. col. 334 et seq. (8 July 1958). See pp. 253–4, below.

38 See the *Report of the Select Committee of Parliamentary Privilege,* paras. 80–91, H.C. 34 (1967–8), where it is suggested that the decision in the London Electricity Board Case should be reversed by legislation.

39 Qualified privilege depends, not on the law of Parliament, but on the ordinary law of libel and slander. Where it exists the person concerned is liable if he was actuated by malice; otherwise he has the same protection as in the case of absolute privilege.

40 May, op. cit., pp. 77–81.

41 *Wason* v. *Walter* (1868) L.R. 4 Q.B. 73.

42 *Cook* v. *Alexander* [1973] 3 W.L.R. 617 (C.A.).

43 A case in which privilege did not apply was *R.* v. *Creevey* (1813) 1 M. & S. 273. An M.P. made a speech in the House and garbled reports of it appeared in the newspapers. The M.P. then sent a correct report to the editor of a newspaper with the request that it be published. It was published and the M.P. was convicted of criminal libel on the basis of the speech. The House of Commons declined to take any action over the matter: C.J. (1812–13) 604; 26 H.C. Deb., col. 898 (1812–13).

44 (1839) 9 Ad. & E. 1. See below, pp. 250–3.

45 E.g. the resolution of 3 March 1762.

46 821 H.C. Deb., 5s., col. 993 (16 July 1971).

47 The privilege is not affected by an adjournment of the House and the forty-day period applies even after a dissolution.

48 Captain Ramsay's case, *Report from the Committee of Privileges,* H.C. 164 (1939–40).

49 See above, p. 185.

50 *Stourton* v. *Stourton* [1963] p. 302.

51 H.C. 34 (1967–8), para. 98. The Select Committee also proposed (ibid. paras. 102–4) that another privilege – that of exemption from attendance as a witness in court, which applies in both civil and criminal cases during the same periods of time as the

immunity from civil arrest – be abolished except where the Speaker considers that the member's attendance in the House should have priority. This proposal has also not been put into effect but since this privilege is usually waived, reform in this case is not so important.

52 For a full list see the *Report from the Select Committee on Parliamentary Privilege*, para. 113, H.C. 34 (1967–8).

53 For example, the reluctance of the courts to interfere in the procedure for the redistribution of seats is at least partly the result of this privilege: see above, pp. 37–8.

54 See above, pp. 49–50.

55 See above, p. 44.

56 (1884) 12 Q.B.D. 271.

57 In certain circumstances the member was permitted to make an affirmation but it was held by the Court of Appeal that this provision did not apply to Bradlaugh: *Clarke* v. *Bradlaugh* (1881) 7 Q.B.D. 38.

58 At p. 277.

59 At pp. 280–1.

60 It is interesting to note in this connection that it was expressly provided in the Parliament Act 1911 (sections 1(1), 1(3), 2(2) and 3), that the question whether the correct procedure is followed in any case where the Act applies is decided not by the courts but by the Speaker.

61 (1842) 8 Cl. & F. 710. See also *Lee* v. *Bude and Torrington Junction Railway Co.* (1871) L.R. 6 C.P. 576. See now *British Railways Board* v. *Pickin* [1974]. 1 All E.R. 609 (H.L.).

62 At p. 725.

63 May, op. cit., pp. 87–8. The decision in *R.* v. *Graham-Campbell, ex parte Herbert* [1935] 1 K.B. 594, in which it was held that the House did not need a licence to sell liquor, seems to take a remarkably wide view of what constitutes a proceeding in Parliament but the court was probably right in holding that the Licensing Acts were not intended to apply to the Houses of Parliament.

64 The judges were Sir Francis Pemberton and Sir Thomas Jones and they had given a judgment adverse to the views of the House in the case of *Jay and Topham's Case* (1689) 12 St. Tr. 821. The House ordered them to be taken into the custody of the Serjeant at Arms: C.J. (1688–93) 210, 213, 227.

65 *Stockdale* v. *Hansard* (1837) 2 M. & Rob. 9; 3 St. Tr. (N.S.) 725.
66 C.J. (1837) 419.
67 *Stockdale* v. *Hansard* (1839) 9 Ad. & E. 1.
68 *Stockdale* v. *Hansard* (1840) 11 Ad. & E. 253.
69 *Case of the Sheriff of Middlesex* (1840) 11 Ad. & E. 273.
70 This is still the rule today: see May, op. cit., pp. 117–19, and the cases there cited. At one time the courts disclaimed the power to interfere even when the ground of the commitment was actually stated; the contrary view was first put forward by Lord Ellenborough in *Burdett* v. *Abott* (1811) 14 East 1.
71 Stockdale and his solicitor were also imprisoned by the House before the matter finally ended.
72 [1963] P. 302 at 306.
73 *Fifth Report from the Committee of Privileges*, H.C. 305 (1956–7); 591 H.C. Deb. Col. 334 (8 July 1958). See de Smith, 'Parliamentary Privilege and the Bill of Rights' (1958) 21 *M.L.R.* 465.
74 The Select Committee on Parliamentary Privilege recommended that the penal power of the House should not in general be used to prevent persons bringing legal proceedings against M.P.s: H.C. 34 (1967–8) para. 48 (iii). For the Committee's comments on the London Electricity Board Case, see ibid. para. 80 et seq.

CHAPTER 13

1 Its Charter was renewed in 1964 (Cmnd. 2385) and runs until 1976. There was a Supplementary Charter in 1969 (Cmnd. 4096).
2 Ibid., para. 5.
3 See para. 16 of the Charter and paras. 12 and 16 of the Licence and Agreement (*Infra*).
4 Licence and Agreement of 7 July 1969 (Cmnd. 4095).
5 See para. 20 of the Charter.
6 The Television Act 1954.
7 The Independent Broadcasting Authority Act 1973, s. 1(1).
8 Cmnd. 4095 (1969), para. 13(2).
9 Ibid., 13(3).
10 Ibid., 13(4).
11 See Street, *Freedom, the Individual and the Law* (3rd edn, 1972), p. 75 and Wilson, *Cases and Materials on Constitutional and Administrative Law* (1966), p. 447.

12 This was done to prevent the Welsh service producing its own series of party political broadcasts. See the Annual Report and Accounts of the BBC, 1955–6 (Cmnd. 9809, 1956), p. 7.

13 This also applied to the IBA. See Street, op. cit., pp. 82–4.

14 Cmnd. 4095 (1969), para. 19(1).

15 Harman Grisewood, *One Thing at a Time* (1968), p. 199.

16 The Independent Broadcasting Authority Act 1973, s. 4(1) (a). For the extent to which the courts can review a decision of the IBA on this matter see *A.G. v. IBA* [1973] 1 All E.R. 689 (C.A.).

17 Ibid., s. 4(1) (b).

18 Ibid., s. 4(3).

19 Ibid., s. 22.

20 Ibid., s. 8(3) and Sch. 2, para. 8.

21 Street, op. cit., pp. 110–11.

22 Cmnd. 3169 (1966), p. 10.

23 Street, op. cit., p. 84.

24 See Martin Harrison in Butler and Pinto-Duschinsky, *The British General Election of 1970* (1971), p. 204.

25 See generally, Martin Harrison, op. cit.; the Annual Report and Accounts of the BBC for 1970–1 (Cmnd. 4824); and R. L. Leonard, *Elections in Britain* (1968), pp. 100–2.

26 See Street, op. cit., pp. 78–9.

27 *The Times*, 4 October 1971.

28 For further details, see Colin Seymour-Ure, *The Press, Politics and the Public* (1968) and Jeremy Tunstall, *The Westminster Lobby Correspondents* (1970).

29 Tunstall, op. cit., p. 124.

30 The rest of this paragraph is based on Seymour-Ure, op. cit. pp. 179–84.

31 He later became editor of the *New Statesman*.

32 For further details of this, and the other cases in this section, see David Williams, *Not in the Public Interest* (1965), chaps. 1 and 4.

33 See also s. 11(2) of the European Communities Act 1972 which provides protection for classified information relating to Euratom.

34 S. 8(1). Sentences of more than 14 years have been imposed in cases in which the charge has been conspiracy to contravene section 1 (in which case there is no limit on the length of imprisonment) or in which the accused has been sentenced to consecutive terms of imprisonment on separate counts.

35 *Chandler* v. *D.P.P.* [1964] A.C. 763. The accused had organized a demonstration at a NATO airfield with the object of grounding the aircraft. They were convicted of conspiring to incite others to commit, and conspiring to commit, a breach of section 1.

36 As amended by the 1920 Act. See especially ss. 8(2) and 10 and Sch. 1.

37 It was held in *Lewis* v. *Cattle* [1938] 2 K.B. 454 that a policeman is included in this description.

38 Authorization need not, however, be express: according to the Home Office, 'the communication of official information is proper if such communication can be fairly regarded as part of the job of the officer concerned'. Senior civil servants exercise a considerable degree of personal judgment in deciding what information may be disclosed; Ministers may authorize themselves. See the *Report of the Departmental Committee on Section 2 of the Official Secrets Act 1911* (Cmnd. 5104, 1972).

39 See the Report by Justice and the British Committee of the International Press Institute entitled *The Law and the Press* (1965), para. 62.

40 See s. 8 of the 1911 Act.

41 Cmnd. 5104 (1972).

42 858 H.C. Deb., cols. 1885 et seq. (29 June 1973).

43 Since the operation of the system does not normally receive publicity, fully up-to-date information cannot always be obtained. The description that follows is based largely on two Government reports – the *Report on Security Procedures in the Public Service* (Cmnd. 1681 of 1962) and the *Report of the Committee of Privy Councillors Appointed to Inquire into 'D' Notice Matters* (Cmnd. 3309 of 1967). The latter report gave details of the system as it operated in 1967; later developments are sometimes difficult to discover.

44 See the *Spectator* of 3 March 1967 and Cmnd. 3309 (1967), p. 6. These Notices were subsequently withdrawn and reworded.

45 The power to do this was given to the Government by section 4 of the Official Secrets Act 1920.

46 See the *Report of the Committee of Privy Councillors Appointed to Inquire into D Notice Matters* (Cmnd. 3309 of 1967).

47 Cmnd. 3312 (1967).

48 Harold Wilson, *The Labour Government 1964–70*, p. 373.

49 See above, p. 82.

50 The Government is not, of course, the only body that might seek

to limit the freedom of the media. Both Parliament and the Courts might use their contempt powers to restrict the activities of the press. For contempt of Parliament, see above, pp. 240-4 and for contempt of court, see above, pp. 185-9.

CHAPTER 14

1 Cmnd. 218 (1957).
2 This Act was replaced by the Immigration Act 1971 but the appeals procedure was continued.
3 For these and subsequent figures relating to 1971 see the report of the Council on Tribunals for 1971-2 (H.C. 13 of 1972-3).
4 By the Redundancy Payments Act 1965, the tribunals were empowered to increase the assessment also.
5 Redundancy Payments Act 1965.
6 As amended by National Insurance Act 1966, s. 9. There is one Chief National Insurance Commissioner and a number of other Commissioners; for difficult cases, three may sit together.
7 Lands Tribunal Act 1949, s. 2(4).
8 Tribunals and Inquiries Act 1971, s. 8.
9 Ibid., s. 7(1).
10 E.g. National Insurance Commissioners must be barristers or advocates of not less than 10 years' standing (National Insurance Act 1966, s. 9(1)). Members of the Lands Tribunal must be lawyers or otherwise professionally qualified (Lands Tribunal Act 1949 s. 2(1)).
11 S. 12.
12 See below, pp. 341-2.
13 See generally R. E. Wraith and G. B. Lamb, *Public Inquiries as an Instrument of Government*.
14 See Wraith and Lamb, op. cit., App. I.
15 The principal statute is now the consolidating Town and Country Planning Act 1971.
16 See now the Act of 1971, ss. 6-21 (as amended).
17 If the local authority and the applicant agree, the dispute can be settled by making written representations to the Minister instead of an inquiry. This is now done for about half the appeals.
18 See the Act of 1971, ss. 22-34 (as amended).
19 See the Act of 1971, s. 35.
20 The Minister has power to revoke the grant of planning permis-

sion but this is rarely done and involves the payment of heavy compensation to the applicant. See the Act of 1971, s. 45.

21 Op. cit., p. 174.

22 E.g. development comprising not more than 30 dwelling-houses (see S.I. 1970 7 No. 1454).

23 See above, p. 275.

24 S. 1(1) (c).

25 Ss. 10, 11.

26 S. 12(1) (b). For the importance of this to judicial review, see below, pp. 341–2.

CHAPTER 15

1 The King could, however, sue in the courts.

2 Except for a tort concerned with the wrongful taking of property.

3 The only exceptions to this at common law are a narrow range of situations in which a defence under the prerogative or the act of state doctrine might arise: see below, pp. 303–8.

4 *Adams* v. *Naylor* [1946] A.C. 543.

5 *Royster* v. *Cavey* [1947] K.B. 204.

6 *Rederiaktiebolaget Amphitrite* v. *The King* [1921] 3 K.B. 500.

7 Ibid., at p. 503.

8 It is important to note that Rowlatt J. held that the Government did not intend to enter into a contract *because* it had no capacity to enter into such a contract. Denning J. (as he then was) was therefore mistaken when he said in *Robertson* v. *Minister of Pensions* [1949] 1 K.B. 227 at 231 that the doctrine of executive necessity was not necessary for the decision in the *Amphitrite*. It should also be noted that Rowlatt J. was careful to distinguish the case where the Government enters into a commercial contract.

9 The only other cases in which the principle has been applied to the Crown are *Board of Trade* v. *Temperley Steam Shipping Co. Ltd* (1926) 26 Lloyd's List Rep. 76, affirmed (1927) 27 Lloyd's List Rep. 230 (C.A.); and *Commissioners of Crown Lands* v. *Page* [1960] 2 Q.B. 274 (C.A.). Both these cases, however, were concerned only with implied terms.

10 *Birkdale District Electric Supply Co.* v. *Southport Corporation* [1926] A.C. 355 and 364.

11 *British Transport Commission* v. *Westmorland C.C.* [1958] A.C. 126. It is not quite clear whether this test must be applied on the basis of the facts as they exist when the contract is made or when the case comes before the court. Since the effect of incompatibility is to make the contract void, it could be argued that the relevant time is when the contract is made (Colin Turpin, *Government Contracts* (1972), p. 24) but there are dicta in the *Westmorland* case which suggest that the latter time may be correct (at pp. 147–8 and 153).

12 [1962] 1 Q.B. 283.

13 See per Devlin J. at pp. 301–3.

14 [1971] 2 All E.R. 277. For a comment on this case, see Evans, (1972) 35 *M.L.R.* 88.

15 The injunction was actually refused on the ground that it would mean granting specific performance of a contract to do continuous acts (managing the airfield) over a period of years. This is a principle which applies in private law as well.

16 [1951] 2 K.B. 476 (C.A.).

17 The by-laws were not to come into effect until 1950 and the corporation was prepared to accept that the contract would be frustrated when this happened because it would be commercially impossible for the company to carry it out. The company, however, wanted the contract terminated in 1948 on the ground that by making the by-laws the corporation had repudiated the contract by anticipatory breach of it.

18 At pp. 484–5.

19 Compare, for example, *Ayr Harbour Trustees* v. *Oswald* (1883) 8 App. Cas. 623 (H.L.) with *Stourcliffe Estates Co. Ltd.* v. *Corporation of Bournemouth* [1910] 2 Ch. 12 (C.A.).

20 Two cases which gave the principle a very wide scope were subsequently criticized in later cases: *In re South Eastern Railway Co. and Whiffen's Contract* [1907] 2 Ch. 366 was criticized in *Stourcliffe Estates Company Ltd.* v. *Corporation of Bournemouth* [1910] 2 Ch. 12 at pp. 20–1 and 23–4; and *York Corporation* v. *Henry Leetham and Sons* [1924] 1 Ch. 557 was criticized in *Birkdale District Electric Supply Co.* v. *Southport Corporation* [1926] A.C. 355 at pp. 366 and 374 (see also the Court of Appeal decision: [1925] Ch. 794 at pp. 820 and 823).

21 See below, pp. 311–12.

22 See P. W. Hogg, 'The Doctrine of Executive Necessity in the Law of Contract' (1970) 44 *Australian L.J.* 154.

23 See *Re Liverpool Taxi Owners' Association* [1972] 2 All E.R. 589 at 594, per Denning M. R. (C.A.).

24 (1865) L.R. 1 Q.B. 173 at pp. 209–10 (*per* Shee J.) Cf the views of Cockburn C.J. at pp. 200–1.

25 *New South Wales* v. *Bardolph* (1934) 52 C.L.R. 455. See further J. D. B. Mitchell *The Contracts of Public Authorities* (1954), pp. 68–75.

26 *Plimmer* v. *Mayor of Wellington* (1884) 9 App. Cas. 699 (P.C.); *Orient Steam Navigation Co.* v. *The Crown* (1925) 21 Ll. L. Rep. 301; *A.-G. to the Prince of Wales* v. *Collom* [1916] 2 K.B. 193 at 204. See further, Farrer, 'A Prerogative Fallacy – "That the Crown is not Bound by Estoppel"' (1933) 49 *L.Q.R.* 511.

27 See above, p. 317.

28 *Rhyl U.D.C.* v. *Rhyl Amusements Ltd.* [1959] 1 W.L.R. 465. (But see now, on the particular point in issue, the Town and Country Planning Act 1959, s. 29.)

29 In the unreported case of *Minister of Agriculture* v. *Hulkin*, quoted by Cassels J. in *Minister of Agriculture* v. *Matthews* [1950] 1 K.B. 148 at 153.

30 [1937] A.C. 610 (P.C.) See also: *The Queen* v. *Blenkinsop* [1892] 1 Q.B. 43 and *Sunderland Corporation* v. *Priestman* [1927] 2 Ch. 107 at 116.

31 Revised Statutes of New Brunswick 1927, c. 127.

32 For another example of this rule see *Commissioners of Customs and Excise* v. *Hebson* (1953) 2 Ll. L. Rep. 382.

33 [1949] 1 K.B. 227.

34 He had appealed from the Minister's decision to the Pensions Appeal Tribunal which affirmed the Minister's decision. He then had a right of appeal to the court.

35 This aspect of the decision has been criticized by Ganz, 'Estoppel and Res Judicata in Administrative Law' [1965] *P.L.* 237 at 244–5.

36 Royal Warrant of 29 June 1940, para. 2(4).

37 He actually based his decision on the doctrine of promissory (equitable) estoppel enunciated in *Central London Property Trust Ltd* v. *High Trees House Ltd* [1947] K.B. 130 but this was unnecessary since it could have been decided on the basis of legal estoppel.

38 At p. 232.

39 [1950] 2 K.B. 16 (C.A.); [1951] A.C. 837 (H.L.).

40 [1951] A.C. 837 at 845.

41 Ibid. at 849.

42 [1962] 1 Q.B. 416. (Div. Ct.)

43 It is not certain that the letter did contain a pure representation of fact – it might be thought that an inference of law was also involved – but the court was prepared to assume that this aspect of the company's case was correct.

44 At p. 424 (*per* Parker C. J.).

45 [1971] 1 Q.B. 222. (C.A.).

46 At p. 230.

47 Ibid.

48 This decision may also be criticized as a misapplication of the doctrine of estoppel. The representation – that the variation was immaterial and planning permission was unnecessary – could not be considered to be a representation of fact. The architect was not misled on any question of fact (he knew the facts much better than the planning officer) but he was given what turned out to be a wrong opinion of law, caused, no doubt, by the planning officer's misunderstanding of the facts.

49 *Supra*.

50 *Supra*.

51 See, as regards the *Southend* case, the Town and Country Planning Act 1947, s. 17 and, as regards the *Westminster* case, the Town and Country Planning Act 1968, s. 43.

52 *Supra*.

53 Under section 64 of the Town and Country Planning Act 1968 (which came into force just before the facts of the *Westminster* case occurred) the planning authority could have delegated power to its officer to make decisions of the kind involved in this case. No such delegation had in fact been made, but Sachs L. J. based his judgment (which was also in favour of the developers) on the idea of an implied delegation. It had been the normal practice for the developers' architect to submit minor alterations in the plans to the planning officer, who would say whether he considered the alterations to be material. It was the continued existence of this practice after section 64 had come into effect that Sachs L. J. regarded as showing that an implied delegation had taken place. There are, however, many objections to this

approach, the most forceful of which is that under sub-section (5) of that section a decision of the planning officer must be communicated in writing to the applicant, and this had not occurred in the case. For a detailed comment, see Evans, (1971) 34 M.L.R. 335.

54 It could be argued that the *ultra vires* doctrine should apply only to acts which are beyond the powers of the authority, and not to acts which could have been performed by the authority but not by the officer in question. But there is no very satisfactory reason why the doctrine should be limited in this way.

55 It has been held in two cases (*Wells* v. *Minister of Housing and Local Government* [1967] 2 All E.R. 1041 (C.A.) and *Re L.* (*A.C.*) (*an infant*) [1971] 3 All E.R. 743) that estoppel can apply to a public authority to prevent its relying on technicalities such as procedural irregularities.

56 Cf *Hedley Byrne & Co. Ltd* v. *Heller & Partners Ltd* [1964] A.C. 465 and *Minister of Housing* v. *Sharp* [1970] 2 Q.B. 223. This suggestion was first put forward by Professor S. A. de Smith; see his *Judicial Review of Administrative Action* (2nd edn) p. 298, n. 77.

57 *Dunn* v. *Macdonald* [1897] 1 Q.B. 555; *The Prometheus* (1949) 82 Ll. L. Rep. 859. See also *Macbeath* v. *Haldimand* (1786) 1 T.R. 172 and *Gidley* v. *Lord Palmerston* (1822) 3 Brod. & B. 275.

58 [1953] A.C. 461.

59 At p. 479.

60 Ibid.

61 Colin Turpin, *Government Contracts* (1972), p. 35.

62 S. 2(1) (a).

63 Or his estate is liable.

64 See Glanville Williams, *Crown Proceedings* (1948) pp. 43–5.

65 It has been suggested (Glanville Williams, op. cit., p. 44) that the object of this provision was to ensure that the Crown would not be liable when the servant could invoke the defence of act of State (discussed below). If this was so, however, the provision was probably unnecessary.

66 S. 38(2).

67 See *Bank voor Handel en Scheepvaart N.V.* v. *Administrator of Hungarian Property* [1954] A.C. 584 (H.L.).

68 As to when a public corporation may be a Crown servant or agent, see Griffith, 'Public Corporations as Crown Servants' (1952) 9 *U. of Toronto L.J.* 169.

69 S. 2(3).

70 S. 38(2).

71 As to policemen, see *Conway* v. *Rimmer* [1968] A.C. 910 at 953 and 974–5 (H.L.) (*dicta*).

72 Judges are normally not personally liable for acts done in their judicial capacity: see above, pp. 183–4. This means that neither the Crown nor the individual judge can be sued.

73 Ss. 2(1) (b), 2(1) (c) and 2(2).

74 (1866) L.R. 1 Ex. 265, affirmed (1868) L.R. 3 H.L. 330.

75 At pp. 308–11.

76 The prerogative is the name given to the special rights and powers of the Monarch which are not shared by any subject. In modern times they are normally exercised on the advice of the Government.

77 It is probably not necessary that war should actually have been declared: thus in *The Broadmayne* [1916] P. 64 a proclamation under the prerogative authorizing the requisitioning of British ships was accepted as valid even though it was made one day before the war began.

78 [1965] A.C. 75.

79 S. 1(1).

80 However, this rule would presumably not apply if the legislation expressly preserved the prerogative, as was the case with s. 9 of the Emergency Powers (Defence) Act 1939.

81 [1920] A.C. 508.

82 See the comments of Lord Morris in *Nissan* v. *A.-G.* [1970] A.C. 179 at 220–1.

83 [1921] 2 A.C. 262.

84 It has been suggested that there are some exceptions to this but it is rather doubtful whether any of these exceptions actually exists. First, there are some dicta in *Johnstone* v. *Pedlar* [1921] 2 A.C. 262 at 293 (*per* Lord Finlay) that the defence might be available against an alien if he were guilty of treasonable activities, but no firm conclusions were reached. Secondly, some writers have thought that the defence might apply to acts committed within the U.K. if the person affected was outside the country: for example where the property within the U.K. of an alien resident abroad was taken by the Crown. (See the authorities cited in Collier, 'Act of State as a Defence against a British Subject' [1968] *C.L.J.* 102 at 112–13.) It would be

rather startling, however, if the Crown could seize goods imported into Britain without the owners having any redress if they were aliens resident abroad. Thirdly, it is sometimes said that the defence can apply to acts against enemy aliens (i.e. citizens of countries at war with the U.K.). It is true that the Crown can intern (*R.* v. *Bottrill, ex p. Kuechenmeister* [1947] 1 K.B. 41) or deport (*Netz* v. *Ede* [1946] Ch. 224) enemy aliens but it is probably better to regard these actions as lawful acts under the prerogative than to say that the courts lack jurisdiction to consider whether they are lawful or not.

85 (1848) 2 Ex. 167.

86 [1970] A.C. 179.

87 Ibid., at p. 227.

88 Ibid., at p. 237.

89 This rule is preserved by the Crown Proceedings Act 1947, s. 40(2) (f).

90 Harry Street, 'The Effect of Statutes Upon the Rights and Liabilities of the Crown' (1948) 7 *U. of Toronto L.J.* 357 at pp. 359–69.

91 *Gorton Local Board* v. *Prison Commissioners* [1904] 2 K.B. 164 n. at 167 n. *per* Day J.

92 [1947] A.C. 58.

93 At p. 61.

94 At p. 63.

95 At pp. 61–2.

96 [1904] 2 K.B. 164.

97 *Clark* v. *Downes* (1931) 145 L.T. 20; *Wirral Estates, Ltd* v. *Shaw* [1932] 2 K.B. 247; *Wheeler* v. *Wirral Estates, Ltd.* [1935] 1 K.B. 294; *Rudler* v. *Franks* [1947] K.B. 530. (See now the Rent Act 1968, ss. 4, 70(3) (a) and 116.)

98 See, for example, the Road Traffic Act 1960, s. 250; the Road Traffic Regulation Act 1967, s. 97; and the Rent Act 1968, s. 116. See also the Crown Proceedings Act 1947, s. 4.

99 See Street, op. cit. (note 90, above), at pp. 373 et seq.

100 [1927] 1 K.B. 269 at 294.

101 Street, op. cit., at pp. 375–8.

102 *Cooper* v. *Hawkins* [1904] 2 K.B. 164.

103 *Bank voor Handel en Scheepvaart N.V.* v. *Administrator of Hungarian Property* [1954] A.C. 584 (H.L.).

104 Ibid. at p. 630.

105 Ibid.

106 Crown Proceedings Act 1947, s. 17.

107 An officer of the Crown is defined in s. 38(2) to include a servant of the Crown (and thus to apply to a Minister).

108 [1955] 1 Ch. 567.

109 S. 21(1).

110 *International General Electric Company of New York Ltd* v. *Commissioners of Customs and Excise* [1962] 1 Ch. 784; *Underhill* v. *Ministry of Food* [1950] 1 All E.R. 591.

111 S. 25.

112 *Duncan* v. *Cammell, Laird & Co.* [1942] A.C. 624 at 635.

113 *Supra.*

114 *Glasgow Corporation* v. *Central Land Board* 1956 S.C. (H.L.) 1. See also *Whitehall* v. *Whitehall* 1957 S.C. 30.

115 See *R.* v. *Snider* (1953) 2 D.L.R. (2d) 9 (Canada); *Corbett* v. *Social Security Commission* [1962] N.Z.L.R. 878 (New Zealand); *Bruce* v. *Waldron* [1963] V.L.R. 3 (Australia).

116 *Re Grosvenor Hotel, London (No. 2)* [1965] Ch. 1210; *Merricks* v. *Nott-Bower* [1965] 1 Q.B. 57; *Wednesbury Corporation* v. *Minister of Housing and Local Government* [1965] 1 W.L.R. 261. But in *Conway* v. *Rimmer* itself the majority in the Court of Appeal felt obliged to follow the *Thetis* doctrine: [1967] 2 All E.R. 1260.

117 [1968] A.C. 910. The comments that follow are based on the judgments in this case.

118 See for example at p. 957 (Lord Morris) and p. 995 (Lord Upjohn).

119 [1972] 2 All E.R. 1057 (H.L.).

120 The Gaming Act 1968, s. 10(3). For another case where similar issues were raised see *R.* v. *Gaming Board for Great Britain, ex parte Benain* [1970] 2 All E.R. 528 (C.A.) discussed below, pp. 331–2.

121 What actually happened was that witness summonses were issued against the Chief Constable and the secretary to the Board requiring the former to produce a copy of the letter and the latter the letter itself. The Attorney-General (acting on behalf of the Home Secretary) then moved the Divisional Court for an order of certiorari to quash the summonses.

122 Ibid., Sch. 2, para. 4(6).

123 See *Duncan* v. *Cammell, Laird* [1942] A.C. 624 at 643; *Gain* v. *Gain* [1962] 1 W.L.R. 1469 and *Broome* v. *Broome* [1955] P. 190.

See also the statement by Lord Kilmuir L.C. in the House of Lords on 6 June 1956 (197 H.L. Deb., 5s., c. 747).

124 See *Rogers* v. *Secretary of State* [1972] 2 All E.R. 1057 at 1060, 1065 and 1066. Another recent case of importance is *Alfred Crompton Ltd* v. *Commissioners of Customs (No. 2)* [1973] 2 All E.R. 1169 (H.L.).

125 In neither *Conway* v. *Rimmer* nor *Rogers* v. *Secretary of State* was this the case. For the contrary view, see the Scottish case of *Whitehall* v. *Whitehall* [1957] S.C. 30.

CHAPTER 16

1 This is not always true where there is a procedural irregularity: in this case the court will have to decide whether the procedural requirement in question is mandatory or merely directory. It is only in the former case that the action taken will be invalid. It is, however, extremely difficult in practice to decide which requirements will be regarded by the courts as mandatory and which will be held to be merely directory (unless the relevant legislation makes this clear). The theory is that only those requirements which are really important will be classified as mandatory but this test is vague.

2 So called, because they were originally mainly used by the King. Proceedings are always brought in the name of the Crown even when the applicant is a private citizen. Habeas corpus is also a prerogative remedy and this is also sometimes used to challenge administrative action; e.g. in deportation cases.

3 (1863) 14 C.B. (N.S.) 180.

4 This case is a good example of a collateral challenge.

5 At p. 194.

6 See the statement by Salmon L. J. in *Re H.K. (An Infant)* [1967] 2 Q.B. 617 at 633.

7 [1964] A.C. 40. (See especially at p. 130 *per* Lord Hodson.) Since this decision the relevant legislation has been changed to give an express right to a hearing. See pp. 133–5.

8 [1967] 2 Q.B. 617.

9 Now replaced by the Immigration Act 1971.

10 At p. 630.

11 *Bates* v. *Lord Hailsham* [1972] 3 All E.R. 1019.

12 [1967] 2 A.C. 337.

13 At p. 349.

14 (1863) 14 C.B. (N.S.) 180.

15 *Durayappah* v. *Fernando* at p. 352.

16 [1964] A.C. 40. See especially pp. 74–9 where Lord Reid expressly rejected the suggestion, put forward by the Privy Council in *Nakkuda Ali* v. *Jayaratne* [1951] A.C. 66 at 78, that natural justice will not apply unless there is a 'superadded' duty to act judicially.

17 *Gaiman* v. *National Association for Mental Health* [1970] 2 All E.R. 362 at 376 (Megarry J.).

18 [1967] 2 Q.B. 617 (discussed above).

19 *R.* v. *Leman Street Police Station Inspector, ex p. Venicoff* [1920] 3 K.B. 72.

20 *Schmidt* v. *Home Secretary* [1969] 2 Ch. 149.

21 Immigration Act 1971, Part II. There are certain cases in which there is no right of appeal (see ss. 13(5), 14(3) and 15(3) and (4)) but it appears that an informal hearing will be given in these cases.

22 *Cooper* v. *Wandsworth Board of Works* (1863) 14 C.B.N.S. 180 (discussed above). See also *Local Government Board* v. *Arlidge* [1915] A.C. 120 at 132 (*per* Viscount Haldane L.C.); *Errington* v. *Minister of Health* [1935] 1 K.B. 249 (both housing cases); and *R.* v. *Birmingham City Justice, ex p. Chris Foreign Foods (Wholesalers) Ltd.* [1970] 3 All E.R. 945 (food unfit for human consumption).

23 *Durayappah* v. *Fernando* [1967] 2 A.C. 337 at 350–1; *Re Pergamon Press Ltd* [1970] 3 All E.R. 535.

24 There are a number of cases concerning trade unions: see, for example, *Taylor* v. *National Union of Seamen* [1967] 1 W.L.R. 532 and *Edwards* v. *SOGAT* [1970] 3 W.L.R. 713.

25 C/f *Pett* v. *Greyhound Racing Association* [1968] 2 All E.R. 545 and [1969] 2 All E.R. 221 (inquiry into doping of greyhound which could result in the trainer losing his licence). In *R.* v. *Gaming Board for Great Britain, ex. p. Benaim* [1970] 2 All E.R. 528 natural justice (in a rather basic form) was held to apply to the *granting* of a licence.

26 [1953] 1 W.L.R. 1150.

27 [1951] A.C. 66.

28 See *per* Denning M.R. in *R.* v. *Gaming Board for Great Britain, ex p. Benaim* [1970] 2 All E.R. 528 at 533.

29 *Ridge* v. *Baldwin* [1964] A.C. 40; *Re Godden* [1971] 3 All E.R. 20. Both these cases concerned police officers (the first was a chief constable and the second a chief inspector).

30 But in *Malloch* v. *Aberdeen Corporation* [1971] 2 All E.R. 1278 (H.L.) it was held that a Scottish school-teacher could not be dismissed without a hearing even though he was dismissable at pleasure.

31 For the impact of the Industrial Relations Act 1971 on this question see *Earl* v. *Slater and Wheeler Ltd,* [1973] 1 All E.R. 145 (N.I.R.C.).

32 *Enderby Town F.C.* v. *Football Association Ltd.* [1971] 1 All E. R. 215.

33 But it has been held not to apply to a charity incorporated as a company limited by guarantee: *Gaiman* v. *National Association* for *Mental Health* [1970] 2 All E.R. 362.

34 *John* v. *Rees* [1970] 1 Ch. 345.

35 *Glynn* v. *Keele University* [1971] 2 All E.R. 89; see also *Ex parte Bolchover, The Times,* 7 October 1970.

36 *R.* v. *Aston University Senate, ex p. Roffey* [1969] 2 Q.B. 538.

37 *Vidyodaya University of Ceylon* v. *Silva* [1964] 3 All E.R. 865.

38 See *Malloch* v. *Aberdeen Corporation* [1971] 2 All E.R. 1278 at 1295 (*per* Lord Wilberforce) (H.L.). In many British universities today there are regulations granting members of staff a right to a hearing if they are threatened with dismissal.

39 See below, pp. 350–4.

40 See *Abbott* v. *Sullivan* [1952] 1 K.B. 189 at 198 (*per* Denning L. J.) (C.A.); *Lee* v. *Showmen's Guild of Great Britain* [1952] 2 Q.B. 329 at 342 (*per* Denning L. J.) (C.A.); *Bonsor* v. *Musicians' Union* [1954] 1 Ch. 479 at 485–6 (*per* Denning L. J.) (C.A.); *Edwards* v. *SOGAT* [1971] Ch. 354 at 376–7 (*per* Denning M. R.) and 381–2 (*per* Sachs L. J.) (C.A.); *Enderby Town Football Club* v. *The Football Association* [1971] 1 All E.R. 215 at 219 (*per* Denning M. R.) (C.A.). For some of the older authorities, including some contrary to those above, see Citrine's *Trade Union Law* (3rd edn 1967) pp. 283–4.

41 *Re Liverpool Taxi Owners' Association* [1972] 2 All E.R. 589 (C.A.).

42 *Jeffs* v. *New Zealand Dairy Production and Marketing Board* [1967] 1 A.C. 551 (P.C.).

43 See *Pett* v. *Greyhound Racing Association No. 1* [1968] 2 All E.R.

545; *ditto No. 2* [1969] 2 All E.R. 221; *Enderby Town F.C.* v. *Football Association* [1971] 1 All E.R. 215 (C.A.).

44 For a full discussion, see J. E. Alder, 'Representation before Tribunals' [1972] P.L. 278.

45 [1970] 2 All E.R. 528 (C.A.).

46 See Sch. 2, para. 4(5) and (6).

47 For another case in which the courts protected the Board's informants, see *Rogers* v. *Secretary of State* [1972] 2 All E.R. 1057 (H.L.), discussed above, pp. 315–16.

48 In another case in which a similar decision was reached, Lord Denning M. R. said that in certain rare cases the evidence of a witness may be so confidential that it could not be put to those affected by it, even in general terms; he considered that in such a case it should be ignored by the decision-maker in making his decision: *Re Pergamon Press Ltd* [1970] 3 All E.R. 535 at 540. A different view was, however, tentatively expressed in the House of Lords by Lord Salmon in *Rogers* v. *Secretary of State* [1972] 2 All E.R. 1057 at 1069. He considered that the information should be taken into account even though the applicant could not be told anything about it.

49 If this could be proved it would be a ground for setting aside the decision even if the decision-maker was not obliged to follow natural justice. See below, pp. 344–50.

50 (1852) 3 H.L.C. 759.

51 [1933] 2 K.B. 696.

52 (1858) EL, BL & EL 101 (= 120 E.R. 445).

53 [1897] 2 Q.B. 468.

54 *Taylor* v. *National Union of Seamen* [1967] 1 All E.R. 767.

55 *Re Godden* [1971] 3 All E.R. 20 (C.A.).

56 *Cooper* v. *Wilson* [1937] 2 K.B. 309. This rule did not, however, apply at common law to judges, who in the past sometimes participated in appeals against their own decisions.

57 [1970] 1 W.L.R. 937.

58 But they decided against the teacher on other grounds.

59 [1969] 1 Q.B. 577 (C.A.).

60 Ibid. at p. 599.

61 *R.* v. *Camborne Justices, ex. p. Pearce* [1955] 1 Q.B. 41 at 51.

62 S. 35.

63 See *Wilkinson* v. *Barking Corporation* [1948] 1 K.B. 721 at 728 (*per* Scott L. J.

64 This happened when the courts of Saskatchewan had to determine the constitutional question whether the provincial legislature could tax the salaries of Saskatchewan judges: *Re The Constitutional Questions Act* [1936] 4 D.L.R. 134 (Sask. C.A.). This case went on appeal to the Privy Council (where the decision of the Saskatchewan Court of Appeal was confirmed): *The Judges* v. *A.G. for Saskatchewan* (1937) 53 T.L.R. 464.

65 *R.* v. *Nailsworth Licensing Justices, ex p. Bird* [1953] 1 W.L.R. 1046.

66 There may be exceptions to this rule in certain cases.

67 It is assumed that the courts interpret the provision according to its normal meaning. In special circumstances it is possible that the courts might decide that Parliament intended the Minister to be the judge of whether X was so; in this case the courts would accept his decision as correct.

68 His decision will be open to challenge if he satisfies himself as to something other than X (*Maradana Mosque Trustees* v. *Mahmud* [1967] A.C. 13 at 25 (P.C.)) and it is even possible that the courts might quash his decision if he had no evidence before him that X was so or if his decision was grossly unreasonable: see *Ashbridge Investments Ltd* v. *Minister of Housing and Local Government* [1965] 3 All E. R. 371 (C.A.); *Coleen Properties Ltd* v. *Minister of Housing and Local Government* [1971] 1 All E.R. 1049 (C.A.). More difficult problems arise if the formula – 'If the Minister has reason to believe that X is so . . .' is employed. This might be interpreted as meaning 'If the Minister is satisfied that he has reason to believe . . .' (subjective condition) or it may mean that reasonable grounds must in fact exist and they must have been known to the Minister when he made his decision. Here the court decides whether there are reasonable grounds. For the former interpretation see the wartime decision of *Liversidge* v. *Anderson* [1942] A.C. 206 (H.L.) and for the latter (and more normal) interpretation see *Nakkuda Ali* v. *Jayaratne* [1951] A.C. 66 (P.C.).

69 See D.M. Gordon, 'The Relation of Facts of Jurisdiction' (1929) 45 *L.Q.R.* 459.

70 For example *R.* v. *Bolton* (1841) 1Q.B. 66 (113 E.R. 1054).

71 [1951] 2 K.B. 1.

72 At p. 10.

73 Ibid. at p. 6 (*per* Lord Goddard C. J.).

74 Ibid. *per* Devlin J. at p. 10.

75 See the decision of the House of Lords in *Anisminic* v. *Foreign Compensation Commission* [1969] 2 A.C. 147 which suggests that almost any error on a question of law might be regarded by the courts as going to jurisdiction.

76 [1922] 2 A.C. 128 at 151. See also *R.* v. *Ludlow, ex p. Barnsley Corporation* [1947] 1 K.B. 634 at 639 (*per* Lord Goddard C. J.) and the authorities there cited.

77 See, for example, *Allison* v. *General Medical Council* [1894] 1 Q.B. 750, and *Coleen Properties Ltd* v. *Minister of Housing and Local Government* [1971] 1 All E.R. 1049 (C.A.). See further H. W. R. Wade, *Administrative Law* (3rd edn 1971), pp. 98–101.

78 [1951] 1 K.B. 711; affirmed [1952] 1 K.B. 338 (C.A.).

79 [1952] 1 K.B. 338 at 352.

80 *R.* v. *Medical Appeal Tribunal, ex p. Gilmore* [1957] 1 Q.B. 574 (C.A.).

81 This provision also applies to a decision taken by a Minister in a matter in which there was provision for a statutory inquiry.

82 In the case of *R.* v. *Chertsey Justices, ex p. Franks* [1961] 2 Q.B. 152 it was held that under the common law oral reasons given by a magistrate may form part of the record; but this seems rather hard to accept.

83 In two decisions by Megaw J. (*Re Poyser and Mills' Arbitration* [1964] 2 Q.B. 467 and *Givaudan & Co. Ltd* v. *Minister of Housing and Local Government* [1966] 3 All E.R. 696) it was held that failure to give reasons, where there is a statutory obligation to do so, is in itself an error of law so as to allow the decision to be quashed. But this view was rejected by the Divisional Court in *Mountview Court Properties Ltd* v. *Devlin* (1970) 21 P. & C.R. 689. This seems the better view.

84 See especially the Tribunals and Inquiries Act 1971, s. 13.

85 The discussion that follows does not apply to a discretionary power stemming from the Royal Prerogative. The courts can consider whether a prerogative power exists but they cannot investigate the way it is exercised.

86 A power granted to a Minister may, however, normally be exercised in his name by civil servants. See above, pp. 88–9.

87 The rules mentioned in this paragraph are not limited to discretionary decisions: they also apply to decisions of fact and law. Thus the courts will intervene if a tribunal refuses to consider

a case, or improperly delegates the power of decision, or ¦
under the dictation of another person. An obvious exampl(
this would be if a magistrate took orders from someone else as
to how he should decide a case.

88 [1970] 3 All E.R. 871.

89 See *Lavender's* case (above) and *Stringer* v. *Minister of Housing and
Local Government* [1971] 1 All E.R. 65.

90 See *R. v. Port of London Authority, ex p. Kynoch Ltd* [1919] 1 K.B.
176 at 184 (*per* Bankes L. J.). Bankes L. J. made a distinction
between 'policies' and 'rules' but this has not been adopted in
the text because it is felt that there is no great difference between
the two in this context: see *British Oxygen Co.* v. *Minister of
Technology* [1971] A.C. 610 at 625 (*per* Lord Reid).

91 In some cases the courts might order an authority to rescind an
improper rule or policy: see *R.* v. *Metropolitan Police Commissioner, ex p. Blackburn* [1968] 2 Q.B. 118 (C.A.).

92 [1897] 1 Q.B. 132.

93 [1905] A.C. 426.

94 At p. 432.

95 [1963] 2 Q.B. 243 (C.A.).

96 Article 20(2) (b) of the Aliens Order 1953 (S.I. 1671) empowered the Secretary of State to make a deportation order
against an alien if he deemed it to be 'conducive to the public
good' to do so.

97 For a detailed consideration of these problems, see S. A. de
Smith, *Judicial Review of Administrative Action* (2nd edn 1968),
pp. 308–12.

98 Ibid., p. 320.

99 [1925] A.C 578.

100 [1955] 1 Ch. 210. (C.A.).

101 At p. 236.

102 See *Associated Provincial Picture Houses Ltd* v. *Wednesbury Corporation* [1948] 1 K.B. 223 at 229 (*per* Lord Greene M. R.).

103 S. A. de Smith, *Judicial Review of Administrative Action* (2nd edn
1968) p. 331.

104 *Associated Provincial Picture Houses Ltd* v. *Wednesbury Corporation*
[1948] 1 K.B. 223 at pp. 229–30 (*per* Lord Greene M. R.).

105 *The Times*, 14 October 1972; (1972) 116 S.J. 862.

106 Thus it was held in *Edinburgh and Dalkeith Railway* v. *Wauchope*
(1842) 8 Cl. & F. 710 (8 E.R. 279) that a private Act of

Parliament could not be challenged on the ground that due notice had not been given to persons affected by it (as required by the Standing Orders of the House of Commons). See now also *Pickin* v. *British Railways Board* [1974] 1 All E.R. 609 (H.L.).

107 For a discussion of the parliamentary aspects of delegated legislation, see below, pp. 215-18.

108 See generally J. A. G. Griffith and H. Street, *Principles of Administrative Law* (4th edn 1967), pp. 103-9.

109 *R.* v. *Sheer Metalcraft Ltd* [1954] 1 Q.B. 586.

110 [1937] A.C. 139. See also *Chester* v. *Bateson* [1920] 1 K.B. 829 and *Commissioners of Customs and Excise* v. *Cure & Deeley Ltd* [1962] 1 Q.B. 340.

111 (1922) 38 T.L.R. 781 (H.L.).

112 Taken from the judgment of Atkin L. J. in the Court of Appeal: (1921) 37 T.L.R. 884 at 886 (affirmed by the House of Lords (1922) 38 T.L.R. 781).

113 [1920] 1 K.B. 854.

114 At p. 866.

115 [1917] A.C. 260.

116 [1898] 2 Q.B. 91.

117 At pp. 99-100 (*per* Lord Russell of Killowen C. J.).

118 On the same principle a clash between two subordinate legislative instruments should be resolved by holding that the one with the later parent Act prevails.

119 This point seems to have been overlooked in *R.* v. *Aston University Senate, ex p. Roffey* [1969] 2 Q.B. 538.

120 *R.* v. *Electricity Commissioners, ex p. London Electricity Joint Committee Company Ltd.* [1924] 1 K.B. 171 at 205 (C.A.).

121 See *Schmidt* v. *Secretary of State for Home Affairs* [1969] 2 Ch. 149 at 170 (C.A.); *R.* v. *Gaming Board for Great Britain, ex p. Benaim* [1970] 2 Q.B. 417 at 430 (C.A.).

122 See *R.* v. *Commissioners of Customs and Excise, ex p. Cooke and Stevenson* [1970] 1 All E.R. 1068 at 1072 and the authorities there cited. For further discussion, see S. A. de Smith, *Judicial Review of Administrative Action* (2nd edn 1969) pp. 574-7.

123 Crown Proceedings Act 1947, s. 21. See *Merricks* v. *Heathcoat-Amory and the Minister of Agriculture* [1955] Ch. 567. See also pp. 311-12.

124 [1957] 1 Q.B. 574 at 583 (C.A.).

125 Ibid., at p. 586 (and authorities there cited).

126 Compare *Institute of Patent Agents* v. *Lockwood* [1894] A.C. 347 at 359–61 with *Minister of Health* v. *The King* (*On the Prosecution of Yaffe*) [1931] A.C. 494 at 501–3.

127 See *Yaffe's* case, above.

128 A proviso relating to Northern Ireland is omitted. A similar provision for Scotland is contained in sub-section (2). The significance of 1 August 1958 is that this was when a previous Act, the Tribunals and Inquiries Act 1958, came into effect.

129 [1956] A.C. 736.

130 [1969] 2 A.C. 147.

131 It should be noted that the Tribunals and Inquiries Act 1958, s. 11 (3) expressly excluded decisions by the Foreign Compensation Commission from the scope of its provisions regarding ouster clauses.

132 A decision containing an error of law on the face of the record is generally regarded as being merely voidable. For the meaning and significance of this term, see below, pp. 364–7.

133 S. 3. For the way this provision came to be inserted in the Act, see above, p. 232.

134 Review on the ground of natural justice is also excluded from the scope of the ouster clause: see s. 3(10).

135 S. 3(3).

136 The Tribunals and Inquiries Act 1971 would not apply to this Act since it was passed after 1 August 1958.

137 See *R.* v. *Aston University Senate, ex p. Roffey* [1969] 2 Q.B. 538.

138 *R.* v. *Nailsworth Licensing Justices, ex p. Bird* [1953] 1 W.L.R. 1046. See above, p. 336.

139 [1971] 2 All E.R. 89. See also *Ex parte Bolchover, The Times*, 7 October 1970.

140 For a dictum in an earlier case casting some doubt on this approach, see *Ridge* v. *Baldwin* [1964] A.C. 40 at 68 (*per* Lord Reid).

141 This may occur if a new right is created by statute and the statute also provides the means by which it is to be enforced. See *Pasmore* v. *Oswaldtwistle U.D.C.* [1898] A.C. 387 (mandamus refused).

142 Compare, for example, *R.* v. *Cotham* [1898] 1 Q.B. 802 (certiorari and mandamus) and *Durayappah* v. *Fernando* [1967] 2 A.C. 337 (P.C.) (certiorari).

143 There is old authority to the effect that if a defect of jurisdiction is apparent on the face of the proceedings, an application for

prohibition may be brought by anyone and the court must grant the remedy: see S. A. de Smith, *Judicial Review of Administrative Action* (2nd edn 1968), pp. 427–8. Where the defect is not apparent on the face of the proceedings, the position is the same as in the case of certiorari.

144 [1970] 1 All E.R. 1068 (Div. Ct.).

145 *R. v. Groom, ex p. Cobbold* [1901] 2 K.B. 157 (Div. Ct).

146 [1970] 3 All E.R. 460 (Div. Ct).

147 It was provided by s. 266(2) of the Local Government Act 1933 that contracts made by a local authority had to be made in accordance with its standing orders.

148 The Court decided to grant mandamus but to delay its effect for a period of 14 days: if the Corporation suspended its standing orders within this time (which it had power to do) mandamus would not issue. The applicants therefore won a pyrrhic victory.

149 [1903] 1 Ch. 109.

150 *Attorney-General (on the relation of McWhirter)* v. *Independent Broadcasting Authority* [1973] 1 All E.R. 689 (C.A.). It is very unlikely that there would be insufficient time to obtain the Attorney-General's permission since he is prepared, where necessary, to give a decision within a matter of hours.

151 [1966] 2 All E.R. 196.

152 *R. v. Hendon R.D.C., ex p. Chorley* [1933] 2 K.B. 696. In *Prescott* v. *Birmingham Corporation* [1955] Ch. 210 (C.A.) a ratepayer was given a declaration that a scheme by the Corporation to allow old people to travel free on buses was *ultra vires*; however, the issue of *locus standi* was not argued.

153 This rule has now been changed by the Nullity of Marriage Act 1971, s. 5.

154 *Healey* v. *Minister of Health* [1955] 1 Q.B. 221; *Punton* v. *Minister of Pensions and National Insurance* (No. 2) [1964] 1 All E.R. 448 (C.A.).

155 (1852) 3 H.L.C. 759. See also *Metropolitan Properties Co. Ltd* v. *Lannon* [1969] 1 Q.B. 577 at 600 (Lord Denning M. R.).

156 (1863) 14 C.B.N.S. 180.

157 [1964] A.C. 40.

158 [1967] 2 A.C. 337.

159 This is a different principle from that of *locus standi* and would be applicable even in collateral proceedings (where no question of *locus standi* could arise).

160 See, for example, the remarks of Lord Morris [1964] A.C. 40 at 125.

161 See *R. v. Nailsworth Licensing Justices, ex p. Bird* [1953] 1 W.L.R. 1046 (bias).

162 Or that the decision is initially valid but is retrospectively invalidated if the person affected takes steps to challenge it.

163 *Durayappah* v. *Fernando* [1967] 2 A.C. 337 at 354.

164 For example *Ridge* v. *Baldwin* [1964] A.C. 40.

165 *R. v. Medical Appeal Tribunal, ex p. Gilmore* [1957] 1 Q.B. 574 (C.A.).

166 [1969] 2 A.C. 147. See above, p. 359.

CHAPTER 17

1 In 1961 Finland became an associate member; Ireland became a member in 1970.

2 Ireland, Norway and Denmark also agreed to join at the same time. Referenda were held in all these countries; membership was approved in Ireland and Denmark but not in Norway. So only Ireland and Denmark came in with Britain.

3 These policies are set out in Article 3 and are elaborated in succeeding articles in the Treaty.

4 Article 9 (EEC).

5 See Articles 110–16 (EEC).

6 See Articles 48–73 (EEC).

7 See Article 48 (2) (EEC); see also Regulations 1612/68 and 1251/70 and the Directives of 25 February 1964 and 15 October 1968.

8 The basic treaty provisions are Articles 38–47 (EEC).

9 See Articles 74–84 (EEC).

10 See Articles 85–90 (EEC). Other provisions concerned with the competition are found in Articles 91–4 (EEC).

11 See Articles 100–2 (EEC).

12 Article 99 (EEC).

13 See Articles 103–16 (EEC).

14 See Articles 117–28 (EEC).

15 Article 149 (EEC).

16 The equivalent of the Commission in the ECSC Treaty was called the 'High Authority'.

17 Treaty Establishing a Single Council and a Single Commission of the European Communities (1965) (Merger Treaty).

18 Article 10 of the Merger Treaty, as amended by the Council Decision of 1 January 1973 altering the number of Members of the Commission, (1973) *Official Journal*, Vol. 16, No. L2/28.

19 Article 11 of the Merger Treaty.

20 Article 10 (2) of the Merger Treaty.

21 Article 144 (EEC).

22 Article 12 of the Merger Treaty.

23 Article 14 of the Merger Treaty and Article 16 of the Accession Treaty.

24 See Articles 193-8 (EEC) (as amended).

25 Article 10 of the Merger Treaty.

26 Article 17 of the Merger Treaty.

27 Article 2 of the Merger Treaty as amended by Article 5 of the Council decision of 1 January 1973 adjusting the documents concerning the accession of New Member States, (1973) *Official Journal*, vol. 16, No. L2/1.

28 Article 148(1) (EEC).

29 Article 148(2) (EEC), as amended by Article 8 of the Council Decision of 1 January 1973 adjusting the documents concerning the accession of New Member States, (1973) *Official Journal*, vol. 16, No. L2/1.

30 Article 237 (EEC).

31 See the statements issued after the extraordinary Council session of 28 and 29 January 1966 (the Luxemburg Accords) in which there was a divergence of views between the French delegation and the others.

32 Article 137 (EEC).

33 Article 138(1) (EEC).

34 Article 138(2) (EEC) as amended by Article 4 of the Act of the Council of 1 January 1973 adjusting the documents concerning the accession of New Member States, (1973) *Official Journal*, vol. 16, No. L2/1.

35 Article 138(3) (EEC).

36 Article 144 (EEC).

37 Ibid.

38 See, for example, Article 140 (EEC).

39 Articles 165 and 167 (EEC) as amended by Articles 9 and 10 of the Council Decision of 1 January 1973 adjusting the documents

concerning the accession of New Member States, (1973) *Official Journal*, vol. 16, No. L2/1.

40 Article 167 (EEC).

41 Article 167 (EEC).

42 Article 166 (EEC) as amended by Article 1 of the Council Decision of 1 January 1973 increasing the number of Advocates-General, (1973) *Official Journal* vol. 16, No. L2/29.

43 The Queen's Proctor in some ways has similar functions.

44 Article 167 (EEC) as amended by Article 19 of the Act annexed to the Treaty of Accession.

45 Articles 6 and 8 of the Protocol to the EEC Treaty on the Statute of the Court of Justice of the European Economic Community.

46 Article 165 (EEC) and Article 15 of the Protocol on the Statute of the Court of Justice as amended by Article 20 of the Act annexed to the Treaty of Accession.

47 See, for example, Article 220 (EEC). Conventions between Member States which are not made under provisions in the Treaties, might in some cases also be a source of Community law.

48 There is also a general power under Article 235 (EEC) to take 'the appropriate measures' to attain Community objectives.

49 Article 190 (EEC).

50 Article 191 (EEC).

51 Direct effectiveness may be different from direct applicability. See J. A. Winter, 'Direct Applicability and Direct Effect' (1972) 9 C.M.L. Rev. 134.

52 [1963] C.M.L.R. 105. (C.M.L.R. = Common Market Law Reports).

53 *Lütticke* v. *Hauptzollamt Sarrelouis* [1971] C.M.L.R. 674; *Salgoil* v. *Ministry of Foreign Commerce of the Italian Republic* [1969] C.M.L.R. 181. For annotation, see Brinkhorst, (1969) 6 C.M.L. Rev. 478 (especially at 484–6). (C.M.L.Rev. = Common Market Law Review).

54 *Grad* v. *Finanzamt Traunstein* [1971] C.M.L.R. 1.

55 *S.A.C.E.* v. *Ministry of Finance of the Italian Republic* [1971] C.M.L.R. 123. For comment on this and the *Grad* case, see Brinkhorst (1971) 8 C.M.L. Rev. 386.

56 Article 192 (EEC). The person on whom the fine is imposed can appeal to the European Court under Article 172 or 173 (EEC).

57 Article 164 (EEC).
58 See J. Mertens de Wilmars and I. M. Verougstraete, 'Proceedings against Member States for Failure to Fulfil their Obligations' (1970) 7 C.M.L. Rev. 385 at 388.
59 Article 169 (EEC). The procedure is somewhat different under ECSC Treaty: see Article 88. See also Articles 93, 180 and 225 of the EEC Treaty.
60 Article 170 (EEC).
61 If the Commission has not delivered an opinion within three months, the absence of an opinion will not prevent proceedings being brought before the Court: Article 170.
62 See Chapter 16.
63 See above, pp. 361–4.
64 Article 173 (EEC) second paragraph.
65 See above, p. 317.
66 Article 173 (EEC).
67 Ibid.
68 See above, pp. 344–8.
69 In certain cases it might be possible to bring proceedings after the time limit has expired: see *Commission* v. *French Republic* [1970] C.M.L.R. 43.
70 Article 175 (EEC).
71 Article 176 (EEC).
72 For the distinction between a direct challenge and a challenge in collateral proceedings, see above, p. 318.
73 These provisions apply to a tribunal as well as a court.
74 Article 177 (EEC).
75 See Article 20 of the Statute of the Court of Justice of the EEC.
76 Article 181 (EEC).
77 Article 178 (EEC).
78 Article 215 (EEC).
79 Article 179 (EEC). The limits of this jurisdiction depend on the Staff Regulations and Conditions of Employment for Community Employees.
80 Article 172 (EEC).
81 See s. 1(2), (3) and (4) and Sch. I, Pt I.
82 These are:

1. The ECSC Treaty (1951);
2. The EEC Treaty (1957);

3. The Euratom Treaty (1957);
4. The Convention on certain Institutions common to the European Communities (1957);
5. The Treaty establishing a single Council and a single Commission of the European Communities (1965);
6. The Treaty amending certain Budgetary Provisions of the Treaties establishing the European Communities and of the Treaty establishing a single Council and a single Commission of the European Communities (1970);
7. The Treaty relating to the accession of the United Kingdom to the EEC and Euratom (1972); and
8. The Decision of the Council relating to the accession of the U.K. to the ECSC.

83 Under Article 3(1) of the Act of Accession (annexed to the Treaty of Accession), the U.K. agreed to accede to all ancillary treaties entered into by the old Member States.

84 A treaty between one of the Communities and a third country would not need to be specified in an Order in Council if the U.K. was not a co-signatory; such a treaty would still be a Community treaty.

85 An Order in Council may specify that other treaties are Community Treaties and this will be conclusive. It is not, however, necessary that other treaties be so specified, nor need such an Order in Council be approved by Parliament.

86 See Schedule II. If it is not approved in draft by each House, it is subject to annulment in pursuance of a resolution by either House.

87 S. 2(4).

88 See Schedule II.

89 Three months if tried summarily.

90 See Articles 187 and 192 of the EEC Treaty.

91 The European Communities (Enforcement of Community Judgments) Order 1972 (S.I. 1972 No. 1590).

92 It is assumed that the provisions of the conflicting U.K. statute are unambiguous. If their meaning is unclear the courts would, of course, try to interpret them in such a way as to avoid a conflict.

93 It could be argued that this would not be so if the Community legislation was enacted after the British statute. In this case Parliament would not have known, when it passed the statute,

that it would conflict with Community law. It could be argued that the statute was not intended to prevail over Community law and should therefore be regarded as containing an implied provision that it was subject to Community law. The basis of this argument is section 2(4) of the European Communities Act: this section could be regarded as laying down a new rule of statutory interpretation that the courts are to presume that Acts of Parliament are intended to be subject to Community law unless the contrary is expressly stated. This approach does not seem totally consistent with the traditional concept of parliamentary sovereignty but it might be adopted by the courts as a half-way house to the full acceptance of the supremacy of Community law. (We are indebted to our colleague J. M. Evans for suggesting this argument.)

94 *Blackburn* v. *A.-G.* [1971] 2 All E.R. 1380 at 1382 (C.A.).

95 See, for example, the decision of the Belgian *Cour de Cassation* in *Minister for Economic Affairs* v. *S.A. Fromagerie Franco–Suisse 'Le Ski'* (1972) 11 C.M.L. Rev. 330; 86 *Journal des Tribunaux* 460 (1971). See further, Bebr 'Law of the European Communities and Municipal Law' (1971) 34 M.L.R. 481.

Bibliography

This list contains only the basic works; further references are given in the notes.

1. Introduction

S. A. de Smith, *Constitutional and Administrative Law* (2nd edn 1973).

O. Hood Phillips, *Constitutional and Administrative Law* (5th edn 1973).

E. C. S. Wade and Godfrey Phillips, *Constitutional Law* (8th edn 1970 by E. C. S. Wade and A. W. Bradley).

W. I. Jennings, *The Law and the Constitution* (5th edn 1959).

R. F. V. Heuston, *Essays in Constitutional Law* (2nd edn 1964).

L. S. Amery, *Thoughts on the Constitution* (1948).

W. Bagehot, *The English Constitution* (1963 edn).

A. V. Dicey, *Introduction to the study of the Law of the Constitution* (10th edn 1965).

G. Marshall and G. Moodie, *Some Problems of the Constitution* (5th edn 1971).

J. P. Mackintosh, *The Government and Politics of Britain* (2nd edn 1971).

J. A. G. Griffith and H. Street, *Principles of Administrative Law* (5th edn 1973).

2. Political Parties

R. T. McKenzie, *British Political Parties* (2nd rev. edn 1963).

S. H. Beer, *Modern British Politics* (1965).

A. Ranney, *Pathways to Parliament* (1965).

M. Rush, *The Selection of Parliamentary Candidates* (1969).

Peter Pulzer, *Political Representation and Elections in Britain* (2nd edn 1970).

P. Paterson, *The Selectorate* (1967).

3. General Elections

Erskine May, *Parliamentary Practice* (18th edn 1971).

Peter Pulzer, *Political Representation and Elections in Britain* (2nd edn 1970).

4. The Government

J. P. Mackintosh, *The British Cabinet* (2nd edn 1968)

W. I. Jennings, *Cabinet Government* (3rd edn 1959).

I. Gilmour, *The Body Politic* (Rev. edn 1971).

M. Nicholson, *The System* (1967).

New Whitehall Services (Royal Institute of Public Administration).

5. The Civil Service

W. J. M. Mackenzie and J. W. Grove, *Central Administration in Britain* (1957).

Richard Chapman, *The Higher Civil Service in Britain* (1970).

R. G. S. Brown, *The Administrative Process in Britain* (1970).

There is a great deal of information in the volumes accompanying The Fulton Report (especially vols. 3 and 4): *The Civil Service* (published by H.M.S.O. 1968–9) vol. 1: *The Report of the Committee* (Cmnd. 3638, 1968); vol. 2: *Report of a Management Consultancy Group*; vol. 3: *Surveys and Investigations*; vol. 4: *Factual, Statistical and Explanatory Papers*; vol. 5: *Proposals and Opinions*.

6. Local Authorities and Public Corporations

R. Buxton, *Local Government* (2nd edn 1973).

W. O. Hart, *Introduction to the Law of Local Government and Administration* (9th edn 1973).

J. A. G. Griffith, *Central Departments and Local Authorities* (1966).

W. A. Robson, *Nationalized Industry and Public Ownership* (2nd edn 1962).

D. Coombes, *The Member of Parliament and the Administration* (1966).

J. A. G. Griffith and H. Street, *Principles of Administrative Law* (5th edn 1973) Chapter 7.

7. The Police

T. A. Critchley, *A History of the Police in England and Wales, 900–1966* (1967).

Geoffrey Marshall, *Police and Government* (1965).

D. W. Pollard, 'The Police Act 1964' [1966] *P.L.* 35.

D. E. Regan, 'The Police Service: An Extreme Example of Central Control over Local Authority Staff' [1966] *P.L.* 13.

The Report of the Royal Commission on the Police (Cmnd. 1728, 1962).

8. Police Powers

Harry Street, *Freedom, the Individual and the Law* (3rd edn 1972), Chaps 1 and 2.

Ian Brownlie, *The Law Relating to Public Order* (1968).

David Williams, *Keeping the Peace* (1967).

Glanville Williams, 'Requisites of a Valid Arrest' [1954] *Crim. L. Rev.* 6.

Glanville Williams, 'Arrest for Felony at Common Law' [1954 *Crim. L. Rev.* 408.

Glanville Williams, 'Arrest for Breach of the Peace' [1954] *Crim. L. Rev.* 578.

Glanville Williams, 'The Interpretation of Statutory Powers of Arrest Without Warrant' [1958] *Crim. L. Rev.* 73, 154.

D. A. Thomas, 'The Execution of Warrants of Arrest' [1962] *Crim. L. Rev.* 520, 597.

Glanville Williams, 'Demanding Name and Address' (1950) 66 *L.Q.R.* 465.

D. A. Thomas, 'Police Powers II – Arrest: A General View' [1966] *Crim. L. Rev.* 639.

D. A. Thomas, 'Police Powers III – The Law of Search and Seizure: Further Ground for Rationalization' [1967] *Crim. L. Rev.* 3.

L. H. Leigh, 'Recent Developments in the Law of Search and Seizure' (1970) 33 *M.L.R.* 268.

Report of the Committee of Privy Councillors Appointed to Inquire into the Interception of Communications (Cmnd. 283/1957).

9. The Judiciary and the Administration of Justice

Harry Street, *Freedom, the Individual and the Law* (3rd edn 1972), pp. 154–78.

R. M. Jackson, *The Machinery of Justice in England* (6th edn 1972).

G. J. Borrie and N. V. Lowe, *The Law of Contempt* (1973).

Amnon Rubinstein, 'Liability in Tort of Judicial Officers' (1964) 15 *U. of Toronto L.J.* 317.

Bernard Dickens, 'Control of Prosecutions in the United Kingdom' (1973) 22 *I.C.L.Q.* 1.

10. The House of Commons

Erskine May, *Parliamentary Practice* (18th edn 1971).

P. G. Richards, *The Backbenchers* (1972).

P. G. Richards, *Parliament and Conscience* (1970).

C. K. Allen, *Law and Orders* (3rd edn 1965).

S. A. Walkland, *The Legislative Process in Great Britain* (1968).

D. C. Rowat, *The Ombudsman* (2nd edn 1968).

H. Mitchell and P. Birt, *Who does what in Parliament* (annual).

D. N. Chester and N. Bowring, *Questions in Parliament* (1962).

J. A. G. Griffith and H. Street, *Principles of Administrative Law* (5th edn 1973) Chaps. 2 and 3.

11. The House of Lords

Erskine May, *Parliamentary Practice* (18th edn 1971).

P. A. Bromhead, *The House of Lords and Contemporary Politics* (1958).

Bernard Crick, *The Reform of Parliament* (Rev. 3rd edn 1970), Chaps. 5 and 6.

J. R. Vincent, 'The House of Lords' (1966) XIX *Parliamentary Affairs* 475 and (1967) XX *Parliamentary Affairs* 178.

House of Lords Reform, Cmnd. 3799 (1968).

12. Parliamentary Privilege

Erskine May, *Parliamentary Practice* (18th edn 1971), Chaps. 5–11.

The Report from the Select Committee on Parliamentary Privileges, H.C. 34 (1967–8).

Geoffrey Wilson, *Cases and Materials on Constitutional and Administrative Law* (1966), Chap. 7.

13. Politics and the Mass Media

Harry Street, *Freedom, the Individual and the Law* (3rd edn 1972), Chaps. 3 and 4.

Colin Seymour-Ure, *The Press, Politics and the Public* (1968).

David Williams, *Not in the Public Interest* (1965), Chaps. 1, 4 and 5.

14. Special Tribunals and Local Inquiries

W. A. Robson, *Justice and Administrative Law* (3rd edn 1951).

H. W. R. Wade, *Administrative Law* (3rd edn 1971).

R. E. Wraith and G. B. Lamb, *Public Inquiries as an Instrument of Government* (1971).

J. A. G. Griffith and H. Street, *Principles of Administrative Law* (5th edn 1973), Chap. 4.

15. Governmental Liability

J. D. B. Mitchell, *The Contracts of Public Authorities* (1954).

Harry Street, *Governmental Liability* (1954).

Colin Turpin, *Government Contracts* (1972).

Glanville Williams, *Crown Proceedings* (1948).

Rogerson, 'On the Fettering of Public Powers' [1971] *P.L.* 288.

Andrews, 'Estoppels against Statutes' (1966) 29 *M.L.R.* 1.

Ganz, 'Estoppel and Res Judicata in Administrative Law' [1965] *P.L.* 237.

Treitel, 'Crown Proceedings: Some Recent Developments' [1957] *P.L.* 321.

Collier, 'Act of State as a Defence against a British Subject' [1968] *C.L.J.* 102.

Gilmour, 'British Forces Abroad and Responsibility for their Actions' [1970] *P.L.* 120.

Griffith, 'Public Corporations as Crown Servants' (1952) 9 *U. of Toronto L.J.* 169.

Street, 'The Effect of Statutes upon the Rights and Liabilities of the Crown' (1948) 7 *U. of Toronto L.J.* 357.

16. Judicial Review

S. A. de Smith, *Judicial Review of Administrative Action* (3rd edn 1973).

H. W. R. Wade, *Administrative Law* (3rd edn 1971).

J. A. G. Griffith and H. Street, *Principles of Administrative Law* (5th edn 1973).

17. The European Community

D. Lasok and J. W. Bridge, *An Introduction to the Law and Institutions of the European Communities* (1973).

P. S. R. F. Mathijsen, *A Guide to European Community Law* (1972).

Anthony Parry and Stephen Hardy, *EEC Law* (1973).

D. G. Valentine, *The Court of Justice of the European Communities* (1965)

Bebr, 'Law of the European Communities and Municipal Law' (1971) 34 *M.L.R.* 481.

Mertens de Wilmars and Verougstraete, 'Proceedings against Member States for Failure to Fulfil their Obligations' (1970) 7 *C.M.L. Rev.* 385.

J. A. Winter, 'Direct Applicability and Direct Effect' (1972) 9 *C.M.L. Rev.* 425.

Mitchell, Kuipers and Gall, 'Constitutional Aspects of the Treaty and Legislation relating to British Membership' (1972) 9 *C.M.L. Rev.* 134.

Trindade, 'Parliamentary Sovereignty and the Primacy of the Community Law' (1972) 35 *M.L.R.* 375.

Wade, 'Sovereignty and the European Communities' (1972) 88 *L.Q.R.* 1.

Cases

Statutes

Index